SAP® MM
HANDBOOK

THE JONES & BARTLETT LEARNING SAP® BOOK SERIES

SAP® R/3® FI Transactions
V. Narayanan (978-1-934015-01-8) © 2007

Upgrading SAP®
Maurice Sens (978-1-934015-15-5) © 2008

SAP® FI/CO Questions and Answers
V. Narayanan (978-1-934015-22-3) © 2008

SAP® ABAP™ Handbook
Kogent Learning Solutions, Inc. (978-0-7637-8107-1) © 2010

SAP® ABAP™ Questions and Answers
Kogent Learning Solutions, Inc. (978-0-7637-7884-2) © 2010

SAP® MM Questions and Answers
Kogent Learning Solutions, Inc. (978-0-7637-8144-6) © 2010

SAP® SD Questions and Answers
Kogent Learning Solutions, Inc. (978-0-7637-8198-9) © 2010

SAP® ERP® Financials and FICO Handbook
Surya N. Padhi (978-0-7637-8080-7) © 2010

SAP® SD Handbook
Kogent Learning Solutions, Inc. (978-1-934015-34-6) © 2011

SAP® MM Handbook
Kogent Learning Solutions, Inc. (978-1-934015-36-0) © 2011

For more information on any of the titles above, please visit us online at http://www.jblearning.com/. Qualified instructors, contact your Publisher's Representative at 1-800-832-0034 or info@jblearning.com to request review copies for course consideration.

SAP® MM HANDBOOK

Kogent Learning Solutions, Inc.

JONES & BARTLETT
LEARNING

World Headquarters
Jones & Bartlett Learning
40 Tall Pine Drive
Sudbury, MA 01776
978-443-5000
info@jblearning.com
www.jblearning.com

Jones & Bartlett Learning
Canada
6339 Ormindale Way
Mississauga, Ontario L5V 1J2
Canada

Jones & Bartlett Learning
International
Barb House, Barb Mews
London W6 7PA
United Kingdom

Jones & Bartlett Learning books and products are available through most bookstores and online booksellers. To contact Jones & Bartlett Learning directly, call 800-832-0034, fax 978-443-8000, or visit our website, www.jblearning.com.

Substantial discounts on bulk quantities of Jones & Bartlett Learning publications are available to corporations, professional associations, and other qualified organizations. For details and specific discount information, contact the special sales department at Jones & Bartlett Learning via the above contact information or send an email to specialsales@jblearning.com.

Production Credits

Publisher: David Pallai
Production Director: Amy Rose
Editorial Assistant: Molly Whitman
Production Assistant: Rebekah Linga
Associate Marketing Manager: Lindsay Ruggiero
V.P., Manufacturing and Inventory Control:
   Therese Connell

Composition: diacriTech
Art Rendering: diacriTech
Cover and Title Page Design: Scott Moden
Cover Image: © Ken Toh/Dreamstime.com
Printing and Binding: Malloy, Inc.
Cover Printing: Malloy, Inc.

Library of Congress Cataloging-in-Publication Data

SAP MM handbook / Kogent Learning Solutions, Inc.
   p. cm.
   Includes index.
   ISBN-13: 978-1-934015-36-0 (hardcover)
   ISBN-10: 1-934015-36-9 (hardcover)
   1. Materials management–Data processing. 2. SAP ERP. 3. Integrated software. I. Kogent Learning Solutions, Inc.
   TS161.S37 2011
   658.70285–dc22

                          2010017558

6048
Printed in the United States of America
14 13 12 11 10   10 9 8 7 6 5 4 3 2 1

CONTENTS AT A GLANCE

TABLE OF CONTENTS

INTRODUCTION

Congratulations on buying the *SAP MM Handbook*! This book is designed to provide comprehensive content on various concepts of the SAP system and the MM module. Introduced by SAP AG, Germany, the SAP system forms an indispensable part of any business enterprise with respect to enterprise resource planning. The pace of technological enhancements is getting faster day by day leading to the extensive use of the SAP system. Today, many companies are using SAP technologies to perform their daily business activities.

ABOUT THIS BOOK

In the *SAP MM Handbook*, you will find as much knowledge about the MM module as can fit between the covers. Hundreds of topics are discussed theoretically as well as practically in different chapters of this book. The book also covers SAP R/3®, concepts of the MM module, data access in the SAP system, system architecture, implementation of procurement and the verification process under various business scenarios, and system administration.

This book is ideal for beginners who intend to familiarize themselves with the MM module, as it covers the very basics that teach you how to perform different tasks in the SAP system. An added advantage is that it also serves professionals who are already familiar with the SAP system and want to enhance their skills, as it deals in depth with the advanced concepts of the MM module. It describes the techniques and procedures that are most frequently employed by users when working with the SAP R/3 software.

The book is divided into easy-to-understand topics, with each topic addressing different programming issues in the MM module, such as:

- Overview of the MM module
- Organizational structure within SAP software
- Classifying materials in the MM module
- Master data in the MM module
- The purchasing process in the MM module
- Material requirement planning process implemented in the MM module
- The inventory management process in the MM module

- The invoice verification process in the MM module
- The inventory valuation process in the MM module
- Key configurations in the MM module
- Transaction codes related to the MM module

This is just an indicative list—there is lot more inside. The book gives special coverage to the MM module implemented in the mySAP™ ERP software, more than any other book dedicated to the subject. In addition, the book helps you to learn to implement the procurement process and invoice verification process under various real business scenarios.

Our sole intent has been to provide a book with in-depth and sufficient information so that you enjoy reading and learning from it. Happy reading!

HOW TO USE THIS BOOK

In this book, we have employed the mySAP ERP software to implement business processes. You must, therefore, install the mySAP ERP software on your system to implement the applications provided in the book. This book begins with the basics of the SAP system and makes you familiar with its user interface. After that, it discusses the implementation of concepts relating to the MM module as well as the implementation of various business processes, such as procurement and invoice verification under various business scenarios. This book consists of nine chapters and four appendices that provide detailed information about the MM module.

CONVENTIONS

There are a few conventions followed in this book that need to be noted. The *SAP MM Handbook* provides you with additional information on various concepts in the form of NOTES:

Note: A collective number is a number that is assigned to a group of RFQs that are created for a single product. It helps you to search an RFQ and identify the product.

Every figure contains a descriptive caption to enhance clarity:

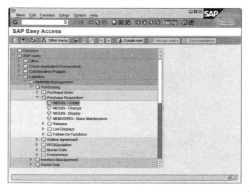

FIGURE 5.2   **Creating a Purchase Requisition**

In this book, table captions are placed immediately after the table, as shown:

UI Element	Description
Document Type	Specifies the document type that defines internal or external number ranges for a purchase requisition. For example, the NB document type is used for the standard purchase requisition and TB for the transport order.
Purchase Requisition	Specifies a unique key to identify a purchase requisition.
Source Determination	Indicates an existing source of supply for a material.
Item Category	Specifies a key number that represents the process of controlling a material or service.
Acct Assignment Cat.	Specifies the account assignment category for an item.
Delivery Date	Specifies a date on which the goods have to be delivered.

Continued

UI Element	Description
Plant	Specifies a key that determines which plant would receive the ordered goods.
Storage Location	Specifies the identification numbers of the storage locations where the material is stored.
Purchasing Group	Specifies a key number assigned to a buyer or group of buyers performing the purchasing activities.
Material Group	Specifies a key number assigned to a group of materials having the same attributes.
Req. Tracking Number	Specifies a number to track and monitor the procurement of required materials.
Requisitioner	Specifies the person or the organization for whom the material is ordered.
Supplying Plant	Specifies a plant that supplies the material.

TABLE 5.1   UI elements of Create: Purchase Requisition: Initial Screen

OTHER RESOURCES

Other useful HTML links where you can find texts related to the MM module with helpful tutorials are as follows:

- http://help.sap.com/
- http://sapbrainsonline.com/TUTORIALS/FUNCTIONAL/MM_tutorial.html
- http://help.sap.com/printdocu/core/Print46c/EN/data/pdf/MMIM/MMIM.pdf
- http://www.sapstudymaterials.com/
- http://www.erpgenie.com/sap/sapfunc/mm.htm

INTRODUCING THE SAP MM MODULE

Systems Applications and Products in Data Processing (SAP) is business software that can be customized according to the requirements of a user. SAP software is being used in many organizations today because of its ability to integrate various applications, with each application representing a specific business area, such as planning, manufacturing, and distribution. This integration helps with the easy transfer of data between applications and provides quick access to information for an organization. This easy transfer of data between applications helps in automatically updating the business processes in the SAP system. The SAP system provides both functional as well as technical modules. The technical modules, such as Advanced Business Application Programming (ABAP™), help in generating various queries according to what the business requires. However, the functional modules, such as Sales and Distribution (SD), Materials Management (MM), and Production Planning (PP), are used to perform day-to-day business transactions. SAP provides a common platform for all these modules to perform various business activities. These modules communicate with each other so that any change made in one module is instantly communicated to the other modules, ensuring effective transfer of information. The SAP system was introduced as Enterprise Resource Planning (ERP) software designed to coordinate all the resources, information, and activities to automate business processes, such as order fulfilment or billing.

In the present era, the SAP R/3® system is a market leader in ERP software. It facilitates the flow of information between all the processes of a company's supply chain, from purchases to sales, including accounting and human resources. The SAP R/3 system can be broadly classified into various groups, which are logistics, financial/management accounting and reporting, human resources, and cross-application functions.

The chapter discusses the need for and history of SAP applications, focusing on the circumstances that necessitated its development, and how its introduction helped improve system performance and business efficiency. In addition, the chapter focuses on the SAP Graphical User Interface (GUI), also known as the SAP screen, used to perform all tasks, including creating material master data and generating bills as well as invoices. Further, the various functional modules of the SAP R/3 system are introduced. Toward the end, the chapter introduces the MM module and explains the relationship of the MM module with SAP software and its other modules.

INTRODUCTION TO SAP APPLICATIONS

SAP was developed by the SAP AG company, Germany, where SAP stands for Systeme, Anwendungen und Produkte in der Datenverarbeitung. The basic idea behind developing SAP was to address the need to introduce standard application software that helps in real-time business processing. A standard SAP system is divided into three systems, namely, Development, Quality Assurance, and Production. The Development system helps customize data in an SAP system, the Quality Assurance system performs the final testing before SAP applications are used in the production system, and finally the Production system helps perform the day-to-day business activities.

In this section, we discuss the following topics to start exploring an SAP system:

- The need for SAP Applications
- History of SAP Software
- SAP R/3 Architecture
- SAP Graphical User Interface (GUI)
- SAP Customizing Implementation Guide

Now, let's discuss each of these topics in detail.

The Need for SAP Applications

Before the advent of SAP software, the computer system used to automate and integrate all facets of business operations, including planning, manufacturing, and sales, was known as an ERP system or simply ERP. In the term ERP, E stands for Enterprise, which includes a firm or company; R stands for Resource, which involves the four Ms, i.e., man, machine, material, and money; and P stands for Planning, which means efficient use of the available resources.

An ERP system is used to integrate several data sources and processes, such as manufacturing, controlling, and distribution of goods of a company. This integration is achieved by using various hardware and software components. An ERP system is primarily module based, which implies that it consists of various modular software applications or modules. A software module in an ERP system automates a specific business area or module of an enterprise, such as finance or sales and distribution. A common database is used to store data related to all the modules of a company, such as sales and distribution, production planning, and plant maintenance. In this way, the data can be accessed, shared, and maintained easily.

Before the advent of the ERP system, each department of a company had its own customized automation mechanism. As a result, the business modules were not interconnected or integrated, and updating as well as sharing data across these modules was a big problem. Let's take an example to understand this concept better. Suppose the Financial/Accounting (FI) and MM modules of an enterprise have their respective customized automation mechanisms. In such a setup, if a purchase is made, its status would be automatically updated in the MM module. However, the purchase invoice of the purchased item would not be updated in the FI module automatically. Consequently, the invoice details of the purchased item would need to be manually updated in the FI module, increasing the probability of errors and asynchronous business processes. These problems were fixed with the help of the integration feature provided in the ERP system.

Another benefit of the ERP system is that it helps synchronize and update data related to the business modules. Ideally, an ERP system uses only a single, common database to store information related to various modules of a company, such as SD, PP, and MM.

After discussing the benefits of an ERP system, let's now have a look at some of its major drawbacks, which are as follows:

- Customization of ERP software is restricted because you cannot easily adapt ERP systems to a specific workflow or business process of a company.
- After an ERP system is established, switching to another ERP system is very costly.
- The ERP system is not clearly associated with the defined roles of the employees in a company. In addition, you do not get the exact status of company resources while an ERP system is processing a transaction. This can lead to problems in accountability, lines of responsibility, and the morale of employees.
- Some large organizations may have multiple departments with separate as well as independent resources, missions, and chains-of-command. The consolidation of the resources and missions into a single enterprise may limit the benefits of the ERP system.

SAP was introduced to overcome all these drawbacks of contemporary ERP systems.

Now that we see the need for SAP applications, let's analyze the timeline history of SAP software, which led to the introduction of the SAP R/1, R/2, R/3, and mySAP™ ERP systems.

History of SAP Software

The evolution of the SAP system has not only removed the bottlenecks of using the ERP system, but also led to improved system performance and business efficiency by integrating individual applications. In other words, an SAP system ensures data consistency throughout the system, in addition to removing the drawbacks of contemporary ERP systems. In this section, we explore the history of SAP based on the various versions of SAP, which are as follows:

- SAP R/1
- SAP R/2

- SAP R/3
- mySAP ERP Application

Introducing SAP R/1

The development process of SAP software began in 1972, with five IBM employees, Dietmar Hopp, Hans-Werner Hector, Hasso Plattner, Klaus Tschira, and Claus Wellenreuther in Mannheim, Germany. A year later, the first financial and accounting software was developed. This software formed the basis for continuous development of other software components, which later came to be known as the SAP R/1 system. Here, R stands for real-time data processing and 1 indicates the single-tier architecture, which means that the three networking layers, Presentation, Application, and Database, which the SAP system architecture depends upon, are implemented on a single system. SAP R/1 ensures efficient and synchronous communication among different business modules within a company.

Introducing SAP R/2

The SAP R/2 system, introduced in 1980, was based on the two-tier architecture and was designed to work on mainframe databases, such as DB/2, IMS, and Adabas. The mainframe computer in SAP R/2 used the time-sharing feature to integrate the functions or business areas of an enterprise, such as accounting, manufacturing processes, supply chain logistics, and human resources. The two-tier client-server architecture of the SAP R/2 system enabled an SAP client to connect to an SAP server to access the data stored in the SAP database. SAP R/2 was particularly popular with large European multinational companies that required real-time business applications, with built-in multi-currency and multi-language capabilities. Keeping in mind that SAP customers belong to different nations and regions, the SAP R/2 system was designed to handle different languages and currencies. The SAP R/2 system delivered a higher level of stability as compared to the earlier version.

Note: Time sharing implies that multiple users can access an application concurrently; however, each is unaware that the application is being accessed by other users.

Introducing SAP R/3

SAP R/3, based on the client-server model, was officially launched on July 6, 1992. This version is compatible with multiple platforms and operating systems, such as UNIX® and Microsoft® Windows®. SAP R/3 introduced a new era of business software—from the mainframe computing architecture to the three-tier architecture consisting of the Database layer, the Application layer (business logic), and the Presentation layer. The three-tier architecture of the client-server model is preferred to the mainframe computing architecture as it allows you to make changes or scale a particular layer in the client-server model without making changes in the entire system.

The SAP R/3 system is customizable software with predefined features that you can turn on or off according to your requirements. It contains various standard tables to execute various types of processes, such as reading data from database tables or processing the entries stored in a table. You can configure the settings of these tables according to your requirements. The data related to these tables is managed with the help of the dictionary of the SAP R/3 system, which is stored in an SAP database and can be accessed by all of the SAP application programs.

The SAP R/3 system integrates all the business modules of a company so that information, once entered, can be shared across these modules. It is a highly generic and comprehensive business application system, especially designed for companies having different organizational structures and lines of business.

The SAP R/3 system can run on various platforms, such as Microsoft Windows and UNIX, and supports various relational databases of different database management systems, such as Oracle®, Adabas®, Informix®, and Microsoft® SQL Server®. The SAP R/3 system uses these databases to handle the queries of the users.

Introducing the mySAP ERP Application

SAP introduced the mySAP ERP application as a follow-up to the SAP R/3 software. With the passage of time, there was a need for a business suite that would run on a single database and offer a preconfigured system with various scenarios. This led to the introduction of the mySAP Business Suite, which includes various applications, such as mySAP ERP, mySAP™ Supply Chain Management (SCM), mySAP™ Customer Relationship Management (CRM), mySAP™ Supplier Relationship Management (SRM), and mySAP™ Product Lifestyle Management (PLM).

This chapter primarily explores the mySAP ERP application of the mySAP Business Suite.

The mySAP ERP application categorizes business operations into the following three core functional areas:

- Logistics
- Financial
- Human Resources

To learn more about the core and other functional areas of the mySAP ERP, refer to the section *Introducing the SAP Modules*. This book focuses on the latest release of the mySAP ERP application, i.e., ECC 6.0.

Now, let's explore the architecture of the SAP R/3 system.

The SAP R/3 Architecture

As stated earlier, the SAP R/3 system evolved from the SAP R/2 system, which was a mainframe. The SAP R/3 system is based on the three-tier architecture of the client-server model. Figure 1.1 shows the three-tier architecture of the SAP R/3 system.

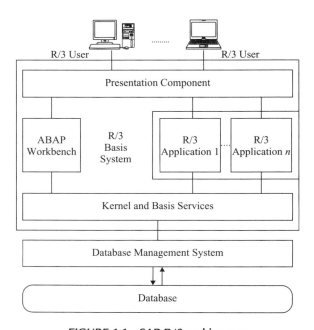

FIGURE 1.1 **SAP R/3 architecture**

Figure 1.1 shows how the R/3 Basis system forms a central platform within the R/3 system. The architecture of the SAP R/3 system distributes the workload among multiple R/3 systems. The link between these systems is established with the help of a network. The SAP R/3 system is implemented in such a way that the Presentation, Application, and Database layers are distributed among individual computers in the SAP R/3 architecture.

The SAP R/3 system consists of the following three types of views:

- Logical view
- Software-oriented view
- User-oriented view

Now, let's describe these views in detail one by one.

The Logical View

The logical view represents the functionality of the SAP system, which is controlled by the R/3 Basis component. In order to control the tasks performed by the SAP system, the R/3 Basis component provides the following services:

- **Kernel and Basis services**—Provides a runtime environment for all R/3 applications. The runtime environment may be specific to the hardware, operating system, or database. The runtime environment is mainly written in either C or C++, though some parts are also written in the ABAP programming language. The tasks of the Kernel and Basis services are as follows:

  - Executing all R/3 applications on software processors (virtual machines).
  - Handling multiple users and administrative tasks in the SAP R/3 system, which is a multi-user environment.When users log on to the SAP system and run applications within it, they are not directly connected to the host operating system, since the R/3 Basis component is the actual user of the host operating system.
  - Accessing the database in the SAP R/3 system. The SAP R/3 Basis system is connected to a database management system (DBMS) and the database itself. R/3 applications do not communicate with the database directly; rather, these applications communicate with the database through the administration services provided by the R/3 Basis system.
  - Facilitating communication of SAP R/3 applications with other SAP R/3 systems and with non-SAP systems. You can access SAP R/3

applications from an external system by using the Business Application Programming Interface (BAPI).

▫   Monitoring and controlling the SAP R/3 system while it is running.

■ **ABAP Workbench service**—Provides a programming environment to create ABAP programs by using various tools, such as the ABAP Dictionary, ABAP Editor, and Screen Painter.

■ **Presentation Components service**—Facilitates user interaction with SAP R/3 applications by using the presentation components (interfaces) of these applications.

The Software-Oriented View

The software-oriented view displays various types of software components that collectively constitute the SAP R/3 system. It consists of SAP GUI components and Application servers as well as a Message server, all parts of the SAP R/3 system. As the SAP R/3 system is a multi-tier client-server system, the individual software components are arranged in tiers. These components act as either clients or servers based on their position and role in a network. Figure 1.2 shows the software-oriented view of the SAP R/3 architecture.

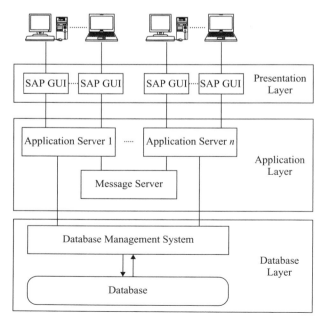

FIGURE 1.2   **Software-oriented view**

As shown in Figure 1.2, the software-oriented view of the SAP R/3 system consists of the following three layers:

- The Presentation layer
- The Application layer
- The Database layer

Now, let's discuss these layers in detail.

The Presentation Layer

The Presentation layer consists of one or more servers that act as an interface between the SAP R/3 system and its users, who interact with the system with the help of well-defined SAP GUI components. Using these components, users can enter a request to perform any task, for example, to display the contents of a database table. The Presentation layer then passes the request to an Application server, where it is processed, and then the result is sent back, where it is then displayed to the user in the Presentation layer. While an SAP GUI component is running, it is also connected to a user's SAP session in the R/3 Basis system.

Note: The servers in the Presentation layer are referred to as Presentation servers in the chapter.

The Application Layer

The Application layer executes the application logic in the SAP R/3 architecture. This layer consists of one or more Application servers and Message servers. Application servers are used to send user requests from the Presentation server to the Database server and retrieve information from the Database server as a response to these requests. Application servers are connected to Database servers with the help of a local area network (LAN). An Application server provides a set of services, such as processing of the flow logic of screens and updating data in the database of the SAP R/3 system. However, a single Application server cannot handle the entire workload of business logic on its own. Therefore, the workload is distributed among multiple Application servers.

Figure 1.3 shows the location of the Application server between the Database and Presentation servers:

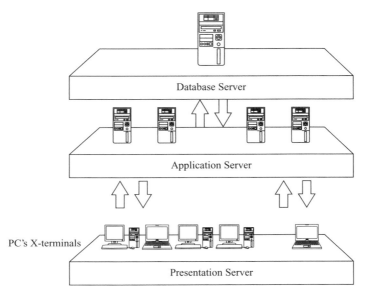

FIGURE 1.3   **Application server**

The Message server component of the Application layer (Figure 1.3) is responsible for communicating between the Application servers. This component also contains information about Application servers and how the workload is distributed among them. It uses this information to select an appropriate server when a user sends a request for processing.

The separation of the three layers of the SAP R/3 system makes the system highly scalable, with the load being distributed among the layers. This distribution of load enables the SAP R/3 system to handle multiple requests simultaneously. The control of a program moves back and forth between the three layers when a user interacts with the program. When the control of the program is in the Presentation layer, the screen is displayed to accept the inputs from the user, and the Application layer becomes inactive for the program. That is, any other application can use the Application layer during this time.

As soon as the user enters the input on the screen, the control of the program shifts to the Application layer to process the input, and the Presentation layer becomes inactive, which means that the SAP GUI (user interface of the SAP R/3 system) cannot accept any kind of input. In other words, until the Application layer completes processing the input and calls a new screen, the SAP GUI is inactive. The process of presenting a new screen to the user is known as a dialog step. Dialog steps are processed in the Application layer, as shown in Figure 1.4.

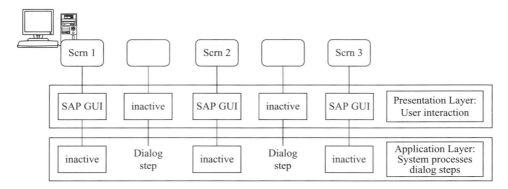

FIGURE 1.4   **A dialog step**

The Database Layer

The Database layer of the SAP R/3 architecture contains the central database system, which contains two components, DBMS and the database itself. The SAP R/3 system supports various databases, such as Adabas® D™, DB2/400™ (on AS/400), DB2/Common Server™, DB2/MVS™, Informix, Microsoft SQL Server, Oracle®, and Oracle® Parallel™ Server.

The database in the SAP R/3 system stores all information in the system, except the master and transaction data. Apart from this, the components of ABAP application programs, such as screen definitions, menus, and function modules, are stored in a special section of the database, known as Repository or Repository Objects. The database also stores control and customization data, which govern how the SAP R/3 system functions. Distributed databases are not used in the SAP R/3 system because the system does not support them.

Note: Master data is the core data and is essential to execute the business logic. Data about customers, products, employees, materials, and suppliers are examples of master data. Transaction data refers to the information about an event in a business process, such as generating orders, invoices, and payments.

The User-Oriented View

The user-oriented view displays the GUI of the R/3 system in the form of windows on the screen. These windows are created by the Presentation layer. To view these windows, start the SAP GUI utility, known as the SAP Logon program. After starting the SAP Logon program, select an SAP R/3 system from the SAP Logon screen. The SAP Logon program then connects to the Message server of the R/3 Basis system in the selected SAP R/3 system and retrieves the address of a suitable Application server, i.e., the Application server with the lightest load. The SAP Logon program then starts the SAP GUI connected to the Application server.

The SAP GUI displays the logon screen, in which you need to specify the user name and password. After logging on successfully, the initial screen of the R/3 system appears. This initial screen starts the first session of the SAP R/3 system.

Figure 1.5 shows the user-oriented view of the SAP R/3 system.

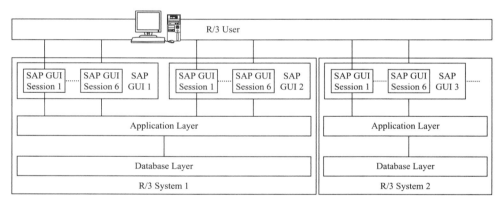

FIGURE 1.5 **User-oriented view**

You can open a maximum of six sessions within a single SAP GUI. Each session acts as an independent SAP GUI. In addition, you can simultaneously run different applications on multiple open R/3 sessions. The processing in an opened R/3 session is independent of the other opened R/3 sessions.

After discussing the SAP architecture, let's explore the SAP GUI, which is used to perform various day-to-day business transactions.

The SAP Graphical User Interface (GUI)

The SAP GUI is a standard SAP user interface that displays menus to perform various business activities. The initial screen of the SAP GUI is known as the **SAP Easy Access** screen. There are numerous SAP GUIs in ECC for users who do not access the SAP menu directly from their systems, such as a standard SAP GUI (also known as the SAP menu) and the Web portal GUI.

Perform the following steps to open the initial screen (**SAP Easy Access** screen) of the SAP GUI:

1. Open the **SAP Logon** screen by selecting **Start** (📧) > **All Programs** > **SAP Front End** > **SAP Logon** (📋), as shown in Figure 1.6.

FIGURE 1.6   **Selecting the SAP Logon option**

The **SAP Logon** screen appears, as shown in Figure 1.7:

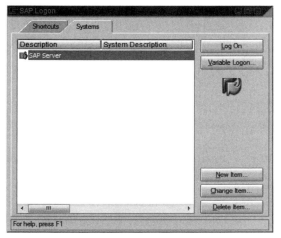

FIGURE 1.7 **Displaying the SAP Logon screen**

2. Click the **Log On** button on the **SAP Logon** screen (Figure 1.7).

The **SAP** screen (first screen of the SAP system) where logon details are entered appears, as shown in Figure 1.8:

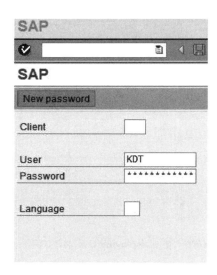

FIGURE 1.8 **Displaying the SAP screen for entering logon details**

The **SAP** screen (Figure 1.8) includes the following fields:

- **Client**—Enables you to enter the client number.
- **User**—Enables you to enter the user ID.
- **Password**—Enables you to enter the password provided by your system administrator. You will notice that as you enter the password, asterisks appear in the field rather than the characters you type. As a security measure, the system does not display the values entered in the Password field.
- **Language (optional)**—Enables you to set the language in which you want to display screens, menus, and fields.

3. Enter the values in all the fields of the SAP screen; for instance, enter your client ID, user name, and password. In our case, we have entered KDT as the user name and sapmac as the password, as shown in Figure 1.8. Now, press the ENTER key. The **SAP Easy Access** screen appears, as shown in Figure 1.9:

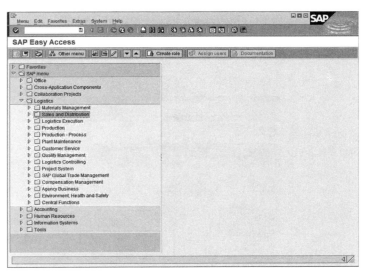

FIGURE 1.9   **Displaying the SAP GUI screen**

The **SAP Easy Access** screen serves as a gateway to work with SAP and contains all the development tools provided by SAP. Figure 1.9 shows various SAP menus, such as **Office, Cross-Application Components, Collaboration Projects**, and **Logistics**.

> **Note:** As this book focuses on the MM module, we will primarily deal with the Materials Management submenu provided under the Logistics menu.

Let's now discuss the SAP Customizing Implementation Guide, which provides the subcategories of the three core functional areas, discussed in the *Introducing the mySAP ERP Application* section.

The SAP Customizing Implementation Guide

The SAP Customizing Implementation Guide is the backbone of the mySAP ERP system and helps in determining how the system functions. It is a customizing screen introduced with the SAP R/3 system, which is used to perform various activities in the mySAP ERP system.

Perform the following steps to open the SAP Customizing Implementation Guide:

1. Open the **SAP Easy Access** screen (Figure 1.9).
2. Enter SPRO as the transaction code in the command field text box located on the standard toolbar of the SAP GUI, and press the ENTER key, as shown in Figure 1.10:

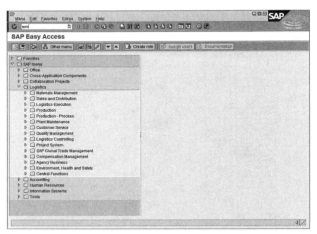

FIGURE 1.10   **Entering the transaction code**

> **Note:** The transaction codes used in the SAP system are not case-sensitive.

The **Customizing: Execute Project** screen appears (Figure 1.11).

3. Click the **SAP Reference IMG** button, as shown in Figure 1.11:

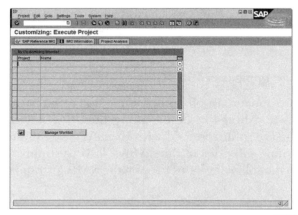

FIGURE 1.11   Displaying the Customizing: Execute Project screen

The **Customizing Implementation Guide** screen appears, as shown in Figure 1.12:

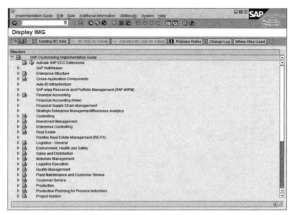

FIGURE 1.12   Displaying the Customizing Implementation Guide screen

Figure 1.12 shows the **Customizing Implementation Guide** screen, which displays the categories of the mySAP ERP application, such as Financial, Human Resources, and Logistics. These categories (functional areas) are further subdivided into applications or modules to perform various business operations depending on their specific business areas, such as finance, sales and distribution, and materials management.

Let's now discuss the modules of the mySAP ERP system.

INTRODUCING THE SAP MODULES

The mySAP ERP application provides various SAP modules to handle the day-to-day business activities of a company, such as recording the payment of invoices, controlling financial accounts, and managing production resources. As the mySAP ERP system works within a single system, all its modules are interrelated with each other. In other words, the processed data of one module can be used as input by the other modules. The various SAP modules used to perform specific business activities are as follows:

- Financial/Accounting
- Controlling
- Investment Management
- Project System
- Human Capital Management
- Sales and Distribution
- Materials Management
- Production Planning
- Logistics Execution
- Quality Management
- Warehouse Management
- Customer Service

Each module is designed to perform some specific tasks, for instance, the SD module helps manage sales and distribution tasks; whereas the FI module is used to keep track of all finances and accounts.

Now, let's discuss each of these modules in detail one by one.

The Financial/Accounting Module

The FI module is designed to handle the financial and accounting-related tasks of a company. This module helps to create and maintain financial records, such as the general ledger, accounts payable, and accounts receivable. It also helps to automatically post journal entries of sales, production, and payments.

The book records designed in this module help the management assess the real financial situation of the company, enabling it to make better decisions and strategic planning.

Table 1.1 describes the submodules of the FI module:

Submodule	Description
Accounts Receivable	Records the account postings for customer sales activities and helps generate a customer analysis report. It also integrates with the General Ledger and Cash Management submodules to facilitate the recording of financial transactions performed in business.
Accounts Payable	Records the account postings for vendor purchase activities and generates automatic postings in the General Ledger module.
Asset Accounting	Manages the records related to the fixed assets of a company. This module sets a fixed value for depreciation of each fixed asset of the company.
Bank Accounting	Manages all bank transactions of the company.
Consolidation	Generates a financial overview based on the financial statements defined for various entities of a company.
Funds Management	Allows the management of a company to set budgets for revenues and expenses.
General Ledger	Records all account postings that display the real-time situation of the financial accounts of a company.
Special Purpose Ledger	Generates ledgers for reports based on the data collected from both internal and external applications.
Travel Management	Manages travelling activities, such as booking trips and managing the expenses of a trip.

TABLE 1.1   The submodules of the FI module

Now, let's discuss the Controlling (CO) module of the mySAP ERP system.

The Controlling Module

The CO module is designed for planning, reporting, and monitoring business operations in an organization. The information generated by this module helps management make important business decisions. It is the most crucial module among all the SAP modules, as it not only helps control transactions made in the other modules but also provides an analysis report for various business tasks.

Table 1.2 describes the components of the CO module:

Components	Description
Cost Element Accounting	Provides cost- and revenue-related information of a company
Cost Center Accounting	Provides information about the costs incurred by the defined cost centers of a company
Internal Orders	Helps evaluate costs of a specific task in a company
Activity-Based Costing	Provides information based on a procedure or activity of a cost center
Product Cost Controlling	Analyzes the production cost of a product to decide its market price
Profitability Analysis	Allows review of the profit-related information of a company
Profit Center Accounting	Helps to generate a detailed profit-loss report

TABLE 1.2   Components of the CO module

Now, let's discuss the Investment Management (IM) module of the mySAP ERP system.

The Investment Management Module

The IM module is designed to manage various investment securities, such as shares and bonds, to meet investment goals for the benefit of the investors of a company. This module enables program management in SAP, which refers to the process of defining a hierarchy for multiple projects. This ensures effective planning and controlling of the costs that include budget authorization. The IM module also integrates with other modules, such as CO and Assets Management (AM), and helps manage the capital investment and budget of a company. The following tasks are performed in the IM module:

- Generating Appropriation Requests (ARs) for master data
- Planning for AR variants
- Planning for AR cost or revenue
- Approving ARs
- Implementing ARs
- Processing investment data periodically
- Creating reports for investment data
- Defining investment management programs
- Defining investment program structures

After discussing the IM module, let's describe the role of the Project System (PS) module in the mySAP ERP system.

The Project System Module

The PS module helps management handle both small as well as large-scale projects. For instance, it can handle large-scale projects, such as building a factory, and small-scale projects, such as organizing a schedule for recruitments. To ensure the completion of a project within time and budget constraints, a project manager in a company needs to define an organizational form for the project in the PS module.

The PS module is integrated with the other modules of the mySAP ERP system, so that you can plan and execute all the tasks associated with a project. This integration means that the PS module constantly accesses data from all the departments involved in a project. The PS module does not have its own organizational structure; therefore, you need to incorporate the project into the existing structure. This can be done by assigning various elements of the project to the organizational units defined in the FI and logistics modules.

Figure 1.13 shows the organizational structure of a project defined in the PS module:

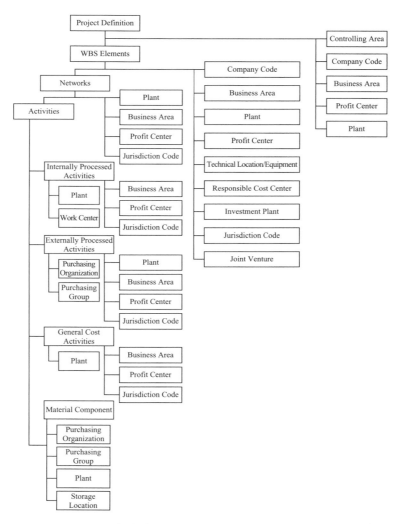

FIGURE 1.13 Displaying the organizational structure of a project

Figure 1.13 shows the organizational structure of a project in which both internally and externally processed activities are specified. It also shows material components that are used to complete the project.

Let's now analyze the role of the Human Capital Management (HCM) module in the mySAP ERP system.

The Human Capital Management Module

The HCM module is designed to plan and control activities related to human resources, and is also known as the Human Resources (HR) module. Employee relations and tasks related to resource planning are also managed by the HCM module. The objective of this module is to maximize the return on investment from the human capital of a company and minimize the risk.

Table 1.3 describes the submodules of the HCM module:

Submodule	Description
Personnel Administration (PA)	Helps to manage and administer human resources in a company
Personnel Development (PD)	Manages the training of personnel to develop human resources in a company
Payroll Management (PY)	Maintains all financial records of salaries, wages, bonuses, and deductions of the employees of a company

TABLE 1.3   Submodules of the HCM module

Let's now discuss the SD module in the mySAP ERP system.

The Sales and Distribution Module

The SD module is one of the logistics modules and helps to manage the sales and distribution activities in a company, such as checking for open sales orders and forecasting future material requirements. The SD module also helps in regulating all activities, starting from receiving the order of a product until the product is delivered to the customer.

The following are the basic features of the SD module:

- **Pricing and taxation**—Evaluates the price of a product under various condition types, such as a rebate or discount granted to a customer

- **Availability check**—Checks the availability of a product in the warehouse
- **Credit management**—Defines the credit limit for a customer during the sale of various products by a company
- **Billing and invoice**—Generates bills or invoices after a sales order for a product is placed
- **Material determination**—Helps determine the details of materials based on a specific condition type
- **Account determination**—Helps determine the details of a customer based on a specific condition type
- **Text processing**—Helps copy text from one document to another

Other business activities, such as packaging, shipping, and the creation of a sales order, are also managed with the help of the SD module.

After discussing the SD module, let's explore the MM module of the mySAP ERP system.

The Materials Management Module

The MM module is designed to procure and manage the material resources of a company. This module mainly deals with the material and vendor master data and handles inventory functions, such as purchasing, inventory management, and reorder processing. The MM module is implemented at the following levels of SAP implementation:

- Client
- Company code
- Plant
- Storage location
- Purchasing organization

The MM module ensures that the required product is available in adequate quantity at the right price. Moreover, this module reduces the working capital by monitoring raw and packaged products regularly.

After understanding the MM module, let's discuss the PP module of the mySAP ERP system.

The Production Planning Module

The PP module is designed to plan the production phase of a product, such as the type of product and the quantity to be produced on the basis of demand. This module deals with the tasks related to the procurement, warehousing, and transportation of materials in a company. The company also plans for the transportation of intermediate products from one stage of production to another at the specified time. The basic features provided by the PP module are as follows:

- Capacity planning
- Master production scheduling
- Material requirements planning

This module also maintains the master data, such as bills of materials, routings, and work centers. Moreover, it helps plan business activities at various stages, such as sales and operation planning and long-term planning.

Table 1.4 describes the submodules of the PP module:

Submodule	Description
PP-Process Industry	Performs business activities of the process industries, such as oil and gas
Production General	Stores the records of various master data, such as bills of materials, routings, and work centers, in a separate component

TABLE 1.4   Submodules of the PP module

After understanding the role of the PP module in the mySAP ERP system, let's discuss the Logistics Execution (LE) module.

The Logistics Execution Module

The LE module is designed to implement the shipping and delivery activities for the SD module. This module works closely with the MM and SD modules.

In the LE module, the warehouse management process is implemented from the MM module, while the processes of delivery, shipping, and transportation are implemented from the SD module. The LE module helps to create the delivery document for a vendor who returns goods. It also allows a company to consolidate outbound delivery activities into the delivery documents. In addition, it helps to standardize output documents and implement these documents in the Transportation module to maintain the details about the goods returned by a vendor.

After discussing the LE module, let's now introduce the Quality Management (QM) module of the mySAP ERP system.

The Quality Management Module

The QM module is designed to check and enhance the quality of products developed by a company. In addition, it also monitors the performance of various processes, such as planning and execution. Quality management is incorporated in every step of the supply chain. This module can also be used as a computer-aided quality system, which includes the following processes to check the quality of a product:

- Quality planning
- Quality inspection
- Quality certificates
- Quality notification
- Quality control
- Audit management
- Test equipment management
- Stability study

The QM module is integrated with the MM and SD modules, as data is needed from these modules to perform quality inspection. This module allows you to transfer or archive information to plan and trace quality-related activities in a company. Even the planning, executing, and evaluating of audits is supported by SAP audit management provided by the QM module.

The following steps should be performed for the audit process:

1. Create an audit plan
2. Create a question list

3. Execute the audit
4. Capture corrective and preventive actions
5. Prepare the documentation (report)
6. Evaluate the documentation

The QM module provides the following interfaces to exchange data with external systems:

- **Inspection Data Interface**—Exchanges the data that needs to be inspected between the QM module and external systems
- **Statistical Data Interface**—Connects the QM module with external evaluation systems

Let's now discuss the Warehouse Management (WM) module of the mySAP ERP system.

The Warehouse Management Module

The WM module divides the storage location defined in the Inventory Management submodule into storage types and storage sections. The storage types are further divided into storage bins. This module maintains records of the movement of goods as well as current stock of the inventory. The WM module provides the following functionalities:

- Defining and managing complex warehousing structures
- Optimizing material flow
- Processing goods receipts, goods issued to customers, and stock transfers
- Characterizing the work process in a warehouse
- Performing work efficiently and at a reasonable cost

The WM module integrates with the MM, PP, QM, and SD modules. The stock posted in the WM module is the same as that posted in the IM module. This module also manages hazardous materials, monitors stock movements, and manages stocks at the storage bin level.

After discussing the WM module, let's now explore the role of the Customer Service (CS) module in the mySAP ERP system.

The Customer Service Module

The CS module provides support for customer services, such as monitoring service calls. In addition, this module helps a company manage its service department, which improves customer service, reduces operating costs, and increases the efficiency of the company. This module is linked to the PM module of the mySAP ERP system.

This ends the discussion of all the modules in the mySAP ERP system; let's now explore the MM module in detail.

EXPLORING THE MM MODULE IN SAP SOFTWARE

In a company, various transactions related to goods or materials, such as maintaining records and invoicing purchase orders, need to be recorded on a regular basis. The SAP system provides the MM module to store all these transaction details in the form of organizational data. The MM module is the core module of the mySAP ERP system, as it helps to implement the supply chain. In addition, this module allows you to plan for future production of material on the basis of the past consumption trends.

The MM module works in close collaboration with the FI module, as the price quoted in an invoice in the MM module is used by the FI module to process various other tasks, such as receiving the payment against the invoice. Apart from the FI module, the data of the MM module is also used by various other modules, such as the PP, CO, FI, QM, SD, PM, and WM modules.

In this section, we will briefly explore the role of the MM module in the mySAP ERP system and the integration of the MM module with the other modules. In addition, the section explores the procurement process followed in the mySAP ERP system.

Role of the MM Module in SAP Software

In the world of business, the movement of goods or material from a vendor to a company, and finally to a customer is called a supply chain. This chain is implemented in the mySAP ERP system with the help of the MM module. In addition, the mySAP ERP system ensures that a company has the right material in the right quantity at the right location at the right time and at a competitive price. The MM module allows a company to control its inventory, forecast customer demand, and keep itself updated on all the transactions of the supply chain. The following steps define the flow of material-related information in the mySAP ERP system:

1. Identifying the need for the materials or goods through the Material Requirement Planning (MRP) process followed in the PP module or by a sales order created in the SD module.
2. Forwarding the purchase requirement document that contains the details of the required materials to the vendor.
3. Receiving the material from the vendor, after which the material may be sent for quality inspection with the help of the QM module.
4. Storing the material (verified by the quality department) in the warehouse by using the WM module.
5. Entering the details of the material to be produced in the production order document.
6. Shipping the final goods to the customer's destination. The shipping and delivery details are processed in the SD module of the mySAP ERP system.

   The instant transfer of information among various modules of the SAP system facilitates the smooth functioning of the preceding steps. The MM module helps to transfer the information, such as order details, the status of the inventory in the storage location, and the delivery status, to other modules. Consider a scenario where a customer places an order of 50 items in a company. Now suppose that 20 items are already available in the warehouse; therefore, the company has to manufacture 30 items to fulfill the order. The details of this order are maintained in the SD module of the mySAP ERP system, which are further forwarded to the MM module after checking the availability of the items in the stock. This movement of details from one module to another is known as flow of information. The instant flow of information in the mySAP ERP system reflects the real situation of a company. The company can share such real-time information with various parties, such as customers, vendors, and shareholders. This in turn helps the company have a distinct competitive advantage over other companies.

   After understanding the role of the MM module in SAP, let's explore the integration of this module with the other modules of the mySAP ERP system.

Integration of the MM Module with Other Modules

The transfer of information from one module to another in the mySAP ERP system helps in the integration of these modules. For instance, when an order for an item is placed by a customer, the details of the order are transmitted to the mySAP ERP system. Next, the availability of the item is checked in the stock on the basis of the details of the order. If the item is not available in the stock, the information is forwarded to the MRP tool. This tool allows you to plan the procurement of material in a company. The various modules provide the following information to the MRP tool:

- Information related to production schedules
- Information regarding the material to be produced
- Information related to the request for material, which is available in the procurement system

The information available in the procurement system is used to create the production order document in which the delivery dates of materials are specified. These delivery dates are communicated to the vendors for confirmation. The vendors, in turn, inform the company about the delivery status of the material. On receiving the required materials against an order, the materials are stored in the storage locations of the company and the details of the transaction are transferred to the WM module. Moreover, the information about the availability of the materials in the storage location is transferred to the PP module so that the materials can be used for final production.

After understanding the importance of the integration of modules in the mySAP ERP system, let's explore the procurement process, which plays an important role in materials management.

Exploring the Procurement Process in the MM Module

The process of purchasing the required quantity of goods or materials by a company from another company at the optimum cost is known as procurement. The procurement process also monitors the activities related to quality inspection of the received material, invoice verification, and release of the invoice for payment. Procurement in a company can be both internal and external. Internal procurement refers to the process of purchasing material or services from internal sources, such as a plant or storage location of the company. On the other hand, external procurement refers to the process of purchasing material or services from an external supplier or vendor. The following steps define the procurement process in the MM module:

1. Determining materials requirements either manually or through the MRP process
2. Checking whether or not the stock is available
3. Maintaining the master data, in case of a new product
4. Identifying the sources for supplying material, if the stock is not available
5. Maintaining vendor details in the mySAP ERP system
6. Negotiating the terms and conditions of an order with the vendor
7. Placing a purchase order
8. Discussing the delivery status with the vendor
9. Receiving the goods in the warehouse
10. Issuing the goods to the distribution department
11. Paying the vendor for the delivery of goods

With this, we come to the end of the procurement process in the MM module of the SAP ERP system. The implementation of the preceding steps is discussed in the following chapters of the book.

SUMMARY

The chapter has explored the need for, history, and architecture of the SAP system, with a detailed discussion of its various versions, such as R/1, R/2, and R/3. The evolution of the mySAP ERP system as a follow-up product of the SAP R/3 system was also described in detail. Next, you learned about various features and functions of the SAP GUI and SAP Customizing Implementation Guide. The chapter further explored various SAP modules, such as FI, CO, MM, and SD, along with their submodules. Towards the end, the integration of the MM module with other modules in the mySAP ERP system was explained in detail.

In the next chapter, you will learn how to define the organizational structure in the mySAP ERP system.

Chapter 2

WORKING WITH THE ORGANIZATIONAL STRUCTURE

An organizational structure is a hierarchy that represents the units of an organization and the relationships among these units. The organizational structure provides a clear understanding of the organizational units and their functions. Production, distribution, and storage of raw materials as well as finished goods are some of the activities that are performed in an organization. An appropriate organizational structure facilitates these activities by localizing their execution centers, such as factory, outlet, and storage locations, within an organization specific to material management. In other words, the organizational structure provides a clear insight of an organization.

An organization needs to properly manage its units to flawlessly execute its activities and maximize the operational efficiency. The organizational structure represents the units of an organization in the structured form. As a result, tasks such as managing the organization's business process, assigning roles and responsibilities to the units, and setting economic autonomy among the units may be efficiently done. In other words, if an organization is properly structured, it can be easily managed.

The accurate representation of an organizational structure is helpful in the day-to-day operations of the organization. For example, the regular activity of transferring the material stock to the production unit or from production to the testing unit becomes an easier task if the concerned staff is familiar with the organizational structure; otherwise, any misunderstanding may lead to unwanted delay in the production or testing of materials. To provide adequate security in an organization, the clear understanding of the organizational structure is required. In other words, the appropriate and timely deployment of security personnel in an organization is possible if its organizational structure is known. In addition, you can establish intensive security zones in highly sensitive organizations, such as nuclear reactors, power plants, and government establishments, after understanding their organizational structure.

In this chapter, you learn about the organizational structure in an enterprise world. Next, the implementation of organizational structure in the mySAP ERP system is discussed in detail, including its different units, such as client, company code, plants, purchasing organization, and storage locations. In the end, an overview of the organizational structure in the mySAP ERP system under different business scenarios is discussed.

EXPLORING AN ORGANIZATIONAL STRUCTURE IN THE ENTERPRISE WORLD

An enterprise is a large establishment having different types of units. Each unit of an enterprise is responsible for implementing a distinct business process, such as production, sales, and purchasing. You can better understand the units of an enterprise and their functions by studying its organizational structure. As a result, upgrading of the existing units may be easily planned.

The organizational structure of an enterprise helps in various circumstances, such as providing corporate insurance policies to employees. Moreover, the organizational structure helps the management in determining the capital, allocating resources, and finalizing staffs to set up additional units in an enterprise. It facilitates the secured and timely transfer of data among the organizational units when establishing newer units or rearranging older units. In addition, any delays in business operations arising due to insufficient or wrong supply of resources to the concerned units can be avoided.

The organizational structure results in decentralization of the overall workings of the organization. It clearly divides the roles and responsibilities among each organizational unit, such as the production unit, inventory, and assembling utilities. It also facilitates the deployment of skilled personnel, such as sales managers, production controllers, and security officers, in an organization. It also quickens the process of decision making and improves the operational efficiency in day-to-day work. For example, the production house does not need management approval to handle common business operations related to the specific unit.

The formation of organizational structure requires correct assessment of the organizational units, proper planning, and clear understanding of the business processes followed in the organization. It also depends on various factors, such as size of an organization, nature of work, relationship among the units, and coupling between organizational units. The enterprise organizational structures are defined on the basis of the following factors:

- **Functional**—Defines an organizational structure in terms of functions or workings of the organizational units. The resulting organizational structure represents the functions of the organizational units in a hierarchy.
- **Geographical**—Defines an organizational structure in terms of the location of various units in a region. The resulting organizational structure represents the geographical locations of different units in a hierarchy.
- **Products**—Defines an organizational structure in terms of the products manufactured or output delivered. The resulting organizational structure represents the hierarchy of products or outputs.
- **Hybrid**—Defines an organizational structure by combining two or more different organizational structures. Different organizations are combined to form a hybrid organizational structure if they are serviced by a single vendor or they manufacture a common product.
- **Matrix**—Defines an organizational structure where the tasks of organizational units are not apparent.

Figure 2.1 shows the organizational structure on the basis of functions of an enterprise:

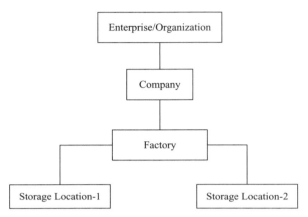

FIGURE 2.1   **Representing an organizational structure**

Based on Figure 2.1, the units of that particular organization are as follows:

- **Enterprise (Organization)**—Represents the topmost level in the organizational structure. The business centers, such as companies, factories, and storage locations, are placed under enterprise.
- **Company**—Represents an autonomous unit of an enterprise that conducts the entire business operation under its own control. In addition, for each company, separate accounting statements are prepared by the management to assess its profitability.
- **Factory**—Represents the separate units of an organization where the goods are manufactured or assembled. Apart from the manufacturing facility, a factory can also contain a sales office or maintenance unit.
- **Storage Location**—Represents a location under factory used to store raw materials, finished goods, scraps, tools, and utilities.

In other words, the organizational structure represents different units of an enterprise in an accurate and informative way. The organizational structure improves the organizational work, interoperability, and exchange of information among various units.

Let's now discuss the implementation of the organizational structure in the mySAP ERP system.

IMPLEMENTING AN ORGANIZATIONAL STRUCTURE IN THE MYSAP ERP SYSTEM

The basic objective of installing the mySAP ERP system in an organization is to automate its business processes, such as materials management, inventory management, or financial accounting. The mySAP ERP system implements the physical organizational structure and creates an equivalent organizational structure in terms of various units, such as client, company code, and plant. The adequate representation of the organizational structure in the mySAP ERP system provides a clear understanding of the organizational units. In addition, it also helps in formulating controlled and accurate business process implementations.

Note that in comparison with the physical organizational structure, the implementation of organizational structure in the mySAP ERP system is logical. The organization where the mySAP ERP system is installed is referred to as the client. The organizational structure in the mySAP ERP system consists of a hierarchy with the client at the topmost level, followed by company code, plant, and storage location. Figure 2.2 shows the organizational structure in the mySAP ERP system:

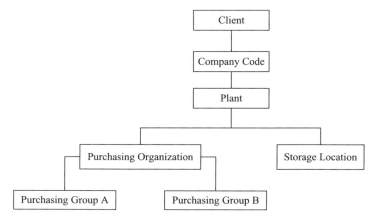

FIGURE 2.2   Displaying an organizational structure in the mySAP ERP system

In Figure 2.2, the client is present at the topmost level of the organizational structure. It is followed by a company code that represents a company under that client. A company represented by a company code executes the business process with the help of its subordinate units, such as plants and storage locations. For each company code, financial accounts are created to calculate the overall profit or loss. Financial accounts need to be complete as well as legal. Financial accounts are considered complete when they provide a clear view of the organization's financial conditions. In addition, financial accounts are legal when they are prepared by authorized personnel and endorsed by the management.

A plant represents a factory under a company where tasks such as production, sales, repair, maintenance, and servicing are performed. Storage locations are used to store the stocks of raw materials, finished products, and scraps. In an organization, storage location can be set up at the plant level. Similarly, a purchasing organization is used to carry out the purchasing process in the organization. Purchasing groups refer to the groups or persons that deal with materials or services purchased through a purchasing organization. The completion of the purchasing process requires contribution from the members of the purchasing groups, such as suppliers, vendors, and the staffs of the purchasing organization. A purchasing organization may have different purchasing groups.

The mySAP ERP system represents various organizational units, such as client, company code, plants, and storage locations. You need to define the organizational units in the mySAP ERP system to implement an organizational structure. At first, you need to define a client, which represents a company or group of companies in the real world. The client is termed as an independent organizational as well as legal entity in the mySAP ERP system.

Next, you need to define rest of the units of the organizational structure, such as plants, storage locations, and purchasing organizations. In addition, a warehouse is also defined in the mySAP ERP system if it is maintained in the organization. After defining the organizational units, you can assign them to each other to establish a relationship between them. For example, after creating a client, company code, and plant in an organization, you can assign the company code to the client and the plant to the company code.

In this section, we discuss the implementation of the following units of the organizational structure in the mySAP ERP system:

- Client
- Company code
- Plant
- Storage location
- Warehouse
- Purchasing organization

Let's start by discussing clients.

Client

As discussed, the client refers to the organization where the mySAP ERP system is installed to implement the business process. For example, let's consider an enterprise named XYZ Corps, which contains a number of subsidiary companies, such as XYZ Medicals and XYZ Hotels. If the mySAP ERP system is installed centrally in XYZ Corps and its services are accessed by the subsidiary companies, then XYZ Corps is treated as a client. If the mySAP ERP system is installed for each subsidiary company, then these companies are treated as individual clients. In other words, an organization that represents the highest entity is referred to as a client in the mySAP ERP system.

The organizational structure varies in size, work plan, and goals of the specific companies under the client. The mySAP ERP system defines the following standard clients:

- **Client 000**—Works as a reference client and does not contain any master data. It is used to perform system specific tasks, such as upgrading the mySAP ERP system and updating client dependent data. You cannot delete it from the mySAP ERP system.
- **Client 001**—Works similar to client 000 and is client dependent.
- **Client 066**—Enables the mySAP ERP system to remotely access the customer's system. In addition, it is also used to improve mySAP ERP system performance and customer support.

The implementation of the organizational structure in the mySAP ERP system is expensive; thereby, proper care is required while creating a client in the mySAP ERP system. A balanced approach in examining the organization is required before creating a client. If the organization is not properly observed, valuable information or elements may not be covered under a client. On the other hand, if over observation of the organization is made, the entities covered under a client may be repeated, and data redundancy and wasted effort may result.

You can define a client in the mySAP ERP system on the basis of the following factors:

- **Organizational Structure**—Creates a client on the basis of an organizational structure. As a result, the highest level of organizational entity is referred to as a client. Other organizational units are formed on the basis of the client.
- **Business Environment**—Creates a client on the basis of the business environment of the organization. As a result, the business process followed in the organization is referred to as a client.
- **Technical Environment**—Creates a client on the basis of master data. As a result, the client is decided on the details of the master data, such as storage location and sales area.
- **Work Environment**—Creates a client on the basis of work area.

After installing the mySAP ERP system in the organization with a default client, the additional clients, such as development, training, production, and quality, are created.

The configuration of the mySAP ERP system changes according to the modifications made in an organization. You can use the Implementation Guide (IMG) tool to configure the changes in the mySAP ERP system. To manage the changes made by IMG, you can use the Correction and Transport System (CTS) tool. This tool manages changes by recording the changes and change requests in the mySAP ERP system. After configuring the changes in the mySAP ERP system, the change request is communicated to the other clients with the help of CTS.

After discussing the client structure in detail, let's discuss the implementation of company code in the mySAP ERP system.

Company Code

Company code refers to the organizational units under a client. For example, XYZ Medicals and XYZ Hotels are the company codes of XYZ Corps. In the mySAP ERP system, you can create and implement independent business entities as separate company codes. You can implement company codes in the mySAP ERP system by performing the following tasks:

- Creating a company code
- Assigning a company code

Let's discuss these tasks in detail.

Creating a Company Code

Company code is the most important entity of the organizational structure. Perform the following steps to create a company code:

1. Click the **IMG Activity** (⊕) icon after navigating the following menu path:

Menu Path

SAP Customizing Implementation Guide > Enterprise Structure > Definition > Financial Accounting > Edit, Copy, Delete, Check Company Code. The resulting **Display IMG** screen is shown in Figure 2.3:

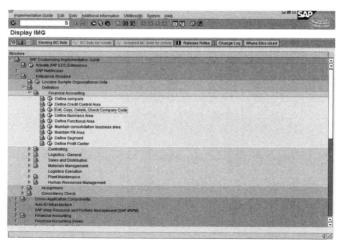

FIGURE 2.3   Displaying the menu path to create a company code

The **Choose Activity** dialog box appears (Figure 2.4).

2. Select the **Edit Company Code Data** activity from the **Choose Activity** dialog box and click the **Choose** push button, as shown in Figure 2.4:

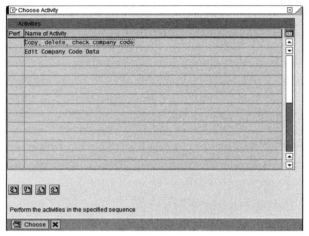

FIGURE 2.4   Displaying the Choose Activity dialog box

The **Change View "Company Code": Overview** screen appears, displaying the existing company codes along with the company name, as shown in Figure 2.5:

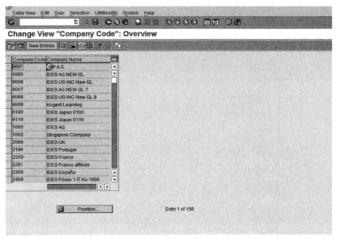

FIGURE 2.5   Displaying the Change View "Company Code": Overview screen

3. Click the **New Entries** button to create a new company code. The **New Entries: Details of Added Entries** screen appears, as shown in Figure 2.6:

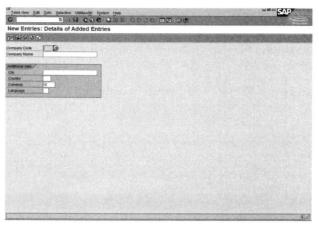

FIGURE 2.6   **Displaying the New Entries: Details of Added Entries screen**

4. Enter the details, such as company code, company name, city, country code, currency, and language. In our case, we have entered company code as `1919`, company name as `Kogent Solutions`, city as `New Delhi`, country code as `IN`, currency as `INR`, and language as `EN` (Figure 2.7).
5. Click the **Save** (⊟) icon to save the company code in the mySAP ERP system, as shown in Figure 2.7:

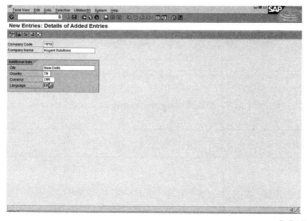

FIGURE 2.7   **Entering the company code details**

Note: If the details of the company code are saved for the first time, the **Edit Address: 1919** dialog box appears, where you can enter the address details of the company code.

6. Click the **Back** (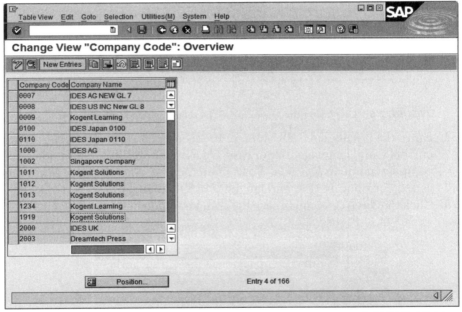) icon in the **New Entries: Details of Added Entries** screen (Figure 2.7).

The **Change View "Company Code": Overview** screen appears, displaying the newly created company code (1919), as shown in Figure 2.8:

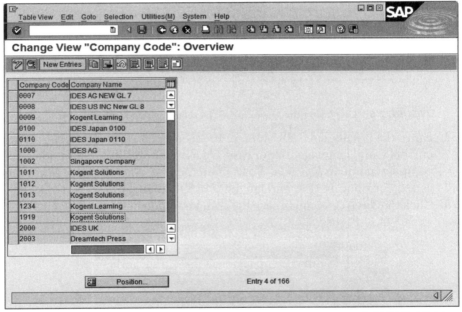

FIGURE 2.8   Displaying the company code details

Note: You can also create a company code by using the OX15 transaction code.

After creating the company code, you can edit various details of it, such as company name, currency, country, city, and language. Perform the following steps to edit the details of company code:

1. Select the **Edit Company Code Data** activity (Figure 2.4).

The **Change View "Company Code": Overview** screen appears (Figure 2.8).

2. Double-click the 1919 company code (Figure 2.8).

The **Change View "Company Code": Details** screen appears, as shown in Figure 2.9:

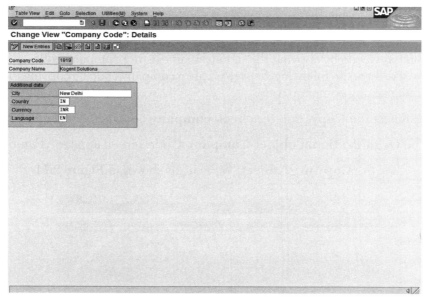

FIGURE 2.9   Displaying the Change View "Company Code": Details screen

3. Modify the detail that you want to edit. In our case, we have changed the city of the company code from New Delhi to Pune (Figure 2.10).
4. Click the **Save** (■) icon to save the edited data. The **Data was saved** message appears, as shown in Figure 2.10:

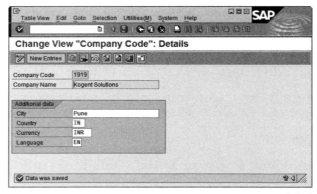

FIGURE 2.10 Displaying edited attributes of the 1919 company code

Apart from creating and editing a company code, you can also create a new company code by copying the details of an existing company code.

Perform the following steps to create a company code by copying the details of an existing company code:

1. Select the **Copy, delete, check company code** activity (Figure 2.4).

The **Organizational object Company Code** screen appears (Figure 2.11).

2. Click the **Copy org. object** (🖻) icon, as shown in Figure 2.11:

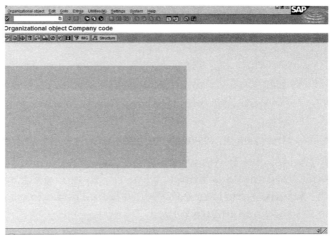

FIGURE 2.11 Displaying the Organizational object Company Code screen

The **Copy** dialog box appears (Figure 2.12).

3. Enter the company code from which you want to create the new company in the **From Company Code** text box. In our case, we have entered 1000 (Figure 2.12).
4. Enter the company code that would be created by copying the existing company code in the **To Company Code** text box. In our case, we have entered 2200 (Figure 2.12).
5. Click the **Continue** (☑) icon to complete the process of creating the company code by copying an existing one, as shown in Figure 2.12:

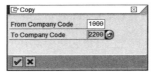

FIGURE 2.12   **Displaying the Copy dialog box**

The **Complete org. object** dialog box appears, prompting you to continue the copying process (Figure 2.13).

6. Click the **Yes** button, as shown in Figure 2.13:

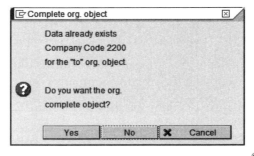

FIGURE 2.13   **Displaying the Complete org. object dialog box**

The **G/L accounts in company code 2200** dialog box appears (Figure 2.14).

7. Click the **Yes** button, as shown in Figure 2.14:

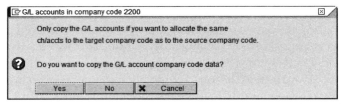

FIGURE 2.14 **Displaying the G/L accounts in company code 2200 dialog box**

The **Change local currency** dialog box appears (Figure 2.15).

8. Click the **No** button, as shown in Figure 2.15:

FIGURE 2.15 **Displaying the Change local currency dialog box**

The **Information** dialog box appears and confirms the successful creation of a company code by copying the existing company code (Figure 2.16).

9. Click the **Continue** (☑) icon, as shown in Figure 2.16:

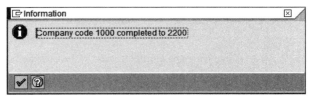

FIGURE 2.16 **Displaying the Information dialog box**

The **Organizational object Company code** screen appears, displaying the 1000 company code that was selected to create the new company code, as shown in Figure 2.17:

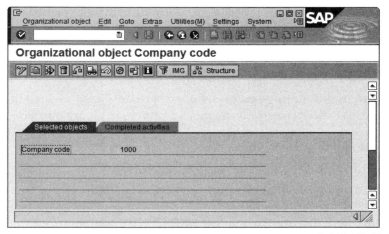

FIGURE 2.17   Selecting an existing company code to create a new company code

> **Note:** You can view the details of the activities performed to create a new company code by selecting the **Completed activities** tab of the **Organizational object Company code** screen (Figure 2.17).

Now, after creating the company code, you can assign it to different units of the organizational structure, such as plant. Let's learn how to assign the company code to different units.

Assigning the Company Code

The business processes of an organization are executed under a company code. For example, plants and storage locations are established under a company code to execute the production as well as storage of materials. Therefore, the company code is assigned to plants as well as storage locations in the mySAP ERP system.

In addition to plants and storage locations, you can also assign a company code to the following units:

■   **Credit control area**—Refers to a logical area in the mySAP ERP system that controls and manages centralized credit control policy in the organization. It is used to define credit information for each customer. You can create the credit control area by navigating the following menu path:

Menu Path

SAP Customizing Implementation Guide > Enterprise Structure > Assignment > Financial Accounting > Assign company code to credit control area

- **Financial management area**—Represents a logical area in the mySAP ERP system for financial planning in an organization. Proper budgeting or allocation of funds is required for the smooth functioning of a company code.

To assign the company code to the relevant units, you need to select a unit to which you want to assign the company code and save the configuration in the mySAP ERP system.

Now, let's discuss plants in the mySAP ERP system.

Plant

A plant is a centralized location in an organization where production, servicing, and maintenance are performed. The definition of plants in the mySAP ERP system varies according to the production planning and materials management concepts. For example, a plant is defined as a location containing the valuated material stocks according to materials management and a location for production according to production planning. In addition, the stocks under a plant are evaluated at the plant level.

After understanding the company code and plant descriptions, you need to learn to valuate the material stocks either at the company code or plant level by using the valuation levels. The stock valuation level represents levels at which stocks are evaluated in an organization. The valuation level of stocks may be either at the company code or the plant level. The evaluation of the stock at the plant level is carried out for production, planning, or costing.

You can valuate stocks by determining the stock valuation level. To determine the correct valuation level of stocks, you need to properly manage the stocks either on the basis of quantity or value. If the stocks are managed on the basis of the quantity, the stock movements, such as goods issue or goods receipt, are recorded in the mySAP ERP system, and the quantities of materials are updated accordingly. However, if the stock materials are managed on the basis of the value, the financial accounting entries are updated for each stock movement.

Navigate the following menu path to determine the stock valuation level:

Menu Path

SAP Customizing Implementation Guide > Enterprise Structure > Definition > Logistics-General > Define valuation level. The resulting **Display IMG** screen is shown in Figure 2.18:

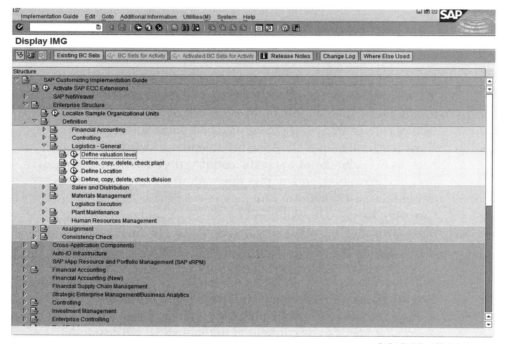

FIGURE 2.18   Displaying the menu path to determine the stock valuation level

Note: After defining the valuation level, it cannot be changed either from the company code to the plant level, or vice versa.

Now, let's discuss the steps to create a plant.

You need to perform the following tasks while implementing plants in the mySAP ERP system:

- Define a plant
- Assign the plant to a company code

Let's discuss these in detail.

Defining a Plant

As discussed, a plant is an important unit of an organizational structure; therefore, it should be defined appropriately in the mySAP ERP system. A plant is defined on the basis of the following units:

- **Factory Calendar**—Refers to a calendar that contains the information about the plant's activities, such as the planning, production, assembly, and delivery processes. In other words, a factory calendar forms the basis of scheduling various business activities during a period. A factory calendar is defined on the basis of the calendar of a specific country, production planning, resource allocation, and market fluctuation. Different countries around the world use different factory calendars.
- **Country Keys**—Determines the code of a country where the plant is located or intended to be set up. The mySAP ERP system contains the country keys of most countries. If a country key is not defined, it can be configured in the mySAP ERP system.
- **Region Keys**—Represents a country key and references the specific regions under the country key. If a key is not already defined, it needs to be configured in the mySAP ERP system.

If you want to define a plan based on a factory calendar, you must first create the factory calendar. Perform the following steps to create a factory calendar:

1. Click the **Activity** (⊕) icon after navigating the following menu path:

Menu Path

SAP Customizing Implementation Guide > Sales and Distribution > Master Data > Business Partners > Customers > Shipping > Define Customer Calendars, as shown in Figure 2.19:

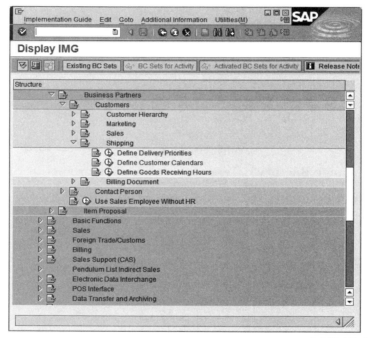

FIGURE 2.19   Displaying the menu path to create a factory calendar

The **SAP Calendar: Main Menu** screen appears (Figure 2.20).

2. Select the **Factory calendar** radio button (Figure 2.20).
3. Click the **Change** push button, as shown in Figure 2.20:

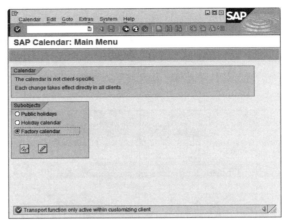

FIGURE 2.20   Displaying the SAP Calendar: Main Menu screen

The **Change Factory Calendar: Overview** screen appears (Figure 2.21).

4. Click the **Create** push button, as shown in Figure 2.21:

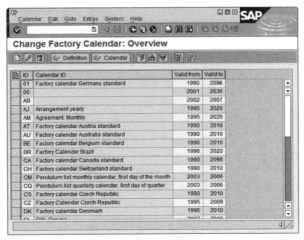

FIGURE 2.21   Displaying the Change Factory Calendar: Overview screen

The **Change Factory Calendar: Details** screen appears (Figure 2.22).

5. Enter the ID and description of the factory calendar. In our case, we have entered DX as the factory calendar ID and DXL Groups Factory Calendar as the description (Figure 2.22).
6. Enter a holiday calendar ID in the **Holiday Calendar ID** text box. In our case, we have entered US as the holiday calendar ID (Figure 2.22).
7. Click the **Save** (🖫) icon, as shown in Figure 2.22:

FIGURE 2.22   Displaying the Change Factory Calendar: Details screen

The **Change Factory Calendar: Details** dialog box appears (Figure 2.23).

8. Click the **Continue** (☑) icon, as shown in Figure 2.23:

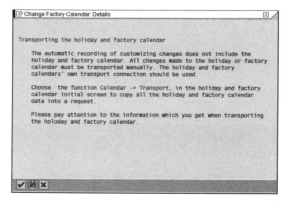

FIGURE 2.23   Displaying the Change Factory Calendar: Details dialog box

The status bar displays a message indicating the successful creation of the factory calendar, as shown in Figure 2.24:

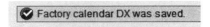

FIGURE 2.24   **Displaying a message after creating a factory calendar**

9. Click the **Display** push button to view the newly created factory calendar (Figure 2.20).

The **Display Factory Calendar: Overview** screen appears, displaying the DX factory calendar, as shown in Figure 2.25:

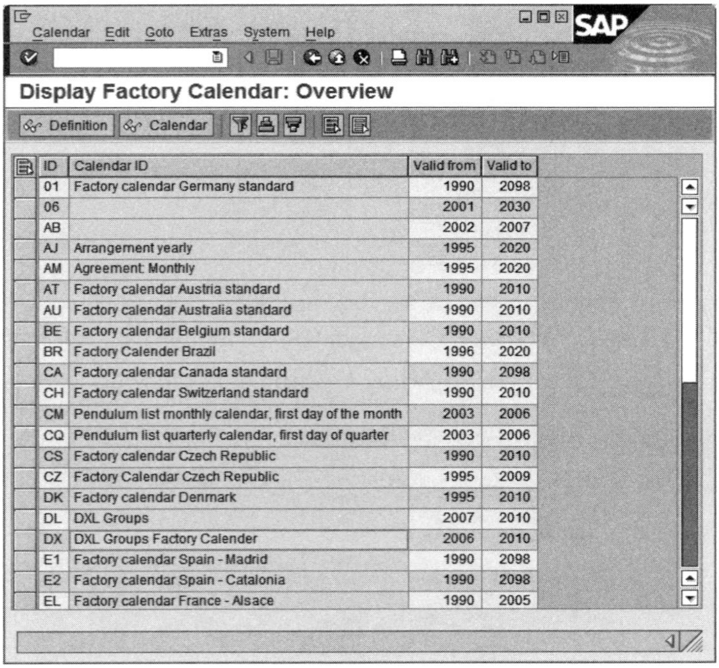

ID	Calendar ID	Valid from	Valid to
01	Factory calendar Germany standard	1990	2098
06		2001	2030
AB		2002	2007
AJ	Arrangement yearly	1995	2020
AM	Agreement: Monthly	1995	2020
AT	Factory calendar Austria standard	1990	2010
AU	Factory calendar Australia standard	1990	2010
BE	Factory calendar Belgium standard	1990	2010
BR	Factory Calender Brazil	1996	2020
CA	Factory calendar Canada standard	1990	2098
CH	Factory calendar Switzerland standard	1990	2010
CM	Pendulum list monthly calendar, first day of the month	2003	2006
CQ	Pendulum list quarterly calendar, first day of quarter	2003	2006
CS	Factory calendar Czech Republic	1990	2010
CZ	Factory Calendar Czech Republic	1995	2009
DK	Factory calendar Denmark	1995	2010
DL	DXL Groups	2007	2010
DX	DXL Groups Factory Calender	2006	2010
E1	Factory calendar Spain - Madrid	1990	2098
E2	Factory calendar Spain - Catalonia	1990	2098
EL	Factory calendar France - Alsace	1990	2005

Display Factory Calendar: Overview

Calendar   Edit   Goto   Extras   System   Help

FIGURE 2.25   **Displaying the Display Factory Calendar: Overview screen**

After creating the factory calendar, perform the following steps to define a plant:

1. Click the **IMG Activity** (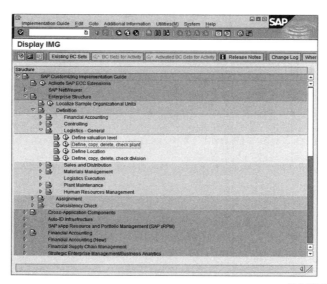) icon after navigating the following menu path:

Menu Path

SAP Customizing Implementation Guide > Enterprise Structure > Definition > Logistics-General > Define, copy, delete, check plant. Figure 2.26 shows the navigated menu path in the **Display IMG** screen:

FIGURE 2.26   **Displaying the menu path to define a plant**

The **Choose Activity** dialog box appears (Figure 2.27).

2. Select the **Define Plant** activity to create a new plant and click the **Choose** push button, as shown in Figure 2.27:

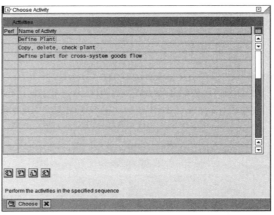

FIGURE 2.27 Displaying the Choose Activity dialog box to define a plant

The **Change View "Plants": Overview** screen appears (Figure 2.28).

3. Click the **New Entries** button, as shown in Figure 2.28:

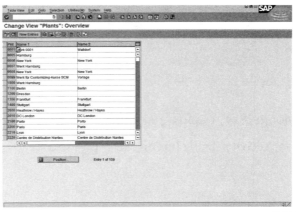

FIGURE 2.28 Displaying the Change View "Plants": Overview screen

The **New Entries: Details of Added Entries** screen appears (Figure 2.29).

4. Enter the details, such as plant name (say DXL) and factory calendar (say AM) in the **New Entries: Details of Added Entries** screen (Figure 2.29).

5. Click the **Save** (□) icon, as shown in Figure 2.29:

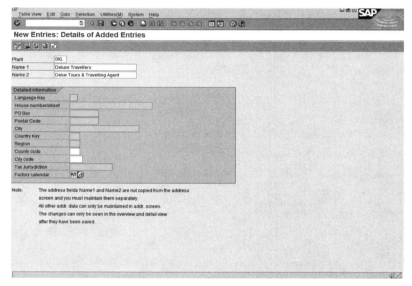

FIGURE 2.29   **Entering the details to create a new plant**

The **Edit address: DXL** dialog box appears (Figure 2.30).

6. Enter the details, such as the name, street address, post box address, and communication address of the DXL plant in the **Edit address: DXL** dialog box (Figure 2.30).

7. Click the **Continue** (☑) icon to copy the address details of the DXL plant into the mySAP ERP system, as shown in Figure 2.30:

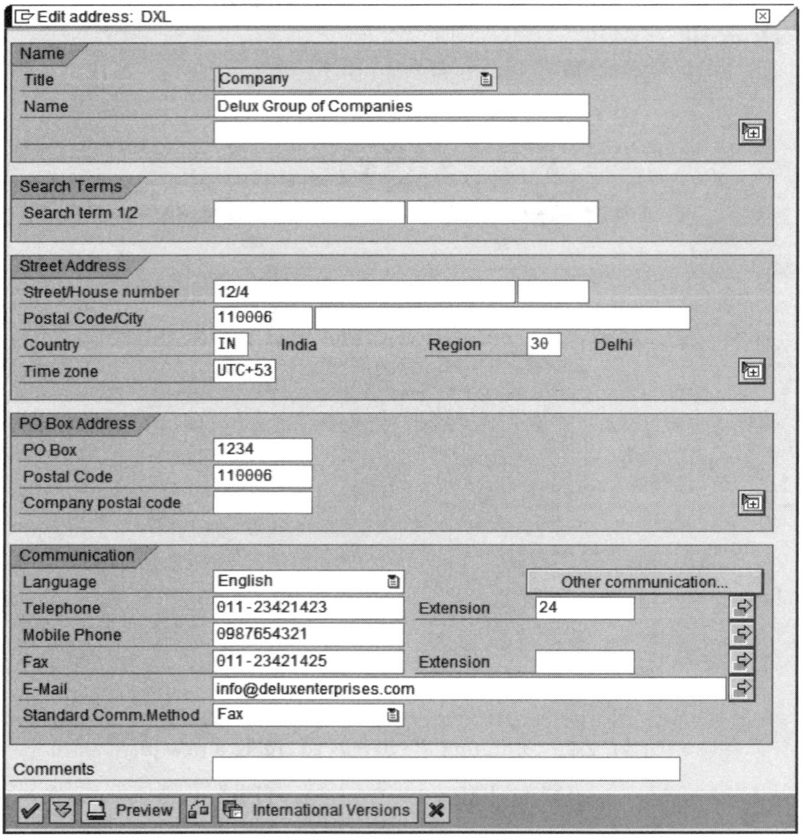

FIGURE 2.30 Displaying the Edit address: DXL dialog box

The **Data was saved** message appears on the status bar of the **New Entries: Details of Added Entries** screen, as shown in Figure 2.31:

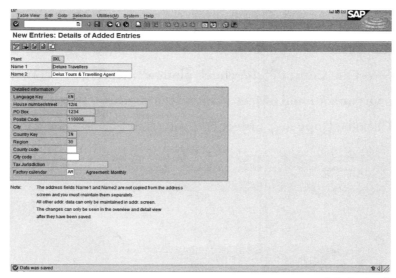

FIGURE 2.31   Saving the plant details

8. Click the **Back** (⬅) icon in the **New Entries: Details of Added Entries** screen (Figure 2.31).

The **Change View "Plants": Overview** screen appears, displaying the details of the DXL plant, as shown in Figure 2.32:

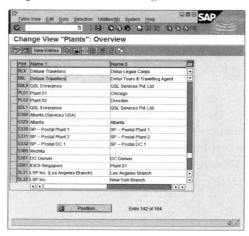

FIGURE 2.32   Displaying the plant details

You can also create a plant by copying the details of an existing plant. Perform the following steps to create a new plant by copying the details of an existing plant:

1. Select the **Copy, delete, check plant** activity (Figure 2.27).

The **Organizational object Plant** screen appears (Figure 2.33).

2. Click the **Copy org. object** (🖼) icon, as shown in Figure 2.33:

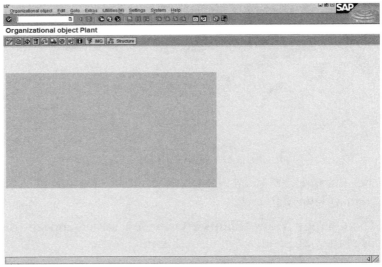

FIGURE 2.33   Displaying the Organizational object Plant screen

The **Copy** dialog box appears (Figure 2.34).

3. Enter the plant code from which you want to create a new plant in the **From Plant** text box. In our case, we have entered DXL (Figure 2.34).
4. Enter the plant code that would be created after copying an existing plant in the **To Plant** text box. In our case, we have entered QSL1 (Figure 2.34).
5. Click the **Continue** (☑) icon to complete the process of creating a plant by copying an existing plant, as shown in Figure 2.34:

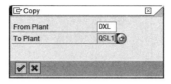

FIGURE 2.34   **Displaying the Copy dialog box to create a plant**

The **Information** dialog box appears and displays a message indicating successful creation of a plant code by copying an existing plant code (Figure 2.35).

6. Click the **Continue** (✅) icon, as shown in Figure 2.35:

FIGURE 2.35   **Displaying the Information dialog box**

The **Organizational object Plant** screen appears, displaying the DXL plant code that was selected to create a new plant, as shown in Figure 2.36:

FIGURE 2.36   **Selecting an existing plant to create a new plant**

Note: You can view the details of the completed activities by selecting the **Completed activities** tab of the **Organizational object Plant** screen (Figure 2.36).

After defining a plant, let's now discuss how to assign the plant to a company code for further implementation of the organizational structure.

Assigning the Plant to a Company Code

Perform the following steps to assign the plant to a company code:

1. Navigate the following menu path and click the **IMG Activity** (⊕) icon:

Menu Path

SAP Customizing Implementation Guide > Enterprise Structure > Assignment > Logistics-General > Assign plant to company code. Figure 2.37 shows the preceding navigated menu path in the **Display IMG** screen:

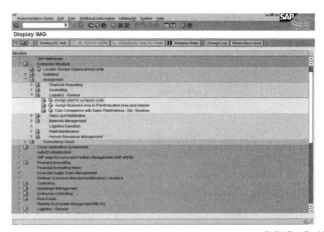

FIGURE 2.37   Displaying the menu path to assign the plant to a company code

The **Change View "Assignment Plant – Company Code": Overview** screen appears (Figure 2.38).

2. Click the **New Entries** button, as shown in Figure 2.38:

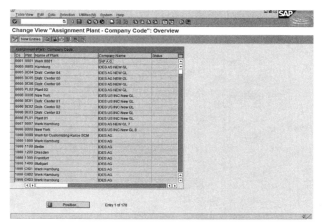

FIGURE 2.38   **Displaying the Change View "Assignment Plant - Company Code": Overview screen**

The **New Entries: Overview of Added Entries** screen appears (Figure 2.39).

3. Enter the company code and plant code in the **CoCd** and **Plnt** fields, respectively. In our case, we have entered 1919 as the company code and DXL as the plant code (Figure 2.39).

4. Click the **Save** (🖫) icon, as shown in Figure 2.39:

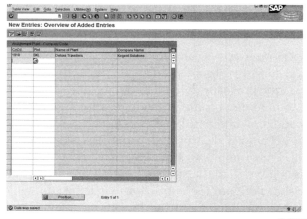

FIGURE 2.39   **Assigning the DXL plant to the 1919 company code**

The **Change View "Assignment Plant – Company Code": Overview** screen appears, displaying the DXL plant that is assigned to the 1919 company code, as shown in Figure 2.40:

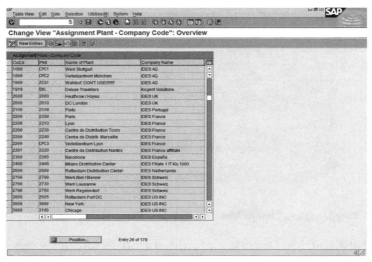

FIGURE 2.40 **Displaying plant and company code details**

Let's now discuss the implementation of storage locations in the mySAP ERP system.

Storage Location

A storage location is a physical place that is used to store a variety of items, such as raw materials, finished goods, and repair parts. In an organizational structure, a storage location is usually defined under a plant. However, you can define the storage location under a company code to store items that are not reserved for the production or manufacturing process, such as office equipment, stationary, or computers. The size of a storage location varies depending upon the material to be stored. For example, to store computer chips, a small storage location is required as compared to the storage location required to store an aircraft.

There is no standard technique for managing storage locations. However, some organizations implement the inventory monitoring process to manage them. The inventory monitoring process uniquely defines the area under the storage location in the mySAP ERP system. This prevents the storage of similar items in two different areas. On the other hand, the storage location can also be managed by dividing the storage area into different parts, such as storage bin and cabinet.

The advantages of managing storage locations include adequate storage of materials and goods, low inventory holding cost, and prevention of waste. Moreover, timely and uninterrupted supply of materials is ensured by managing the storage locations effectively. Poor management of storage locations is a common problem faced by organizations. The organizations either do not define the storage location or define it incorrectly. As a result, the materials are stored at places not defined for them. To overcome this problem, assessment of the current stock, rechecking of the storage facilities, and proper investigation of the stock movements are completed.

In this section, you learn to perform the following tasks:

- Define a storage location
- Edit storage location details
- Create the storage location automatically

Let's learn all these in detail.

Defining a Storage Location

Each storage location is uniquely defined in the mySAP ERP system and assigned to a specific plant. Defining the storage location in the mySAP ERP system not only assures the exact representation of the storage location in an organization, but also indicates that the materials are physically stored in that storage location. Perform the following steps to define a storage location in the mySAP ERP system:

1. Navigate the following menu path and click the **IMG Activity** (⊕) icon:

Menu Path

SAP Customizing Implementation Guide > Enterprise Structure > Definition > Materials Management > Maintain storage location.

Figure 2.41 shows the preceding navigated menu path in the **Display IMG** screen:

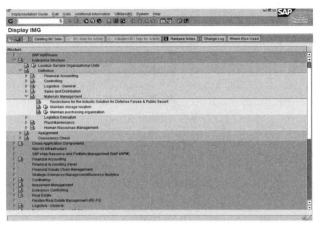

FIGURE 2.41   Displaying the menu path to Maintain storage locations

The **View Cluster Maintenance: Initial Screen**, displaying the **Determine Work Area: Entry** dialog box, appears (Figure 2.42).

2. Enter the plant code of the plant under which you want to create the storage location, in the **Plant** text box. In our case, we have entered DXL (Figure 2.42).

3. Click the **Continue** (✓) icon, as shown in Figure 2.42:

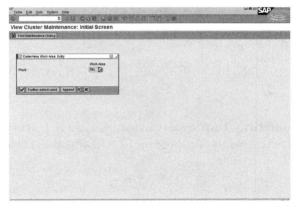

FIGURE 2.42   Displaying View Cluster Maintenance: Initial Screen

The Change View "Storage locations": Overview screen appears (Figure 2.43).

5. Click the **New Entries** button, as shown in Figure 2.43:

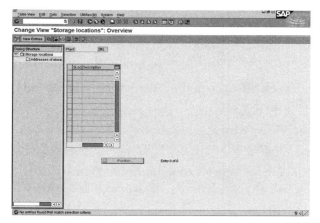

FIGURE 2.43 **Displaying the Change View "Storage Locations": Overview screen**

The **New Entries: Overview of Added Entries** screen appears (Figure 2.44).

6. Enter the unique number and description for a new storage location in the **SLoc** and **Description** fields, respectively. In our case, we have entered 101 as the unique storage location number and DXL Storage Loc as its description (Figure 2.44).
7. Click the **Save** (🖫) icon to save the entered data, as shown in Figure 2.44:

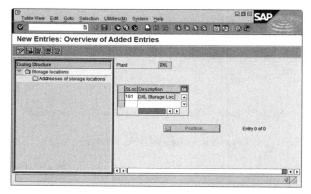

FIGURE 2.44 **Displaying the newly created storage location**

In Figure 2.44, you can see that the `101` storage location has been created under the `DXL` plant. Let's now learn to edit the details of an existing storage location.

Editing Storage Location Details

After creating a storage location, you can edit its details, such as name, address, and city. Perform the following steps to edit the details of a storage location:

1. Click the **Back** (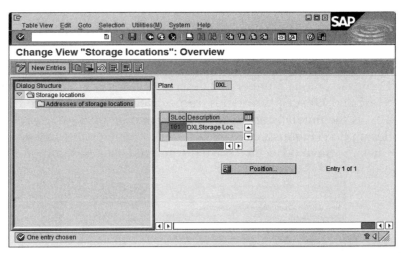) icon in the **New Entries: Overview of Added Entries** screen (Figure 2.44).

The **Change View "Storage locations": Overview** screen appears, displaying the `101` storage location number assigned to the `DXL` plant (Figure 2.45).

2. Select the `101` storage location number (Figure 2.45).
3. Double-click the **Addresses of storage locations** folder, as shown in Figure 2.45:

FIGURE 2.45   Displaying the 101 storage location

The **New Entries: Overview of Added Entries** screen appears (Figure 2.46).

4. Enter a unique number for the `101` storage location under the `DXL` plant in the **No.** field. In our case, we have entered `1` (Figure 2.46).
5. Click the **Address** (⬛) icon, as shown in Figure 2.46:

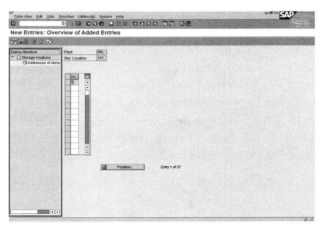

FIGURE 2.46   **Entering the address number of the 101 storage location**

The **Edit address: 1** dialog box appears (Figure 2.47).

6. Enter the desired address details for the `101` storage location in the
   Edit address: 1 dialog box (Figure 2.47).
7. Click the **Copy** (Enter) (✅) icon to copy the records into the mySAP ERP
   system, as shown in Figure 2.47:

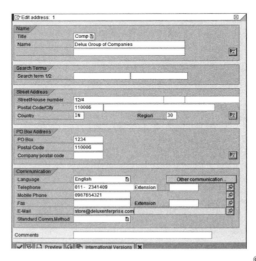

FIGURE 2.47   **Displaying the Edit Address: 1 dialog box**

Figure 2.47 shows the address of the storage location that is edited and copied into the mySAP ERP system.

Now, after editing the address of the storage location, let's discuss how to create a storage location automatically.

Creating a Storage Location Automatically

In the mySAP ERP system, a storage location can be created automatically for goods movement and plants. Perform the following steps to automatically create a storage location in the mySAP ERP system on the basis of plant:

1. Navigate the following menu path and click the **IMG Activity** (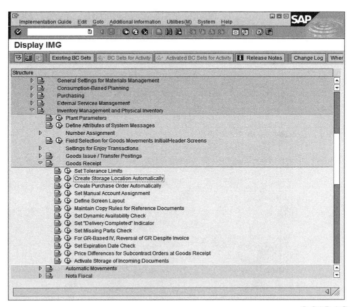) icon:

Menu Path

SAP Customizing Implementation Guide > Materials Management > Inventory Management and Physical Inventory > Goods Receipt > Create Storage Location Automatically. Figure 2.48 shows the preceding menu path in the **Display IMG** screen:

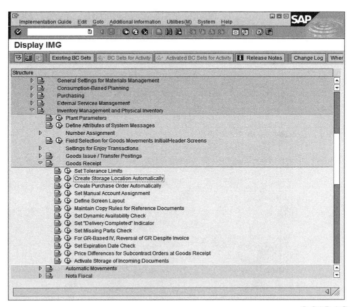

FIGURE 2.48   Displaying the menu path to Create Storage Location Automatically

The **Create Storage Loc. Automatically** screen appears, displaying the options to automatically create the storage location on the basis of plant as well as movement type (Figure 2.49).

2. Click the **Plant** button, as shown in Figure 2.49:

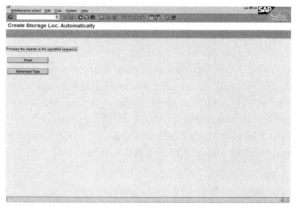

FIGURE 2.49   Displaying the Create Storage Loc. Automatically screen

The **Change View "Autom. Creation of SLoc per Plant": Overview** screen appears, displaying the names of the plants for which storage locations have been created automatically, as shown in Figure 2.50:

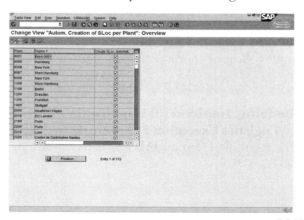

FIGURE 2.50   Displaying the Change View "Autom. Creation of SLoc per Plant": Overview screen

After discussing the storage location in detail, let's discuss the implementation of a warehouse in the next subsection.

Warehouse

A warehouse is an important part of an organization that is used to store finished products, semi-finished goods, scraps, and tools. It also contains separate storage types to store a particular type of material, such as bulk, liquids, chemicals, and metal ores. The storage types can be further divided into storage bins and cabinets. Warehouses are primarily implemented by the Sales and Distribution (SD) module of the mySAP ERP system. As per the Materials Management (MM) module specifications, a warehouse is implemented as one of the storage locations in the mySAP ERP system.

You need to perform the following activities to implement the warehouse organizational unit in the mySAP ERP system:

- Create a warehouse
- Assign the warehouse to plants and storage locations
- Create the storage types

Let's discuss all these in detail.

Creating a Warehouse

In comparison to an internal storage location, warehouses are established at an offshore site near shipping locations. In addition, every goods movement in the warehouse is recorded in the mySAP ERP system.

Perform the following steps to create a warehouse:

1. Navigate the following menu path and click the **IMG Activity** (⊕) icon:

Menu Path

SAP Customizing Implementation Guide > Enterprise Structure > Definition > Logistics Execution > Define, copy, delete, check warehouse number. The resulting **Display IMG** screen is shown in Figure 2.51:

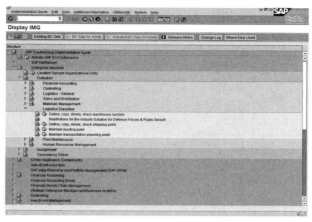

FIGURE 2.51   **Displaying the menu path to create a warehouse**

The **Choose Activity** dialog box appears (Figure 2.52).

2. Select the **Define warehouse number** activity and click the **Choose** push button, as shown in Figure 2.52:

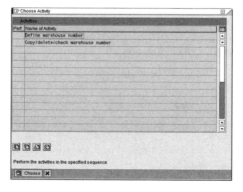

FIGURE 2.52   **Displaying the Choose Activity dialog box to define a warehouse number**

The **Change View "Define warehouse number": Overview** screen appears (Figure 2.53).

3. Click the **New Entries** button, as shown in Figure 2.53:

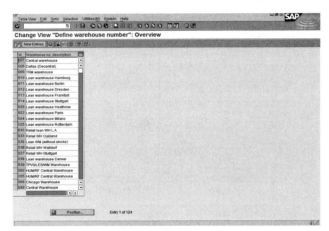

FIGURE 2.53   Change View "Define warehouse number": Overview screen

The **New Entries: Overview of Added Entries** screen appears (Figure 2.54).

4. Enter a unique number and description for a warehouse in the **WhN** and **Warehouse no. description** fields, respectively. In our case, we have entered 888 in the **WhN** field and DXL Warehouse in the **Warehouse no. description** field (Figure 2.54).

5. Click the **Save** (⧉) icon, as shown in Figure 2.54:

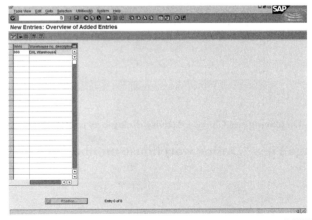

FIGURE 2.54   Defining a warehouse number

6. Click the **Back** (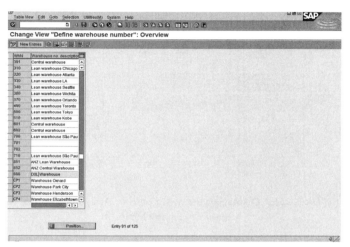) icon in the **New Entries: Overview of Added Entries** screen (Figure 2.54).

The **Change View "Define warehouse number": Overview** screen appears, displaying the newly created warehouse (888), as shown in Figure 2.55:

FIGURE 2.55   Displaying the 888 warehouse number

Now, after creating the warehouse, let's assign the warehouse to a plant or storage location.

Assigning the Warehouse to a Plant or Storage Location

As discussed, a warehouse is created offshore to store finished products and packaging materials for dual purposes, such as for exporting or transferring to a storage location or plant. Therefore, the warehouse must be assigned to plants or storage locations.

Perform the following steps to assign a warehouse to a plant or storage location:

1. Navigate the following menu path and click the **IMG Activity** (⊕) icon:

Menu Path

SAP Customizing Implementation Guide > Enterprise Structure > Assignment > Logistics Execution > Assign warehouse number to plant/ storage location.

The resulting **Display IMG** screen is shown in Figure 2.56:

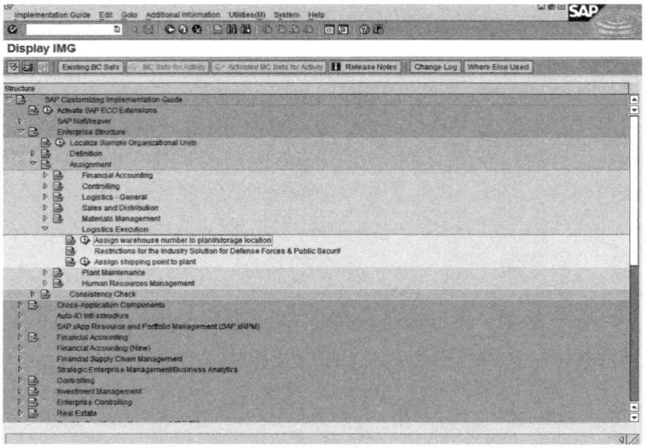

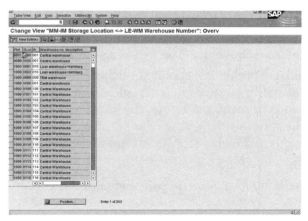

FIGURE 2.56   Displaying the menu path to Assign warehouse to
a plant or storage location

The **Change View "MM-IM Storage Location <-> LE-WM Warehouse Number":** Overview screen appears (Figure 2.57).

2. Click the **New Entries** button, as shown in Figure 2.57:

FIGURE 2.57   Displaying Change View "MM-IM Storage Location <-> LE-WM
Warehouse Number": Overview screen

The **New Entries: Overview of Added Entries** screen appears (Figure 2.58).

3. Enter a plant code, storage location code, and warehouse number in the **Plnt**, **SLoc**, and **WhN** fields, respectively. In our case, we have entered DXL as the plant code, 101 as the storage location code, and 888 as the warehouse number (Figure 2.58).

4. Click the **Save** (🖫) icon, as shown in Figure 2.58:

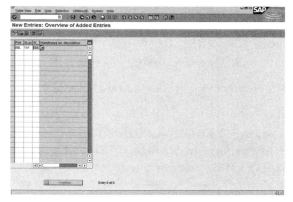

FIGURE 2.58   **Assigning warehouse to a plant or storage location**

The 888 warehouse number has been assigned to the DXL plant and 101 storage location, as shown in Figure 2.59:

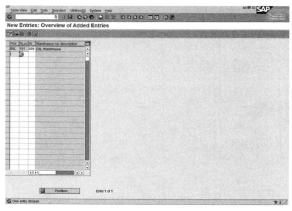

FIGURE 2.59   **Displaying the warehouse assigned to a plant and storage location**

After assigning the warehouse to a plant or storage location, let's learn how to create storage types.

Creating Storage Types

The cost incurred in setting up of a warehouse is high; therefore, it is advisable to efficiently manage warehouse space. In the mySAP ERP system, the storage space of a warehouse is logically divided in separate units, which are called storage types. Each storage type is used to store a unique type of material. In the mySAP ERP system, default storage types are assigned a unique number from 900 to 999.

Perform the following steps to create storage types:

1. Navigate the following menu path and click the **IMG Activity** (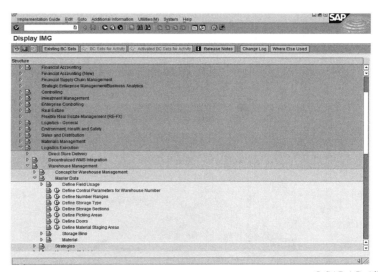) icon:

Menu Path

SAP Customizing Implementation Guide > Logistics Execution > Warehouse Management > Master Data > Define Storage Type. The resulting **Display IMG** screen is shown in Figure 2.60:

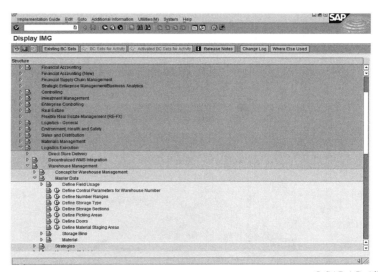

FIGURE 2.60   Displaying the menu path to create storage types

The **Change View "Storage type definition": Overview** screen appears (Figure 2.61).

2. Click the **New Entries** button, as shown in Figure 2.61:

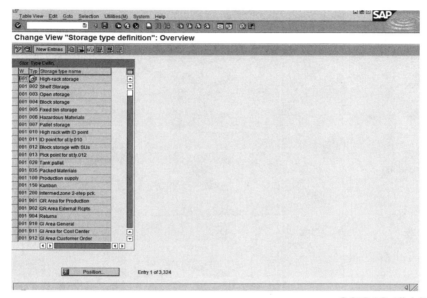

FIGURE 2.61   Displaying the Change View "Storage type definition":
Overview screen

The **Change View "Storage type definition": Details** screen appears (Figure 2.62).

3. Enter the warehouse number under which you want to create the storage type in the **Whse number** field. In our case, we have entered 888 (Figure 2.62).

4. Enter the storage type in the **Storage type** field. In our case, we have entered 003 (Figure 2.62).

5. Click the **Save** () icon, as shown in Figure 2.62:

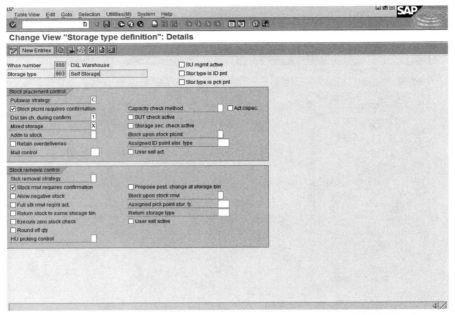

FIGURE 2.62   Displaying the Change View "Storage type definition": Details screen

The **Data was saved** message appears, as shown in Figure 2.63:

FIGURE 2.63   Displaying the status bar

6. Click the **Back** () icon in the **Change View "Storage type definition": Details** screen (Figure 2.62).

The **Change View "Storage type definition": Overview** screen appears, displaying the newly created storage type, 003, as shown in Figure 2.64:

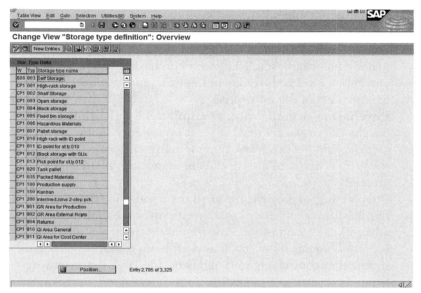

FIGURE 2.64   **Displaying the list of storage types**

After learning about the warehouse, let's discuss the purchasing organization.

Purchasing Organization

A purchasing organization is responsible for performing all the purchase activities centrally in an organization. It helps to perform the tasks required to complete the purchase process, such as studying the requirements of the purchase, preparing the purchase requisition and request of quotation documents, analyzing the documents, and preparing purchase orders. In a large organization, purchasing can be done at different levels, starting from the enterprise level. Therefore, the purchasing organizations can be established at the following levels:

- **Purchasing organization at enterprise level**—Refers to the purchasing organization that is set up at the highest level in an enterprise. At this level, the purchasing organization executes the purchasing activities for all the units of an enterprise, such as companies, plants, storage locations, and warehouses. One of the most common advantages of this level is the facility to closely monitor the purchasing process. On the other hand, the major concern of establishing the purchasing organization at the enterprise level is the delay in finalizing the purchasing process for the units of the enterprise.

- **Purchasing organization at company level**—Refers to the purchasing organization that is set up for each company in an organization. At this level, the purchasing organization executes the purchasing activities of the company under which it is created.

- **Purchasing organization at plant level**—Refers to the purchasing organizations that are set up at the plant level. It is advisable to set up purchasing organizations at the plant level for large organizations, such as petroleum refineries, crude oil production companies, and highly customized manufacturing firms. In all these organizations, a purchasing organization is established on the basis of various important factors, such as availability of the raw materials, distance between the raw material producing organization as well as the plant, and timely availability of the raw materials.

- **Reference purchasing organization**—Refers to the strategic purchasing organization that monitors the purchasing processes followed in an organization. It helps the management and purchasing organizations decide whether to continue or halt the purchasing process. The reference purchasing organization can also help analyze the purchasing process cleared by other purchasing organizations and negotiate with the vendor to get the best deal. In addition, the decision made by the reference purchasing organization regarding discounts and special conditions is accepted by all the purchasing organizations throughout the organization. Therefore, the reference purchasing organization can be critically important from the strategic view. This implies that the reference purchasing organization has more decisive powers than the other purchasing organizations.

You need to perform the following tasks to implement a purchasing organization in the mySAP ERP system:

- Create a purchasing organization
- Assign the purchasing organization to a plant
- Create the purchasing group

Let's discuss these in detail.

Creating a Purchasing Organization

Perform the following steps to create a purchasing organization:

1. Navigate the following menu path and click the **Activity** (⊕) icon:

Menu Path

SAP Customizing Implementation Guide > Enterprise Structure > Definition > Materials Management > Maintain purchasing organization. The resulting **Display IMG** screen is shown in Figure 2.65:

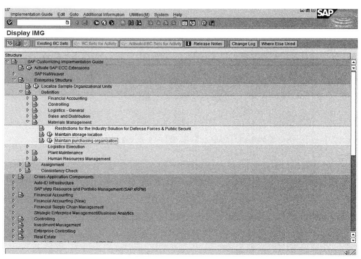

FIGURE 2.65 Displaying the menu path to create a purchasing organization

The **Change View "Purchasing Organizations": Overview** screen appears (Figure 2.66).

2. Click the **New Entries** button to create the new purchasing organization, as shown in Figure 2.66:

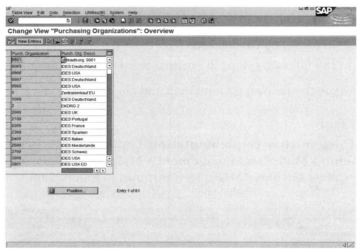

FIGURE 2.66 Displaying the Change View "Purchasing Organizations": Overview screen

The **New Entries: Overview of Added Entries** screen appears (Figure 2.67).

3. Enter a number and description for the purchasing organization in the **Purch. Organization** and **Purch. Org. Descr.** fields, respectively. In our case, we have entered 777 as the purchasing organization number and DXL Purchasing Co. as the description (Figure 2.67).

4. Click the **Save** (⊡) icon to save the details of the purchasing organization, as shown in Figure 2.67:

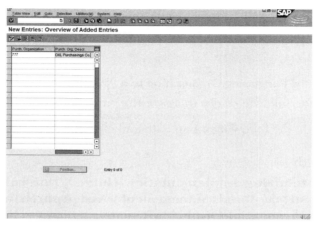

FIGURE 2.67   Creating the 777 purchase organization

5. Click the **Back** (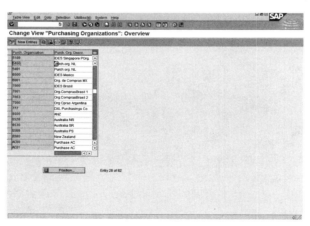) icon to view the new purchasing organization (Figure 2.67).

The **Change View "Purchasing Organizations": Overview** screen appears, displaying the purchasing organization, 777, as shown in Figure 2.68:

FIGURE 2.68   Displaying the Change View "Purchasing Organizations": Overview screen

After creating the purchasing organization, you can assign the purchasing organization to a plant. Let's discuss how to assign the purchasing organization to a plant.

Assigning the Purchasing Organization to a Plant

Perform the following steps to assign the purchasing organization to a plant:

1. Navigate the following menu path and click the **Activity** (⊕) icon:

Menu Path

SAP Customizing Implementation Guide > **Enterprise Structure** > **Assignment** > **Materials Management** > **Assign purchasing organization to plant**. The resulting **Display IMG** screen is shown in Figure 2.69:

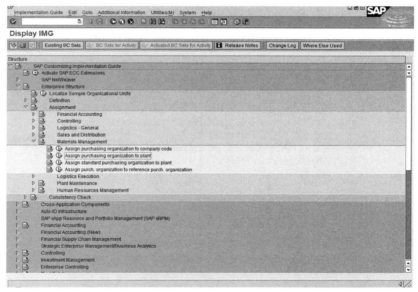

FIGURE 2.69   Displaying the menu path to assign a purchasing organization to a plant

The **Change View "Assign Purchasing Organization to Plant": Overview** screen appears (Figure 2.70).

2. Click the **New Entries** button, as shown in Figure 2.70:

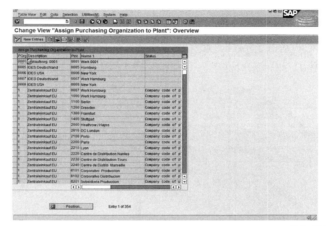

FIGURE 2.70   **Displaying the Change View "Assign Purchasing Organization
to Plant": Overview screen**

The **New Entries: Overview of Added Entries** screen appears (Figure 2.71).

3. Enter the purchasing organization number and plant code in the **POrg** and
Plnt fields, respectively. In our case, we have entered 777 as the purchasing
organization number and DXL as the plant code (Figure 2.71).
4. Click the **Save** (🖫) icon, as shown in Figure 2.71:

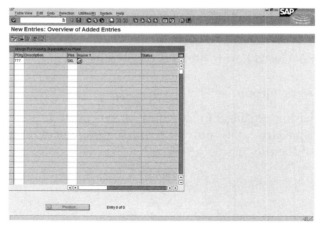

FIGURE 2.71   **Assigning the 777 purchasing organization to the DXL plant**

5. Click the **Back** (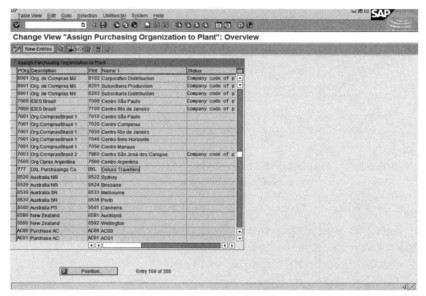) icon to view the purchasing organization that has been assigned to the DXL plant (Figure 2.71).

The **Change View "Assign Purchasing Organization to Plant": Overview** screen appears, displaying the purchasing organization, 777, which is assigned to the DXL plant, as shown in Figure 2.72:

FIGURE 2.72   **Displaying purchase organizations assigned to plants**

Let's now learn how to create a purchasing group.

Creating a Purchasing Group

The purchasing organization contains various persons or groups dealing with materials that are being purchased in the organization. To implement the activities of the purchasing organization, you can create purchasing groups in the mySAP ERP system. Perform the following steps to create a purchasing group:

1. Navigate the following menu path and click the **Activity** (⊕) icon:

Menu Path

SAP Customizing Implementation Guide > Materials Management > Purchasing > Create Purchasing Groups. The resulting **Display IMG** screen is shown in Figure 2.73:

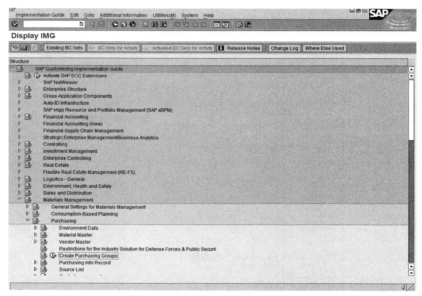

FIGURE 2.73 Displaying the menu path to Create Purchasing Groups

The **Change View "Purchasing Groups": Overview** screen appears (Figure 2.74).

2. Click the **New Entries** button, as shown in Figure 2.74:

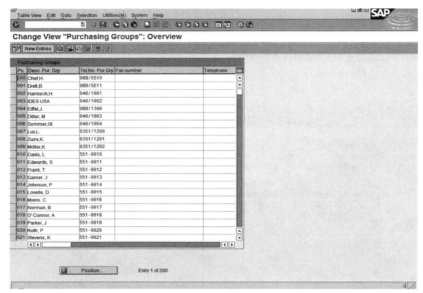

FIGURE 2.74 Displaying the Change View "Purchasing Groups": Overview screen

The **New Entries: Overview of Added Entries** screen appears (Figure 2.75).

3. Enter the details for creating the purchasing group. In our case, we have entered 44 as the purchasing group number, DXL Purchasing Gro as a description, 011-23323235 as a telephone number, 011-33232245 as a fax number, and 011-23476543 as an additional telephone number (Figure 2.75).

4. Click the **Save** (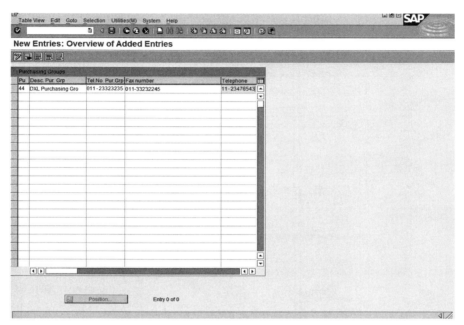) icon to save the details of the purchasing group, as shown in Figure 2.75:

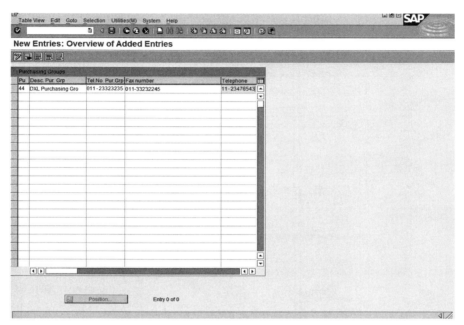

FIGURE 2.75   **Entering details of a purchasing group**

5. Click the **Back** (⬅) icon to view the new purchasing group (Figure 2.75).

The **Change View "Purchasing Groups": Overview** screen appears, displaying the newly created purchasing group named 44, as shown in Figure 2.76:

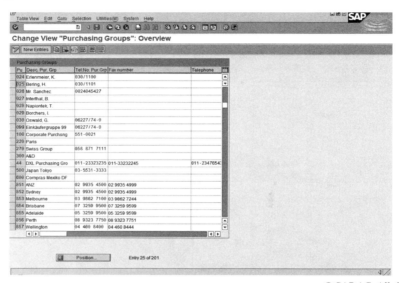

FIGURE 2.76   **Displaying the 44 purchasing group**

After discussing the implementation of organizational units in the mySAP ERP system, let's analyze the organizational structures under various business scenarios.

ANALYZING THE ORGANIZATIONAL STRUCTURE UNDER VARIOUS BUSINESS SCENARIOS

In a real business scenario, the organizational structure may depend on various factors, such as requirements, planning, purchasing, and resource availability. These factors have a significant role in deciding the resulting organizational structure and its business process implementation. In addition to the preceding factors, the organizational structure also depends on the purchasing organization, due to massive investments in its establishment. The major decisions regarding the establishment of purchasing organizations is whether to establish them at the plant or company code level and whether to create a reference purchasing organization. In this section, we discuss the business scenarios involving the purchasing organizations established at the following levels:

- Individual purchasing organization at plant level
- Single purchasing organization for multiple plants
- Cross company code purchasing organization at plant level
- Reference purchasing organization

Now, let's discuss these one by one.

Individual Purchasing Organization at Plant Level

As discussed, the purchasing organization is an important factor that greatly influences an organizational structure. Let's consider a situation where each plant of a company code has a separate purchasing organization. This type of organizational structure is followed in organizations where the business processes are highly customized. Each plant is allocated a distinct set of tasks independent of the other plants in the company code. It helps to maintain the operational efficiency and uninterrupted supply of materials to the individual plants. The organizational structure that includes an individual purchasing organization for each plant is shown in Figure 2.77:

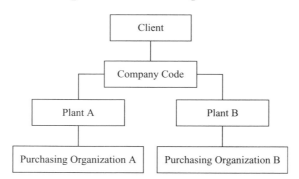

FIGURE 2.77   **Displaying individual purchasing organizations**

Let's now discuss a situation in which multiple plants can use the service of a single purchasing organization.

Single Purchasing Organization for Multiple Plants

Let's consider an organizational structure based on the situation where the single purchasing organization is assigned to more than one plant. The decision to set up this type of organizational structure is based on various factors, such as a common vendor supplying materials to all the plants. In this organizational structure, the purchasing processes of the underlying plants become faster due to their centralized processing. In contrast, the plants may have to wait until their purchasing process is approved, which may affect the production process. Figure 2.78 displays the organizational structure in which a single purchasing organization is assigned to multiple plants:

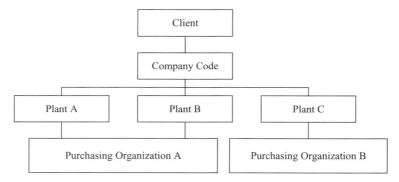

FIGURE 2.78   **Displaying single purchasing organization assigned to multiple plants**

Figure 2.78 represents an organizational structure with a single purchasing organization named A, which is assigned to the A and B plants. In this situation, the purchasing organization, A, is entitled to execute the purchasing processes for the A and B plants.

Let's now consider a situation in which the purchasing organization may be assigned to the plants of different company codes.

Cross Company Code Purchasing Organization at Plant Level

There may be a situation when a common purchasing organization is established across different company codes. As a result, plants of different company codes use the services of the common purchasing organization to complete their purchasing process. The decision to set up such an organizational structure is based on various factors, such as market fluctuation and increased demand of a product. Moreover, if the entire organization is overhauled or a common security, manufacturing, or software system is installed in the organization, a cross company code purchasing organization may be set up. Setting up a common purchasing organization across company codes is an administrative decision. Figure 2.79 represents an organizational structure based on the cross company code purchasing organization:

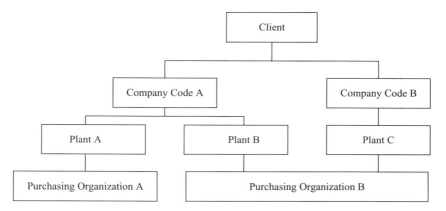

FIGURE 2.79   **Displaying an organizational structure with cross company code purchasing organization**

Figure 2.79 displays an organizational structure that uses a common purchasing organization for plants of separate company codes. Company code A contains plants A and B as well as purchasing organization A; whereas, company code B contains plant C and purchasing organization B. Plant B is assigned to the purchasing organization B of company code B. Therefore, the purchasing process of plant B is executed by purchasing organization B, which belongs to company code B.

Now, let's consider a different business scenario with a reference purchasing organization next.

Reference Purchasing Organization

The centralized purchasing organizations that are set up to monitor the purchasing processes across the organization are called reference purchasing organizations. A reference purchasing organization is more powerful than the individual purchasing organizations, since it is set up at the corporate level. Moreover, it can negotiate with a vendor and create a purchasing plan or formulate a global agreement that is applicable for all the purchasing organizations. An organizational structure based on the reference purchasing organization is shown in Figure 2.80:

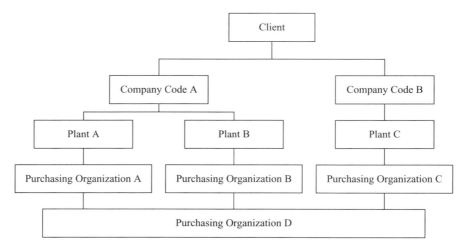

FIGURE 2.80   Displaying the organizational structure based on the reference purchasing organization

In Figure 2.80, the purchasing organizations A, B, and C are assigned to the plants of company codes A and B. Purchasing organization D is a reference purchasing organization assigned to all the other purchasing organizations. Any change or decision made by purchasing organization D is applicable to the rest of the purchasing organizations.

Let's now summarize the concepts learned in the chapter.

SUMMARY

In this chapter, we discussed the organizational structure of an organization in detail, including the units, such as company, factory, and storage location. Next, implementation of the organizational structure in the mySAP ERP system was discussed in detail, including the creation of organizational units, such as client, company code, and plants. In the end, an analysis of the organizational structure under various business scenarios was discussed.

The next chapter discusses the classification of materials in the MM module.

CLASSIFYING MATERIALS IN THE MM MODULE

3

A classification system refers to a technique used to categorize various entities or materials in a structured format. This system is used extensively in a number of companies and institutions to organize different materials and records in an alphabetical, hierarchical, numerical, ideological, spatial, or chronological order. For example, the Dewey Decimal classification system is used to arrange books in a library and the Linnaean classification system is used to arrange animals in a zoo. As the mySAP™ Enterprise Resource Planning (ERP) system deals with a huge amount of data and information generally spread over various modules, a classification system is required to differentiate and categorize this data under various groups. Consider a scenario where a company purchases 500 rubber balls of three different sizes, weights, and colors. As the cost of a ball varies according to its size and weight, the company intends to sell the balls at three different prices. In this case, the classification system of the mySAP ERP system helps to sort the balls according to their characteristics and place them under three different price groups, facilitating the process of managing, processing, and maintaining records.

The chapter acquaints you with the key terms used in the basic material classification system, such as objects, classes, and class types. These terms help in classifying and differentiating one object from another. Next, you learn to configure the material classification system in the mySAP ERP system.

Let's explore key terms used in the material classification system of the Materials Management (MM) module of the SAP® system.

EXPLORING THE MATERIAL CLASSIFICATION SYSTEM

As already learned, the material classification system of the mySAP ERP system is used to arrange various objects, such as the materials and vendor master data of a company. This system not only facilitates storing and maintaining records of the materials, but also helps you to search for a particular record from thousands of records stored in the database of the company, which can save a lot of time and effort.

The following key terms of the material classification system are used to categorize and arrange materials and records in the mySAP ERP system:

- Objects
- Classes
- Characteristics
- Class types
- Class hierarchies

Let's now discuss these key terms in detail.

Objects

An object is defined as a pattern or instance of a class. For example, Maruti 800, Zen, and Tata Indica are objects and car is their class. An object can represent a real world entity, such as a person or place, or a programming entity, such as constants, variables, and memory locations. The three main characteristics of an object are state, behavior, and identity.

The state of an object can be described as a set of attributes and their values. For example, an account has a set of attributes, such as account number, account type, name, and balance, each having a value of its own. The behavior of an object refers to the changes that occur in its attributes for a specific period of time. For example, a washing machine is in the static state of behavior when it is switched off. However, it displays a change in behavior when you switch it on to wash the clothes. Each object has a unique identity that distinguishes it from other objects. Two objects may exhibit the same behavior; however, they may or may not have the same state.

Objects can interact with each other by sending messages. For example, if employee and salary are two objects in a program, the employee object may send a message to the salary object to confirm the tax deduction from the salary. The object that receives the message is called a receiver, and the set of actions performed by a receiver is represented by a method.

An object can be used as a user-defined data type and is also known as the variable of the type class. After defining a class, you can create any number of objects belonging to that class. The objects are associated with the data of the class to which they are assigned. There are three types of objects in the SAP MM module—vendor, material, and batch—that are associated with their corresponding classes.

Classes

A class is a prototype that defines the data and behavior common to the objects of a specific type. In a class, data is represented by class attributes and the behavior of an instance of the class is provided by class methods. In other words, we can say classes describe objects.

In the SAP MM module, a class is used to define characteristics of the objects associated with it. For example, a vehicle hardware trading company may define material classes for the tires, engine, and chassis (body of a vehicle) of a car.

Characteristics

In the SAP MM module, the characteristic component of a classification system specifies the properties of objects that are grouped together in a class. In other words, a characteristic represents a property, such as the length, color, or weight of an object. A class contains a number of characteristics and their values. For example, the mobile class may have color and size characteristics. The values of the color characteristic may be red and blue; while the values of the size characteristic may be 3 inches, 2 inches, and 4 inches.

Class Types

A class type is used to define objects associated with a class. It specifies whether objects should be classified under one class or different classes.

Table 3.1 lists some important class types available in the mySAP ERP system:

Class Type	Class Name	Description
001	Material	Represents the material class of the MM module
002	Equipment	Represents the equipment class of the MM module
010	Vendor	Represents the vendor class of the MM module
011	Customer	Represents the customer class of the MM module
017	Document Management	Represents the document management class of the MM module
042	Funds	Represents the funds class of the MM module
AUP	Audit Partner	Represents the audit partner class of the MM module

TABLE 3.1   Class types of the MM module

Note: After creating a class, you cannot change its class type.

Class Hierarchies

In the MM module, class hierarchies represent a list of superior and subordinate classes that are inherited or extended from a class. For example, in an organization, the superior class is represented by the employee class having two subordinate classes—part-time employees and full-time employees.

Navigate the following menu path to create a class hierarchy:

Menu Path

SAP menu > Cross-Application Components > Classification System > Environment > Reporting > Class Hierarchy, as shown in Figure 3.1:

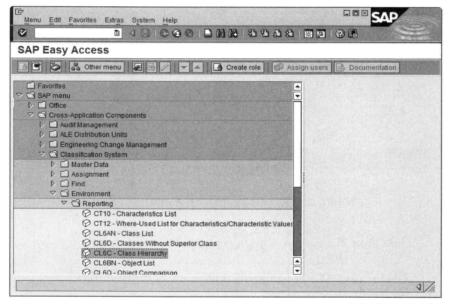

FIGURE 3.1   **Displaying the CL6C – Class Hierarchy activity**

Now, double-click the **CL6C – Class Hierarchy** option in the **Reporting** folder to create a class hierarchy.

The **Class Hierarchy** screen appears, as shown in Figure 3.2:

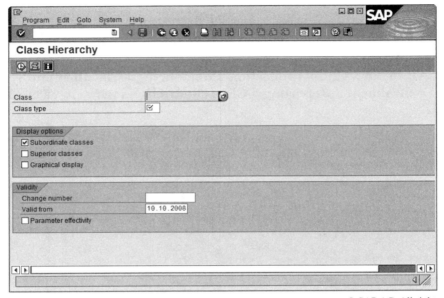

FIGURE 3.2   **Displaying the Class Hierarchy screen**

The **Class Hierarchy** screen contains the following fields:

- **Class**—Allows you to specify a number to represent a class hierarchy
- **Class type**—Allows you to specify a number that represents a class type, such as 001 for material class and 002 for equipment class
- **Change number**—Allows you to specify a number used in the **Change Master Record** screen of a class hierarchy
- **Valid from**—Allows you to enter the date from which the class hierarchy is made valid

The **Class Hierarchy** screen also contains the following check boxes:

- **Subordinate classes**—Specifies whether or not all classes in the class hierarchy are displayed under the superior class
- **Superior classes**—Specifies whether or not all classes in the class hierarchy are displayed over the subordinate class
- **Graphical display**—Specifies whether or not the class hierarchy is displayed in a graphical format
- **Parameter effectivity**—Specifies whether or not you want to open the **Class Hierarchy** dialog box to select data for a class hierarchy

Note: You can also create a class hierarchy by using the CL6C transaction code.

Let's now learn to configure the basic material classification system in the mySAP ERP system.

CONFIGURING THE MATERIAL CLASSIFICATION SYSTEM

Depending upon the characteristics of materials, the material classification system of the MM module classifies them in an alphabetical, hierarchical, numerical, or chronological order. You can also set your own criteria to categorize materials having similar characteristics, such as price, date of procurement, and type.

The process to configure the material classification system in the mySAP ERP system involves the following broad-level steps:

1. Creating characteristics
2. Creating classes
3. Assigning objects to classes

Now, let's discuss all these steps in detail.

Creating Characteristics

As you know, a characteristic represents a property, such as length, color, or weight, of an object that distinguishes it from other objects. Perform the following steps to create a characteristic of an object in the mySAP ERP system:

1. Navigate the following menu path to create a characteristic in the MM module (Figure 3.3):

Menu Path

SAP menu > Cross-Application Components > Classification System > Master Data > Characteristics

2. Double-click the **CT04 – Characteristics** option in the **Master Data** folder to create a characteristic, as shown in Figure 3.3:

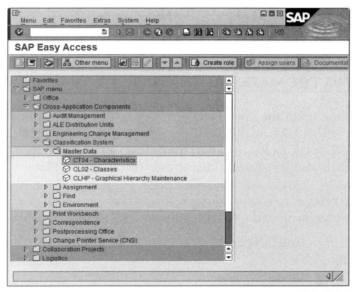

FIGURE 3.3   Displaying the CL04 – Characteristics activity for a classification system

The **Characteristics** screen is displayed (Figure 3.4).

> **Note:** In the mySAP ERP system, the CT04 transaction code is also used to define characteristics.

3. Enter Goods to Deliver in the **Characteristic** field and click the **Create** (□) icon (Figure 3.4).
4. Enter the date in the **Valid From** field and press the ENTER key. In our case, we have entered 13.10.2008, as shown in Figure 3.4:

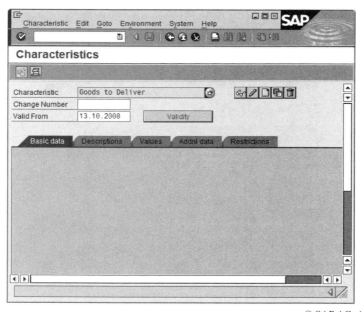

FIGURE 3.4   **Displaying the Characteristics screen**

In Figure 3.4, the following fields are displayed:

- **Characteristic**—Allows you to specify the name of a characteristic
- **Change Number**—Allows you to specify a number used to identify a master record that needs to be changed
- **Valid From**—Allows you to specify the date from which the validity period of an object starts

After entering the date, the **Create Characteristic** screen appears with the **Basic data** tab activated (Figure 3.5).

5. Enter Goods to Deliver in the **Description** text box under the **Basic data** tab (Figure 3.5).
6. Select an option from the **Chars Group** drop-down list. In our case, we have selected the **AUTOMOTIVE** option (Figure 3.5).
7. Select an option from the **Data Type** drop-down list. In our case, we have selected the **Character Format** option (Figure 3.5).
8. Enter 5 in the **Number of Chars** field (Figure 3.5).
9. Select the **Single Value** radio button, as shown in Figure 3.5:

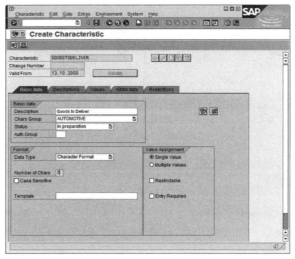

FIGURE 3.5 Displaying the Create Characteristic screen

Figure 3.5 displays the following fields in the **Basic data** tab:

- **Description**—Allows you to enter the details of a characteristic
- **Auth. Group**—Allows you to define a key that specifies whether or not a user is allowed to maintain a characteristic

The following drop-down lists are also displayed in the **Create Characteristic** screen:

- **Chars Group**—Allows you to select the name of the group with similar characteristics

- □ **Status**—Allows you to select a status of the object related to the characteristic (released, locked, or in preparation)
- □ **Data Type**—Allows you to select the data type for your charateristic, such as character, numeric, date, or time

The following check boxes are also displayed in Figure 3.5:

- □ **Case Sensitive**—Specifies whether or not the values entered in a characteristic are written in lower case
- □ **Restrictable**—Specifies whether or not the values entered in a characteristic are restricted while configuring a variant
- □ **Entry Required**—Specifies whether or not the entered value is assigned to a characteristic

The following radio buttons are also displayed in Figure 3.5:

- □ **Single Value**—Specifies whether or not a value is assigned to a characteristic
- □ **Multiple Values**—Specifies whether or not multiple values are assigned to a characteristic

10. Click the **Save** (🖫) icon to save the created characteristic (Figure 3.5).

The GOODSTODELIVER characteristic is created, as shown in Figure 3.6:

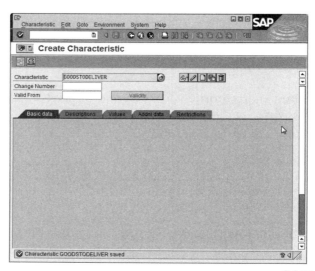

FIGURE 3.6   **Displaying the message after the successful creation of a characteristic**

You can display the details of the GOODSTODELIVER characteristic by clicking the **Display** (⚙) icon (Figure 3.6). The **Display Characteristic** screen appears, as shown in Figure 3.7:

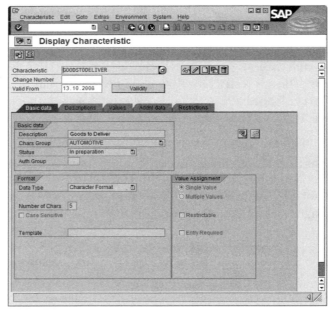

FIGURE 3.7 **Displaying the Display Characteristics screen**

The desired characteristic is created and displayed. Let's now learn how to create classes.

Creating Classes

You have already learned that a class is a group of similar objects that describes the characteristics of an object. Perform the following steps to create a class in the mySAP ERP system:

1. Navigate the following menu path to create a class in the mySAP ERP system (Figure 3.8):

Menu Path

SAP menu > Cross-Application Components > Classification System > Master Data > Classes

2. Double-click the **CL02 – Classes** option in the **Master Data** folder to create a class, as shown in Figure 3.8:

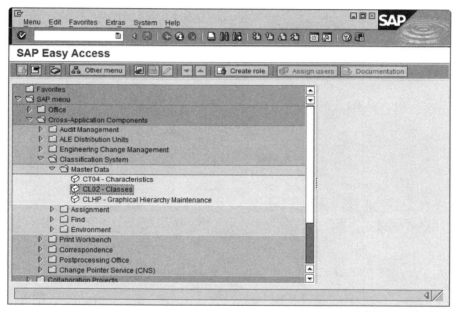

FIGURE 3.8 **Displaying the CL02 – Classes activity for a Classification System**

The **Class** screen appears (Figure 3.9).

Note: The CL02 transaction code is also used to create a class in the mySAP ERP system.

3. Enter a name for the class in the **Class** field. In our case, we have entered MYCLASS (Figure 3.9).
4. Enter a number, say 004, in the **Class** type field (Figure 3.9).

5. Enter a date, say `13.10.2008`, in the **Valid from** field (Figure 3.9).
6. Click the **Create** (□) icon, as shown in Figure 3.9:

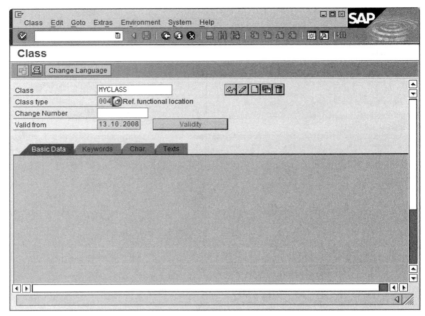

FIGURE 3.9   Displaying the Class screen

The **Create Class:** screen appears with the **Basic Data** tab activated (Figure 3.10).
In Figure 3.9, the following fields are displayed:

- **Class**—Allows you to specify a name to identify a class
- **Class type**—Allows you to specify a number to identify a class type, such as 001 for material class, 002 for equipment class, and 007 for code groups
- **Change Number**—Allows you to specify a number to identify the master record that needs to be changed
- **Valid from**—Allows you to specify a date from which the validity period of an object starts

7. Enter the description of the object that you are creating in the **Description** field under the **Basic Data** tab. In our case, we have entered `Car model` (Figure 3.10).

8. Select an option from the **Status** drop-down list. In our case, we have selected the **In preparation** option (Figure 3.10).
9. Select an option from the **Class group** drop-down list. In our case, we have selected the **TPPE** option (Figure 3.10).
10. Enter the validity date in the **Valid From** field under the **Basic Data** tab. In our case, it is 13.10.2008 (Figure 3.10).
11. Enter the date up to which you want the class to remain valid in the **Valid to** field under the **Basic Data** tab. In our case, it is 31.12.9999 (Figure 3.10).
12. Select the **Do not check** radio button (Figure 3.10).
13. Click the **Save** (■) icon, as shown in Figure 3.10:

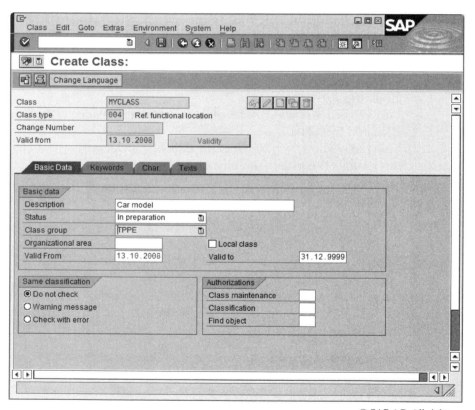

FIGURE 3.10   **Displaying the Create Class: screen**

In Figure 3.10, the following fields are displayed under the **Basic Data** tab:

- **Description**—Allows you to enter the description of a class
- **Organizational area**—Allows you to assign characteristics of a class to the functional area of a company
- **Class maintenance**—Allows you to specify whether or not a user is allowed to maintain a class
- **Classification**—Allows you to specify a classification authorization group that determines whether or not a user is allowed to assign objects to a class
- **Find object**—Allows you to specify an authorization group to find objects

In Figure 3.10, the following drop-down lists are displayed under the **Basic Data** tab:

- **Status**—Allows you to select a status (release, locked, or in preparation) that represents the current status of an object.
- **Class group**—Allows you to select a string that is used to group similar classes
- **Valid From**—Allows you to select the date from which objects can be allocated to a class
- **Valid to**—Allows you to select the date at which the validity of allocating an object to a class should expire

In Figure 3.10, the following radio buttons are displayed under the **Basic Data** tab:

- **Do not check**—Specifies whether or not the mySAP ERP system checks for identical characteristic values
- **Warning message**—Specifies whether or not a warning message is displayed while assigning different objects to the same class
- **Check with error**—Specifies whether or not an error message is displayed while assigning different objects with the same characteristic value to the same class

In addition, the **Create Class:** screen also contains the **Local class** check box, which specifies whether or not a class is defined with a local class.

As a result of clicking the **Save** (🖫) icon in Figure 3.10, the MYCLASS class is created. The **Class type 004: Class MYCLASS created** message appears, as shown in Figure 3.11:

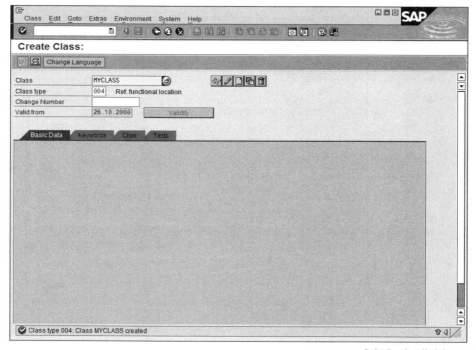

FIGURE 3.11   Displaying the Create Class: screen with the MYCLASS class

You can display the details of the MYCLASS class by clicking the **Display** (⊗) icon (Figure 3.11). The **Display Class:** screen appears, as shown in Figure 3.12:

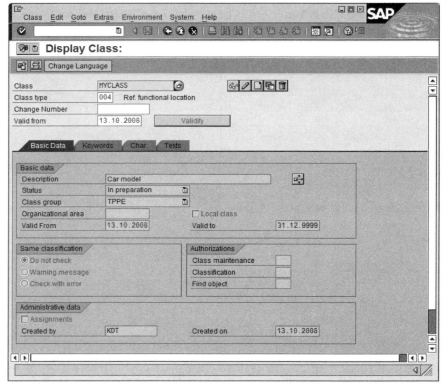

FIGURE 3.12   **Displaying the Display Class: screen**

After learning to create a class, let's learn how to assign objects to classes.

Assigning Objects to Classes

The process of assigning objects to a class or classes is used either while creating the material master record or classifying objects in the mySAP ERP system.

Perform the following steps to assign an object to classes:

1. Navigate the following menu path in the mySAP ERP system (Figure 3.13):

Menu Path

SAP menu > Cross-Application Components > Classification System > Assignment > Assign Object to Classes

2. Double-click the **CL20N – Assign Object to Classes** option in the **Assignment** folder, as shown in Figure 3.13:

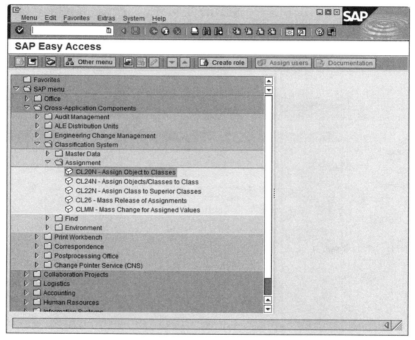

FIGURE 3.13   Displaying the CL20N – Assign Object to Classes activity

Note: Apart from the preceding menu path, you can also use the CL20N transaction code to assign an object to a class or classes in the mySAP ERP system.

The **Assign Object to Classes** screen appears (Figure 3.14).

3. Enter a class type in the **Class Type** field and press the ENTER key. In our case, we have entered 011 as the class type (Figure 3.14).

The **Customer** field is displayed in the **Assign Object to Classes** screen (Figure 3.14).

4. Enter a customer code in the **Customer** field and press the ENTER key. In our case, we have entered FOREIGN00 as the customer code (Figure 3.14).
5. Enter the class name in the **Class** field. In our case, we have entered CATALOG_VIEW_CUST (Figure 3.14).
6. Select the **Standard class** check box (Figure 3.14).
7. Enter a status code in the **Status** field. In our case, we have entered 3 as status code (Figure 3.14).
8. Enter an item number, say 55, in the **Item No.** field (Figure 3.14).
9. Click the **Save** (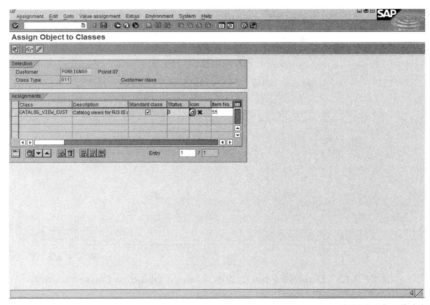) icon, as shown in Figure 3.14:

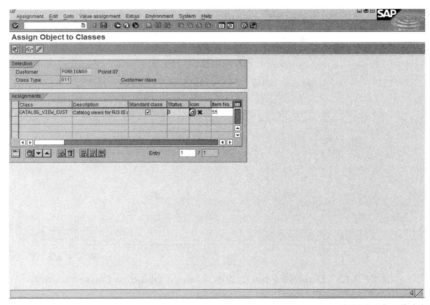

FIGURE 3.14   **Displaying the Assign Object to Classes screen**

The **Assign Object to Classes** screen displays the following fields:

□ **Class Type**—Allows you to specify the code of the class that needs to be assigned to an object

- Customer—Allows you to specify a customer number to identify a customer or vendor when assigning an object to a class
- Class—Allows you to specify a class name corresponding to the class type specified in the **Class Type** field
- Description—Allows you to describe the process of assigning an object to a class
- Standard class—Specifies whether or not a class can access information related to the classification and characteristics of an object
- Status—Allows you to specify a number representing the current status of an object
- Icon—Shows the icons corresponding to the status displayed in the **Status** field
- Item No.—Allows you to specify an item number

When you click the **Save** (⊟) icon in Figure 3.14, the CATALOG_VIEW_CUST object is assigned to the FOREIGN00 customer class. The **Saving changes to assignments** message appears, as shown in Figure 3.15:

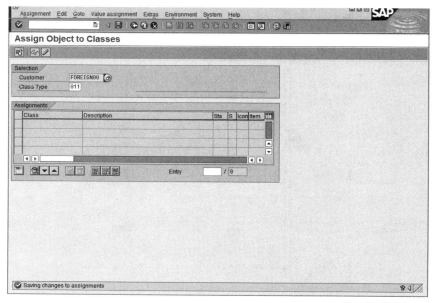

FIGURE 3.15   **Displaying the message after assigning an object to a class or classes**

You can view the details of the CATALOG_VIEW_CUST object assigned to the FOREIGN00 customer class by performing the following steps:

1. Enter a customer code, say FOREIGN00, in the **Customer** field displayed on the **Display Object to Classes** screen (Figure 3.16).
2. Enter the type of the class in the **Class Type** field. In our case, we have entered 011 (Figure 3.16).
3. Click the **Display all assignments** (⚙) icon to display whether or not the object is assigned to the class, as shown in Figure 3.16:

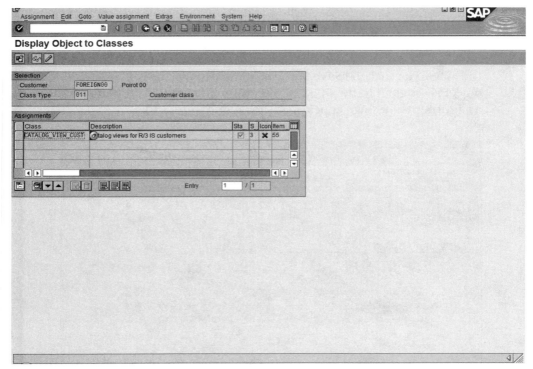

FIGURE 3.16 **Displaying the Display Object to Classes screen**

Figure 3.16 shows that the CATALOG_VIEW_CUST object is assigned to the FOREIGN00 customer class.

Let's now summarize the main points discussed in this chapter.

SUMMARY

In this chapter, you learned about key terms used in the material classification system to classify or identify materials. The material classification system helps you to arrange and classify the materials in a structured order, such as alphabetical, numerological, and chronological. You also learned how to configure the material classification system in the MM module of the mySAP ERP system. You can configure the material classification system by creating characteristics and classes for a material, and by assigning objects to classes.

The next chapter describes the process of implementing the purchasing process in the MM module.

4

WORKING WITH MASTER DATA IN THE MM MODULE

As you know, the Materials Management (MM) module of the SAP® system maintains the records of various activities and processes relating to material procurement, material codification, and production, such as purchasing materials, storing and mantaining them, and making payments to the vendor for supplying the materials and services. Separate records, called master records, are maintained for each of these processes in the SAP database to store the required information, such as the name and address of customers and vendors, the type of materials and products, and the level or other details of the storage locations. For example, the record that contains all the details about a material, such as day and date of purchase, material type, quantity, and price at which the material is purchased, is called the material master record. Similarly, the record maintaining the details of the vendor from whom the material is purchased is known as the vendor master record. Depending upon their specific requirements, the information stored in these master records is shared by all the departments of an organization. Sharing of master data not only eliminates the problem of repeated processing of similar data but also minimizes the chance of errors, as all the departments access data from the same source. Creating masters is the first step in any implementation, as it reduces redundancy and unifies the codification across the organization. It allows for the tracking of the details of availability of materials at any place and at any point of time, ensuring the smooth confirmation of orders. It also improves governance and planning efficiency in the organization.

In this chapter, you will learn about the various types of master data, such as vendor and material master data, maintained in the MM module of the mySAP™ ERP system. You also will learn about various records maintained in the MM module, such as purchasing information records, the source list, batch management data, and quota arrangement.

Let's first learn to work with vendor master records.

WORKING WITH THE VENDOR MASTER RECORD

A vendor is a person, company, or organization that sells or supplies material or services to a purchasing organization. The vendor master record in SAP can be defined as a data file that contains the vendor-related information required by an organization for day-to-day business operations. The vendor master record is maintained by the purchasing as well as the accounting department of an organization; however, the data maintained by these departments is different. For instance, the purchasing department records the data of the materials supplied by the vendor; whereas, the accounting department keeps track of the financial transactions made with the vendor. However, some basic information, such as the name and address of a vendor, the mode and terms of payment, and the currency in which the vendor would be paid by the organization is maintained by both departments.

Depending upon the information it contains, the data of the vendor master record can be placed under the following three categories:

■ **General Data**—Comprises general information about vendors, such as their names, addresses, and contact numbers. The general data is always maintained at the client level so that the lower-level organizational units can access it easily.

- **Accounting Data**—Comprises the financial data of the vendor, such as tax information, bank details, payment terms, and payment methods. The accounting data is maintained by the accounting department of the organization and is created at the company code level. You can maintain the accounting data by using the FK01, FK02, and FK03 transaction codes.
- **Purchasing Data**—Comprises the purchasing data, such as terms, date, and location of delivery. The purchasing data is maintained by the purchasing department of the organization. You can maintain the purchasing data by using the MK01, MK02, and MK03 transaction codes.

You can also maintain the accounting and purchasing data together in the vendor master record by using the XK01, XK02, and XK03 transaction codes.

In this section of the chapter, you will learn to create the vendor master record, explore the data for the vendor master record, change the vendor master record, display the vendor master record, delete the vendor master record, and block or unblock the vendor master record.

Let's first learn to create the vendor master record.

Creating the Vendor Master Record

The vendor master record is a record that stores all the information about a vendor that is selected to supply one or more materials to the organization. As the data of the vendor master record is shared by many of the SAP system modules, the person responsible for maintaining it should make sure that the data in the record is not only correct but also checked and updated regularly.

Let's perform the following steps to create the vendor master record:

1. Navigate the following menu path in the SAP Graphical User Interface (GUI):

Menu Path

SAP menu > Logistics > Materials Management > Purchasing > Master Data > Vendor > Central > XK01 – Create.

Figure 4.1 shows the preceding menu path:

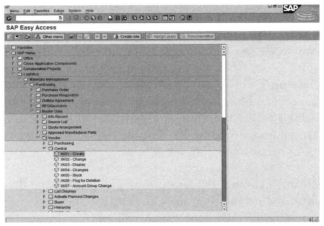

FIGURE 4.1 Displaying the menu path to create a new vendor

The **Create Vendor: Initial Screen** appears, as shown in Figure 4.2:

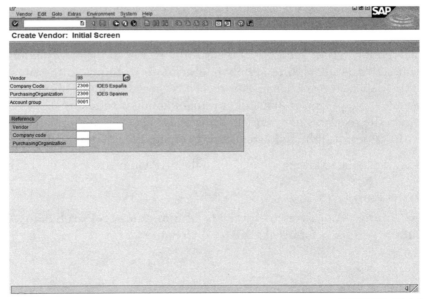

FIGURE 4.2 Displaying the Create Vendor: Initial Screen

Note: You can also use the XK01 transaction code to access the **Create Vendor: Initial Screen**.

2. Enter the vendor account number in the **Vendor** text box.
3. Enter the company code of the vendor in the **Company Code** text box.
4. Enter the purchasing organization of the vendor in the **Purchasing Organization** text box.
5. Enter the account group of the vendor in the **Account group** text box.
6. Press the ENTER key or click the **Enter** (🗹) icon on the standard toolbar of SAP GUI. The **Create Vendor: Address** screen appears, as shown in Figure 4.3:

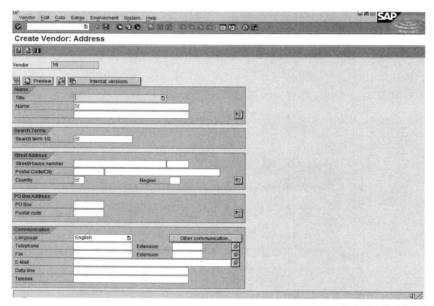

FIGURE 4.3   **Entering address of the new vendor**

7. Enter the address of the vendor in the required fields in the **Create Vendor: Address** screen and press the ENTER key.

The **Create Vendor: Control** screen appears, as shown in Figure 4.4:

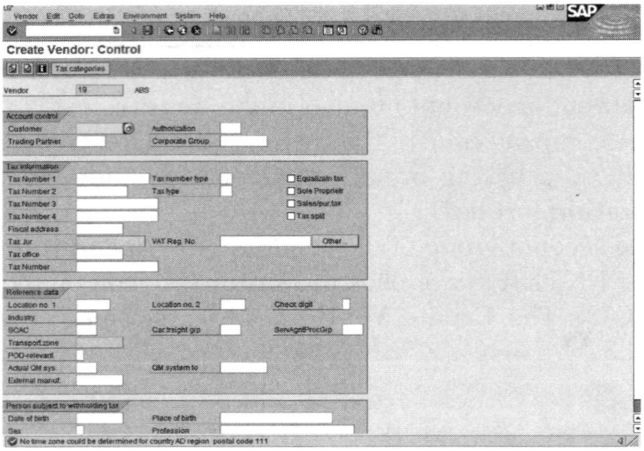

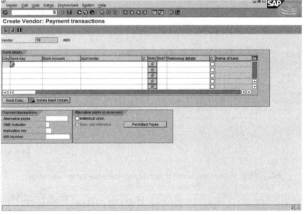

FIGURE 4.4 **Providing the accounting information**

8. Enter the accounting information of the vendor in the **Create Vendor: Control** screen and press the ENTER key.

The **Create Vendor: Payment transactions** screen appears, as shown in Figure 4.5:

FIGURE 4.5 **Providing the payment transaction details**

9. Enter the payment transaction details in the **Create Vendor: Payment** transactions screen and press the ENTER key.

The **Create Vendor: Accounting information Accounting** screen appears, as shown in Figure 4.6:

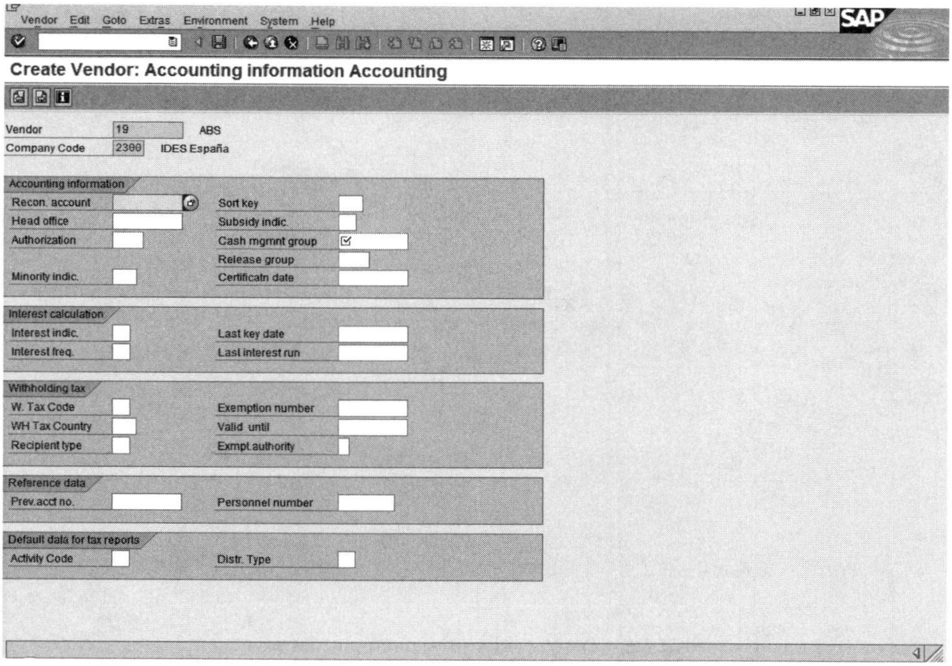

FIGURE 4.6   Providing the account details

10. Enter the account details of the vendor in the **Create Vendor: Accounting information Accounting** screen and press the ENTER key.

The **Create Vendor: Payment transactions Accounting** screen appears, as shown in Figure 4.7:

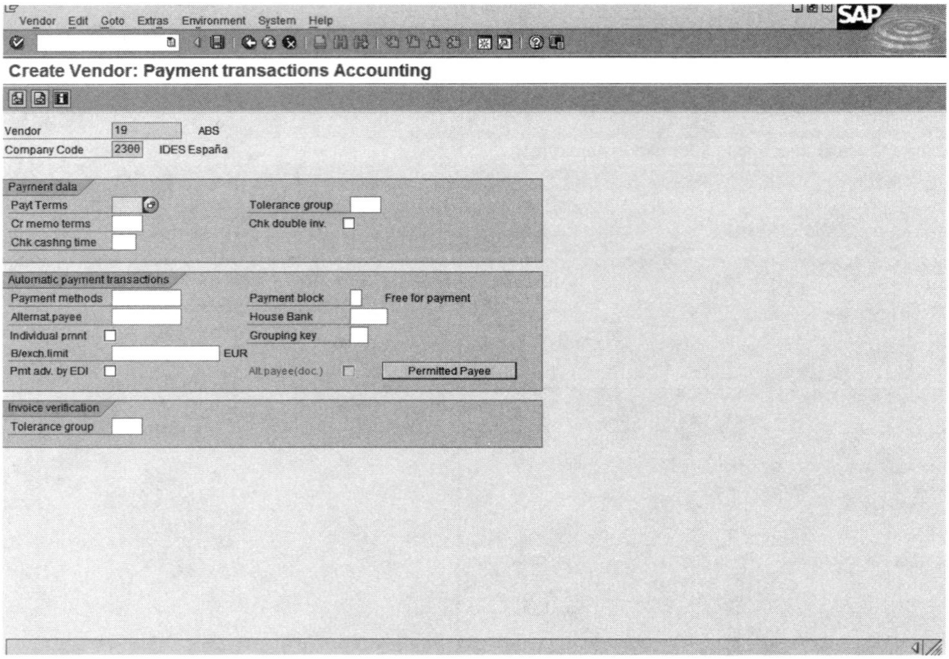

FIGURE 4.7   Providing the payment details

11. Enter the payment details in the **Create Vendor: Payment transactions Accounting** screen and press the ENTER key. The **Create Vendor: Correspondance Accounting** screen appears.

12. Enter the dunning data and the correspondence data of the vendor in the **Create Vendor: Correspondance Accounting** screen and press the ENTER key.

The **Create Vendor: Puchasing data** screen appears, as shown in Figure 4.8:

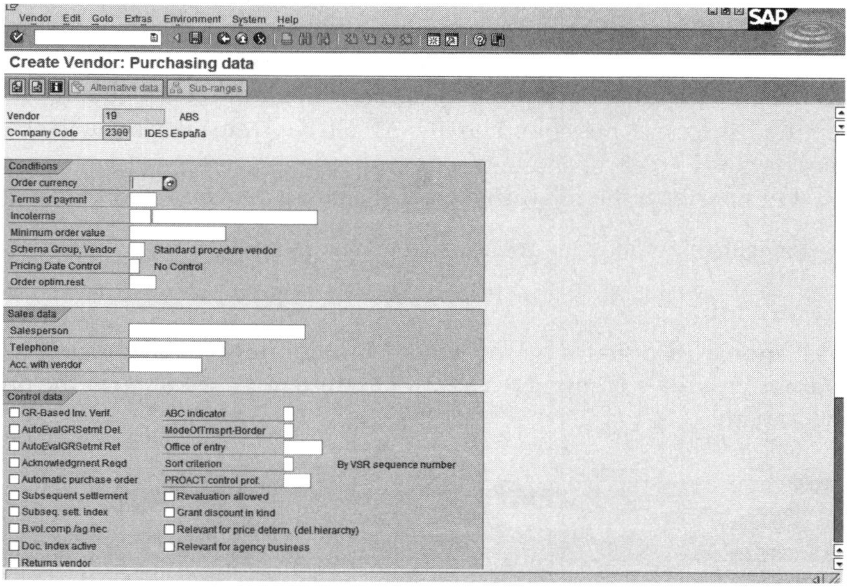

FIGURE 4.8   **Providing the purchasing data**

13. Enter the purchasing data of the goods in the **Create Vendor: Purchasing data** screen and press the ENTER key.

The **Create Vendor: Partner functions** screen appears.

14. Enter the necessary partner roles of the vendor in the **Create Vendor: Partner functions** screen and click the **Save** (⊞) icon on the standard toolbar to save the vendor information.

After creating the vendor master record in the MM module of the mySAP ERP system, let's now learn how to change the data in the vendor master record.

Changing the Vendor Master Record

As the vendor master record consists of sensitive and important information and has a significant impact on the purchase and account-related activities of the organization, any sort of incorrect data can lead to serious problems. Therefore, for the smooth functioning of all these activities, any incorrect entry should be rectified as soon as possible. The mySAP ERP system allows you to change the vendor master record, as and when required.

Let's perform the following steps to change the vendor master record:

1. Navigate the following menu path in the SAP GUI:

Menu Path

SAP menu > Logistics > Materials Management > Purchasing > Master Data > Vendor > Central > XK02 – Change. Figure 4.9 shows the preceding menu path:

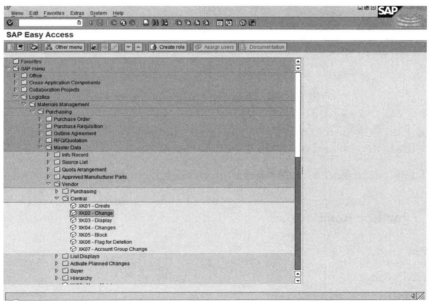

FIGURE 4.9 Displaying the menu path to change vendor information

The **Change Vendor: Initial Screen** appears, as shown in Figure 4.10:

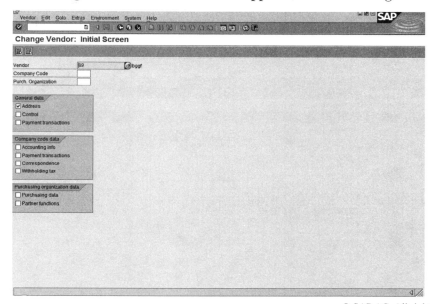

FIGURE 4.10   Displaying the Change Vendor: Initial Screen

Note: You can also use the XK02 transaction code to access **Change Vendor: Initial Screen**.

Figure 4.10 shows that the **Change Vendor: Initial Screen** contains some check boxes that you need to select to specify the data that you want to change. These check boxes are placed under the following three categories:

- **General data**—Allows you to change the general data about the vendor, such as address, control, and details of payment transactions
- **Company code data**—Allows you to change the company code data of the vendor, such as accounting information, payment transactions, and the withholding tax
- **Purchasing organization data**—Allows you to change purchasing information, such as purchasing data and partner functions

2. Enter the account number of the vendor whose details you want to modify in the **Vendor** text box (Figure 4.10).
3. Press the ENTER key or click the **Enter** (☑) icon on the standard toolbar.

The **Change Vendor: Address** screen appears, as shown in Figure 4.11:

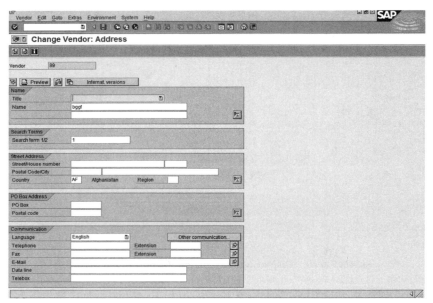

FIGURE 4.11   Changing the vendor information

4. In the **Change Vendor: Address** screen, make the necessary changes and click the **Save** (💾) icon to save the modified vendor information.

Displaying the Vendor Master Record

After making the necessary changes in the vendor master record, you can verify whether or not the changes have been successfully updated by displaying the vendor master record.

Let's perform the following steps to display the vendor master record:

1. Navigate the following menu path in the SAP GUI:

Menu Path

SAP menu > Logistics > Materials Management > Purchasing > Master Data > Vendor > Central > XK03 – Display. Figure 4.12 shows the preceding menu path:

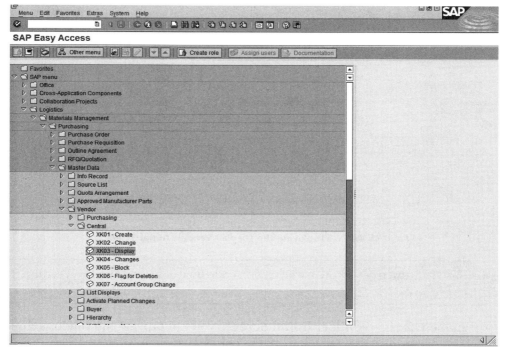

FIGURE 4.12   Displaying the menu path to display vendor information

The **Display Vendor: Initial Screen** appears, as shown in Figure 4.13:

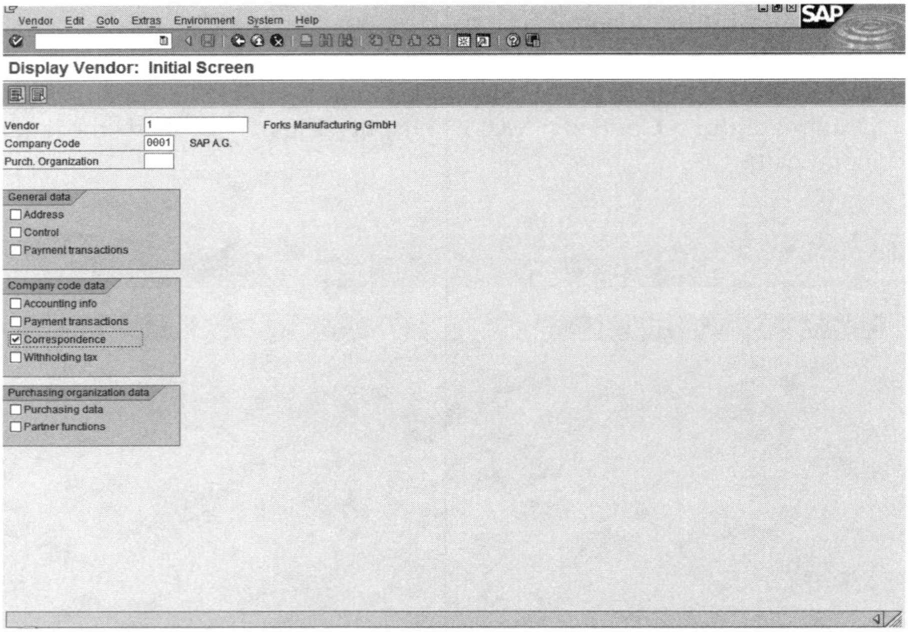

FIGURE 4.13 Displaying the Display Vendor: Initial Screen

Note: You can also use the XK03 transaction code to access the **Display Vendor: Initial Screen**.

In the **Display Vendor: Initial Screen**, you can provide the vendor account number to view the general data, the company code to view company data, or the purchasing organization code to view the purchasing organization data of the vendor.

2. Enter the account number of the vendor whose information you want to view in the **Vendor** text box (Figure 4.13).
3. Enter the vendor company code in the **Company Code** text box (Figure 4.13).

4. Select the **Correspondence** check box in the **Company code data** group and press the ENTER key.

The **Display Vendor: Correspondence Accounting** screen appears, as shown in Figure 4.14:

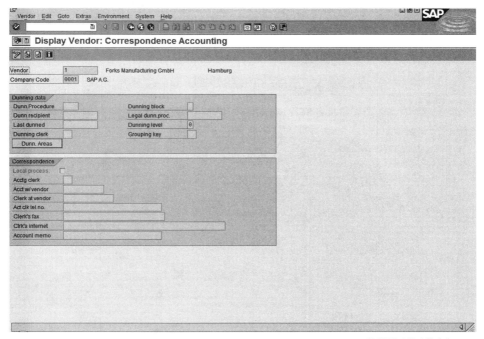

FIGURE 4.14   **Displaying the Correspondance Accounting details of the vendor**

After learning to display various types of vendor information, let's learn how to delete the vendor master record.

Deleting the Vendor Master Record

There can be instances in which your organization might decide not to have any more transactions with a particular vendor. In such a situation, the best option is to delete the corresponding vendor master record.

Let's perform the following steps to delete the vendor master record:

1. Navigate the following menu path in the SAP GUI:

Menu Path

SAP menu > Logistics > Materials Management > Purchasing > Master Data > Vendor > Central > XK06 – Flag for Deletion. Figure 4.15 shows the preceding menu path:

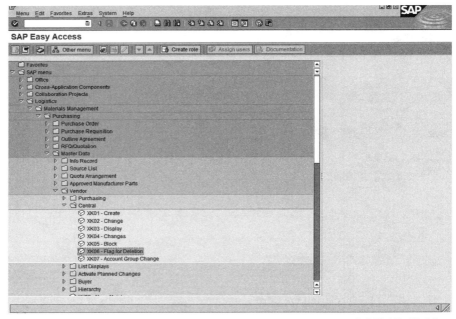

FIGURE 4.15   Displaying the menu path to delete vendor information

The **Flag for Deletion Vendor: Initial Screen** appears, as shown in Figure 4.16:

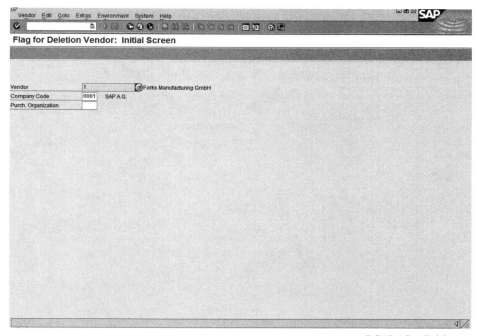

FIGURE 4.16 Displaying the Initial Screen to delete a vendor

Note: You can also use the XK06 transaction code to access the **Flag for Deletion Vendor: Initial Screen**.

2. Enter the account number of the vendor whose information you want to delete in the **Vendor** text box (Figure 4.16).
3. Enter the company code of the vendor in the **Company Code** text box (Figure 4.16).
4. Press the ENTER key or click the **Enter** (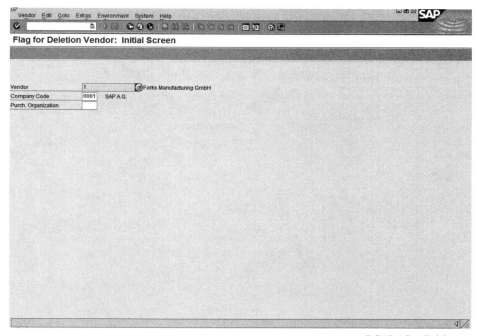) icon on the standard toolbar.

The **Flag for Deletion Vendor: Details** screen appears, as shown in Figure 4.17:

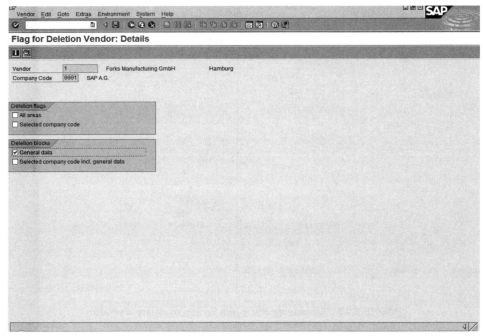

FIGURE 4.17   **Specifying the fields to be deleted**

The mySAP ERP system provides you the option to delete the entire master record at once or some selected fields. The **Flag for Deletion Vendor: Details** screen allows you to specify the deletion flags or deletion blocks for the information that you want or do not want to delete, respectively. The **Deletion flags** group contains the following options:

- **All areas**—Specifies that all the details entered in the vendor master record will be deleted

    ☐ **Selected company code**—Specifies that only the company code data of the vendor master record will be deleted

In the **Deletion blocks** group, you can specfiy the fields of the vendor master record that you do not want to delete. The **Deletion blocks** group contains the following options:

    ☐ **General data**—Specifies that the general data in the vendor master record will not be deleted

    ☐ **Selected company code incl. general data**—Specifies that the data specific to the company code will not be deleted

5. Select the **General data** check box in the **Deletion blocks** group and click the **Save** (🖫) icon to save the changes.

    Now, let's proceed to learn how to block or unblock the vendor master record.

Blocking or Unblocking the Vendor Master Record

After the vendor master record is created and entered in the SAP database, you can block it to prevent unauthorized access or tampering with the stored information. Blocking the vendor master records makes it uneditable. In other words, no more posting or purchasing data can be entered in it.

    Let's perform the following steps to block the vendor master record:

1. Navigate the following menu path in the SAP GUI:

Menu Path

SAP menu > Logistics > Materials Management > Purchasing > Master Data > Vendor > Central > XK05 – Block.

Figure 4.18 shows the preceding menu path:

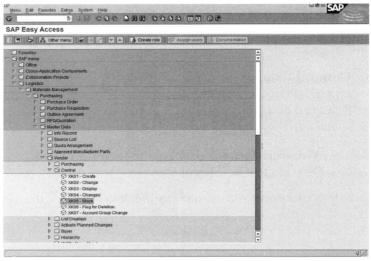

FIGURE 4.18   Displaying the menu path to block vendor information

The **Block/Unblock Vendor: Initial Screen** appears, as shown in Figure 4.19:

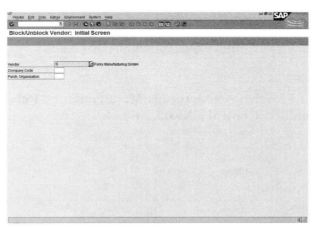

FIGURE 4.19   Displaying the Initial Screen to block vendor information

Note: You can also use the XK05 transaction code to access the **Block/Unblock Vendor: Initial Screen**.

2. Enter the account information of the vendor in the **Vendor** text box and press the ENTER key.

The **Block/Unblock Vendor: Details** screen appears, as shown in Figure 4.20:

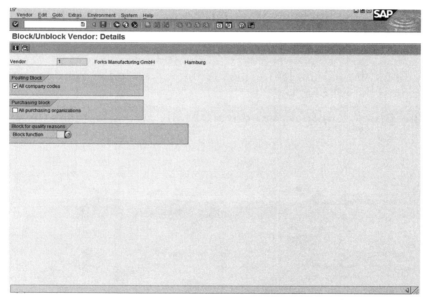

FIGURE 4.20 **Providing details to block vendor information**

The **Block/Unblock Vendor: Details** screen contains the following check boxes:

□ **All company codes**—Prevents users from posting new items in the vendor account

□ **All purchasing organizations**—Indicates whether or not the vendor master record is blocked for all departments of the company

3. Select the **All company codes** check box in the **Posting Block** group (Figure 4.20).

4. Click the **Save** (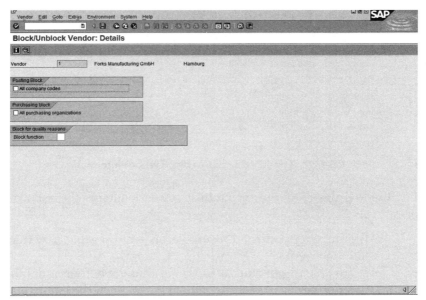) icon to save the changes and block the vendor.

After blocking a particular vendor, let's now learn how to unblock a blocked vendor master record.

Perform the following steps to unblock a blocked vendor master record:

1. Navigate the following menu path in the SAP GUI (Figure 4.18):

Menu Path

SAP menu > Logistics > Materials Management > Purchasing > Master Data > Vendor > Central > XK05 – Block. The **Block/Unblock Vendor: Initial Screen** appears (Figure 4.19).

2. Enter the account information of the vendor in the **Vendor** text box and press the ENTER key.

The **Block/Unblock Vendor: Details** screen appears, as shown in Figure 4.21:

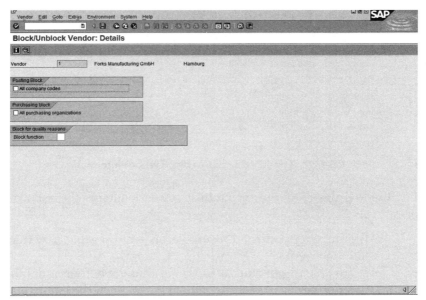

FIGURE 4.21 **Unblocking a vendor record**

3. Uncheck the **All company codes** check box in the **Posting Block** group (Figure 4.21).
4. Click the the **Save** (⊞) icon to save the changes and unblock the vendor.

In this section of the chapter, you have learned about the vendor master record. Now, let's learn about material master data in the SAP MM module.

WORKING WITH THE MATERIAL MASTER DATA

In the SAP MM module, material master data refers to all the material master records that are stored in the system. In other words, material master data consists of the description of all the materials that an organization not only purchases but also produces and keeps in its stock. The material master data acts as a central database of information for the materials in an organization.

Maintaining the details of all the materials at a central location not only minimizes the risk of data redundancy but also allows other departments of the organization to share this data among themselves. The other departments of the organization can use the material master data to perform various tasks, such as invoice verification and inventory management. The material master record is used by different departments of an organization, and each department requires different information about the material. For example, the purchasing department might require only the price of the material to perform price control functions; whereas, the sales department might require the sales data to prepare the sales graph of a given period of time.

To facilitate locating the relevant data, various fields have been provided in the **Create Material (Initial Screen)**. Every department can easily locate and access the data required by it by entering the relevant details in these fields.

While creating the material master record, the first screen that appears is the **Create Material (Initial Screen)**, as shown in Figure 4.22:

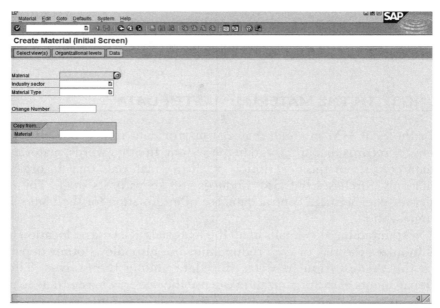

FIGURE 4.22 **Creating the material master record**

Note: You can use the MM01 transaction code to access the **Create Material (Initial Screen)** screen.

The **Create Material (Initial Screen)** allows you to specify various attributes, such as material number, industry sector, and material type, to locate the required data. Let's explore each of these attributes next.

The Material Number

A material number is used to uniquely identify a material in the SAP system. It is a unique 18 character field, which is assigned to each material in either of the following two ways:

- **Internally**—Refers to the number that the mySAP ERP system assigns to a material while creating its master record
- **Externally**—Refers to the number that is assigned to a material by the person who creates its master record

> **Note:** With the SAP R/3 system, you can define one external and one internal number range for each material type or even a group of materials.

The Industry Sector

Depending upon the industrial use of a material, you need to assign an industry sector to it. The different predefined industry sectors included in the SAP R/3 system are:

- Aerospace and defence
- Beverage
- Chemical industry
- Food and related products
- Mechanical engineering
- Pharmaceuticals
- Plant engineering and construction
- Retail
- Service provider
- Agriculture, mining, and manufacturing
- Infrastructure

You can also create a new industry sector apart from these predefined sectors.

The Material Type

The materials having common features are grouped together and assigned a material type. For example, in the mySAP ERP system, all the raw materials are grouped together under the ROH group, finished products are grouped under FERT, and semi-finished products are grouped under HALB.

Assigning a material type to a material while creating the material master record helps in:

- Assigning a material number
- Assigning the material number range
- Controlling the price of the materials
- Determining the account in which the entry of the material is to be made
- Updating the plants with the value and quantity of the material
- Determining the sequence of screens that should appear after the **Create Material (Initial Screen)**

Table 4.1 lists different material types used while creating the material master data:

Material Type	Description	Transaction Code
DIEN – Services	Refers to the services that are procured from external sources and cannot be stored, such as legal services or garbage collection.	MMS1
FERT – Finished Good	Refers to the products created by the organization. It does not contain any purchasing information as the products are not purchased.	MMF1
HALB – Semi-Finished Goods	Refers to the products that are procured from external sources and then assembled or processed internally and sold as finished products.	MMB1
HAWA – Trading Goods	Refers to the materials that are purchased from the vendors and then sold, without any internal operation being performed on the material.	MMH1
HIBE – Operating Supplies	Refers to the materials that are used in the production process, such as lubricants or compressed air. It contains only the purchasing information and not the sales information.	MMI1

Continued

Material Type	Description	Transaction Code
IBAU – Maintenance Assembly	Refers to a set of logical elements that are used to assemble technical objects into clearly defined units. For example, a car is a technical object and the parts of a car, such as the engine and axles, are maintenance assemblies.	MMP1
KMAT – Configurable Material	Refers to the material type that is used for all variant configuration materials. A variant configuration material is a material that has variables, such as the length of a chain or a belt.	MMK1
LEER – Empties	Refers to the material that is used for packing purposes and can be returned to the manufacturer, such as a crate or drum.	MML1
LEIH – Returnable Packaging	Refers to the reusable packaging material that is used to pack finished goods. The customer is obliged to return the packaging material to the vendor.	MMG1
NLAG – Non-Stock Material	Refers to the consumable material that is not held in stock and not recorded in the inventory.	MMN1
ROH – Raw Material	Refers to the material that is used to produce finished goods. If the raw material is sold, no sales data is maintained for the same.	MMR1
UNBW – Non-Valuated Material	Refers to the material that is managed on quantity basis and not by value.	MMU1
VERP – Packaging Material	Refers to the packaging material that is offered free of charge to the customer in the delivery process.	MMV1
WETT – Competitive Products	Refers to the product that is used by the sales department to monitor the products of the competitor.	MMW1

TABLE 4.1   Material types used in creating material master data

After discussing the material types present in the mySAP ERP system, let's learn to configure, change, and define the number range of a material type.

Configuring the Material Type

To assign a material type to a material, you first need to configure the material type.

You can configure the material type by navigating the following menu path:

Menu Path

IMG > Logistics-General > Material Master > Basic Settings > Material Types > Define Attributes of Material Types. Figure 4.23 shows the preceding menu path:

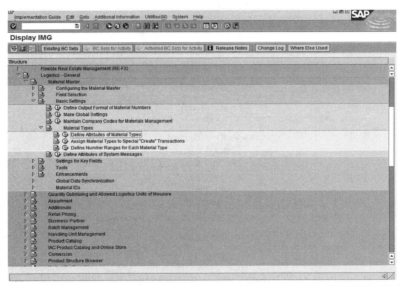

FIGURE 4.23   Defining material types

The **Change View "Material types": Overview** screen appears, as shown in Figure 4.24:

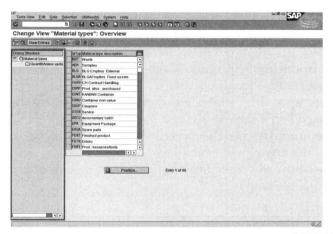

FIGURE 4.24   Displaying the initial Overview screen

In the **Change View "Material types": Overview** screen, select a material type, say DIEN, and click the **Quantity/value updating** link. The **Change View "Quantity/value updating": Overview** screen appears, displaying the content of the folder of the DIEN material type, as shown in Figure 4.25:

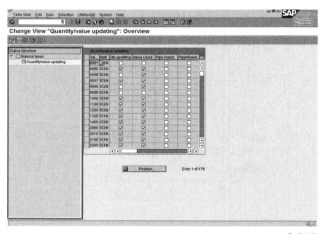

FIGURE 4.25   Displaying the valuation areas for a material type

In the **Change View "Quantity/value updating": Overview** screen, you can configure the following four fields of the material type:

- **Qty updating**—Specifies whether or not the material can be managed on a quantity basis
- **Value updating**—Specifies whether or not the material can be managed on a value basis
- **Pipe. mand.**—Specifies whether or not the material is subject to mandatory pipeline handling
- **Pipe allowed**—Specifies whether or not the material is subject to pipeline handling

> **Note:** The best way to create a new material type is to select and copy an existing material type to the new material type. This method helps in reducing the amount of configuration required while creating a new material type.

Changing the Material Type

At times, you may need to change the material type of a material. For example, a material that was initially being used for in-house production may now need to be sold. In such a situation, its material type needs to be changed from ROH to HAWA.

Let's perform the following steps to change the material type of a material:

1. Navigate the following menu path in the SAP GUI:

Menu Path

SAP menu > Logistics > Materials Management > Material Master > Material > MMAM – Change Material Type. Figure 4.26 shows the preceding menu path:

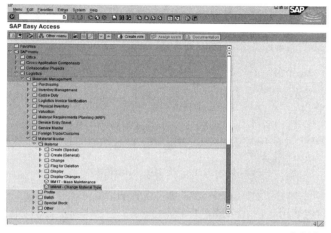

FIGURE 4.26   **Displaying the menu path to change the material type**

The **Change Material Type: Initial Screen** appears, as shown in Figure 4.27:

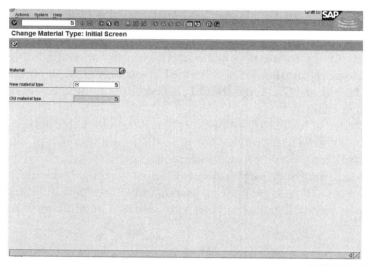

FIGURE 4.27   **Changing the material type**

Note: You can also use the MMAM transaction code to access the **Change Material Type: Initial Screen**.

2. Enter the number of the material whose material type you want to change in the **Material** text box (Figure 4.27).
3. Enter the new material type of the material in the **New material type** text box (Figure 4.27).
4. Enter the old material type of the material in the **Old material type** text box (Figure 4.27).
5. Click the **Save** (⊟) icon to save the changes.

The mySAP ERP system imposes certain restrictions while changing the material type of a material.

The following are the areas in which restrictions are imposed while changing the material type in the material master record:

- **Price**—Specifies that the new material type can only allow standard price in case the old material type does not have any specific price control
- **PRT view**—Specifies that if the old material type has a PRT view, it should also be maintained in the new material type
- **Configurability**—Specifies that if the old material type is not configurable, the new material type is also not configurable
- **Inspection plan**—Specifies that inspection plans, if allowed in the old material type, should also be implemented in the new material type
- **Process indicator**—Specifies that if the old material type is being used as a process indicator, the new material type should also be used as a process indicator
- **Manufacturer part indicator**—Specifies that if the old material type is being used as a manufacturer part indicator, the new material type should also be used as a manufacturer part indicator

Now, let's learn to define a number range for the material type.

Defining a Number Range for the Material Type

After configuring the material type of a material, you need to define a number range for the material type. The following are the ways to define a number range:

- **Internal number assignment**—Refers to the number that is assigned by the system within a number range interval
- **External number assignment**—Refers to the number that is assigned by the user within a number range interval

Let's now learn to create the material master record

Creating a Material Master Record

The material master record comprises all the information that the company needs to manage a material. The data stored in the material master record is descriptive in nature, as it contains information, such as the name, size, or dimension of the material. The material master record also contains data that the system uses to perform various control functions on a material, such as MRP type and price control.

The following are the three ways to create a material master record:

- The immediate process
- The scheduling process
- The special process

Let's now discuss each of these in detail.

The Immediate Process

The immediate process helps you to create the material master record immediately. In this process, you just need to enter the basic information about the material to create its master record.

Let's perform the following steps to create the material master record using the immediate process:

1. Navigate the following menu path in the SAP GUI:

Menu Path
SAP menu > Logistics > Materials Management > Material Master > Material > Create (General) > MM01 – Immediately. Figure 4.28 shows the preceding menu path:

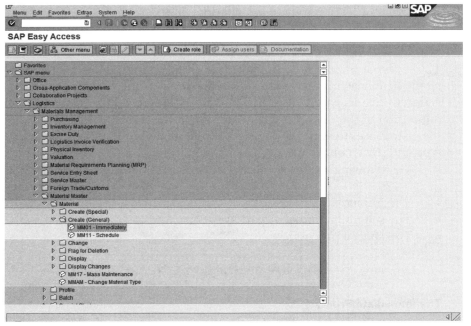

FIGURE 4.28 Displaying the menu path to create the material master record

The **Create Material (Initial Screen)** appears, as shown in Figure 4.29:

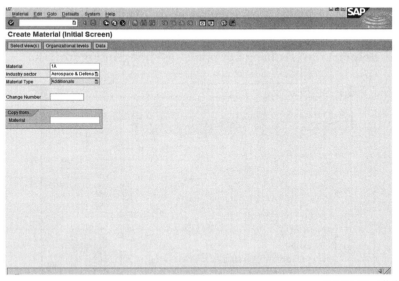

FIGURE 4.29   **Displaying the Create Material (Initial Screen)**

Note: You can also use the `MM01` transaction code to access the **Create Material (Initial Screen)**.

The **Create Material (Initial Screen)** contains the following fields:

- **Material**—Allows you to enter the material number.
- **Industry sector**—Allows you to enter the industry in which the material will be used.
- **Material Type**—Allows you to enter the type of material.
- **Change Number**—Allows you to enter the number if the customer is using Engineering Change Management. This is is an optional field.
- **Copy from Material**—Allows you to enter the material number of a material, which provides information about the new material. This is an optional field.

2. Enter the required information in the **Material, Industry sector**, and **Material Type** text boxes and press the ENTER key.

The **Select View(s)** dialog box opens, as shown in Figure 4.30:

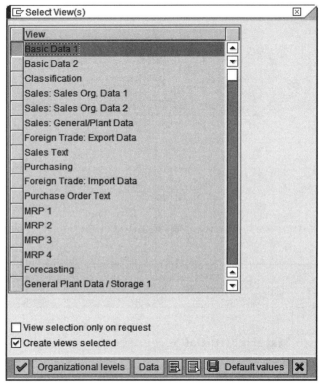

FIGURE 4.30   **Displaying the Select View(s) dialog box**

Note: In the **Select View(s)** dilaog box, you can describe the screens that you require to enter detailed information about a material.

3. Select the **Basic Data 1** option from the **View** list box of the **Select View(s)** dialog box and press the ENTER key.

The **Create Material** screen appears, as shown in Figure 4.31:

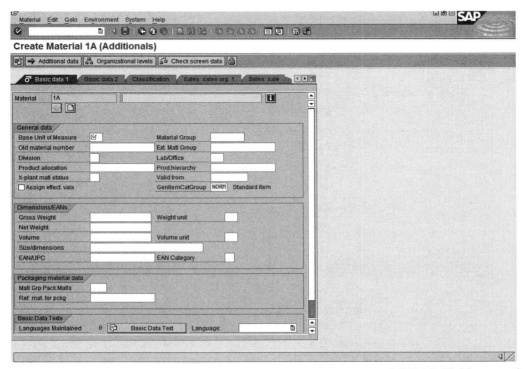

FIGURE 4.31 **Entering basic data**

4. Enter the required information about the new material in the relevant fields and press the ENTER key.

The **Create Material** dialog box appears, containing the summary of the new material master record, as shown in Figure 4.32:

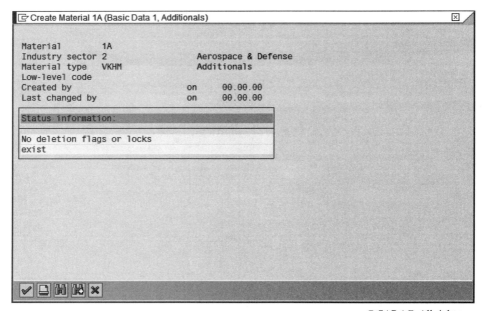

FIGURE 4.32   Summarizing the record

5. Click the **Enter** (☑) icon.
6. Click the **Save** (🖫) icon to save the changes.

The Scheduling Process

In the mySAP ERP system, instead of creating the material master record immediately, you can schedule it to be created at a later date. This is known as the scheduling process, where you can enter the information about the material for which you want to create the material master record and specify the date on which you want the material to be created in the records. The data of the new material is saved and created in the records on the specified date.

Let's perform the following steps to create the material master record using the scheduling process:

1. Navigate the following menu path in the SAP GUI:

Menu Path

SAP menu > Logistics > Materials Management > Material Master > Material > Create (General) > MM11 – Schedule. Figure 4.33 shows the preceding menu path:

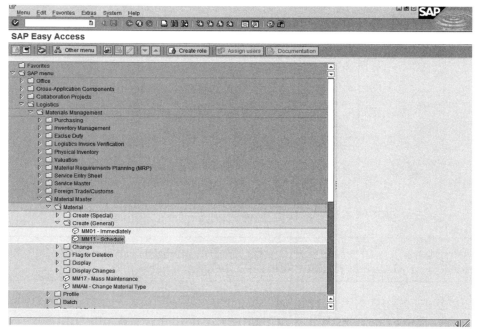

FIGURE 4.33 Displaying the menu path for scheduling creation of the material master data

The **Schedule Creation of Material (Initial Screen)** appears, as shown in Figure 4.34:

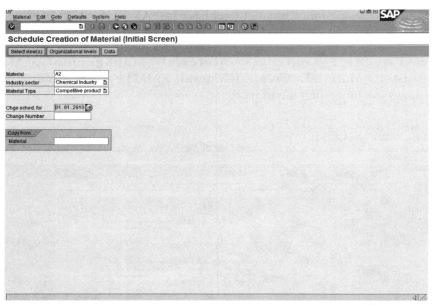

FIGURE 4.34   Creating material using the scheduling process

> **Note:** You can also use the `MM11` transaction code to access the **Schedule Creation of Material (Initial Screen)**.

2. Enter the material number in the **Material** text box (Figure 4.34).
3. Enter the industry in which the material will be used in the **Industry sector** text box (Figure 4.34).
4. Enter the type of material in the **Material Type** text box (Figure 4.34).
5. Enter the date on which the material is scheduled to be created in the **Chge sched. for** text box (Figure 4.34).
6. Enter a number to identify the change master record in the **Change Number** text box (Figure 4.34). This is an optional field.

> **Note:** A change master record consists of data such as the reason for changing the material master record and the administrative data of the material master record.

7. Enter the material number of a material, which provides information about the new material in the **Copy from Material** text box (Figure 4.34). This is an optional field.
8. Enter the required information in the **Material, Industry sector, Material Type**, and **Chge sched. for** text boxes and press the ENTER key.

The **Select View(s)** dialog box opens, as shown in Figure 4.35:

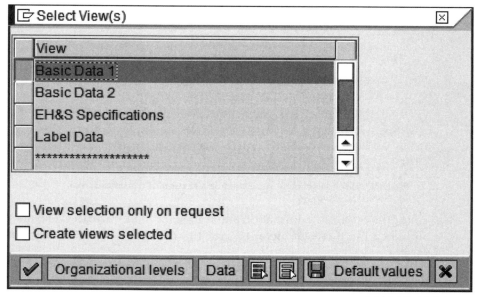

FIGURE 4.35   **Selecting a view to create master record**

9. Select the **Basic Data 1** option from the **View** list box of the **Select View(s)** dialog box and press the ENTER key.

The **Schedule Creation of Material** screen appears, as shown in Figure 4.36:

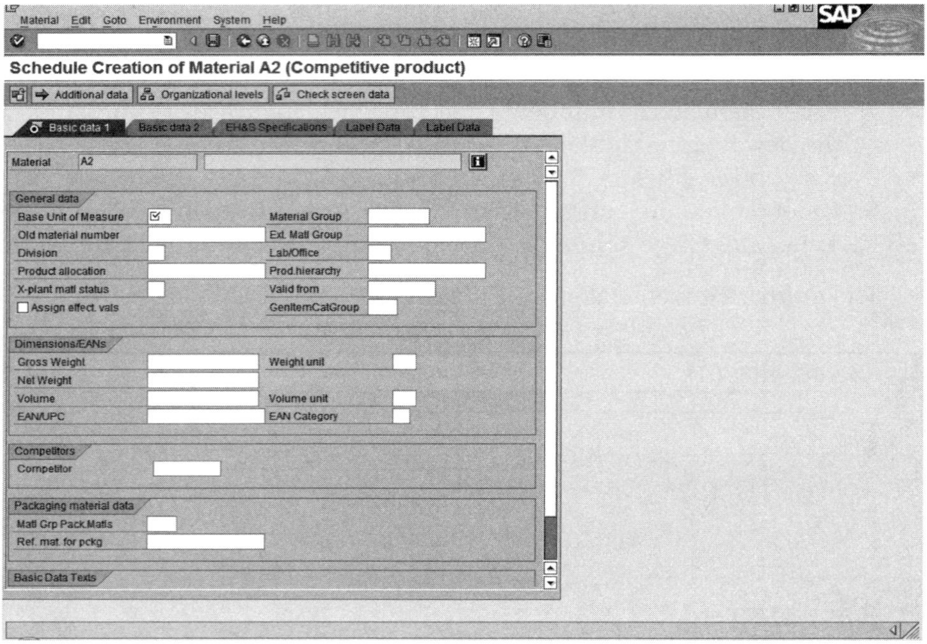

FIGURE 4.36   Displaying the Schedule Creation of Material screen

10. Enter the required information about the new material in the relevant fields and click the **Save** (■) icon to save the changes and create the material master record.

The Special Process

In the discussion above about the immediate and scheduling processes, you learned to create records for general materials. In other words, in both these processes, you need to specify the type of material in the intial screen. The special process of creating the material master record is used in situations where the type of the material has already been decided. In such cases, you need not mention the material type.

Let's perform the following steps to create the material master record by using the special process:

1. Navigate the following menu path in the SAP GUI:

Menu Path

SAP menu > Logistics > Materials Management > Material Master > Material > Create (Special). Figure 4.37 shows the preceding menu path:

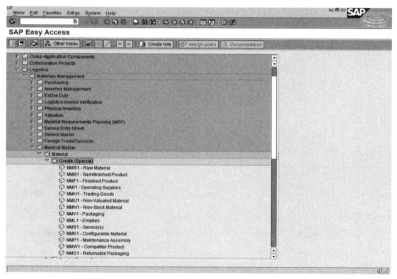

FIGURE 4.37   Displaying the menu path to create a material master record using
the special process

A list of material types appears.

2. Select the type of material whose record you want to create from this list. In this case, we have selected the **MMR1 – Raw Material** option.

The **Create Raw Material (Initial Screen)** appears, as shown in Figure 4.38:

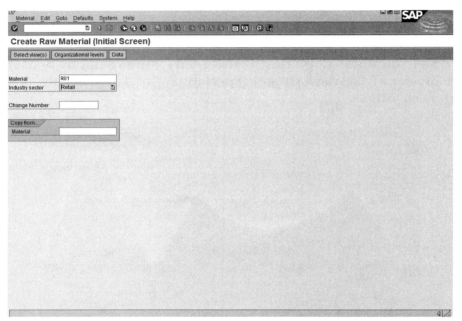

FIGURE 4.38   Creating a master material record for raw material

> **Note:** Refer to Table 4.1 for the list containing all the transaction codes to create different material types using the special process.

3. Enter the required information in the **Material** and **Industry sector** text boxes and press the ENTER key.

The **Select View(s)** dialog box opens, as shown in Figure 4.39:

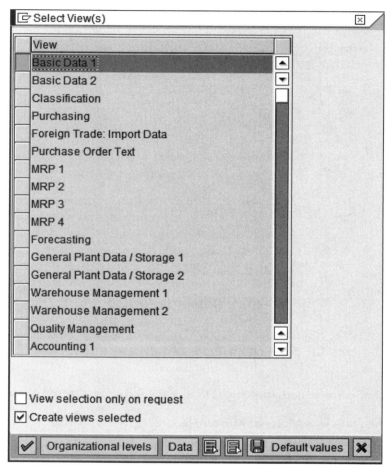

FIGURE 4.39   **Selecting a view to create a raw material master record**

4. Select the **Basic Data 1** option from the **View** list box of the **Select View(s)** dialog box and press the ENTER key.

The **Create Raw Material** screen appears, as shown in Figure 4.40:

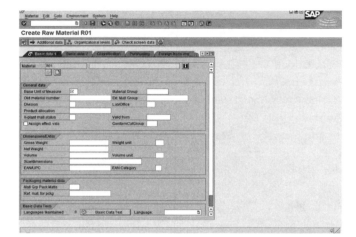

FIGURE 4.40 **Entering basic data**

5. Enter the required information about the new material in the relevant fields and click the **Save** (🖫) icon to save the changes and create the material master record.

Let's now explore the various tabs contained in the **Create Material** screen.

Exploring the Data in a Material Master Record

You have already learned that while creating the material master record for a material, you need to enter various types of information in the **Create Material** screen, such as the material description, the base unit of measure of the material, and the material group. The **Create Material** screen also contains various tabs, and each tab contains specific fields. Apart from the initial screen, you need to enter the relevant details about the material in these fields. You can enter the following types of information in the **Create Material** screen:

- Basic data
- Classification data
- Purchasing data
- Forecasting data
- Sales organization data

- Sales general data
- Work scheduling data
- Production resources/tools data
- Warehouse management data
- MRP data
- Accounting data
- Quality management data
- Costing data

Let's now discuss each of these in detail.

Basic Data

The basic data tabs—**Basic data 1** and **Basic data 2**—allow you to enter the basic information about the material that you want to create.

Figure 4.41 shows the **Basic data 1** tab:

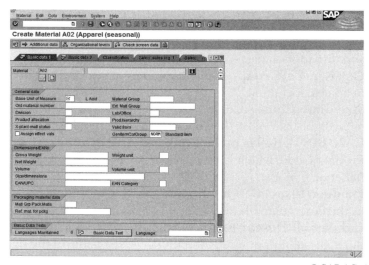

FIGURE 4.41   **Displaying the Basic data 1 tab**

The following are the noteworthy UI elements of the **Basic data** (1 and 2) tabs:

- **Material**—Defines the material. It accepts a 40-characters long maximum description of new material.
- **Base Unit of Measure**—Defines the unit of measure, which is the lowest level of measure for the material. For example,

a sheet of steel may be sold as a single sheet or in pallets; the base unit of measure will always be the same in both cases.

- **Material Group**—Groups similar materials. This is an important field as it helps in searching for a material.
- **Old material number**—Refers to the number that helps you manage the material in other ERP systems.
- **Division**—Allows the organization to organize its sales structure. At the organizational level, you can assign each material only one division so that the different areas of the distribution channel are easily identified.
- **Lab/Office**—Refers to the laboratory or office from which one can identify the people responsible for creating the bill of the purchased material.
- **X-plant matl status**—Allows the person responsible for data entry of the material to enter a status of the material, which is valid for all the clients.
- **Prod. hierarchy**—Groups materials based on different characteristics. It is an alphanumeric field and used in the sales and distribution part of a company.
- **GenItemCatGroup**—Generates an item type of the material in a sales document.
- **Size/dimensions**—Contains information about the gross and net weights as well as the volume of the material.
- **EAN/UPC**—Refers to the European Article Number/Universal Product Code, which is used to identify the manufacturer of the material.
- **Product/Inspection memo**—Refers to the product or inspection memo of the material.
- **Ind. Stand. Desc.**—Enters the industry standard description of the material. For example, the ISO or ANSI name of the material.
- **Basic material**—Allows a basic material to be selected, under which the new material can be grouped.
- **DG indicator profile**—Specifies whether or not the new material should be classified as a dangerous good.
- **Environmentally rlvt**—Specifies if the new material is safe for shipping.
- **Highly viscous and In bulk/liquid**—Specifies that the transport document of the specific material is influenced by customer reports, if customer reports are created.

- **Design Drawing fields**—Helps in creating a design document, which includes fields such as document, document type, document version, page number, document chapter, page format, and number of sheets.
- **Cross-plant CM**—Identifies a configurable material.
- **Packaging material**—Groups the materials using the same packaging material.

Classification Data

Classification data, entered in the **Classification** tab, helps you to search for a specific material. For example, while searching for a material, the values entered in the classes of each material are searched and the materials having the specified set of features are listed.

While entering classification data for a material in the **Classification** tab, you first need to select the class type from the **Class Type** dialog box, as shown in Figure 4.42:

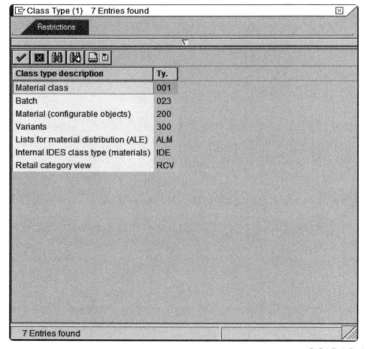

FIGURE 4.42   Displaying the Class Type dialog box

The class type is a type of grouping, which is predefined in SAP and is assigned to a class depending on its function.

The classes in the classification data help in grouping the characteristics of the material.

Purchasing Data

The **Purchasing** tab contains the fields to enter the purchasing information of the material. This tab is displayed when you assign a material type to a material record for personal consumption, i.e., consumption within the organization, such as raw materials.

Figure 4.43 displays the **Purchasing** tab:

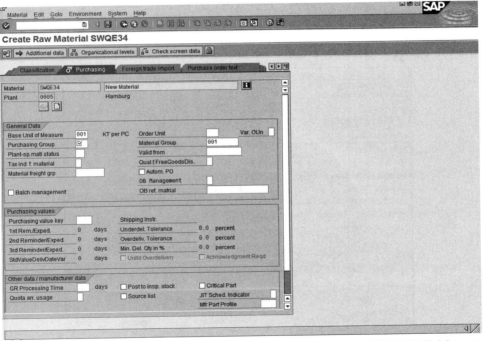

FIGURE 4.43   **Displaying the Purchasing tab**

The following are the noteworthy UI elements of the **Purchasing** tab:

- **Base Unit of Measure**—Defines the unit of measure, which is carried forward from the **Basic Data** tab.
- **Order Unit**—Defines the unit of measure in which the material can be purchased.
- **Var. OUn**—Refers to the variable order unit that allows you to change the unit of measure for the purchase order after the material master record is created.
- **Plant-sp matl status**—Refers to the plant specific material status that defines the status of the material at the plant level.
- **Tax ind. f. material**—Refers to the tax indicator for the material that determines the tax code of the material.
- **Qual.f.FreeGoodsDis.**—Specifies if a discount is available for the material.
- **Material freight grp**—Provides transportation information to companies and agents.
- **Autom. PO**—Generates a purchase order automatically when purchase requisitions are converted to purchase orders.
- **Batch management**—Allows batches to be created for the material.
- **Purchasing value key**—Defines the remainder days, tolerance limit, and shipping instructions required for purchasing a material.
- **GR Processing Time**—Defines the number of working days that are required for inspecting the received material for quality.
- **Post to insp. stock**—Indicates whether or not the material requires an inspection check.
- **Source list**—Indicates that there is a requirement to maintain a source list for procurement. This is an important field for the purchasing department.
- **Quota arr. usage**—Defines the way in which the quota arrangement is used for purchasing. It specifies the sources of supply for a purchase requisition.

Forecasting Data

In the **Forecasting** tab, you need to enter the forecast and consumption values of the material. This screen is displayed only when the material type is applicable for forecasting.

Figure 4.44 displays the **Forecasting** tab:

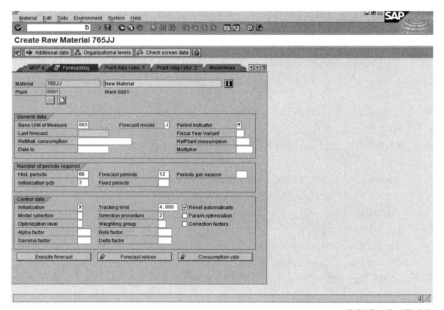

FIGURE 4.44   Displaying the Forecasting tab

The following are the noteworthy UI elements of the **Forecasting** tab:

- **Forecast model**—Forecasts the requirements for the material.
- **Period Indicator**—Specifies the time period for which various forecasted consumption values are held.

- **Fiscal Year Variant**—Describes the number of posting periods for the fiscal year.
- **RefMatl: consumption**—References a material that is used for consumption.
- **RefPlant: consumption**—Refers to the plant on whose consumption data the forecast for the material is dependent.
- **Multiplier**—Specifies the percentage of the consumption of reference material that is to be used for the production of new material.
- **Forecast periods**—Specifies the period over which the forecast will be calculated.
- **Fixed periods**—Helps in avoiding fluctuations in forecast calculation.
- **Intialization pds**—Allows the mySAP ERP system to intialize the forecast.
- **Tracking limit**—Specifies the amount by which the forecast value can deviate from the actual value.
- **Reset automatically**—Specifies that the forecast should be reset if the tracking limit is exceeded.
- **Model selection**—Selects the foreacast model. This field is active only when the user wants the system to select the model automatically.
- **Selection procedure**—Defines how the system should select the optimum forecast model.
- **Optimization level**—Helps in making the forecast more accurate.

Sales Organization Data

The **Sales** (**1** and **2**) tabs allow you to enter the information related to the organization that is selling the material. You should note that a particular material may be sold by different sales organizations. Therefore, the data for each material may differ.

Figure 4.45 displays the **Sales** tab screen:

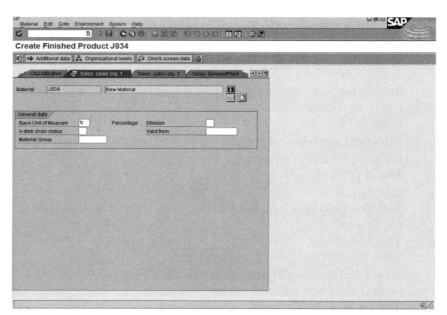

FIGURE 4.45 Displaying the Sales tab

The following are the noteworthy UI elements of the **Sales** tabs:

- **Sales Unit**—Refers to the unit of measure in which the material is to be sold.
- **Variable Sales Unit Not Allowed Indicator**—Specifies whether or not the sales unit of measure can be changed by the sales representative.
- **Cross-Distribution Chain Material Status**—Checks whether or not the material can be used in the distribution channels.
- **Delivering Plant**—Specifies the default plant where the material is to be delivered.
- **Minimum Order Quantity**—Specifies the minimum quantity that a customer can order.
- **Miminum Delivery Quantity**—Specifies the minimum quantity that a supplier can deliver.

- **Delivery Unit**—Specifies the minimum unit of quantity for delivery.
- **Material Group**—Defines the material for sales department analysis.

Sales General Data

The **Sales: General/Plant** tab allows you to enter data pertaining to either a particular material or plant.

Figure 4.46 shows the **Sales: General/Plant** tab screen:

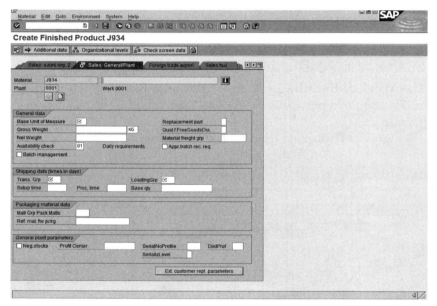

FIGURE 4.46 Displaying the Sales: General/Plant tab

The following are the noteworthy UI elements of the **Sales: General/ Plant** tab:

- **Replacement part**—Specifies whether or not the material is a replacement part.
- **Availability check**—Checks the availability of a material.
- **Appr. batch rec. req.**—Specifies that the batch record has to be entered for performing certain activities. The activities

include changing the batch status from restricted to unrestricted or making the decision concerning inspection of the goods received from the production department.

- **Trans. Grp**—Groups the materials that have similar transport requirements, such as trucks, rails, or tanker.
- **LoadingGrp**—Groups the materials that have similar loading requirements, such as crane or trolley.
- **Setup time**—Specifies the time for procuring equipment.
- **Neg. stocks**—Specifies the situation in which the stock has not been marked as paid in the inventory. You can set this indicator if there is a requirement to allow the material to be stocked in a negative stock situation.

Work Scheduling Data

The **Work scheduling** tab helps the user to enter the work scheduling information of a particular plant. The work scheduling data is managed at the plant level.

Figure 4.47 displays the **Work scheduling** tab:

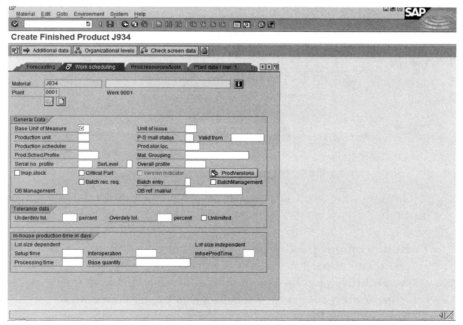

FIGURE 4.47   Displaying the Work scheduling tab

The following are the noteworthy UI elements of the **Work scheduling** tab:

- **Production unit**—Specifies the unit of measure for a material in the production process.
- **Production scheduler**—Calculates the capacity requirement for a material during a scheduling process.
- **Prod.stor.loc.**—Specifies the storage location where the finished goods will be stored after production.
- **Prod.Sched.Profile**—Provides configuration for activities such as capacity planning, availability check, goods reciept, and transport type.
- **Underdely tol.**—Specifies the percentage of under-delivery tolerance.
- **Overdely tol.**—Specifies the percentage of over-delivery tolerance.
- **Setup time**—Determines the dates for planned orders.

Production Resources/Tools Data

Production resources/tools (PRTs) are the movable resources of an organization, such as documents, measurement instruments, and engineering drawing tools. These resources are generally used to perform an activity on a regular basis. The **Prod. resources/tools** tab contains information about PRTs.

Figure 4.48 shows the **Prod. resources/tools** tab:

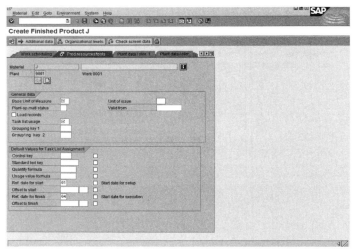

FIGURE 4.48   Displaying the Prod. resources/tools tab

The following are the noteworthy UI elements of the **Prod. resources/ tools** tab:

- **Task list usage**—Specifies the task list in which PRTs can be used.
- **Grouping key 1 and 2**—Defines groupings for PRTs.
- **Control key**—Specifies how PRTs are used in the task list.
- **Standard text key**—Allows the plant maintenance department to define a standard text for PRTs.
- **Quantity formula**—Calculates the number of required PRTs.
- **Offset to start**—Specifies the offset between the reference date and the actual production date of PRTs. This field can have either a negative or a positive value. A negative value specifies that the start date is before the reference date. A positive date specifies that the reference date is before the start date.
- **Storage bin**—Specifies the storage location where the material is stored.
- **Temperature conditions**—Specifies the temperature at which the material should be stored.

Warehouse Management Data

The **Warehouse mgmt** (**1** and **2**) tabs allow you to save data related to warehouse management of a material. You can enter warehouse management data at the warehouse or storage type level.

The **Warehouse mgmt** tab is displayed in Figure 4.49:

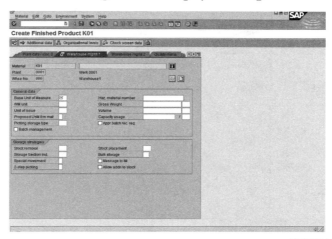

FIGURE 4.49   Displaying the Warehouse mgmt tab

The following are the noteworthy UI elements of the **Warehouse mgmt** tabs:

- **WM unit**—Defines the unit of measure of the material.
- **Stock removal**—Defines the sequence in which the storage type is searched for a material.
- **Stock placement**—Defines the sequence in which the storage type for a material is searched for placing the stock in the warehouse.
- **Storage Section Ind.**—Defines the place where a material is to be placed in reference to the other.
- **Bulk storage**—Defines the way in which the material should be stored in stock.
- **Special movement**—Specifies that the material requires special treatment while being moved from the warehouse.
- **2-step picking**—Helps in minimizing the workload. You can select either 1-step picking or 2-step picking for a material. 1-step picking is ideal for materials that are large and bulky and can be removed from the warehouse at one time. However, in case of multiple small materials, you should select 2-step picking to minimize the workload.
- **Storage bin**—Specifies the storage bin in which the material is added.
- **Maximum bin quantity**—Defines the maximum quantity that can be entered in the storage bin.
- **Minimum bin quantity**—Defines the minimum quantity that can be entered in the storage bin.
- **Replenishment quantity**—Specifies the quantity that should be placed in the storage bin.

MRP Data

MRP data for a particular material is stored at the plant level, implying that MRP data is valid only for a specific plant. Maintaing the MRP data of materials is important as this information specifies how materials are made, planned, and produced in the plant. The **MRP** (**1, 2, 3** and **4**) tabs are used to save the MRP data of a material.

Figure 4.50 shows the **MRP 1** tab:

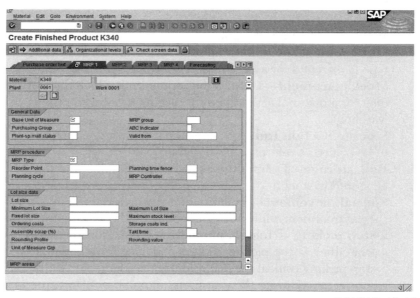

FIGURE 4.50 Displaying the MRP 1 tab

The following are the noteworthy UI elements of the **MRP** tabs:

- **MRP Group**—Combines the special control parameters that are specific to the total planning run.
- **ABC Indicator**—Classifies a material as an A, B, or C part. Classifying the material as an A part specifies that the material is an important part and is of high consumption value. B specifies that the material is of medium consumption value, and C specifies that the material is of low consumption value.
- **MRP Type**—Helps in not only planning a material but also in controlling the MRP parameters that can be maintained for a material.
- **Reorder Point**—Helps in reorder planning, which is decided by the planning department.

- **Planning time fence**—Specifies the period in which no changes can be made to the master plan.
- **Planning cycle**—Determines when the material is to be ordered.
- **MRP Controller**—Specifies the person who is responsible for planning the material.
- **Lot size**—Determines the lot-sizing procedure, which the system uses to calculate the quantity to be produced.
- **Minimum Lot Size**—Specifies the minimum lot size for procurement.
- **Maximum Lot Size**—Specifies the maximum lot size for procurement.
- **Fixed lot size**—Specifies the fixed amount of material that should be ordered, if there is a shortage of material.

Accounting Data

The **Accounting** (**1** and **2**) tabs allow you to enter the accounting data of a material. It allows the accounting department to enter the valuation and price data needed for inventory transactions of a material.

The **Accounting 1** tab is shown in Figure 4.51:

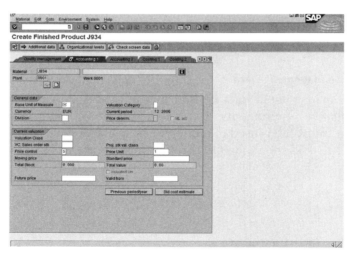

FIGURE 4.51   **Displaying the Accounting 1 tab**

The following are the noteworthy UI elements of the **Accounting** tabs:

- **Valuation Category**—Determines if the stock of material is to be valuated together or separately.
- **ML Active**—Specifies whether or not the material ledger has been activated for the specified material.
- **Valuation Class**—Assigns a material to the general ledger account.
- **Price control**—Helps in stock valuation. There are two options available: V (moving price) and S (standard price). V specifies that the price changes according to goods movement and S specifies that the material is valuated at a constant price.
- **Price Unit**—Specifies the number of units of either the moving price or the standard price.
- **Moving price**—Specifies that the price changes according to the goods movement. It is calculated by dividing the material value by the total stock.
- **Standard price**—Specifies that the material is valuated at a constant price.
- **Future price**—Specifies that the price entered is valid from the date that is entered in the **Valid from** field.

Quality Management Data

Quality management data is used by the quality department to define the basic quality requirements of the material at each plant level. The **Quality management** tab is used to enter quality management data.

Figure 4.52 shows the **Quality management** tab:

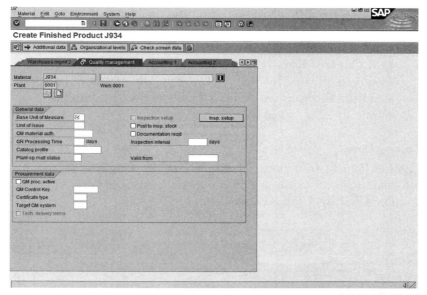

FIGURE 4.52   Displaying the Quality management tab

The following are the noteworthy UI elements of the **Quality management** tab:

- **Post to insp. stock**—Specifies whether or not quality inspection is required for the material
- **QM material auth.**—Restricts any sort of user access to the material-related data
- **Inspection interval**—Allows the quality department to specify the number of days required between different quality inspections

- **Catalog profile**—Notifies about the quality of the material
- **QM proc. active**—Specifies the quality-management aspect of procurement
- **QM Control Key**—Determines the way in which the material would be affected by quality during the procurement cycle
- **Certificate type**—Attaches a quality certificate with the material

Costing Data

Costing data for a material is entered in the **Costing** (**1** and **2**) tabs. The information in these tabs is entered by the costing department.

The **Costing 1** tab is displayed in Figure 4.53:

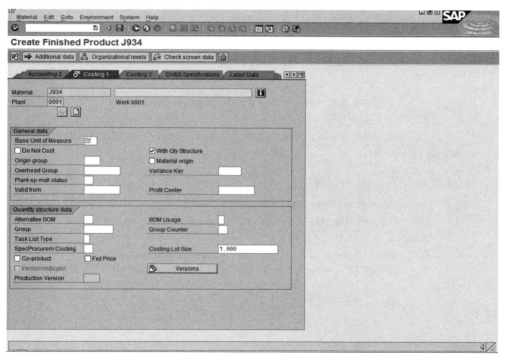

FIGURE 4.53   Displaying the Costing 1 tab

The following are the noteworthy UI elements of the **Costing** tabs:

- **Origin Group**—Helps in subdividing the overhead and material cost
- **Overhead Group**—Applies overhead cost to the materials
- **Group**—Combines the materials having similar production processes
- **Costing Lot Size**—Specifies the lot size for the material, which is used in the product cost estimate

Let's now learn how to modify the material master record.

Changing the Material Master Record

You can change the material master record after it has been created and saved in the SAP database. The following are two ways to change the material master record:

- **Immediately**—Changes the material master record immediately
- **Schedule**—Allows you to set a date on which the material master record should be changed

Let's perform the following steps to change the material master record immediately:

1. Navigate the following menu path in the SAP GUI (Figure 4.54):

Menu Path

SAP menu > Logistics > Materials Management > Material Master > Material > Change > MM02 – Immediately

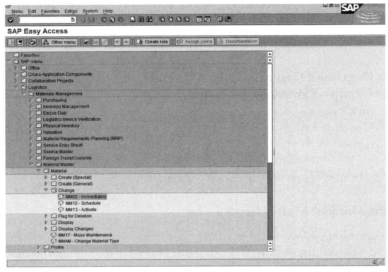

FIGURE 4.54 Displaying the menu path to change the material master record

The **Change Material (Initial Screen)** appears, as shown in Figure 4.55:

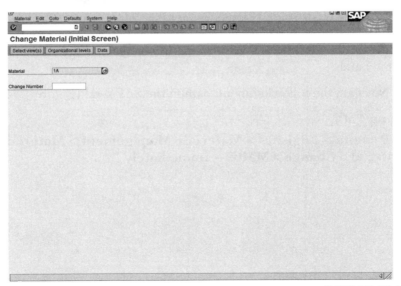

FIGURE 4.55 Changing the material master record

Note: You can also use the MM02 transaction code to access the **Change Material (Initial Screen)**.

2. Enter the number of the material that you want to change in the **Material** text box (Figure 4.55) and press the ENTER key. In this case, we have entered 1A.

The **Select View(s)** dialog box opens, as shown in Figure 4.56:

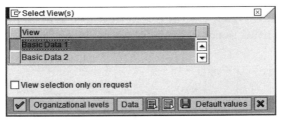

FIGURE 4.56   Selecting view

3. Select the **Basic Data 1** option in the **Select View(s)** dialog box and click the **Continue** (✔) icon.

The **Change Material 1A** screen appears, as shown in Figure 4.57:

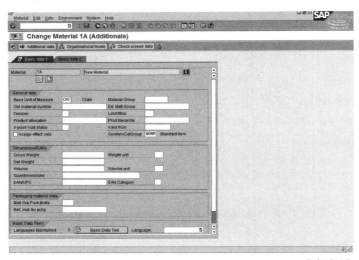

FIGURE 4.57   Entering the new data

4. Enter the new record in the respective text boxes and click the **Save** (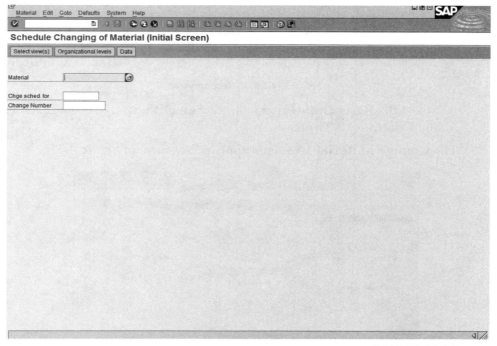) icon to save the changes.

You can schedule a time to change the material master record either by using the `MM12` transaction code or by navigating through the following menu path:

Menu Path

SAP menu > Logistics > Materials Management > Material Master > Material > Change > Schedule. The **Schedule Changing of Material (Initial Screen)** appears, as shown in Figure 4.58:

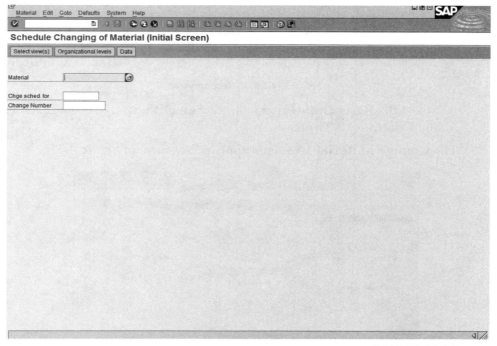

FIGURE 4.58   **Scheduling change of the master material record**

In the **Schedule Changing of Material (Initial Screen)**, you need to enter the following information:

- **Material**—Refers to the material number
- **Chge sched. for**—Refers to the date on which the change is scheduled

Deleting the Material Master Record

You can also delete the master record of a material that is no longer required. Let's perform the following steps to delete the material master record:

1. Navigate the following menu path in the SAP GUI (Figure 4.59):

Menu Path

SAP menu > Logistics > Materials Management > Material Master > Material > Flag for Deletion > MM06 – Immediately

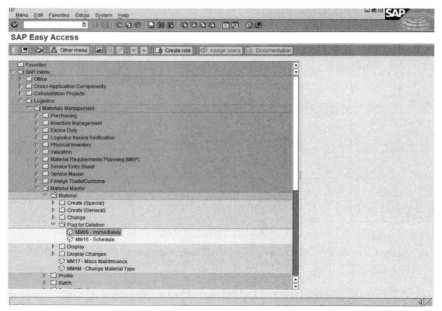

FIGURE 4.59   Displaying the menu path to delete the material master record

The **Flag Material for Deletion: Initial Screen** appears, as shown in Figure 4.60:

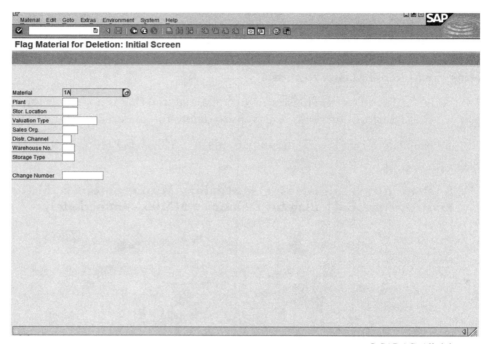

FIGURE 4.60   Displaying the Initial Screen to delete the material master record

Note: You can also use the MM06 transaction code to access the **Flag Material for Deletion: Initial Screen**.

2. Enter the material number in the **Material** text box (Figure 4.60) and press the ENTER key.

The **Flag Material for Deletion: Data Screen** appears, as shown in Figure 4.61:

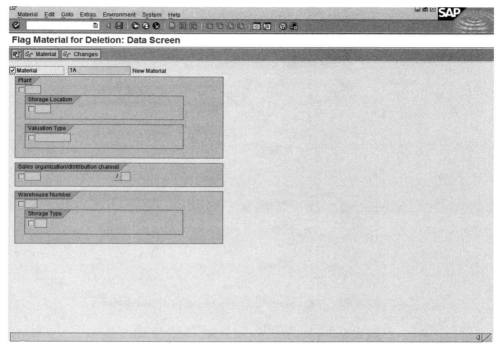

FIGURE 4.61   **Displaying the Data Screen**

3. Select the **Material** check box in the **Flag Material for Deletion: Data Screen** to delete the material at the client level and the lower levels.
4. Press the F11 key to flag the material for deletion.

   A system message indicating that the record has been flagged for deletion appears in the system message line of the screen.

Defining Field Selections

The field selection group of a material helps you to identify whether or not entering a value in a particular field is mandatory or optional. You can define the field selection group in the **Change View "Field Groups": Overview** screen. You can access the **Change View "Field Groups": Overview** screen, as shown in Figure 4.62, by using the OMSR transaction code:

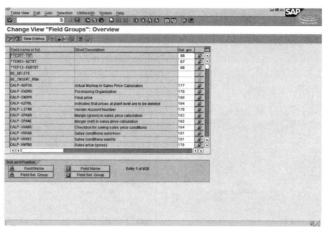

FIGURE 4.62   Displaying the screen to define field selections

In the **Change View "Field Groups": Overview** screen, double-click any transaction to modify the values of its field. When you double-click any transaction, the **Change View "Field Groups": Details** screen opens, as shown in Figure 4.63:

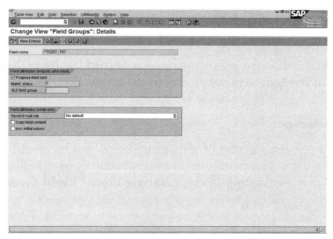

FIGURE 4.63   Displaying the screen to change any field

While defining the field selection for the material master record, you should remember the following points:

- You should not change the field status of the field selection group that has the field reference key with the SAP prefix.
- A new field reference key should begin with Y or Z.
- You cannot change the field reference key for transaction codes and procurement types that are already configured.
- The new field selection groups should be taken from those groups that are not already configured.

Creating Material Groups

You can create different material groups to distinguish various materials. For example, a computer manufacturing organization can classify a computer as a desktop, laptop, or a server, and each classification would have its own individual group.

You can create a material group by accessing the following menu path:

Menu Path

SAP IMG > Logistics – General > Material Master > Settings for Key Fields > Define Material Groups. Figure 4.64 shows the preceding menu path:

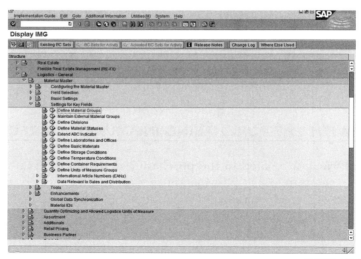

FIGURE 4.64 **Displaying the menu path to create a material group**

The **Change View "Material Groups": Overview** screen appears, as shown in Figure 4.65:

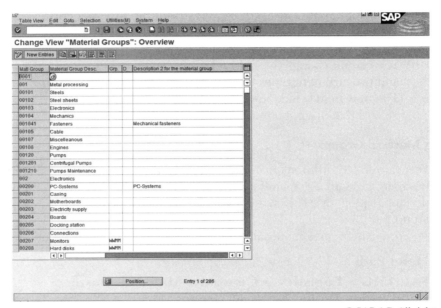

FIGURE 4.65   Displaying the Change View "Material Groups": Overview screen

In the **Change View "Material Groups": Overview** screen, you can group together the materials or services having common attributes.

In this section, you have learned about the material master data. Now let's learn about purchasing information records in SAP MM.

WORKING WITH THE PURCHASING INFORMATION RECORDS

The information related to the purchasing department of an organization is saved in the purchasing information record. In other words, the purchasing information record contains information about a specific material or service that is purchased from a specific vendor. For example, it saves information about the specific terms and conditions of the purchase of each material. The information saved in the purchasing information record is used as default data in some of documents, such as a purchase order. The organization can use the purchasing information record to identify the purchased materials as well as vendors who have supplied them. The purchasing information record serves as a source of information for purchasing and not only saves time but also provides consistent data.

The purchasing information record maintains the following data:

- The current and future price of the material, which includes the gross price, discount, and the freight charges
- The delivery date and time
- The vendor information, which includes information such as the vendor material number and vendor material group
- Detailed information about the material

The purchasing information record can be maintained for the following procurement types:

- **Standard**—Records information supplied by a vendor for a specific material or service
- **Subcontracting**—Records information when the material is in the subcontracting stage
- **Pipeline**—Records information about materials, supplied by utility vendors, such as water and electricity
- **Consignment**—Records information about material supplied by the vendor to be stored at the customer site

Let's first learn to create purchasing information records.

Creating the Purchasing Information Records

In the mySAP ERP system, you can create a purchasing information record with or without entering the details about a purchasing organization. If you do not specify the purchasing organization of the material or service, the purchasing information record is created only with general data. If you enter the information about the purchasing organization along with the material and vendor information, you can access the purchasing data screen. In the purchasing data screen, you can enter information related to a specific purchasing organization.

Let's perform the following steps to create a purchasing information record:

1. Navigate the following menu path in the SAP GUI:

Menu Path
SAP menu > Logistics > Materials Management > Purchasing > Master Data > Info Record > ME11 – Create. Figure 4.66 shows the preceding menu path:

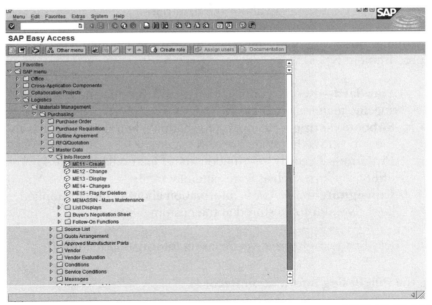

FIGURE 4.66   Displaying the menu path to create a purchasing information record

The **Create Info Record: Initial Screen** appears, as shown in Figure 4.67:

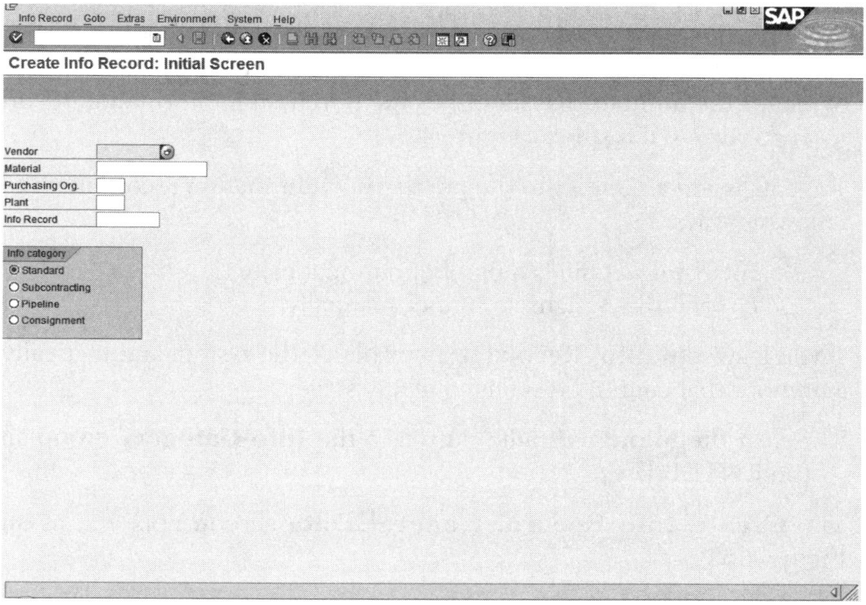

FIGURE 4.67   Displaying the Create Info Record: Initial Screen

---

Note: You can also use the ME11 transaction code to access **Create Info Record: Initial Screen**.

---

2. Enter the vendor number in the **Vendor** text box (Figure 4.67).
3. Enter the material number in the **Material** text box (Figure 4.67).

The **Material** text box allows you to create the purchasing information record in two ways:

- **With material number**—Copies the information, such as price and material description, from the material master to the order item
- **Without material number**—Creates the record without reference to the material master record

4. Enter the purchasing organization of the material in the **Purchasing Org.** text box (Figure 4.67).
5. Enter the name of the plant to receive the ordered goods in the **Plant** text box (Figure 4.67).
6. Enter the number that identifies the purchasing information record in the **Info. Record** text box (Figure 4.67).

You can assign a number to the purchasing information record in either of the following ways:

- **Internal**—Assigns a number automatically
- **External**—Assigns a number manually

If you leave the **Info. Record** text box blank, the system automatically assigns a number that cannot be changed at any stage.

7. Select the **Standard** radio button in the **Info Category** group and press the ENTER key.

The **Create Info Record: General Data** screen appears, as shown in Figure 4.68:

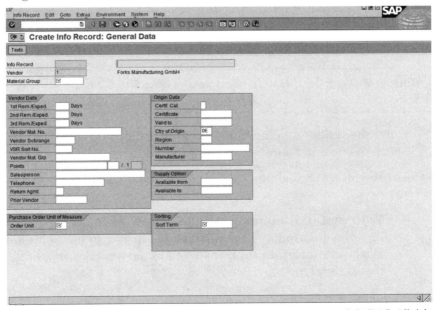

FIGURE 4.68 Entering general data

8. Enter the required information in the **Create Info Record: General Data** screen and press the ENTER key.

The **Create Info Record: Text Overview** screen appears, as shown in Figure 4.69:

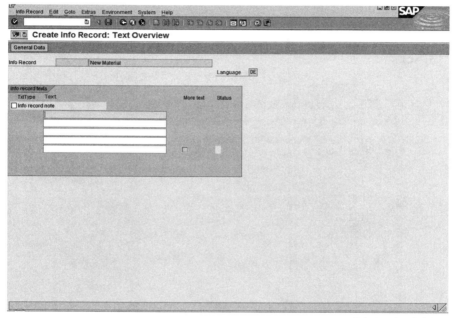

FIGURE 4.69   Displaying the Text Overview screen

9. Enter a short description of the material in the **Create Info Record: Text Overview** screen and click the **Save** (🖫) icon to save the changes.

A system message indicating that the purchasing info record has been created appears in the system message line of the screen.

Configuring the Purchasing Information Records

While configuring the purchasing information record, you can specify the level at which the price of a material should be stored. You can configure purchasing information records by navigating the following menu path:

Menu Path

SAP IMG > Materials Management > Purchasing > Conditions > Define Condition Control at Plant Level. Figure 4.70 shows the preceding menu path:

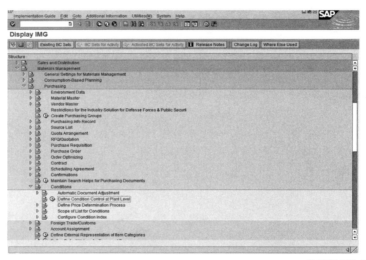

FIGURE 4.70   Displaying the menu path to configure the record

The **Change View "Activate Condition Maintenance for Plant": Overview** screen appears, as shown in Figure 4.71:

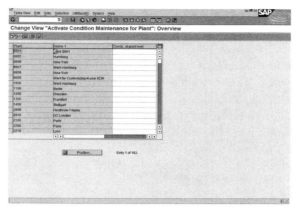

FIGURE 4.71   Displaying the Change View screen

In the **Change View "Activate Condition Maintenance for Plant":
Overview** screen, you can control the conditions at the plant level by selecting
any of the following three options:

- **Conditions allowed at plant level**—Specifies that you have to
  create the purchasing information record relating to the plant at
  the plant level.
- **Conditions are not allowed at plant level**—Specifies that
  it is not necessary to create the purchasing information record
  specifically for the plant at the plant level.
- **Conditions are allowed with or without plant**—Specifies
  that you can create a purchasing information record that is
  either related or not related specifically to a plant. In other
  words, you can create a purchasing information record either at
  the plant level or at the purchasing organization level.

After learning to create and configure purchasing information records,
let's learn about source lists in the SAP MM Handbook.

WORKING WITH SOURCE LISTS

A source list is a type of master data that specifies the sources of supply for a material. In other words, it lists the preferred sources from which the material can be procured. The various uses of a source list are:

- Helps in maintaining a fixed source of supply
- Helps in limiting the source of supply during the source determination process
- Helps in blocking the source of supply

Source lists are maintained where there is more than one source from where the organization can procure materials. These lists can be created either manually or automatically.

Let's perform the following steps to create a source list manually:

1. Navigate the following menu path in the SAP GUI:

Menu Path

SAP menu > Logistics > Material Management > Purchasing > Master Data > Source List > ME01 – Maintain. Figure 4.72 shows the preceding menu path:

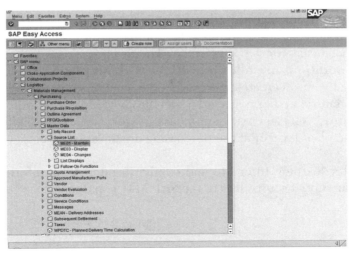

FIGURE 4.72   **Displaying the menu path to create a source list**

The **Maintain Source List: Initial Screen** appears, as shown in Figure 4.73:

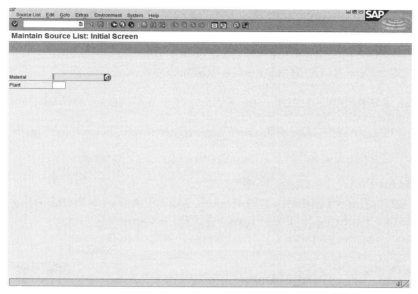

FIGURE 4.73   **Displaying the Maintain Source List: Initial Screen**

Note: You can also use the ME01 transaction code to access the **Maintain Source List: Initial Screen**.

2. Enter the material number in the **Material** text box (Figure 4.73).
3. Enter the corresponding company code in the **Plant** text box (Figure 4.73) and press the ENTER key.

The **Maintain Source List: Overview Screen** appears, in which you need to enter the following information:

- **Valid from**—Specifies the date from which the source list is valid
- **Valid to**—Specifies the date up to which the source list is valid
- **Fixed source**—Specifies that the vendor is the preferred source of supply for the particular material

      □ **Blocked source**—Specifies that the vendor is blocked from supplying a particular material for a specified time

      □ **Agreement**—Specifies that there is an agreement between the vendor and the organization

      □ **MRP**—Specifies whether or not the source of supply should be considered during the planning process

4. Click the **Save** (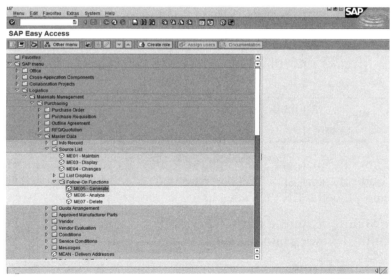) icon to create the source list.

If you want to create the source list automatically, you can use the ME05 transaction code.

Let's perform the following steps to create the source list automatically:

1. Navigate the following menu path in the SAP GUI:

Menu Path

SAP menu > Logistics > Materials Management > Purchasing > Master Data > Follow-On Functions > ME05 – Generate. Figure 4.74 shows the preceding menu path:

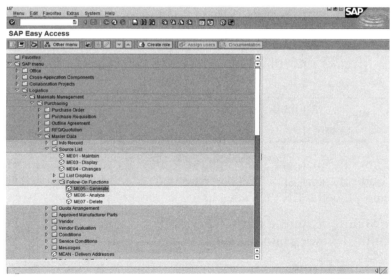

FIGURE 4.74 **Displaying the menu path to create a source list automatically**

The **Generate Source List** screen appears, as shown in Figure 4.75:

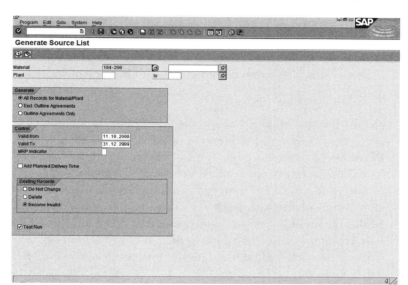

FIGURE 4.75   **Creating a source list automatically**

2. Enter the material number in the **Material** text box (Figure 4.75).
3. Select the **All Records for Material/Plant** radio button in the **Generate** group (Figure 4.75).
4. Enter the validity period in the **Valid from** and **Valid To** text boxes in the **Control** group (Figure 4.75).
5. Select the **Become Invalid** radio button in the **Existing Records** group (Figure 4.75).
6. Select the **Test Run** check box (Figure 4.75).
7. Press the F8 key to create the source list.

Let's now learn about batch management data in the SAP MM Handbook.

WORKING WITH BATCH MANAGEMENT DATA

A batch refers to a collection of material grouped together for various reasons, such as having the same characteristics or being produced on the same day. In SAP MM, a batch is identified by a batch record, which is known as batch management data. The batch record can be determined at various levels, which include:

- **Client level**—Assigns a single batch number for a batch regardless of material or location of the batch.
- **Plant level**—Assigns a batch number that is unique to the plant and material but is not applicable across the organization. This implies that a batch of material can have the same batch number at different plants within the organization.
- **Material level**—Assigns a batch number that is unique to the material across all plants. This implies that if the material is shifted to another plant, the batch information of the material will remain the same.

Note: While creating a batch record, you should note that you can create batch records only for those materials that are to be handled in batches. You should set the Batch Management indicator of a material while creating the material master record, so that the material is allowed to be handled in batches.

To create a batch record, navigate through the following menu path in the SAP GUI:

Menu Path

SAP menu > Logistics > Material Management > Material Master > Batch > MSC1N – Create. Figure 4.76 shows the preceding menu path:

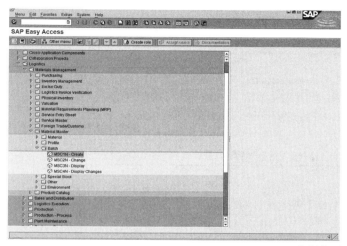

FIGURE 4.76   **Displaying the menu path to create batch records**

The **Create Batch** screen appears, as shown in Figure 4.77:

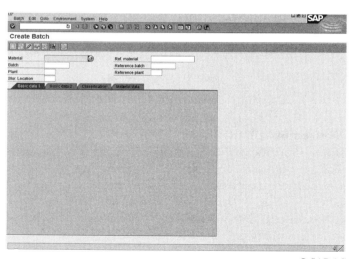

FIGURE 4.77   **Creating batch records**

> **Note:** You can also use the MSC1N transaction code to access the **Maintain Source List: Initial Screen**.

Enter the required information in their respective fields and click the **Save** (🖫) icon to create the batch record.

Let's now learn about quota arrangement in SAP MM.

UNDERSTANDING QUOTA ARRANGEMENT

Quota arrangement in SAP MM is the method for determining the part of the material that can be procured from a specified source. For example, the switches of table lamps scheduled to be produced in a batch can be procured from a particular vendor. To define the quota arrangement for a material, you need to provide the following information:

- **Validity period**—Specifies the validity of the quota arrangement for the specified material
- **Procurement type**—Specifies that the material can be procured either internally or externally
- **Special procurement type**—Specifies that the material can be procured by any of the following three methods:
    - Consignment
    - Subcontracting
    - Third-party procurement
- **Procurement plant**—Refers to the vendor plant
- **Quota**—Specifies the portion of the material that should be procured from the specified source of supply
- **Quota base quantity**—Specifies any additional quota-allocated quantity
- **Quota allocated quantity**—Refers to the total quantity from the purchasing department
- **Quota rating**—Refers to the source of supply, which is used by the system

You can use the MEQ1 transaction code to maintain quota arrangement.

SUMMARY

In this chapter, you have learned about various types of master data that can be maintained in the SAP MM module. First, the vendor master data was discussed, which consists of all the information about the vendors of the organization. You learned to change, display, delete, block, and unblock the vendor master record. Next, you learned about material master data and its main attributes, which include material number, industry sector, and material type. You also learned to create the material master record by immediate, scheduling, and special processes. Next, you learned to create and configure purchasing information records.

The chapter continued with a discussion about source lists, which consist of information about the sources of supply for a material in a particular plant. You also learned about batch management data and the quota arrangement processes in detail.

In the next chapter, you will learn to implement the purchasing process in the SAP MM module.

Implementing the Purchasing Process in the MM Module

5

The purchasing process refers to the process of procuring materials or services required by an organization from an external source. Usually, an agreement, containing all the details of the transactions, such as the type of material, price, and delivery date, is drawn between the purchasing and the selling parties. After the materials or services have been received, the purchasing organization has to pay the vendors or suppliers as per the terms of the agreement. To ensure fair transactions between the parties involved in the purchasing process, the Materials Management (MM) module of the mySAP™ ERP system allows you to generate various documents, such as purchase requisitions, request for quotations (RFQs), quotations, purchase orders (POs), goods receipts, and invoice receipts. Some of these documents are internal documents while others are external. Internal documents are used to store the information for the internal use of an organization. For instance, a purchase requisition, which is used by various departments of an organization to know the services or materials that need to be purchased, is an internal document. On the other hand, external documents are the documents that are created to be sent to vendors. For example, a PO is an external document that is sent by an organization to the vendors for availing materials and services.

In this chapter, you learn how to implement the purchasing process in the MM module. The chapter begins by explaining the complete cycle of the procurement or purchasing process. This process is divided into various phases, such as purchase requisition, quotation, request for quotation, and purchase order. In the purchase requisition phase, you learn to create a purchase requisition document. Next, you learn to create, maintain, and release an RFQ document in the request for quotation phase. In the quotation phase, you learn to enter the quotations of various vendors in the mySAP ERP system and then to compare these quotations to select a vendor for supplying the material. Next, you learn to create a PO document corresponding to the selected vendor in the purchase order phase. You also learn about outline purchase agreements between purchasing organizations and vendors, and vendor confirmations to customers regarding the delivery of material. Toward the end, you learn about the process of procuring services in the MM module.

Let's start by exploring the purchasing process.

EXPLORING THE PURCHASING PROCESS

The purchasing process, also known as the procurement cycle or procure to pay (P2P) cycle, starts with the determination of the requirements for materials or services in an organization, and ends when the payment is made to the supplier.

The various stages involved in the procurement cycle are shown in Figure 5.1:

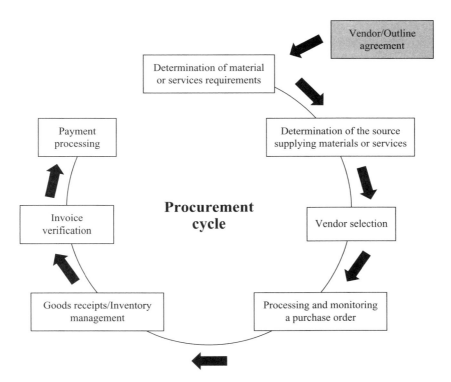

FIGURE 5.1   Displaying the procurement cycle

Let's now discuss each of these stages in detail.

Determining the Material Requirements

The procurement cycle in the mySAP ERP system starts by determining the materials or services that need to be procured from an external source. The material requirements are then recorded in the purchase requisition document, which is forwarded to the purchasing department of the organization. A purchase requisition document is used to notify the purchasing department about the details of the required materials or services, such as their type, the amount or quantity in which the materials are required, and the date by which they must be made available to the organization. Note that in the mySAP ERP system, a purchase requisition document must be approved or released before being passed to the next stage or phase in the purchasing process.

Determining the Source of Supplying the Materials

After determining the requirements of an organization, the next step is to identify the source of supply to fulfill these requirements. This source can be determined by referring to past orders and the existing agreements of the organization with external suppliers and vendors. You can use the ME57 transaction code in the mySAP ERP system to check whether the required material or service can be obtained from an existing contract and agreement. If you do not find a valid contract or agreement, you can create new RFQ documents to be sent to vendors. A RFQ is an external purchasing document that contains all the details of a material, such as price, delivery conditions, and terms of payment that a vendor agrees to while providing the material or service. The RFQ document is sent by a company to a vendor to request for the quotation of the material.

Selecting a Vendor

When the vendors submit their quotations of materials, these quotations are entered in the mySAP ERP system by using the ME47 transaction code. These quotations are then compared for their financial and other feasibilities by using the ME49 transaction code, after which the organization selects a particular vendor to supply the required materials or services. The organization can also send rejection letters to the vendors whose quotations are not selected.

Processing and Monitoring a PO

After selecting a vendor, the organization creates a purchase order (PO) document for the selected vendor. A PO is a legal document that is issued by an organization to a vendor. We learned earlier that a PO contains all the details of the required material or service, such as the description, quantity, delivery date, agreed prices, terms of delivery, and terms of payment. The information to be entered in a PO is retrieved from the purchase requisition or quotation document. You can use the `ME21N` transaction code to create a PO document.

After issuing a PO document to the vendor, the organization monitors whether or not the vendor is delivering the material or service as per the terms and conditions agreed between them. It also checks whether the material or service is received by the concerned person, for instance a warehouse man, who then creates a goods receipt for the received materials.

Generating Goods Receipts

When the concerned person in the organization receives the material or service, he has to post a goods receipt or service acceptance document and update the PO history in the mySAP ERP system. In addition, the mySAP ERP system also generates a reminder in case the goods receipt document is not created corresponding to the item(s) mentioned in the PO document at the specified date.

Verifying the Invoices

After the goods receipt is sent to the vendor, the vendor matches the details with the PO document and generates an invoice. An invoice is a formal document issued by a vendor to an organization for the payment of the material or service that has been provided to the organization. In general, an invoice is attached with a goods receipt or delivery note document and sent to the organization. On receiving an invoice from the vendor, the organization verifies it by performing the following tasks:

1. Comparing the information present in the invoice with that of the original PO document.
2. Checking whether or not the materials or services mentioned in the PO have been received from the vendor.
3. Checking whether or not the goods receipt or service acceptance document has been issued to the vendor. If the goods receipt or service acceptance document has been issued, the invoice receipt document can be posted in the mySAP ERP system.

Processing of Payments

After posting an invoice receipt document, the organization has to pay the vendor as per the terms of payment mentioned in the PO document. The task of payment processing is performed in the Financial Accounting (FI) module. When payment processing is completed, the vendor's account is debited and the organization's account is credited.

Since the purchasing process or procurement cycle starts with the purchase requisition phase, let's now discuss this phase in detail.

EXPLORING THE PURCHASE REQUISITION PHASE

A purchase requisition is an internal document containing the details of the materials or services required by an organization. In the mySAP ERP system, a purchase requisition document can be created directly or indirectly. In the MM module, a purchase requisition document is created directly by executing the ME51N or ME54 transaction code in the command field. Alternately, you can generate a purchase requisition document indirectly in the various modules of SAP, such as Plant Maintenance (PM), Production Planning (PP), and Project System (PS).

Let's first learn to create a purchase requisition document directly.

Creating a Purchase Requisition Directly

A purchase requisition can be created only for those materials or services that have their master records in the mySAP ERP system. In the direct creation process, you need to manually enter the details of the required material or service in a purchase requisition. Perform the following steps to create a purchase requisition:

1. Navigate the following menu path:

Menu Path
SAP menu > Logistics > Materials Management > Purchasing > Purchase Requistion

2. Double-click the **ME51N – Create** option, as shown in Figure 5.2:

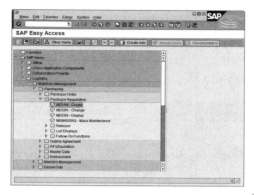

FIGURE 5.2   Creating a purchase requisition

The **Create Purchase Requisition** screen appears (Figure 5.3).

3. Enter the required details, such as material, material description, quantity, unit, delivery date, and plant, in the **Create Purchase Requisition** screen, as shown in Figure 5.3:

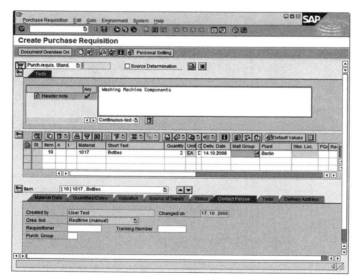

FIGURE 5.3   Specifying the details for a purchase requisition

4. Click the **Save** (🖫) icon to save the details of a purchase requisition (Figure 5.3).

A message indicating the successful creation of the purchase requisition is displayed, as shown in Figure 5.4:

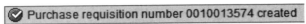

FIGURE 5.4   **Displaying the message after creating a purchase requisition**

You can also create a purchase requisition directly by executing the ME51 transaction code in the command field. The **Create: Purchase Requisition: Initial Screen** appears, as shown in Figure 5.5:

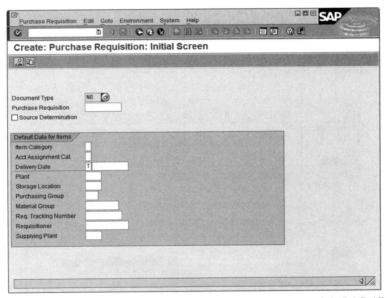

FIGURE 5.5   **Displaying the Create: Purchase Requisition: Initial Screen**

You need to enter the required details in the screen displayed in Figure 5.5 to create a purchase requisition document. Table 5.1 lists the UI elements displayed in **Create: Purchase Requisition: Initial Screen**:

UI Element	Description
Document Type	Specifies the document type that defines internal or external number ranges for a purchase requisition. For example, the NB document type is used for the standard purchase requisition and TB for athe transport order.
Purchase Requisition	Specifies a unique key to identify a purchase requisition.
Source Determination	Indicates an existing source of supply for a material.
Item Category	Specifies a key number that represents the process of controlling a material or service.
Acct Assignment Cat.	Specifies the account assignment category for an item.
Delivery Date	Specifies a date on which the goods have to be delivered.
Plant	Specifies a key that determines which plant will receive the ordered goods.
Storage Location	Specifies the identification numbers of the storage locations where the material is stored.
Purchasing Group	Specifies a key number assigned to a buyer or group of buyers performing the purchasing activities.
Material Group	Specifies a key number assigned to a group of materials having the same attributes.
Req. Tracking Number	Specifies a number to track and monitor the procurement of required materials.
Requisitioner	Specifies the person or the organization for whom which the material is ordered.
Supplying Plant	Specifies a plant that supplies the material.

TABLE 5.1   UI elements of Create: Purchase Requisition: Initial Screen

After creating a purchase requisition document, you may need to perform various activities, such as display or modify the details of a purchase requisition document. Table 5.2 lists the menu paths and transaction codes to perform these activities:

Activity	Menu Path	Transaction Code
Displaying a purchase requisition	SAP menu > Logistics > Materials Management > Purchasing > Purchase Requisition > ME53N – Display	ME53N
Modifying a purchase requisition	SAP menu > Logistics > Materials Management > Purchasing > Purchase Requisition > ME52N – Change	ME52N
Displaying a list of purchase requisitions	SAP menu > Logistics > Materials Management > Purchasing > Purchase Requisition > List Displays > ME5A – General	ME5A

TABLE 5.2   Menu paths and transaction codes to display and modify a purchase requisition document

Let's now learn how to create a purchase requisition indirectly.

Creating a Purchase Requisition Indirectly

A purchase requisition is said to be indirectly created when its data is retrieved from other modules of the mySAP ERP system. You can retrieve data from any of the following modules to create a purchase requisition indirectly:

- **Production Order**—Creates a purchase requisition on the basis of the elements of the production order, namely routing and the Bill of Materials (BOM).
- **Plant Maintenance Order**—Creates a purchase requisition on the basis of a list of operations. These operations provide procedural steps, which serve as a guideline for further course of action. In addition, these operations also specify which materials and equipments are required for each step.

- **Project Systems**—Creates a purchase requisition on the basis of a collection of networks. A network is a set of instructions that guides a user to perform certain tasks. It also provides information about the order of tasks and the date on which these tasks have to be performed.
- **Materials Planning**—Creates a purchase requisition based on consumption of the material.

Let's explore the request for quotation phase in the next section.

EXPLORING THE REQUEST FOR QUOTATION PHASE

At times, a purchasing organization cannot process a purchase requisition for a particular vendor. This may happen when the material supplied by a particular vendor is not used by the purchasing organization because of the bankruptcy or decertification of the vendor. Consider a situation in which an organization that manufactures furniture procures the raw materials, such as wood, from a vendor. Prior to the manufacturing of the furniture, the vendor is declared bankrupt. In such a situation, the organization does not process the purchase requisition for the bankrupted vendor and the RFQ document is issued to a new vendor. As you have already learned, a RFQ is an external document used by a purchasing organization to select a vendor or supplier to avail the material or service. It can be created with or without referencing an already existing RFQ document. In this section, you learn how to:

- Create an RFQ
- Change an RFQ
- Release an RFQ
- Send an RFQ printout to a specific vendor

Creating an RFQ

To create an RFQ, you need to enter the relevant details, such as the type of RFQ, the date of the RFQ, the deadline of the quotation, and the name of the purchasing organization in the **Create RFQ: Initial Screen**.

Let's perform the following steps to create an RFQ in the mySAP ERP system:

1. Navigate the following menu path (Figure 5.6):

Menu Path

SAP menu > Logistics > Materials Management > Purchasing > RFQ/Quotation > Request for Quotation

2. Double-click the **ME41 – Create** option, as shown in Figure 5.6:

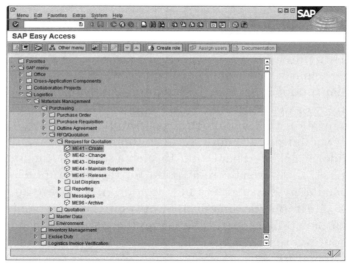

FIGURE 5.6   Displaying the menu path to create an RFQ

The **Create RFQ: Initial Screen** appears (Figure 5.7).

3. Enter the required details in the **RFQ Type, Language Key, RFQ Date, Quotation Deadline, Purchasing Organization**, and **Purchasing Group** fields (Figure 5.7).

4. Click the **Header Details** (⬛) icon, as shown in Figure 5.7:

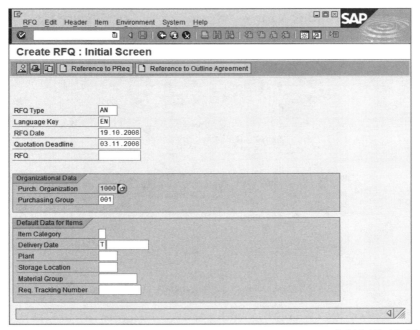

FIGURE 5.7 **Displaying the Create RFQ: Initial Screen**

The **Create RFQ: Header Data** screen appears (Figure 5.8).

Note: You can also use the `ME41` transaction code to access **Create RFQ: Initial Screen**.

5. Enter a collective number in the **Coll.No.** field. In our case, we have entered `Z0_03` (Figure 5.8).

Note: A collective number is a number that is assigned to a group of RFQs that are created for a single product. It helps you to search for an RFQ and identify the product.

6. Click the **Vendor Address** (📧) icon, as shown in Figure 5.8:

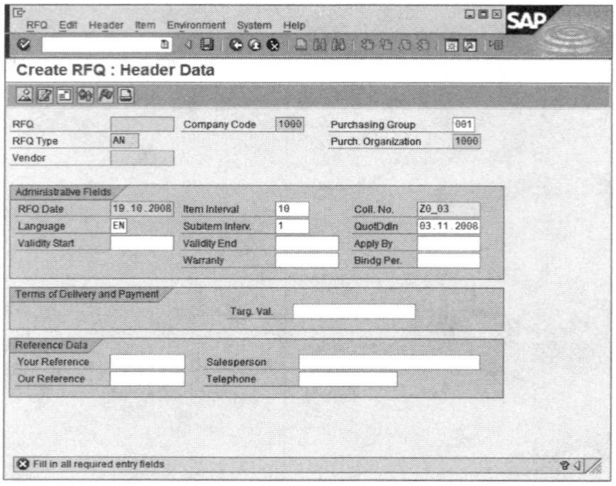

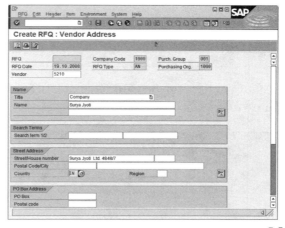

FIGURE 5.8   **Displaying the Create RFQ: Header Data screen**

The **Create RFQ: Vendor Address** screen appears (Figure 5.9).

7. Enter the vendor number, title, name, and address in the **Vendor**, **Title**, **Name**, and **Street Address** fields, respectively (Figure 5.9).
8. Click the **Overview** (👤) icon, as shown in Figure 5.9:

FIGURE 5.9   **Displaying the Create RFQ: Vendor Address screen**

The **Create RFQ: Item Overview** screen appears (Figure 5.10).

9. Enter a material number, quantity, delivery date, and plant number in the relevant fields (Figure 5.10).
10. Click the **Save** (🖫) icon, as shown in Figure 5.10:

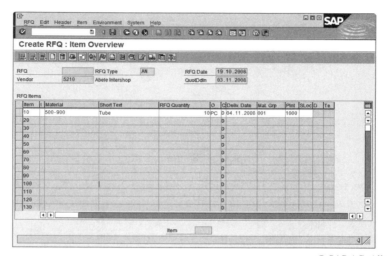

FIGURE 5.10   **Displaying the Create RFQ: Item Overview screen**

11. Press the ENTER key. The status bar displays a message indicating the successful creation of the RFQ document, as shown in Figure 5.11:

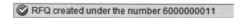

FIGURE 5.11   **Displaying a message after creating an RFQ**

After creating an RFQ document, let's learn how to change it.

Changing an RFQ

You can change an RFQ by executing the ME42 transaction code or navigating the following menu path:

Menu Path

SAP menu > Logistics > Materials Management > Purchasing > RFQ/ Quotation > Request for Quotation > ME42 – Change

The **Change RFQ: Initial Screen** appears, as shown in Figure 5.12:

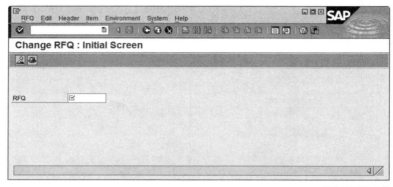

FIGURE 5.12   **Displaying the Change RFQ: Initial Screen**

Select an RFQ number from the valid matchcodes and click the **Overview** (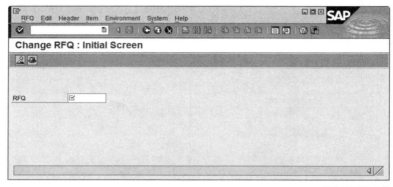) icon. The valid matchcodes to find a valid RFQ number are given as follows:

- Purchasing Documents per Requirement Tracking Number
- Purchasing Documents per Collective Number

In our case, we have selected the RFQ number from the **Purchasing Documents per Collective Number** matchcodes, as shown in Figure 5.13:

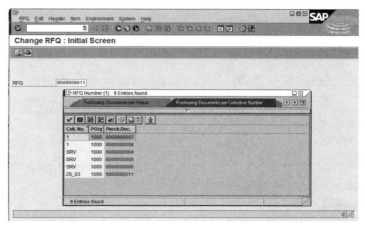

FIGURE 5.13   **Displaying valid matchcodes to find a valid RFQ number**

The **Change RFQ: Item Overview** screen appears (Figure 5.14). In our case, the RFQ number is `6000000011`, as shown in Figure 5.14:

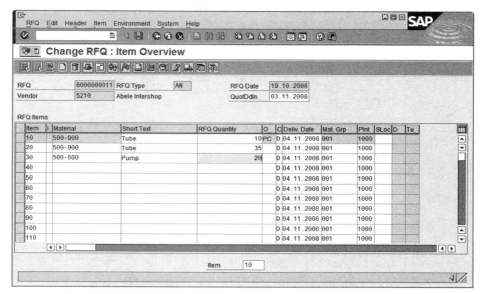

FIGURE 5.14   Displaying the Change RFQ: Item Overview screen

In the **Change RFQ: Item Overview** screen, you can enter one or more line items corresponding to the selected RFQ. If an incorrect line item is entered, you can delete or block it by selecting the **Edit > Delete** or **Edit > Block** option, respectively. You can remove the delete indicator or unblock a line item by selecting the **Edit > Reset Deletion Ind** option.

Let's now learn to release an RFQ.

Releasing an RFQ

After completing the details in an RFQ document, it is released to be issued to a vendor. The release of an RFQ is closely related to a purchase requisition or PO. You can either use the `ME45` transaction code or navigate the following menu path to release an RFQ (Figure 5.6):

Menu Path

SAP menu > Logistics > Materials Management > Purchasing > RFQ/ Quotation > Request for Quotation > Release – ME45. The **Release**

(**Approve**) **Purchasing Documents** screen appears, as shown in Figure 5.15:

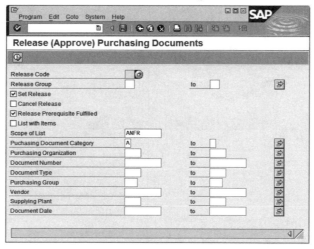

FIGURE 5.15   **Displaying the Release (Approve) Purchasing Documents screen**

You need to enter the relevant details in the user interface (UI) elements shown in Figure 5.15 to release an RFQ. Table 5.3 lists the UI elements displayed in the **Release (Approve) Purchasing Documents** screen:

UI Element	Description
Release Code	Specifies a code for the approval of a purchasing document
Release Group	Represents a collection of multiple release strategies
Set Release	Indicates that the mySAP ERP system uses the default values to process the purchasing documents
Cancel Release	Indicates that the mySAP ERP system uses the default values to cancel the release of purchasing documents

Continued

UI Element	Description
Release Prerequisite Fulfilled	Checks whether or not the prerequisites required to release an RFQ are fulfilled by purchase requisition items or purchasing documents
List with Items	Displays a list of data items in the purchasing document
Scope of List	Specifies the information of a purchasing list
Purchasing Document Category	Specifies a document category that differentiates purchasing documents in the mySAP ERP system
Purchasing Organization	Specifies a purchasing organization
Document Number	Specifies a unique alphanumeric key to identify a purchasing document
Document Type	Represents a document type that differentiates purchasing documents in the mySAP ERP system
Purchasing Group	Represents a key number for a buyer or group of buyers performing purchasing activities
Vendor	Specifies a unique alphanumeric key to identify a vendor
Supplying Plant	Describes a plant that supplies the ordered material
Document Date	Represents the date of creating a purchasing document

TABLE 5.3   The UI elements in the Release (Approve) Purchasing Documents screen

Let's now learn to send an RFQ document to a vendor.

Sending an RFQ Document to a Specific Vendor

After entering the details of an RFQ in the mySAP ERP system, the organization needs to send a printout of the RFQ document to the selected vendor. You can take the printout of the RFQ document by using the ME9A transaction code or navigating the following menu path:

Menu Path

SAP menu > Logistics > Materials Management > Purchasing > RFQ/ Quotation > Request for Quotation > Messages

Double-click the **ME9A – Print/Transmit** option, as shown in Figure 5.16:

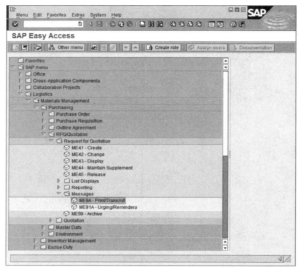

FIGURE 5.16 Displaying the ME9A – Print/Transmit option

The **Message Output** screen appears, as shown in Figure 5.17:

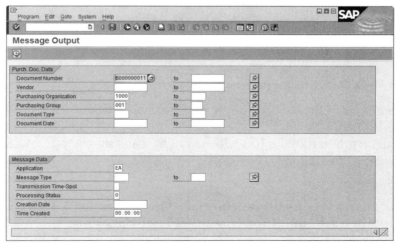

FIGURE 5.17 Displaying the Message Output screen

In the **Message Output** screen, you need to select an RFQ document before printing it. You can select an RFQ on the basis of various criteria, such as **Document Number, Vendor, Purchasing Organization, Purchasing Group, Document Type**, and **Document Date**. In our case, we have selected the `6000000011` document number. Now, click the **Execute** (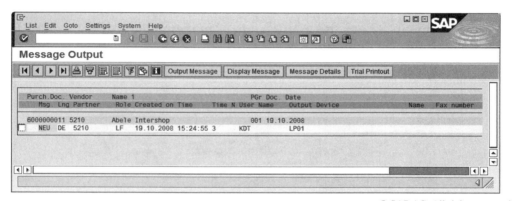) icon. The **Message Output** screen displays the RFQ document details before printing it, as shown in Figure 5.18:

FIGURE 5.18   **Displaying the details of an RFQ document for printing**

Let's explore the quotation phase in the next section.

EXPLORING THE QUOTATION PHASE

The phase in which an organization receives quotations from multiple vendors in response to the RFQ sent by it is known as the quotation phase. After receiving the quotations, the organization first enters all the quotations in the mySAP ERP system and then compares them to select the vendor from whom it would like to purchase the materials. Rejection letters are generated and sent to the unselected vendors. Let's learn how to insert, compare, and reject quotations in the mySAP ERP system.

Inserting a Quotation

After receiving the quotations from vendors, they must be entered in the mySAP ERP system.

Perform the following steps to enter a quotation in the mySAP ERP system:

1. Navigate the following menu path (Figure 5.19):

Menu Path

SAP menu > Logistics > Materials Management > Purchasing > RFQ/Quotation > Quotation

2. Double-click the **ME47 – Maintain** option, as shown in Figure 5.19:

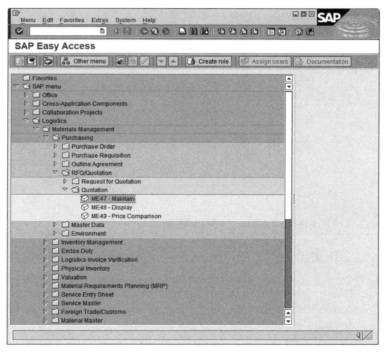

FIGURE 5.19   Displaying the menu path to insert a quotation

The **Maintain Quotation: Initial Screen** appears (Figure 5.20).

3. Enter an RFQ number in the **RFQ** text field. In our case, we have entered `6000000011`, as shown in Figure 5.20:

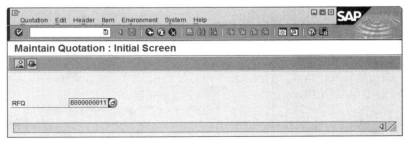

FIGURE 5.20   Displaying the Maintain Quotation: Initial Screen

Note: You can also use the `ME47` transaction code to open the **Maintain Quotation: Initial Screen**.

4. Press the F5 key. The **Maintain Quotation: Item Overview** screen appears (Figure 5.21).
5. Enter the quotation details corresponding to an RFQ in the **Maintain Quotation: Item Overview** screen, as shown in Figure 5.21:

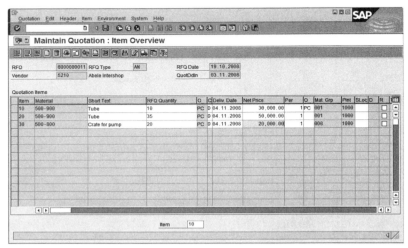

FIGURE 5.21   Displaying the Maintain Quotation: Item Overview screen

In Figure 5.21, you can see the entered bid amount in the **Net Price** column. When a quotation is entered in the mySAP ERP system, the respective RFQ is updated in the system.

6. Click the **Conditions** (▣) icon (Figure 5.21).

The **Change Quotation: Item – Conditions** screen appears (Figure 5.22).

7. Enter discounts, taxes, and other details in the **Change Quotation: Item – Conditions** screen, as shown in Figure 5.22:

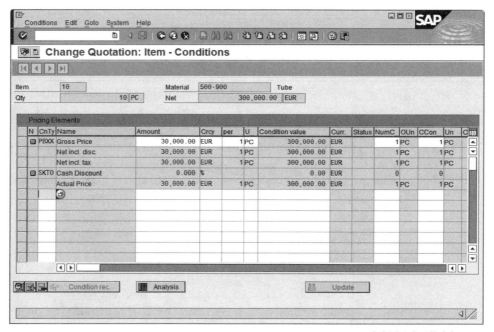

FIGURE 5.22   Displaying the Change Quotation: Item – Conditions screen

8. Click the **Save** (▣) icon to save the changes.

After inserting the quotations in the mySAP ERP system, let's now learn how to compare them.

Comparing Quotations

The purchasing organization compares the quotations to select a vendor for providing the required materials or services. The quotations are compared on the basis of prices of materials provided by vendors. You can compare the quotations entered into the mySAP ERP system by using the ME49 transaction code or navigating the following menu path (Figure 5.19):

Menu Path

SAP menu > Logistics > Materials Management > Purchasing > RFQ/ Quotation > Quotation > ME49 – Price Comparison. The **Price Comparison List** screen appears, as shown in Figure 5.23:

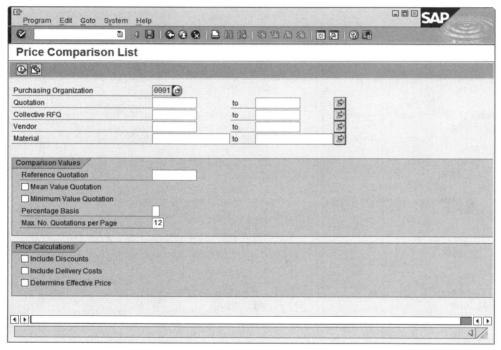

FIGURE 5.23   Displaying the Price Comparison List screen

Figure 5.23 displays various criteria on which the quotations are compared.

Table 5.4 lists the UI elements present in the **Price Comparison List** screen to compare quotations:

UI Element	Description
Purchasing Organization	Represents a purchasing organization
Quotation	Specifies a unique alphanumeric key to identify a purchasing document
Collective RFQ	Specifies a number range that helps manage a collection of multiple RFQs or POs
Vendor	Specifies a unique alphanumeric key to identify a vendor
Material	Specifies a unique alphanumeric key to identify the material
Reference Quotation	Specifies a quotation with which the selected quotations have to be compared
Mean Value Quotation	Indicates the average value of the quotations
Minimum Value Quotation	Indicates the minimum value of the quotations
Percentage Basis	Specifies a value that can be taken as the basis for price comparison
Max. No. Quotations per Page	Represents the maximum number of quotations that can be displayed together
Include Discounts	Indicates whether or not the percentage discount is given on the purchase price in accordance with the terms of payment
Include Delivery Costs	Indicates whether or not the delivery costs are considered in calculating the price
Determine Effective Price	Indicates whether or not the cash discounts and delivery costs are considered in calculating the price

TABLE 5.4   UI elements of Price Comparison List screen

Now, let's learn how to reject quotations in the mySAP ERP system.

Rejecting Quotations

After comparing the quotations of different vendors or bidders, the organization purchasing the material selects a vendor for supplying the material. After selecting the quotation of a particular vendor, the remaining quotations can be flagged as rejected. You can flag a quotation as rejected by using the ME47 transaction code or navigating the following menu path (Figure 5.19):

Menu Path

SAP menu > Logistics > Materials Management > Purchasing > RFQ/ Quotation > Quotation > ME47 – Maintain. The **Maintain Quotation: Item Overview** screen appears. Figure 5.24 shows that a quotation has been rejected in the 6000000011 RFQ:

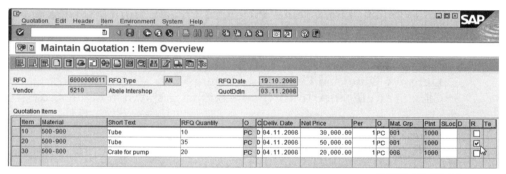

FIGURE 5.24   **Selecting the quotation to be rejected**

In Figure 5.24, the quotation of the item Tube, having an RFQ quantity of 35, is marked as rejected by selecting the **R** check box. A rejected quotation can be printed by using the ME9A transaction code.

Let's learn about the purchase order phase next.

EXPLORING THE PURCHASE ORDER PHASE

In the purchase order phase, PO documents are issued by purchasing organizations to vendors for supplying the required materials or services on specified delivery dates. A PO contains the details of the required materials or services, such as type, quantity, and price.

In this section, you learn how to:

- Create a PO
- Maintain a PO
- Assign accounts to a PO

Creating a PO

A PO document can be created with or without knowing a vendor's details. You can create a PO by executing the ME21 transaction code in the command field.

Perform the following steps to create a PO in the mySAP ERP system:

1. Enter the ME21 transaction code in the command field and press the ENTER key. **The Create Purchase Order: Initial Screen** appears (Figure 5.25).
2. Enter the required details in the **Vendor, Order Type, Purchase Order Date, Purchase Order, Purch. Organization, Purchasing Group, Delivery Date**, and **Plant** fields (Figure 5.25).
3. Click the **Reference to RFQ** push button, as shown in Figure 5.25:

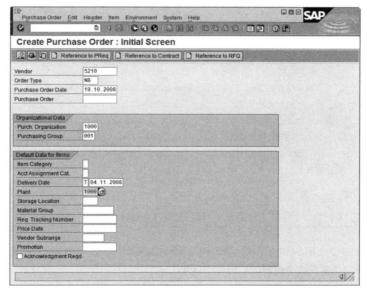

FIGURE 5.25   Displaying Create Purchase Order: Initial Screen

The **Reference to RFQ** dialog box appears (Figure 5.26).

4. Enter an RFQ number in the **RFQ** field. In our case, we have entered 6000000011, as shown in Figure 5.26:

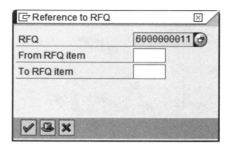

FIGURE 5.26   Displaying the Reference to RFQ dialog box

5. Click the **Enter** (☑) icon. The **Create Purchase Order: Overview: Reference Document Items** screen appears (Figure 5.27).
6. Click the **Adopt + Details** button, as shown in Figure 5.27:

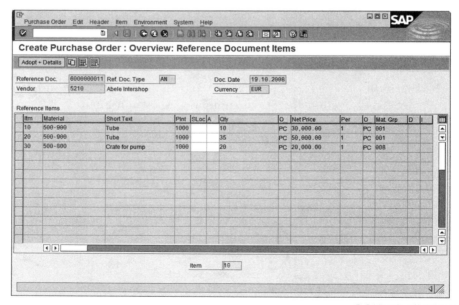

FIGURE 5.27   Displaying the Create Purchase Order: Overview: Reference Document Items screen

The **Create Purchase Order: Item 00010** screen appears (Figure 5.28).

7. Click the **Save** (🖫) icon, as shown in Figure 5.28:

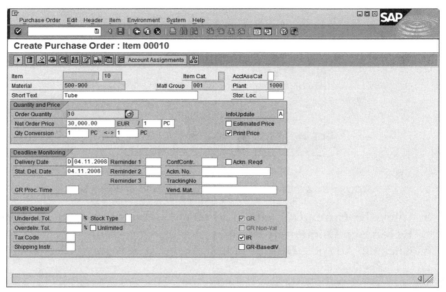

FIGURE 5.28   **Displaying the Create Purchase Order: Item 00010 screen**

8. Press the ENTER key. The status bar diplays a message indicating the successful creation of a PO document, as shown in Figure 5.29:

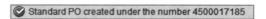

FIGURE 5.29   **Displaying a message after creating a PO**

Note: You can also create a PO by using the ME21N transaction code or traversing the following menu path to create a PO document:

Menu Path

SAP menu > Logistics > Materials Management > Purchasing > Purchase Order > Create > ME21N – Vendor/Supplying Plant Known. When the vendor is unknown, you should use the ME25 transaction code or navigate the following menu path to create a PO document (Figure 5.30):

Menu Path

SAP menu > Logistics > Materials Management > Purchasing > Purchase Order > Create. Double-click the **ME25 – Vendor Unknown** option, as shown in Figure 5.30:

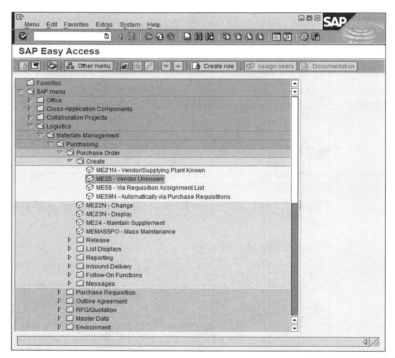

FIGURE 5.30   Displaying the menu path to create a PO

The **Create Purchase Order: Initial Screen** appears, as shown in Figure 5.31:

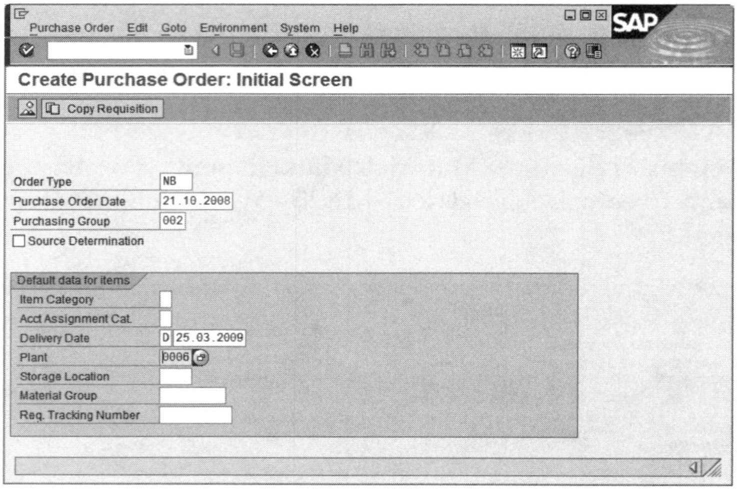

FIGURE 5.31   **Displaying the Create Purchase Order: Initial Screen in case of unknown vendor**

You need to enter the relevant details in the UI elements present in the screen shown in Figure 5.31.

Table 5.5 lists the UI elements in the **Create Purchase Order: Initial Screen**:

UI Element	Description
Order Type	Specifies an identifier that differentiates different kinds of requisitions and POs in the mySAP ERP system
Purchase Order Date	Specifies the date on which the PO is created
Purchasing Group	Specifies a key number assigned to a buyer or group of buyers performing the purchasing activities
Source Determination	Indicates the source of supplying the material
Item Category	Specifies a key that defines the process of controlling the material or service

Continued

UI Element	Description
Acc. Assignment Cat.	Specifies which account assignment data, such as cost center and account number, is necessary for the item
Delivery Date	Indicates that the format of the delivery date will be in the form of a calendar day, week, or month
Plant	Specifies a key that determines which plant of the organization will receive the ordered goods
Storage Location	Specifies a number representing the storage location where the material is stored
Material Group	Specifies a key number assigned to a group of materials having similar attributes
Req. Tracking Number	Specifies a number to track and monitor the procurement of required materials

TABLE 5.5   UI elements of Create Purchase Order: Initial Screen

After creating a PO document, let's now learn how to maintain a PO document.

Maintaining a PO

At times, an organization may need to modify a PO document for numerous reasons. For example, an organization has to modify a PO document if the organization changes the supplier or quantity of the required material. You can change a PO document by using the ME22N transaction code or navigating the following menu path (Figure 5.30):

Menu Path

SAP menu > Logistics > Materials Management > Purchasing > Purchase Order > ME22N – Change. You can also cancel or block a material line item by first selecting it and then clicking the **Delete** (🗑) or **Block** (🔒) icon, respectively. A blocked PO stops the generation of goods receipts corresponding to the line items mentioned in the PO.

Figure 5.32 shows the blocking of a line item in a sample PO, 4500017185:

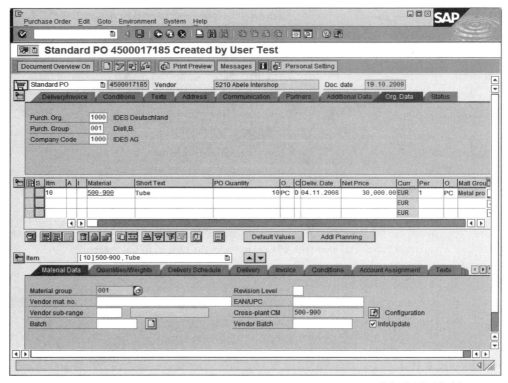

FIGURE 5.32   Displaying the blocking of a line item

Moreover, you can remove the delete indicator or unblock a previously blocked line item by clicking the **Unblock** (🗔) icon.

Note: You can display the details of a PO by using the ME23N transaction code or navigating the following menu path:

Menu Path

SAP menu > Logistics > Materials Management > Purchasing > Purchase Order > ME23N – Display. Let's now learn to assign account assignment categories to a PO.

Assigning Account Assignment Categories to a PO

You can assign one or more account assignment categories to a PO. Each category is associated with an account code, which describes the purpose for creating the PO; for example, the C code is assigned to a PO that is meant to fulfill the requirements of a sales order. To assign an account assignment category to a PO, you need to select its corresponding account code.

You can assign an account code to a PO on the **Create Purchase Order: Initial Screen** by using the ME21 transaction code, as shown in Figure 5.33:

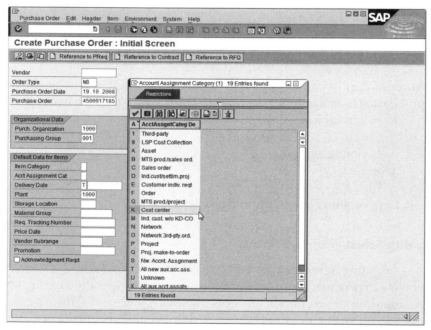

FIGURE 5.33   Assigning an account code to a PO at the Create Purchase Order: Initial Screen

Apart from the already existing account assignment categories, you can create new categories in the mySAP ERP system. To create a new account assignment category, navigate the following menu path:

Menu Path

SAP Customizing Implementation Guide > Materials Management > Purchasing > Account Assignment > Maintain Account Assignment Categories

> **Note:** To open the SAP Customizing Implementation Guide, execute the SPRO transaction code in the command field.

Let's now proceed to explore the outline purchase agreements in the next section.

EXPLORING OUTLINE PURCHASE AGREEMENTS

An outline purchase agreement is a long-term agreement made between a purchasing organization and a vendor. The following are the two types of outline purchase agreement:

- Scheduling agreement
- Contract

Let's explore each of these types in detail.

Working with Scheduling Agreements

A scheduling agreement is created between a purchasing organization and vendor to procure materials on a predefined date specified in the agreement. A scheduling agreement accepts manually entered data or can retrieve data from other documents, such as purchase requisitions, quotations, or contracts. It is mandatory to define an account assignment category, purchasing organization, and purchasing group before creating a scheduling agreement.

You can create a scheduling agreement by using the ME31L transaction code or navigating the following menu path:

Menu Path

SAP menu > Logistics > Materials Management > Purchasing > Outline Agreement > Scheduling Agreement > Create. Double-click the **ME31L – Vendor Known** option, as shown in Figure 5.34:

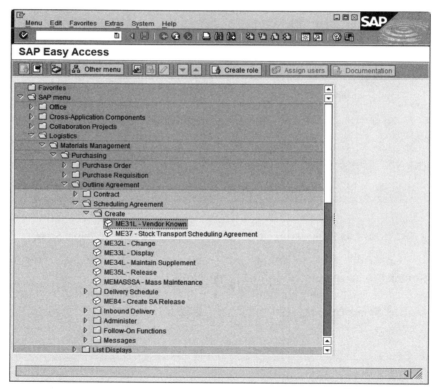

FIGURE 5.34   **Displaying the menu path to create a scheduling agreement**

The **Create Scheduling Agreement: Initial Screen** appears, as shown in Figure 5.35:

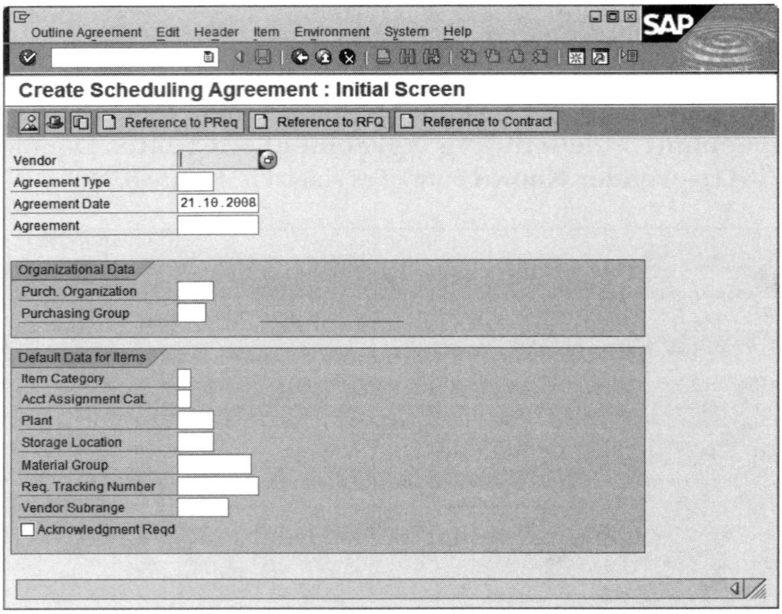

FIGURE 5.35   Displaying the Create Scheduling Agreement: Initial Screen

Enter the relevant details in the **Create Scheduling Agreement: Initial Screen** to create a scheduling agreement.

Table 5.6 lists the UI elements present in **Create Scheduling Agreement: Initial Screen**:

UI Element	Description
Vendor	Represents a unique alphanumeric key to identify a vendor.
Agreement Type	Specifies an outline purchase agreement in the mySAP ERP system.

Continued

UI Element	Description
Agreement Date	Specifies the date of the agreement.
Agreement	Specifies a number of the outline agreement.
Purchasing Organization	Represents a purchasing organization.
Purchasing Group	Specifies a key number assigned to a buyer or group of buyers performing the purchasing activities.
Item Category	Specifies a key that defines the process of controlling the material or service.
Acct. Assignment Cat.	Specifies which account assignment data, such as cost center and account number, is necessary for the item.
Plant	Specifies a key that determines a plant to receive the ordered goods.
Storage Location	Specifies the number representing the storage locations where the material is stored.
Material Group	Specifies a key number assigned to a collection of materials having similar attributes.
Req. Tracking Number	Specifies a number that monitors the procurement of required materials.
Vendor Subrange	Specifies the subdivision of a vendor's product range. For instance, a vendor, Kabir in Mumbai has two subranges: wood and glass. All materials from the wood subrange are ordered in Mumbai. However, if you order materials from the glass subrange, the vendor subrange finds the Chennai ordering address. This is because you have maintained an alternative ordering address of Chennai for the glass subrange.
Acknowledgement Reqd	Determines whether or not the vendor is acknowledged for the purchasing document, such as a PO and outline purchase agreement.

TABLE 5.6   The UI elements of Create Scheduling Agreement: Initial Screen

After creating a scheduling agreement, you may need to perform various activities, such as displaying or modifying the details of a scheduling agreement. Table 5.7 lists the menu paths and transaction codes to perform these activities:

Option	Menu Path	Transaction Code
Change	SAP menu > Logistics > Materials Management > Purchasing > Outline Agreement > Scheduling Agreement > ME32L – Change	ME32L
Display	SAP menu > Logistics > Materials Management > Purchasing > Outline Agreement > Scheduling Agreement > SAP menu > Logistics > Materials Management > Purchasing > Outline Agreement > Scheduling Agreement > ME33L – Display	ME33L
Release	SAP menu > Logistics > Materials Management > Purchasing > Outline Agreement > Scheduling Agreement > SAP menu > Logistics > Materials Management > Purchasing > Outline Agreement > Scheduling Agreement > ME35L – Release	ME35L

TABLE 5.7   Menu paths and transaction codes to perform various operations on a scheduling agreement

Let's now learn to work with contracts in the next section.

Working with Contracts

A contract is an agreement made between a purchasing organization and a vendor to procure the specified quantity of a material over a period of time. There are two types of contracts in the MM module, which are as follows:

- **Quantity contract**—Refers to the agreement made between a purchasing organization and a vendor for a fixed quantity of material or services. For example, a quantity contract between a laptop distributing company and a vendor may state that a vendor has to deliver 25 laptops to an organization in a month.
- **Value contract**—Refers to the agreement made between a purchasing department and a vendor to provide a particular type of material up to a fixed value. For example, a vendor may have

to deliver fast food worth Rs. 50,000 to an organization within the duration of one month. These types of contracts are not based on the quantity but on the value of the material.

Apart from these two types, there is a special type of contract, called a centrally agreed contract, in which a vendor can supply materials or services to several plants of an organization. Such centrally agreed contracts are also called national, group, or corporate contracts.

Let's now learn how to create a contract.

Creating a Contract

You can create a contract by using the ME31K transaction code or navigating the following menu path:

Menu Path

SAP menu > Logistics > Materials Management > Purchasing > Outline Agreement > Contract. Double-click the **ME31K – Create** option, as shown in Figure 5.36:

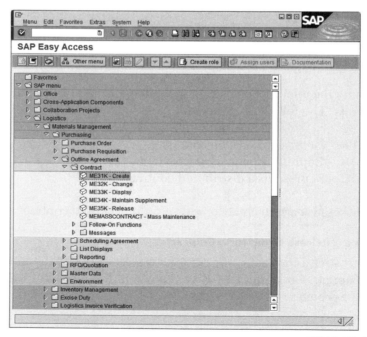

FIGURE 5.36   Displaying the menu path to create a contract

The **Create Contract: Initial Screen** appears, as shown in Figure 5.37:

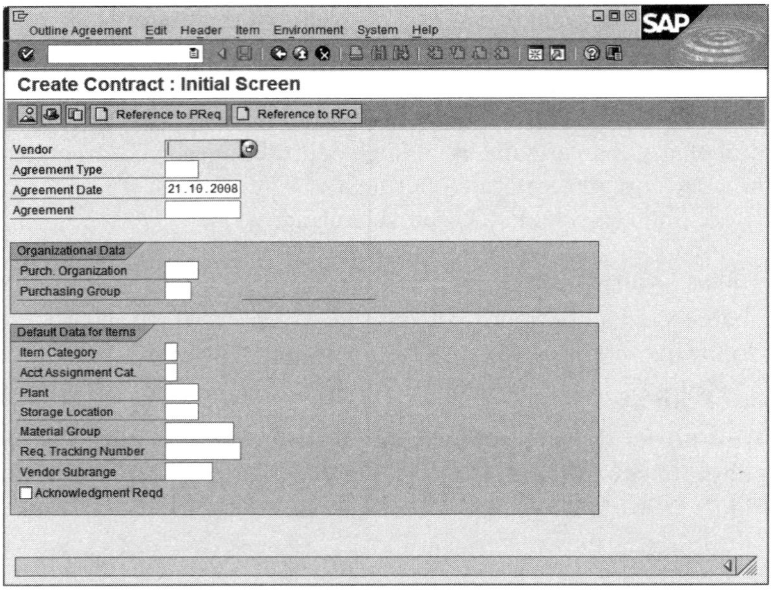

FIGURE 5.37   Displaying the Create Contract: Initial Screen

Enter the relevant details in the **Create Contract: Initial Screen** to create a contract. The following agreement types are used while creating a contract:

- **WK**—Represents a value contract
- **MK**—Represents a quantity contract
- **DC**—Represents a distributed contract

Let's now learn to create a release order against a contract.

Creating a Release Order for a Contract

After creating a contract, a release order is created against the contract to deliver the material. A release order is created from the **Create Purchase Order: Initial Screen**.

Perform the following steps to create a release order with respect to an existing contract:

1. Open the **Create Purchase Order: Initial Screen** by executing the ME21 transaction code in the command field.
2. Click the **Reference to Contract** push button, as shown in Figure 5.38:

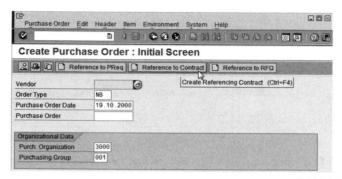

FIGURE 5.38   Displaying the Reference to Contract push button

The **Contract Release Order** dialog box appears (Figure 5.39).

3. Select a contract number in the **Outline Agreement** text field in the **Contract Release Order** dialog box. In our case, we have selected 4600000032 (Figure 5.39).
4. Click the **Continue** (☑) icon, as shown in Figure 5.39:

FIGURE 5.39   Displaying the Contract Release Order dialog box

The **Create Purchase Order: Overview: Contract Items for Release Order** screen appears, as shown in Figure 5.40:

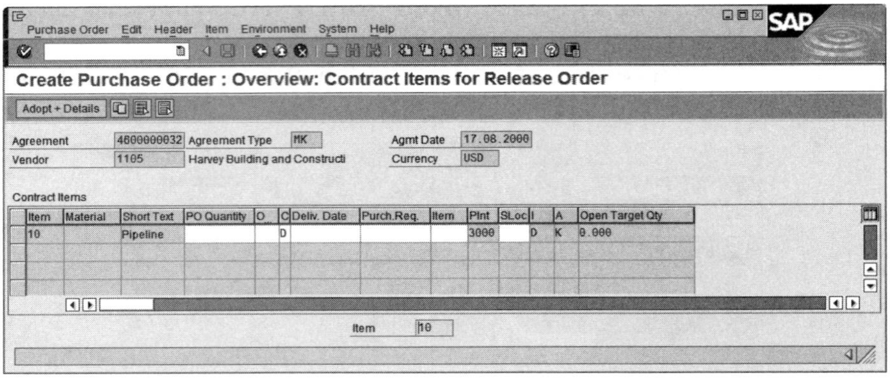

FIGURE 5.40   Displaying the Create Purchase Order: Overview: Contract Items for Release Order screen

In Figure 5.40, you can see the details of a contract release order and specify the quantity of the items against an existing contract.

After creating a contract, you may need to perform various activities, such as displaying or modifying contracts. Table 5.8 lists the menu paths and transaction codes to perform these activities:

Option	Menu Path	Transaction Code
Change	SAP menu > Logistics > Materials Management > Purchasing > Outline Agreement > Contract > ME32K – Change	ME32K
Display	SAP menu > Logistics > Materials Management > Purchasing > Outline Agreement > Contract > ME33K – Display	ME33K

Continued

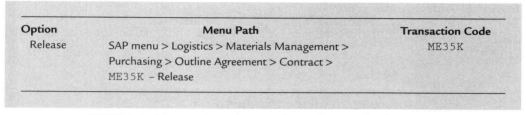

Option	Menu Path	Transaction Code
Release	SAP menu > Logistics > Materials Management > Purchasing > Outline Agreement > Contract > ME35K – Release	ME35K

TABLE 5.8   Menu paths and transaction codes to maintain contracts

After learning to create and work with various outline purchase agreements, let's proceed to learn about vendor confirmations.

CONFIRMING A VENDOR

Vendor confirmations are updated information provided by a vendor to a customer about the delivery of ordered goods. They are defined in the mySAP ERP system when the vendors communicate with the customers regarding a PO or inbound delivery. Vendors can communicate with customers through fax, emails, or Electronic Data Interchange (EDI). These communications can be initiated for the following reasons:

- Order acknowledgement
- Advance ship notification
- Transport confirmation

A vendor confirmation is defined in the mySAP ERP system either manually or automatically (when the confirmation is sent from the vendor using EDI). When a confirmation is entered manually, it is considered an external confirmation; whereas, it is considered an internal confirmation if it is entered automatically.

Let's first learn to configure an external vendor confirmation.

External Vendor Confirmation

You can configure an external vendor confirmation by navigating the following menu path:

Menu Path

SAP Customizing Implementation Guide > Materials Management > Purchasing > Confirmations

Figure 5.41 shows the preceding menu path:

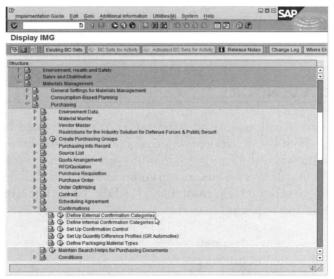

FIGURE 5.41   Defining an external vendor confirmation

Click the **IMG Activity Icon** (⊕) icon beside the **Define External Confirmation Categories** activity (Figure 5.41).

The **Change View "Confirmation Categories": Overview** screen appears, as shown in Figure 5.42:

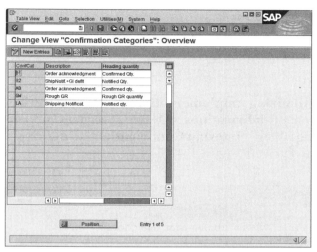

FIGURE 5.42   Displaying the Change View "Confirmation Categories": Overview screen

You can click the **New Entries** ([New Entries]) button to enter a new external confirmation category (Figure 5.42).

Table 5.9 lists the UI elements of the **Change View "Confirmation Categories": Overview** screen.

UI Element	Description
ContCat	Specifies a code for the new category of vendor confirmation
Description	Specifies the description of the category of vendor confirmation
Heading quantity	Represents a heading for the quantity of the vendor confirmation category

TABLE 5.9   UI elements of the Change View "Confirmation Categories": Overview Screen

Now, let's configure an internal vendor confirmation.

Internal Vendor Confirmation

You can configure an internal vendor confirmation by navigating the following menu path:

Menu Path

SAP Customizing Implementation Guide > Materials Management > Purchasing > Confirmations > Define Internal Confirmation Categories. The **Change View "Internal Confirmation Categories": Overview** screen appears, as shown in Figure 5.43:

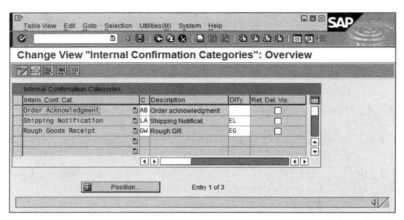

FIGURE 5.43   Displaying the Change View "Internal Confirmation Categories": Overview screen

In the **Change View "Internal Confirmation Categories": Overview** screen, you see various internal confirmation categories, such as **Order Acknowledgement** and **Shipping Notification**. You need to enter relevant details beside one or more of these categories to configure the process of internal vendor confirmation.

Let's learn how to manage external services in the next section.

MANAGING EXTERNAL SERVICES IN THE MM MODULE

External Service Management (ESM) refers to the process of managing the purchasing process of services in the MM module. In the MM module, the data for ESM is stored in the master records, which are located in the central database. These master records are used and processed by multiple applications. In the mySAP ERP system, the information related to the procurement of a service is stored in service master record and standard service catalog.

In this section, you will learn to:

- Explore the service master record
- Explore the standard service catalog
- Set the external services conditions
- Procure services using a PO
- Insert services in the mySAP ERP system

Exploring the Service Master Record

A service master record stores the master data of the purchasing process of services. You can create a service master record in the mySAP ERP system by using the AC03 transaction code or navigating the following menu path:

Menu Path

SAP menu > Logistics > Materials Management > Service Master > Service > AC03 – Service Master. Figure 5.44 shows the preceding menu path:

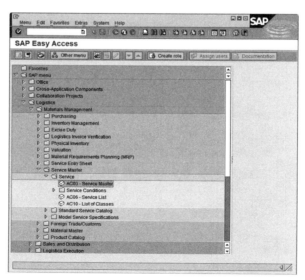

FIGURE 5.44   **Displaying the menu path to create a service master record**

The preceding menu path opens the details of an existing service in the display mode. In our case, the details of the SVCS - 002 service are displayed (Figure 5.45).

Click the **Create** (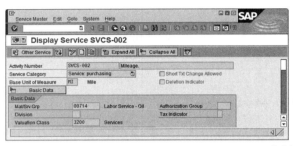) icon to create a new service master record, as shown in Figure 5.45:

FIGURE 5.45   Displaying a service in the display mode

The **Create Service Master Record** screen appears, as shown in Figure 5.46:

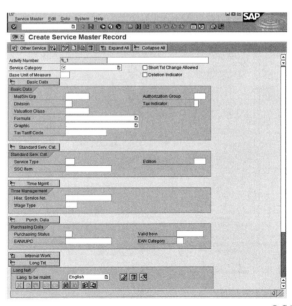

FIGURE 5.46   Displaying the Create Service Master Record screen

Some important fields that need to be filled while creating a service master record through the **Create Service Master Record** screen are as follows:

- **Activity Number**—Specifies a unique number of a service master record that is required to enter, change, or display the information relating to a service. You can define a number range for the activity number by using the ACNR transaction code or navigating the following menu path:

Menu Path

SAP Customizing Implementation Guide > Materials Management > External Service Management > Service Master > Define Number Ranges

- **Service Category**—Specifies a code that differentiates services based on their usage. You can define your own service categories in the mySAP ERP system by navigating the following menu path:

Menu Path

SAP Customizing Implementation Guide > Materials Management > External Service Management > Service Master > Define Service Category

- **Material/Service Group**—Represents a collection of multiple services.
- **Tax Indicator**—Indicates a tax code for purchasing a particular service. You need to enter a tax code for a taxable service.
- **Valuation Class**—Represents the assignment of a service to a group of general ledger (G/L) accounts.
- **Formula**—Represents a formula to calculate the effort required to perform a task. For instance, you can enter a service detail by defining a formula to calculate the number of hours required to rectify a network-related problem. A formula can be defined by up to a maximum of five variables. It can use mathematical functions, for instance sine and cos. You can also define variables of a formula by using system-defined variables, such as ROMS1 (Size 1) and ROMS2 (Size 2). In addition, you can use constants,

Pi (3.1415) and the +, −, *, and / operators. You can define a formula in the mySAP ERP system by navigating the following menu path:

Menu Path

SAP Customizing Implementation Guide > Materials Management > External Service Management > Formula for Quantity Determination > Define Formulas

■   Navigate the following menu path to define variables used in a formula:

Menu Path

SAP Customizing Implementation Guide > Materials Management > External Service Management > Formula for Quantity Determination > Specify Names of Formula Variables

■   **Graphic**—Represents a picture that can be used to provide information about a service.

Exploring the Standard Service Catalog

The Standard Service Catalog (SSC) is a document used to store information about a service that does not have a service master record. Similar to master records, SSCs are stored centrally in the MM module. In addition, SSCs can be divided into various service types, such as masonry, maintenance, and transport services. An SSC document is created by using the ML01 transaction code or navigating the following menu path:

Menu Path

SAP menu > Logistics > Materials Management > Service Master > Standard Service Catalog.

Double click the **ML01 – Create** option, as shown in Figure 5.47:

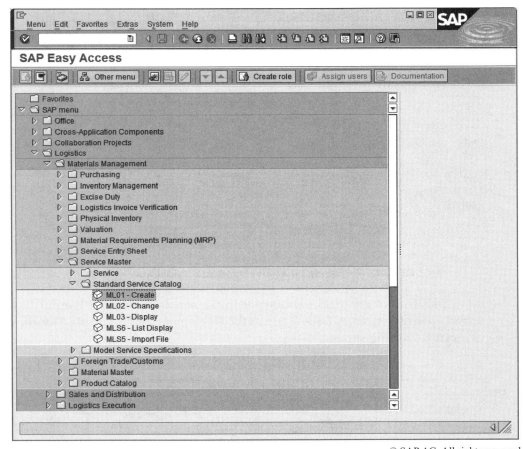

FIGURE 5.47   **Displaying menu path to create an SSC document**

The **Create Standard Service Catalog** screen appears, as shown in Figure 5.48:

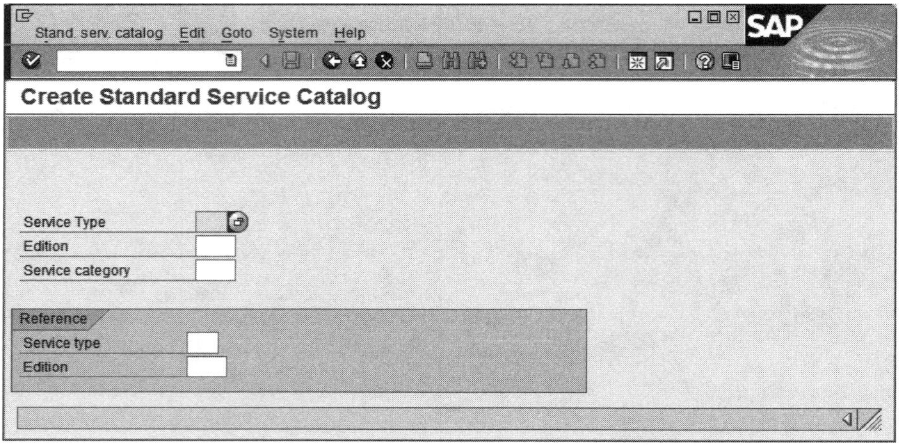

FIGURE 5.48   Displaying the Create Standard Service Catalog screen

You need to enter relevant details in the screen shown in Figure 5.48 to create a service catalog. Table 5.10 lists the UI elements of the **Create Standard Service Catalog** screen:

UI Element	Description
Service Type	Specifies a unique key of a service type
Edition	Specifies the edition of a service type
Service category	Specifies a unique key to differentiate services on the basis of their usage
References	Specifies the references that are used as a key and an edition for the service type

TABLE 5.10   UI elements of the Create Standard Service Catalog screen

Let's now learn to set the external services conditions.

Setting the External Services Conditions

You can also specify the conditions or terms of payment, such as discounts, surcharges, and taxes, for external services. You can enter a condition or term for a service in the mySAP ERP system by using either the `ML45` transaction code or navigating the following menu path:

Menu Path

SAP menu > Logistics > Materials Management > Service Master > Service > Service Conditions > For Service > ML45 – Add

Procuring Services by Using a PO

In SAP, services can be procured in the same way as materials; i.e., by using the **Create Purchase Order: Initial Screen** (the `ME21` transaction code). To create a PO document for a service, use the item category `D`. You can also create a blanket PO to purchase a low-value service at the minimum cost. A blanket PO is created using the `ME21` or `ME21N` transaction code. While creating a blanket PO, you must set the document type as `FO` and the item category as `B` for the limited order.

Inserting Services in the mySAP ERP System

A service entry sheet stores all the records of the transaction of services. This sheet is used to enter information about the partial or full completion of a service in the mySAP ERP system. You can enter data relating to a service in the service entry sheet by accessing the `ML81N` transaction code or navigating the following menu path:

Menu Path

SAP menu > Logistics > Materials Management > Service Entry Sheet > ML81N – Maintain. A service entry sheet is based on the PO document of the service. After selecting a valid PO document for the service, you can view the service number assigned to the service in the PO document. Note that you can save a service entry sheet in the mySAP ERP system only after filling in the details of a service completely.

Now, let's summarize the main topics discussed in this chapter.

SUMMARY

In this chapter, you learned about the purchasing process of materials and services in the MM module. First, the purchasing process cycle was discussed along with its various stages, such as determination of material requirements, vendor selection, and invoice verification. Next, you explored the purchase requisition phase, in which a purchase requisition document is created either directly or indirectly. After that, you learned about the request for quotation phase, in which an RFQ document is created to receive quotations from vendors. Next, the quotation phase was described, in which quotations of various vendors are entered in the mySAP ERP system and compared. The chapter further explored various types of long-term outline purchase agreements between the purchasing organization and vendor. Finally, you learned about the procurement process of external services in the MM module.

In the next chapter, you will learn how to implement material requirements planning in the mySAP ERP system.

Chapter 6

IMPLEMENTING MATERIAL REQUIREMENTS PLANNING

Material requirements planning (MRP) is a process that is used to check the availability of materials in a storage location. The reports generated by this process help a company decide whether the materials required for production are available in the organization or need to be procured from outside. This process helps in identifying the quantity and type of materials required for future production by accessing the bill of material, master production schedules, and inventories. The MRP process ensures the availability of materials for production and delivery to customers; maintains the minimum possible level of inventory; and plans delivery schedules, as well as manufacturing and purchasing activities.

In the SAP® system, MRP is a planning tool used to create either a planned order or purchase requisition for the material to be produced or procured by an organization, respectively. The SAP system uses the master data to create a planned order or purchase requisition. When the material is available within the organization, a planned order is created, which is then converted into a production order by the master scheduler of the SAP system. On the other hand, if the material needs to be procured from outside vendors, a purchase requisition is created.

In this chapter, you will learn how to implement the MRP process in the mySAP™ ERP system on the plant as well as storage location levels. The planning based upon the results of the past consumption trends is known as consumption-based planning (CBP). The chapter also discusses various types of CBP, such as reorder point, forecast-based, and time-phased planning, and how to implement them in the mySAP ERP system.

IMPLEMENTING CONSUMPTION-BASED PLANNING

As already discussed, the process of determining the future material requirements based on the past consumption of a material is known as CBP. In other words, CBP is a material requirements planning method, which identifies future requirements on the basis of the consumption values provided in the material master record. Apart from observing the past consumption trends, an organization can also use a forecast and other statistical procedures to determine future material requirements.

You need to perform the following tasks to implement CBP in the SAP system:

- Define Master Data for CBP
- Implement the Planning Process
- Evaluate the Planning Results

Let's now learn to perform each of these tasks.

Defining Master Data for CBP

In the SAP system, the material master record holds the consumption values for a material, which are calculated on the basis of the unplanned and total consumption. You can view as well as update the consumption values in the material master record, which can be created by performing the following steps:

1. Navigate the following menu path (Figure 6.1):

Menu Path

SAP menu > Logistics > Materials Management > Material Master > Material > Change > MM02 – Immediately

2. Double-click the **MM02 – Immediately** activity, as shown in Figure 6.1:

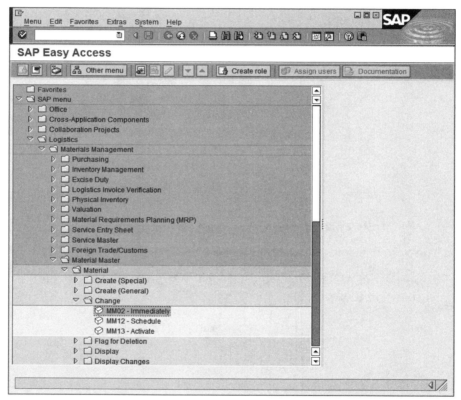

FIGURE 6.1   Displaying the menu path to define material master records for CBP

The **Change Material (Initial Screen)** appears (Figure 6.2).

3. Enter the material number in the **Material** text box. In our case, we have entered 101–200 as the material number (Figure 6.2).

4. Click the **Organizational levels** button, as shown in Figure 6.2:

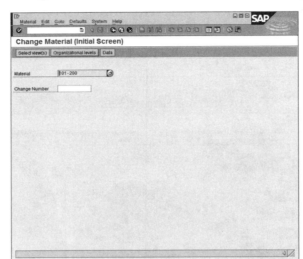

FIGURE 6.2   **Displaying the Change Material (Initial Screen)**

The **Select View(s)** dialog box appears (Figure 6.3).

5. Select the **MRP1** view and click the **Organizational levels** button, as shown in Figure 6.3:

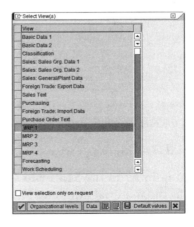

FIGURE 6.3   **Displaying the Select View(s) dialog box**

The **Organizational Levels** dialog box appears (Figure 6.4).

6. Enter the plant details in the **Plant** text box. In our case, we have entered `1000` as the plant code (Figure 6.4).

7. Enter the storage location details in the **Stor. Location** text box and click the **Continue** (☑) icon. In our case, we have entered `0001` as the storage location, as shown in Figure 6.4:

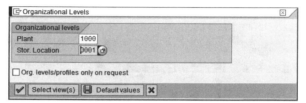

FIGURE 6.4   **Displaying the Organization Levels dialog box**

The details of the `101-200` material is displayed (Figure 6.5).

8. Click the **Additional data** push button in the **Change Material 101–200 (Semi-finished product)** screen, as shown in Figure 6.5:

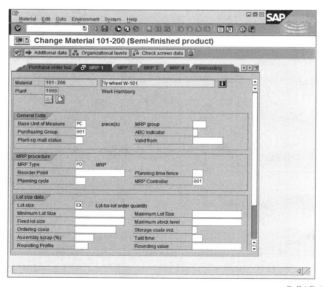

FIGURE 6.5   **Displaying the Change Material 101–200 (Semi-finished product) screen**

The additional details of the product are displayed under various tabs, such as **Inspection text, Basic data text**, and **Consumption** (Figure 6.6).

9. Click the **Consumption** tab. The consumption values are displayed, as shown in Figure 6.6:

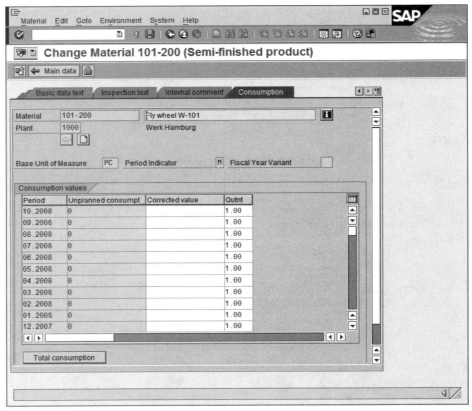

FIGURE 6.6   Displaying the consumption values of the product

You can enter the actual consumption values for a specified period under the **Corrected value** header and click the **Save** (🖫) icon to save the entered details. Figure 6.6 shows the relevant consumption time periods under the **Period** header.

You can define a consumption period for a material by performing the following steps:

1. Navigate the following menu path (Figure 6.7):

Menu Path

SAP menu > Logistics > Materials Management > Material Requirements Planning (MRP) > MRP > Master Data > Planning Calendar > MD25 – Create Periods

2. Double-click the **MD25 – Create Periods** activity, as shown in Figure 6.7:

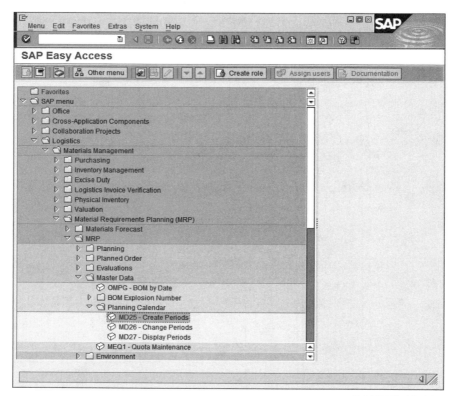

FIGURE 6.7   Displaying the menu path to define a consumption period

The **Create Planning Calendar** screen appears (Figure 6.8).

3. Enter the plant code in the **Plant** text box. In our case, we have entered `0001` as the plant code (Figure 6.8).

4. Enter a unique code for the planning calendar that you need to create and click the **Enter** (✅) icon. In our case, we have entered `002` in the **Planning Calendar** text box, as shown in Figure 6.8:

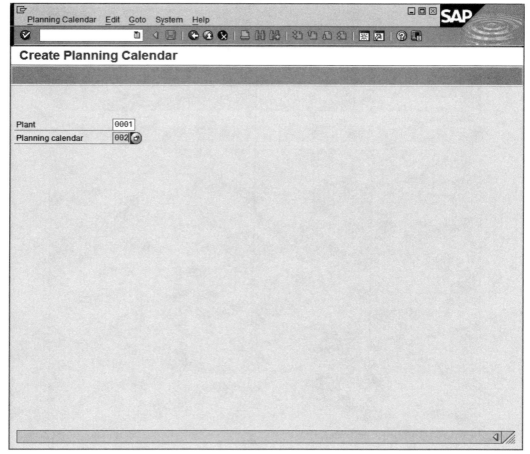

FIGURE 6.8   **Displaying the Create Planning Calendar screen**

The **Create Planning Calendar** screen displays the details to be entered for the new planning calendar (Figure 6.9).

5. Enter the description of the planning calendar. In our case, we have entered `New Planning Calendar` in the **Planning Calendar** text box (Figure 6.9).
6. Select the **Following working day** radio button, as shown in Figure 6.9:

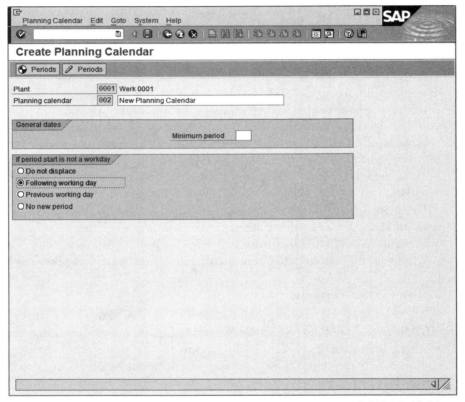

FIGURE 6.9   Displaying the details of a planning calendar

While creating a planning calendar, you need to create certain variables to perform various tasks, such as specifying a weekday to start a period. After creating the required variables, click the **Save** (🖫) icon to save the details of the new planning calendar.

You can display the new planning calendar details by navigating the following menu path:

Menu Path

SAP menu > Logistics > Materials Management > Materials Requirement Planning (MRP) > MRP > Master Data > Planning Calendar > MD27 – Display Periods. Let's now learn how to implement the planning process in the mySAP ERP system.

Implementing the Planning Process in the mySAP ERP System

The planning process in SAP ensures the availability of materials required for production purposes by an organization. To implement the planning process, you first need to calculate the material requirements at either the plant or the storage location level. Consider a scenario where there are two storage locations in an organization, and five plants are allocated to each of them. In such an organizational structure, the material requirements can be calculated for either ten plants or two storage locations. While calculating the material requirements at the plant level, the net requirements are evaluated for each plant and then combined together. However, at the storage location level, the net requirements are calculated individually for each storage location.

We explore how to implement the planning process at these two levels next.

Planning at the Plant Level

While planning for the required materials at the plant level, the mySAP ERP system adds the stocks from all individual plants to determine the total stock at the plant level. Depending upon the available stock, the material requirements are determined and the procurement elements are created for these requirements.

To plan the required materials at the plant level, you first need to set the planning files in the mySAP ERP system by navigating the following menu path:

Menu Path

SAP Customizing Implementation Guide > Materials Management > Consumption-Based Planning > Planning > Activate Material Requirements Planning. Now, click the **Activity** (⊕) icon. The **Activation** screen appears, as shown in Figure 6.10:

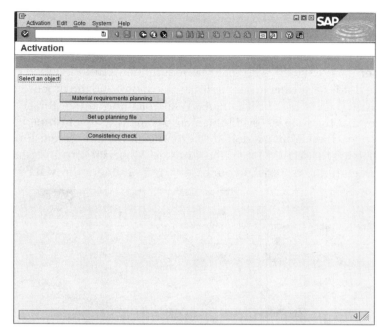

FIGURE 6.10   **Displaying the Activation screen**

You can set the planning file by clicking the **Set up planning file** button. After setting the planning file, the net requirements of each material are calculated by the mySAP ERP system. If the net requirements are not fulfilled by the purchasing and production departments, a procurement proposal is created. While calculating the net requirements, the values are rounded off to achieve the exact net requirements. After calculating the net requirements, the scheduling process begins, which helps to determine the start and finish dates of the procurement proposals. In other words, the mySAP ERP system defines the planned orders, purchase requisitions, and schedule lines that are used to create the procurement proposals. While creating the procurement proposals, you need to assign a supplier from whom the material needs to be procured. Finally, the mySAP ERP system calculates the actual days to supply the material to a vendor.

Let's now learn how to implement the planning process at the storage location level.

Planning at the Storage Location Level

While planning at the storage location level, the mySAP ERP system considers the stocks at either the storage location or the subcontractor level at which the storage locations are assigned. The material requirements are identified on the basis of the total stock available in all the storage locations, and the procurement elements are created for these requirements. While planning at the storage location level, ensure that the reorder level for a material and the replenishment quantities are clearly specified. You can define the reorder level and replenishment quantities by selecting the **MRP4** tab in the **Change Material** screen. Figure 6.11 shows the details of the material, in our case 101-200, under the **MRP4** tab:

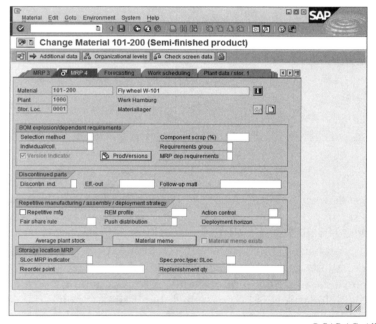

FIGURE 6.11   Displaying the MRP4 view of a material

You need to provide the details for the storage location MRP fields in the material master record to implement planning at the storage location level. Apart from planning at the individual storage location level, you can also exclude a storage location from the planning process. In other words, you can exclude the stock available in a storage location from the total available stock by excluding that storage location. The appropriate MRP indicator needs to be selected to specify that a storage location is excluded. You can select the proper storage location MRP indicator by clicking the icon of the **SLoc MRP Indicator** text box (Figure 6.11). Figure 6.12 shows various MRP indicators:

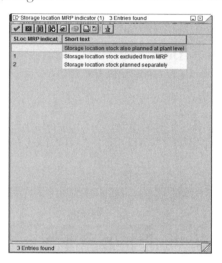

FIGURE 6.12   **Displaying various possible storage location MRP indicators**

The MRP indicator options signify a specific type of planning for a storage location that the mySAP ERP system would follow in the MRP process.

After understanding the planning process at the storage location level, let's learn how to evaluate planning results.

Evaluating Planning Results

An organization can verify whether or not the desired results are achieved by evaluating and analyzing planning results. In the mySAP ERP system, the following two methods are used to evaluate planning results:

- The MRP list
- The stock/requirements list

Let's discuss each of them in detail.

The MRP List

In the mySAP ERP system, the MRP list serves as the initial working document for the MRP controller. The MRP list is a static list that reflects changes in planning results only when the next planning process is implemented. You can display the MRP list of either a single item or all items collectively. Perform the following steps to evaluate planning results on the basis of the MRP list:

1. Double-click the **MD05 – MRP List – Material** activity to display the MRP list of a material after navigating the following menu path (Figure 6.13):

Menu Path

SAP menu > Logistics > Materials Management > Material Requirements Planning (MRP) > MRP > MD05 – MRP List – Material

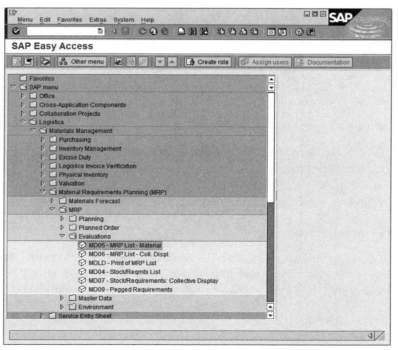

FIGURE 6.13   Displaying the menu path to show the MRP list of a material

The **MRP List: Initial Screen** appears (Figure 6.14).

Note: You can also use the MD05 transaction code to display the MRP list.

2. Enter a material code in the **Material** field. In our case, we have entered 101-200 as the material code (Figure 6.14).
3. Enter a MRP area code in the **MRP Area** field. In our case, we have entered 3000 as the MRP area code (Figure 6.14).
4. Enter a plant code in the **Plant** field. In our case, we have entered 3000 as the plant code (Figure 6.14).
5. Click the **Enter** (☑) icon, as shown in Figure 6.14:

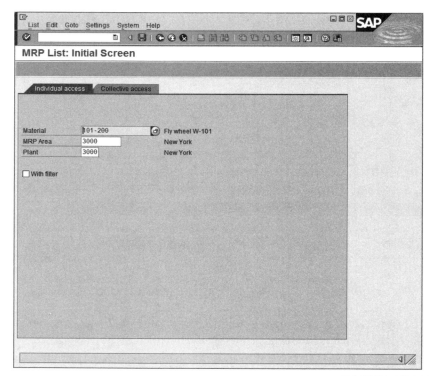

FIGURE 6.14　Displaying the MRP List: Initial Screen

The MRP list of the 101-200 material is displayed, as shown in Figure 6.15:

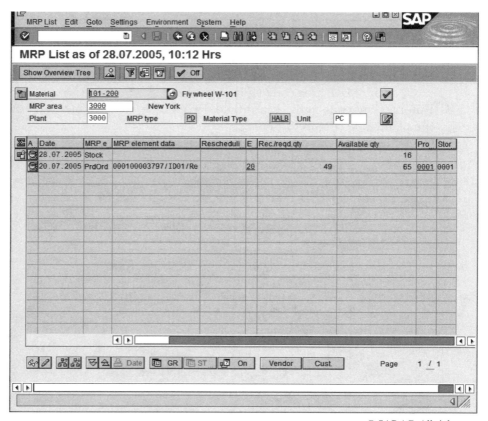

FIGURE 6.15 Displaying the MRP List of the 101–200 Material

Apart from displaying the MRP list of a single material, you can also display the MRP list for all materials collectively. Perform the following steps to evaluate planning results collectively:

1. Click the **Collective access** tab on the **MRP List: Initial Screen** (Figure 6.16). You can display the MRP list collectively on the basis of the MRP controller, product group, or vendor of a material.

2. Enter 3000 as the plant code (Figure 6.16).
3. Enter 002 as the MRP controller code (Figure 6.16).
4. Click the **Enter** (☑) icon, as shown in Figure 6.16:

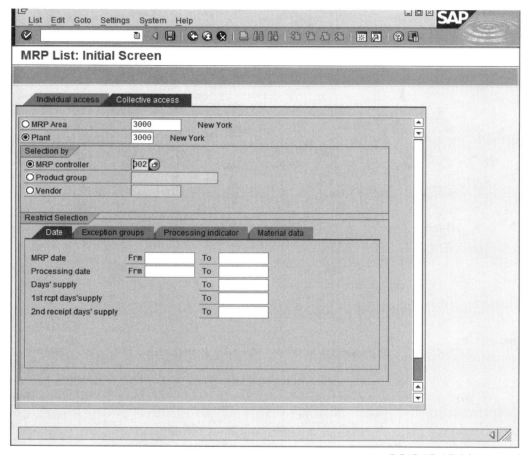

FIGURE 6.16   Displaying the Collective access tab of the MRP List: Initial Screen

The **MRP List: Material List** screen appears, collectively displaying the planning results for the 002 MRP controller, as shown in Figure 6.17:

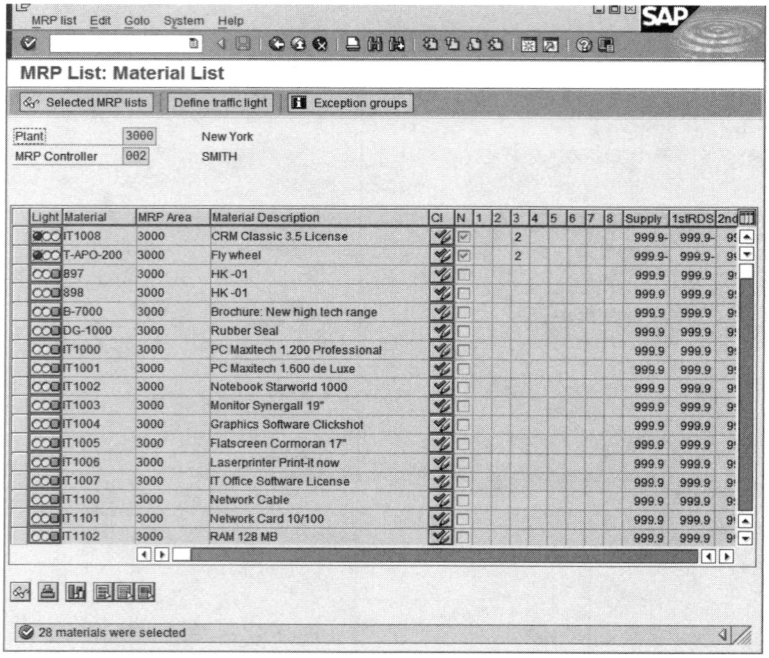

FIGURE 6.17   **Displaying the MRP list collectively on the basis of MRP controller**

Figure 6.17 shows all materials related to the 002 MRP controller. You can evaluate planning results for all materials by double-clicking the supply or stock details of the 101-200 material.

Let's now discuss the stock/requirement list method.

The Stock/Requirements List

The stock/requirements list depicts the current material requirements and available stock. As compared to the MRP list, the stock/requirements list is a dynamic list that is updated each time it is accessed. Perform the following steps to display the stock/requirements list:

1. Navigate the following menu path to display the stock/requirements list of a material (Figure 6.13):

Menu Path

SAP menu > Logistics > Materials Management > Material Requirements Planning (MRP) > MRP > MD04 – Stock/Reqmts

Note: Instead of navigating the preceding menu path, you can also use the MD04 transaction code to display the stock/requirements list.

2. Double-click the **MD04 – Stock/Reqmts** activity (Figure 6.13). The **Stock/Requirements List: Initial Screen** appears (Figure 6.18).
3. Enter IT1008 as the material number in the **Material** field (Figure 6.18).
4. Enter 3000 as the MRP area code in the **MRP Area** text box (Figure 6.18).
5. Enter 3000 as the plant code in the **Plant** text box (Figure 6.18).
6. Click the **Enter** () icon, as shown in Figure 6.18:

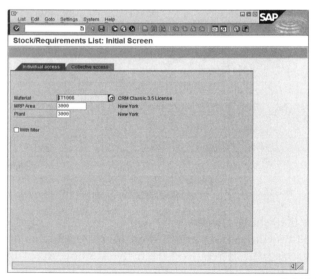

FIGURE 6.18   **Displaying the Stock/Requirements List: Initial Screen**

The stock/requirements list is displayed, as shown in Figure 6.19:

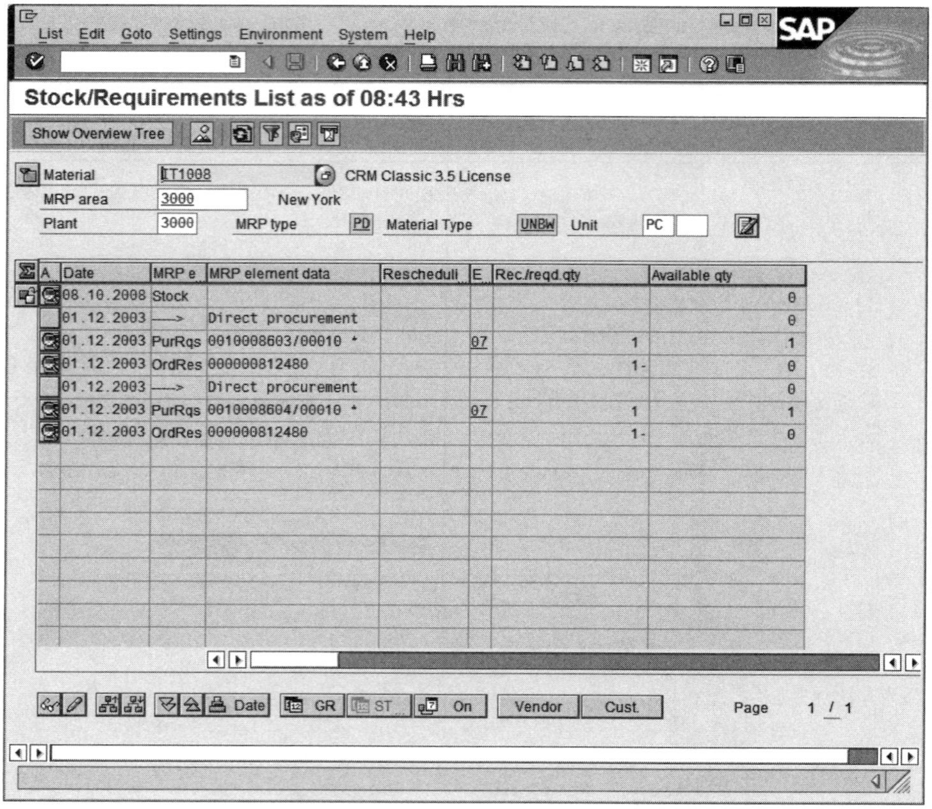

FIGURE 6.19   Displaying the stock/requirements list

Figure 6.19 shows the stock/requirements list of a single material, IT1008. This list allows you to keep a record of the materials that are already available in the stock as well as received from the vendor. Apart from displaying the stock/requirements list of a single material, you can also display the stock/requirements list of all materials of a specific MRP controller collectively. Perform the following steps to display the stock/requirements list of all materials collectively based on a specific MRP controller:

1. Click the **Collective access** tab (Figure 6.18) to display the stock/requirements list of various materials collectively.
2. Enter 002 as the MRP Controller for which the stock/requirements list will be displayed (Figure 6.20).
3. Click the **Enter** (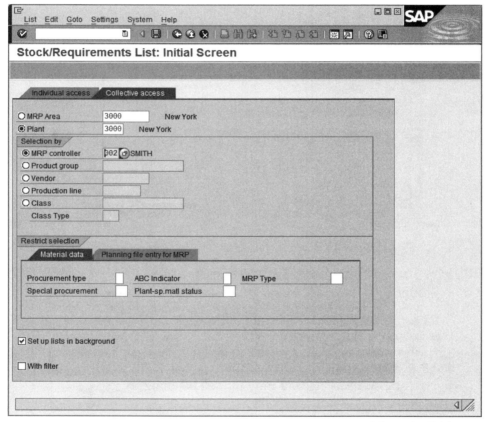) icon, as shown in Figure 6.20:

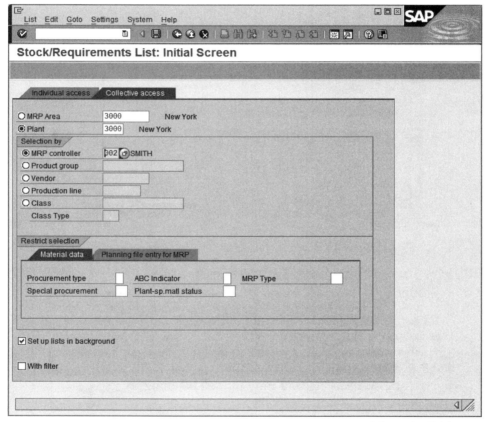

FIGURE 6.20 Displaying the Collective access tab of the Stock/Requirements List: Initial Screen

The **Stock/Requirements List: Material List** screen appears, as shown in Figure 6.21:

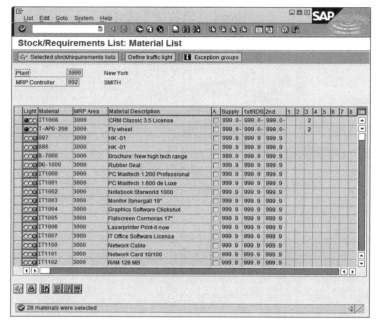

FIGURE 6.21   Displaying the Stock/Requirements List: Material List screen

Figure 6.21 shows the stock/requirements list of the materials categorized on the basis of the `002` MRP controller.

After understanding the methods of evaluating planning results in the mySAP ERP system, let's discuss the types of CBP: reorder point planning, forecast-based planning, and time-phased planning.

IMPLEMENTING REORDER POINT PLANNING

A reorder point is the stock level at which an organization should place new orders with the suppliers to bring the inventory level up. The reorder point includes the average material requirements expected during the replenishment lead time and the safety stock. In other words, a reorder point is equal to the normal consumption during replenishment lead time and the safety stock. With reorder point planning, the mySAP ERP system verifies if the available stock is below the reorder point specified for a material. In other words, the mySAP ERP system verifies whether or not the sum of the stock available in a plant and the firmed receipts is below the reorder point. The procurement is triggered in the mySAP ERP system when the available stock is less than the reorder point value.

When you define the master data of a material in the mySAP ERP system, you need to specify the MRP type in the **MRP1** tab. You can specify the type of reorder planning for a material in the **MRP Type** field available under the **MRP1** tab. For manual reorder point planning, you need to specify the VB SAP standard; whereas, for automatic reorder point planning, the VM standard is used. Apart from the standards, you also need to specify the reorder point value for both manual and automatic reorder point planning of the material.

Let's discuss manual and automatic reorder point planning next.

Manual Reorder Point Planning

With manual reorder point planning, you need to manually enter the reorder point and safety stock values in the material master record of a material. In our case, we specify VB as the MRP type of the 101-200 material and 12 as its reorder point value, as shown in Figure 6.22:

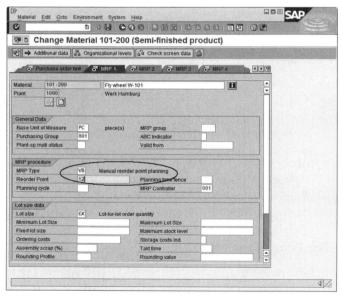

FIGURE 6.22 **Displaying the MRP type VB for manual reorder point planning**

Apart from specifying the MRP type and the reorder point value, as shown in Figure 6.22, you need to provide the safety stock value, which is used to calculate the net requirements of a material. You can specify the safety stock value by clicking the **MRP2** tab, as shown in Figure 6.23:

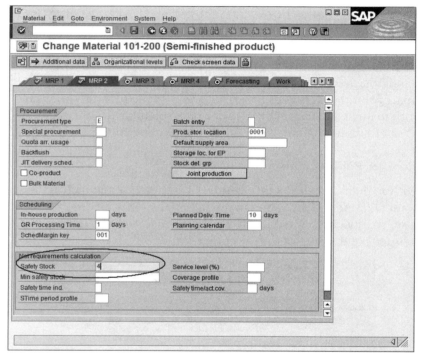

FIGURE 6.23   **Displaying the safety stock value**

After entering the MRP type as manual reorder point planning and defining the reorder point as well as safety stock values, you need to click the **Save** (🖫) icon to save the entered details.

Let's now discuss how to specify automatic reorder point planning.

Automatic Reorder Point Planning

With automatic reorder planning, the mySAP ERP system calculates the reorder and safety stock level on the basis of past consumption values of a material. This helps the mySAP ERP system forecast the future requirements of the material. You can specify automatic reorder point planning for a material by specifying VM as the MRP type while creating the material master record. In our case, we change the MRP type of the 101-200 material to VM and provide the reorder point value, as shown in Figure 6.24:

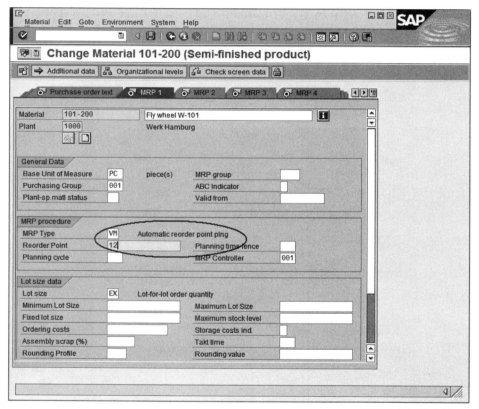

FIGURE 6.24   **Displaying the MRP type VM for automatic reorder point planning**

After changing the MRP type, click the **Save** (🖫) icon to save the changed values of the 101-200 material.

Let's now learn how to implement forecast-based planning for a material.

IMPLEMENTING FORECAST-BASED PLANNING

Similar to reorder point planning, forecast-based planning also uses past consumption values and forecast values to plan for material procurement. During forecast-based planning, future requirements are determined on the basis of the forecasting program selected for a material. In the mySAP ERP system, the VV SAP standard is used to depict that forecast-based planning has been implemented for a material. In our case, we specify the MRP type of the 101-200 material as forecast-based planning, as shown in Figure 6.25:

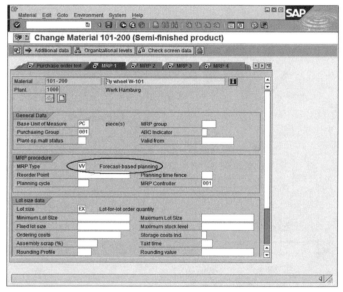

FIGURE 6.25 Displaying the MRP type VV for forecast-based planning

The following are the three phases of the forecast-based planning procedure:

1. In the first phase, the mySAP ERP system automatically generates a forecast value and then ensures that the forecast value covers the available stocks, planned purchases, and planned production. However, if the forecast value is greater than the sum of the available stock, planned purchases, and planned production, the mySAP ERP system generates a procurement proposal that can be either a purchase requisition or a planned order.

2. In the second phase, the purchase requisitions or planned orders are verified against the lot size value defined in the material master record.
3. In the final phase, the mySAP ERP system defines a date for each procurement proposal on which the proposal should be converted into a production process or purchase order.

Apart from forecast-based planning, you also need to learn how time-phased planning is implemented in an organization.

IMPLEMENTING TIME-PHASED PLANNING

In cases where a vendor supplies the material on a specific date or day, time-phased planning is used to plan material requirements. In such situations, you should ensure that the planning date set in the mySAP ERP system is the date on which the vendor supplies the material. In our case, we specify R1 as the MRP type and 001 as the planning cycle for the 101-200 material to implement time-phased planning, as shown in Figure 6.26:

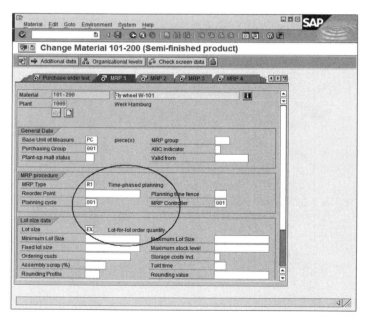

FIGURE 6.26   Displaying the MRP type R1 for time-phased planning

Figure 6.26 shows that the EX SAP standard lot size has been specified in the **Lot size** text box. After specifying the details required for time-phased planning, click the **Save** (▣) icon to save the entered details.

SUMMARY

In this chapter, you learned various methods to implement the CBP process in the mySAP ERP system. You also learned how to implement planning at the plant as well as storage location level. Next, you learned to evaluate planning results based on the MRP and stock/requirements lists. The chapter also discussed various types of CBP procedures implemented in the mySAP ERP system, such as reorder point planning, forecast-based planning, and time-phased planning.

In the next chapter, you will learn how to implement the inventory management process in the MM module.

IMPLEMENTING THE INVENTORY MANAGEMENT PROCESS IN THE MM MODULE

7

Inventory management refers to the process of managing the inventory items of an organization, such as raw materials, finished as well as semi-finished goods, and scrap or obsolete items. The implementation of inventory management in an organization not only ensures an uninterrupted supply of materials and services to a plant but also prevents any interruptions or delays in the production or manufacturing process. Maintaining a correct and up-to-date inventory helps to reduce inventory costs and prevent the blockage of working capital. In addition, inventory management is essential for correct planning and budgeting, as it provides a correct assessment of funds that are allocated to purchase inventory items.

In the mySAP™ ERP system, the inventory management process is implemented on the basis of the structure of an organization. For example, in the case of a client or enterprise organizational unit, the inventory is managed at the plant level. Therefore, in the mySAP ERP system, different types of stock movements are implemented for different organizational units.

In this chapter, you will learn about the implementation of the inventory management process in the mySAP ERP system. Next, you will explore the different stock types that exist in the mySAP ERP system. Thereafter, different types of goods movements that affect inventory are discussed, including goods received, goods issued, goods returned, stock transfer, and reservation. Toward the end, you will learn about physical inventory in detail and the traditional approach to inventory management.

Let's begin by exploring the different stock types in the mySAP ERP system.

EXPLORING THE TYPES OF STOCK

In inventory management, stock is classified into different types depending on its usage. For example, the stock frequently used for production is called the standard stock. Similarly, the goods receipt items are referred to as the goods receipt block stock. In addition, the stock that is not regularly used or the offshore stock that is handled differently is classified as the special stock. Each stock type is handled differently from others.

This section discusses the following stock types that are created in the mySAP ERP system as a part of the inventory management process:

- The standard stock
- The goods receipt block stock
- The special stock

Let's first discuss the standard stock.

The Standard Stock

The standard stock is commonly used in an organization for the production or manufacturing process. It is stored in a common storage area having optimum temperature, light, and humidity conditions. The documentation and accounting entries are similar for all items present in the standard stock, which is divided in the following types:

- **Unrestricted-use stock**—Refers to the type of standard stock that is used for regular production processes. The unrestricted-use stock includes the materials issued to customers after the completion of the purchasing process. Quality evaluation checks are performed for this stock before sending it out for consumption purposes.
- **Quality-inspection stock**—Refers to the standard stock that is under the quality evaluation process. Quality inspectors are appointed by an organization to evaluate the quality of the standard stock. The use of the stock under quality inspection is temporarily suspended until the completion of the quality inspection process. You can block the usage of stock material depending on the results of the quality inspection process. In other words, the materials under quality inspection are transferred to either the unrestricted-use stock or the blocked stock after their quality evaluation. The quality evaluation process should be done in a transparent and responsible manner to prevent errors. Incorrect quality evaluation can lead to severe complications in the production and planning processes. In addition, it may also affect the planning and forecasting of the inventory management process, as the management needs to replace the faulty items immediately.
- **Blocked stock**—Refers to the standard stock that is blocked in the quality inspection process and is not used for production. The primary reason for blocking the standard stock is an unsatisfactory quality evaluation report. Arrangements are made for the earliest replacement of the stock that is blocked due to its damaged condition. Sometimes, items have to be kept in the blocked stock due to some error in their purchasing, taxation, or billing documents. In addition, the materials provided by vendors for promotion are placed in the blocked stock, as these are not used for production purposes. Apart from that, the materials that are transferred by the vendors in the midst of the purchasing process are also placed in the blocked stock. If the materials placed under the blocked stock do not get clearance for use, they are permanently withdrawn from the storage location.

Now, after discussing the standard stock in detail, let's discuss the goods receipt block stock.

The Goods Receipt Blocked Stock

When a stock of materials or goods is initially received from the vendor, it is kept in the goods receipt blocked stock to check whether or not the received materials are as per the order given by the organization. The inappropriate and damaged materials are immediately returned to the vendor while others are transferred to the standard stock.

Perform the following steps to post the goods receipt in the goods receipt blocked stock:

1. Navigate the following menu path (Figure 7.1):

Menu Path

SAP menu > Logistics > Materials Management > Inventory Management > Goods Movement > MIGO – Goods Movement (MIGO)

2. Double-click the **MIGO – Goods Movement (MIGO)** activity, as shown in Figure 7.1:

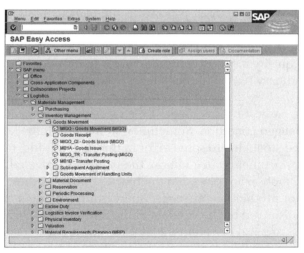

FIGURE 7.1   **Displaying the menu path to post the goods receipt blocked stock**

The Goods Receipt Purchase Order – User Test screen appears (Figure 7.2).

3. Select **Goods Receipt** and **Purchase Order** from the drop-down lists (Figure 7.2).
4. Select the **Rev. GR to blocked** movement type to receive goods against a purchase order. In our case, we have selected 104 (Figure 7.2).
5. Enter the purchase order number, say 4500017174 (Figure 7.2).
6. Click the **Enter** (✓) icon, as shown in Figure 7.2:

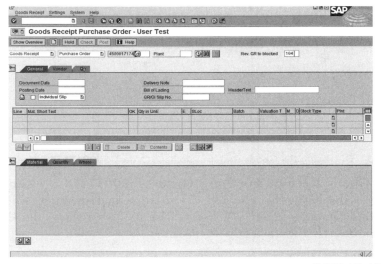

FIGURE 7.2   **Displaying the Goods Receipt Purchase Order – User Test screen**

The Goods Receipt Purchase Order 4500017174 – User Test screen appears (Figure 7.3).

7. Enter the document date in the **Document Date** text box. In our case, we have entered 13.10.2008 (Figure 7.3).
8. Enter the posting date in the **Posting Date** text box. In our case, we have entered 13.11.2006 (Figure 7.3).
9. Check the **Item OK** check box (Figure 7.3).

10. Click the **Check** button, as shown in Figure 7.3:

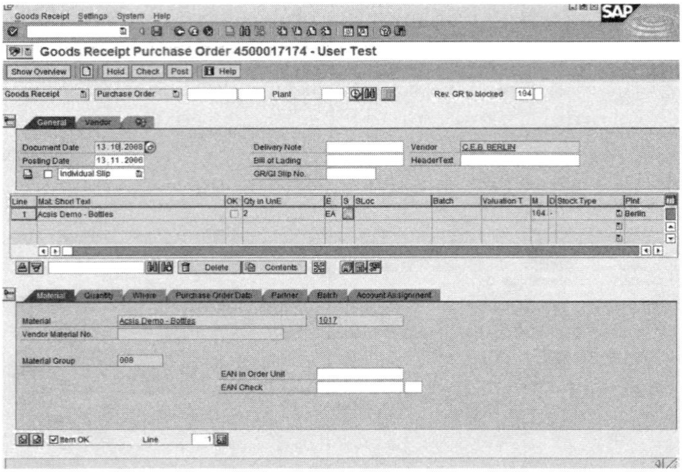

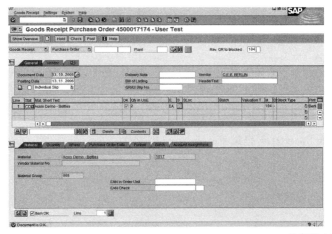

FIGURE 7.3   Displaying the Goods Receipt Purchase Order 4500017174 – User Test screen

The **Goods Receipt Purchase Order 4500017174 – User Test** screen appears, displaying the `Acsis Demo-Bottles` material item, which is received based on purchase order `45000174`. The status bar shows the **Document is O.K**. message (Figure 7.4).

11. Click the **Post** button to post the data in the goods receipt check stock, as shown in Figure 7.4:

FIGURE 7.4   Posting data in the goods receipt check stock

A message appears stating that the data is successfully posted in the mySAP ERP system.

> **Note:** You can also use the `MIGO` transaction code to access the **Goods Receipt Purchase Order – User Test** screen.

If the items of the goods receipt blocked stock are properly verified, they are released and transferred to the standard stock. You can release the goods receipt blocked stock by posting the goods receipt using the `105` movement type. On the other hand, the items of the goods receipt blocked stock are returned to the vendor if they are found defective. You can return the goods receipt blocked stock by posting a goods return with the `124` movement type. The process to post the release of goods is similar to the posting of the goods receipt.

Let's now discuss the special stock.

The Special Stock

The special stock is the stock that is stored outside the enterprise—at the customer's or vendor's premises—and contains items other than raw materials, such as subcontracts, consignments, and returnable packaging materials. You can classify the special stock into the following two types:

- **Company-owned special stock**—Refers to the stock owned by an organization and includes the subcontract stock at the vendor's end, consignment stock at the customer's end, and items that need to be returned to customers or vendors. Sometimes, vendors are provided with items that are used to produce the finished goods. For example, if a vendor is given a housing contract, then the enterprise may provide metal pipes to establish water supply connections in the houses. The materials provided by the enterprise are known as subcontract stock and subcontract purchase orders are created to issue these materials as company-owned special stock. Apart from subcontracts, consignments are another company-owned stock. These are the finished products purchased from a manufacturing company for selling. The consignment stock is referred to as a company-owned stock because while it is stored at the customer end, it is owned by the enterprise. In some cases, the organization sends the packaging material to the customer along with the finished products. For example, enterprises that prepare soft drinks send plastic crates along with the soft drink bottles. The customer has to return them after the items are delivered. These types of returnable packaging materials also come under the company-owned stock.

■ **Externally owned special stock**—Refers to the stock, such as consignments and packaging materials, which is owned by external parties, such as vendors or suppliers. The stock of finished items for which payment is received from customers is also grouped under externally owned stock. In addition, the stock received to undertake a project on behalf of an external company is referred to as externally owned stock. The externally owned stock is stored in the internal storage location along with the regular stock.

Let's discuss the types of goods movement in the next section.

EXPLORING THE TYPES OF GOODS MOVEMENT

Goods movement is the process of moving goods from one location to another. This movement of goods can be categorized as inbound or outbound. In the mySAP ERP system, each of these movements is assigned a unique movement type to prevent the unauthorized movement of goods. The inbound movement of goods refers to the process of transferring goods within an organization, i.e., movement of goods from the standard stock to either the quality-inspection stock or the production units. On the other hand, the process of delivering goods to a customer or vendor is referred as the outbound movement of goods.

Let's now learn how to implement each of these movement categories in the mySAP ERP system.

The Inbound Movement Process

The process of receiving goods from vendors, customers, or through purchase orders is known as the inbound movement process. In this process, the goods receipts are posted in the mySAP ERP system and a material document is created. The MIGO transaction code is used to post inbound movement of goods in the mySAP ERP system. The inbound movement process comprises the following sub-processes:

- **Goods receipt**—Involves the unloading, checking, counting, and posting activities related to the received goods. The financial and inventory records are then updated on the basis of goods receipts. In addition to purchase orders, goods are received through inbound deliveries, stock transfers, and production orders.
- **External demand**—Specifies the details of the required goods, such as quantity and delivery date, which are associated with the inbound movement process.
- **Advanced shipping notification**—Represents the documents supplied by the vendors. These documents contain information regarding the quantity of the materials to be supplied, the pricing, and the delivery date.
- **Delivery monitor**—Supervises the delivery process of all goods receipts and helps in tracking the inbound movement process.
- **Yard management**—Refers to the external management of stock materials before they are transferred to the inventory. This process includes the loading and weighing of materials in a yard. It also provides details about the exact number of items that are delivered, which may be different than the number later loaded into the inventory.

After discussing the inbound delivery process, let's now discuss the outbound delivery process.

The Outbound Movement Process

The process in which goods are moved outside an organization, such as by issuing goods to customers against a sales order, returning goods to vendors, or sending finished products to suppliers and distributors for marketing, is known as the outbound movement process. In the outbound movement process, the Post Goods Issue (PGI) documents are posted by using the `MB51` transaction code. The outbound movement process comprises the following sub-processes:

- **Goods issue**—Refers to the posting of a goods issue for the outbound process. The goods issue sub-process performs the following actions:
  - Reducing the stock by the quantity delivered
  - Changing the value of the stock in the financial accounts
  - Reducing the number of outstanding deliveries
  - Updating the serial numbers of the products after issuing goods from the warehouse
  - Changing the goods issue document
  - Generating the final document for the outbound delivery
- **Delivery process and distribution**—Covers the activities associated with the delivery of goods after which the goods are shipped to the relevant distributors. In some cases, the goods are shipped directly to the customer's end.
- **Delivery documents**—Refers to the creation of the delivery document after the products have been received by the customer. This document includes details such as the purchase order date, the time of delivery, and the actual quantities delivered against the sales order. Any defect in the delivered product is recorded at the time of the delivery of the product.
- **Value-added services**—Refers to the management of internal warehouse activities, such as managing individual products, tasks and resources, and mobile data entry of items.
- **Delivery monitor**—Refers to the management of the outbound movement process, which is similar to the delivery process implemented in the inbound movement process.

Let's now discuss the process of issuing goods in the next section.

ISSUING OF GOODS

Goods issuing refers to the process of transferring goods from stock for a variety of reasons, such as shipping goods to a customer, withdrawing goods for production, returning defective goods to vendors, and sending finished products to distributors. In addition, the transferring of scraps (unused or obsolete materials) from the inventory also comes under the category of issued goods. In this section, you learn to perform the following activities:

- Issuing goods to a production order
- Issuing goods to scrap
- Issuing goods for sampling
- Updating the documents related to a goods issue

Issuing Goods to a Production Order

An organization can determine the type and quantity of raw materials required for producing finished products with the help of the Material Requirements Planning (MRP) tool. After determining the material requirements, the production order is prepared on the basis of the production schedule, the periodic consumption of goods, and the availability of goods. Thereafter, the required quantity of goods is issued to the production unit from the inventory. The following types of goods can be issued against a production order:

- Planned goods
- Unplanned goods

Apart from the process of issuing the preceding types of goods, you will also learn the concept of backflushing.

Issuing Planned Goods

After assessing the goods requirements, an organization can plan and reserve the required goods in the mySAP ERP system. The planned goods are then issued on the basis of this reservation. The MB1A transaction code is used to issue the planned goods against a production order.

Perform the following steps to post the planned goods issue:

1. Navigate the following menu path (Figure 7.5):

Menu Path

SAP menu > Logistics > Materials Management > Inventory Management > Goods Movement > MB1A – Goods Issue

2. Double-click the **MB1A – Goods Issue** activity, as shown in Figure 7.5:

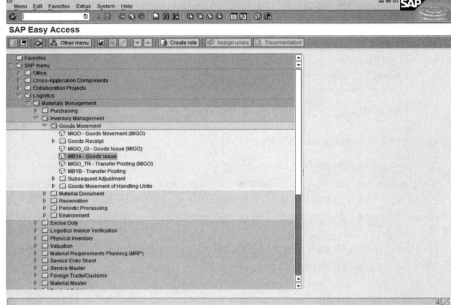

FIGURE 7.5 Posting of a planned goods issue

The **Enter Goods Issue: Initial Screen** appears (Figure 7.6).

3. Enter the document date in the **Document Date** text box. In our case, we have entered 15.10.2006 (Figure 7.6).
4. Enter the posting date in the **Posting Date** text box. In our case, we have entered 15.12.2006 (Figure 7.6).
5. Enter the movement type in the **Movement Type** text box. In our case, we have entered 261 (Figure 7.6).
6. Enter plant in the **Plant** text box. In our case, we have entered 1000 (Figure 7.6).
7. Enter the storage location in the **Storage Location** text box. In our case, we have entered PL01 (Figure 7.6).
8. Click the **Enter** (☑) icon, as shown in Figure 7.6:

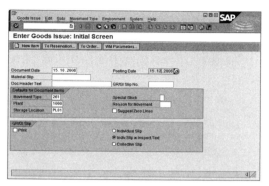

FIGURE 7.6   Displaying the Enter Goods Issue: Initial Screen

The **Enter Goods Issue: New Items** screen appears (Figure 7.7).

9. Enter the order number in the **Order** text box. In our case, we have entered 300020 (Figure 7.7).

10. Enter the name of the material in the **Material** text box. In our case, we have entered T-B106 (Figure 7.7).

11. Enter the quantity in the **Quantity** text box. In our case, we have entered 2 (Figure 7.7).

12. Enter the unit of measurement for the goods in the **UnE** text box. In our case, we have entered PC (Figure 7.7).

13. Click the **Enter** (✅) icon, as shown in Figure 7.7:

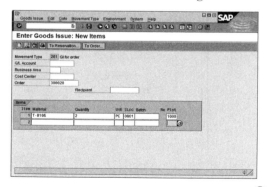

FIGURE 7.7   Displaying the Enter Goods Issue: New Items screen

The **Enter Goods Issue: Collective Processing** screen appears (Figure 7.8).

14. Click the **Save** (▣) icon in the **Enter Goods Issue: Collective Processing** screen to post the transaction for planned goods issue, as shown in Figure 7.8:

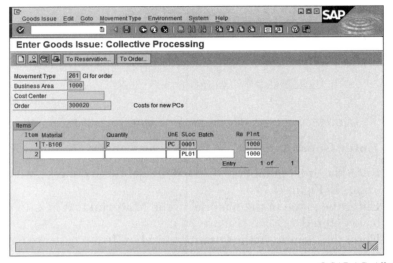

FIGURE 7.8   Displaying the Enter Goods Issue: Collective Processing screen

Let's now learn how to issue unplanned goods in the mySAP ERP system.

Issuing Unplanned Goods

In the mySAP ERP system, you can also issue goods without any prior planning. This is generally required when there is an urgent demand for the goods. The unplanned goods are issued against a bill of materials (BOM) document and posted in the mySAP ERP system. The unplanned goods movement is posted in the mySAP ERP system by using transaction code 261.

Perform the following steps to post an unplanned goods issue:

1. Navigate the following menu path (Figure 7.5):

Menu Path

SAP menu > Logistics > Materials Management > Inventory Management > Goods Movement > MB1A – Goods Issue

2. Double-click the **MB1A – Goods Issue** activity (Figure 7.5). The **Enter Goods Issue: Initial Screen** appears (Figure 7.6).
3. Enter the document date in the **Document Date** text box. In our case, we have entered 18.11.2006 (Figure 7.9).
4. Enter the posting date in the **Posting Date** text box. In our case, we have entered 18.12.2006 (Figure 7.9).
5. Enter the movement type in the **Movement Type** text box. In our case, we have entered 261 (Figure 7.9).
6. Enter the plant in the **Plant** text box. In our case, we have entered 2730 (Figure 7.9).
7. Select the **Goods Issue > Create with Reference > To BOM** option to issue goods as per BOM (unplanned goods), as shown in Figure 7.9:

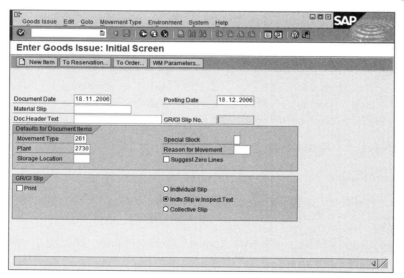

FIGURE 7.9   **Posting an unplanned goods issue**

Let's now discuss the backflushing process.

Backflushing

The process of automatic posting of a production order by the mySAP ERP system is known as backflushing. For example, in the case of the automobile assembly line, production orders for wheels are automatically issued by the mySAP ERP system. The backflushing process is used for materials having a fixed consumption rate, such as the number of wheels in automobile production. This process is also used to calculate the unused materials and scraps that are left after the completion of the production process, which in turn helps to create the revised production order for additional material requirements, if necessary. In the mySAP ERP system, you can flag a material for backflushing by setting an indicator on the material master record. Backflushing is performed only after the completion of the production phase to evaluate the exact amount of scrap.

After learning how to issue goods to a production order, let's discuss the process of issuing goods to scrap.

Issuing Goods to Scrap

As already discussed, scrap refers to the unused or obsolete material in an organization. This includes materials that remain unused beyond their expiry date, unused machines, or the goods damaged during the production process. Scrap is removed from the inventory by creating a goods issue for it. In the mySAP ERP system, you can post the goods issue to scrap by either using the `MB1A` transaction code or the `551` goods movement type.

Perform the following steps to post the goods issue to scrap:

1. Navigate the following menu path (Figure 7.5):

Menu Path

SAP menu > Logistics > Materials Management > Inventory Management > Goods Movement > MB1A – Goods Issue

2. Double-click the **MB1A – Goods Issue** activity (Figure 7.5). The **Enter Goods Issue: Initial Screen** appears (Figure 7.10).
3. Enter the document date in the **Document Date** text box. In our case, we have entered `18.11.2006` (Figure 7.10).
4. Enter the posting date in the **Posting Date** text box. In our case, we have entered `18.12.2006` (Figure 7.10).
5. Enter the plant in the **Plant** text box. In our case, we have entered `1000` (Figure 7.10).
6. Enter the goods movement type in the **Movement Type** text box. In our case, we have entered `551` (Figure 7.10).
7. Click the **Enter** (☑) icon, as shown in Figure 7.10:

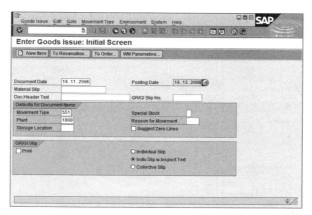

FIGURE 7.10   Entering details to post the goods issue to scrap

The **Enter Goods Issue: New Items** screen appears (Figure 7.11).

8. Enter the name of the material in the **Material** text box. In our case, we have entered T-B106 (Figure 7.11).
9. Enter the quantity in the **Quantity** text box. In our case, we have entered 2 (Figure 7.11).
10. Enter the unit of measurement for the goods in the **UnE** text box. In our case, we have entered PC (Figure 7.11).
11. Click the **Enter** (☑) icon, as shown in Figure 7.11:

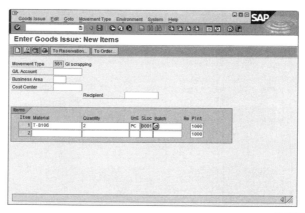

FIGURE 7.11   Posting the goods issue to scrap

The **Enter Goods Issue: New Item 0001** screen appears (Figure 7.12).

12. Click the **Enter** (✓) icon, as shown in Figure 7.12:

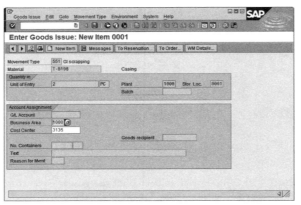

FIGURE 7.12   Displaying the Enter Goods Issue: New Item 0001 **screen**

The **Enter Goods Issue: Collective Processing** screen appears (Figure 7.13).

13. Click the **Save** (🖫) icon to post the transaction for goods that are issued to scrap, as shown in Figure 7.13:

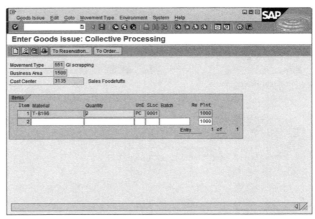

FIGURE 7.13   Displaying Enter Goods Issue: Collective Processing **screen**

Let's discuss how to issue goods for sampling next.

Issuing Goods for Sampling

Some products, such as chemicals, edible items, and electrical appliances need to be extensively tested before being sent for selling and distribution purposes. In other words, before sending the entire stock of the product to the masses, a specific quantity is sent as samples to distributors for testing. In the mySAP ERP system, the goods issued for sampling are posted by using the MB1A transaction code with the 331 movement type.

Perform the following steps to post the goods issue for sampling:

1. Navigate the following menu path (Figure 7.5):

Menu Path

SAP menu > Logistics > Materials Management > Inventory Management > Goods Movement > MB1A – Goods Issue

2. Double-click the **MB1A – Goods Issue** activity (Figure 7.5). The **Enter Goods Issue: Initial Screen** appears (Figure 7.14).
3. Enter the document date in the **Document Date** text box. In our case, we have entered 18.11.2006 (Figure 7.14).
4. Enter the posting date in the **Posting Date** text box. In our case, we have entered 18.12.2006 (Figure 7.14).
5. Enter the goods movement type in the **Movement Type** text box. In our case, we have entered **333** (Figure 7.14).
6. Click the **Enter** () icon, as shown in Figure 7.14:

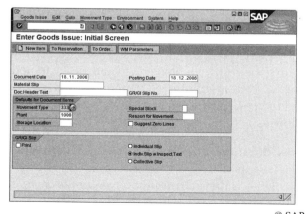

FIGURE 7.14 Entering details to post the goods issue for sampling

The **Enter Goods Issue: New Items** screen appears (Figure 7.15).

7. Enter the appropriate values in the text boxes of the **Enter Goods Issue: New Items** screen and click the **Save** (🖫) icon to post the data, as shown in Figure 7.15:

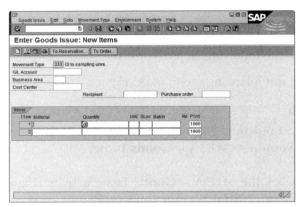

FIGURE 7.15   **Posting the goods issue for sampling**

After issuing goods for sample, let's learn how to post goods issue in the books of accounts.

Updating the Documents Related to a Goods Issue

As discussed earlier, the goods from the stock are issued for various purposes, such as for a production order, scrap, or sampling. While issuing the goods, the books of accounts for material stock, the material document, and the accounting documents are updated in the mySAP ERP system. In addition, you can post the reasons for goods movement and the value of the issued goods. You can also post the issue of goods into other documents, such as goods issue slips, stock changes, and the general ledger accounts.

The following is the list of documents related to the issue of goods:

■   **Material document**—Allows you to provide the quantity of goods to be issued. This document can help verify the actual amount of goods moved from the inventory is correct. The MB03 transaction code is used to post the goods issue in the material document. Perform the following steps to post a goods issue as per a material document:

1. Navigate the following menu path (Figure 7.5):

Menu Path

SAP menu > Logistics > Materials Management > Inventory Management > Goods Movement > MB1A – Goods Issue

2. Double-click the **MB1A – Goods Issue** activity (Figure 7.5). The **Enter Goods Issue: Initial Screen** appears (Figure 7.16).
3. Enter the document date in the **Document Date** text box. In our case, we have entered 18.11.2006 (Figure 7.16).
4. Enter the posting date in the **Posting Date** text box. In our case, we have entered 18.12.2006 (Figure 7.16).
5. Enter the movement type in the **Movement Type** text box. In our case, we have entered 261 (Figure 7.16).
6. Enter the plant in the **Plant** text box. In our case, we have entered 2730 (Figure 7.16).
7. Enter the storage location in **Storage Location** text box. In our case, we have entered 0088 (Figure 7.16).
8. Select **Goods Issue > Create with Reference > To Mat Document**, as shown in Figure 7.16:

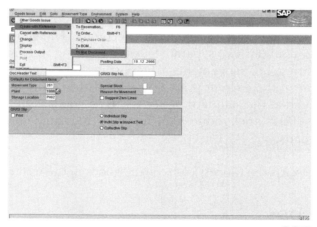

FIGURE 7.16   Posting the goods issue by using a material document

As a result, the material document is created for a goods issue.

After creating the goods issue according to the material document, you can use the MB03 transaction code to display the material document.

- **Accounting documents**—Refers to documents where one posts the financial entries associated with the goods issue. After posting the goods movement in the financial accounts, it is displayed by using the MB03 transaction code.
- **Goods issue slip**—Refers to a document that is used to find the material picked from the storage house for issue. The goods issue slip is the primary document where the issue of goods is posted. The goods issue slip can be of the following types:
  - **Individual slip**—Contains an individual goods issue slip for each material document
  - **Individual slip with inspection text**—Contains a single goods issue slip for each goods issue and includes the description related to the quality inspection
  - **Collective slip**—Contains a single goods issue slip for issuing a collection of goods
- **Stock changes**—Depicts the reduction in the quantity of materials after the goods are issued from the stock. In the case of stock reversal, the stock increases due to the inward goods movements in the stock.
- **General ledger accounts**—Refers to the posting of the goods issue in the general ledger accounts. The general ledger contains two separate sides for posting the inward and outward goods movements. The posting for the goods issue is done at the current price of the goods while the material is valued at the standard price. With the goods issue, the price of the stock reduces by the value and the quantity of the goods.

Let's discuss the process of receiving goods in the next section.

RECEIVING GOODS

Goods are received in the stock as a result of the inward movement of goods, which occurs for a number of reasons, such as:

- Purchase of goods from a vendor against the purchase order
- Defective goods returned by customers
- Sample goods sent by vendors for advertising

Depending on the nature of the material and its value, the goods receipt process can be simple or complex.

For example, the goods receipt process for materials that are not easily consumable, such as iron ore, rocks, and building materials can be simple. However, the goods receipt of chemicals, explosives, radioactive items, and gems are complex as well as restrictive. In this section, the following activities related to the goods receipt are discussed:

- Receiving goods for a purchase order
- Receiving goods without a purchase order
- Receiving goods for a production order
- Receiving goods without a production order
- Receiving goods for by-products
- Receiving free goods

Let's discuss the goods receipt for a purchase order.

Receiving Goods for a Purchase Order

A purchase order is used to receive goods from a vendor. After receiving the goods, the purchase order is posted in the general ledger account.

Perform the following steps to implement the goods received for a purchase order:

1. Navigate the following menu path (Figure 7.1):

Menu Path

SAP menu > Logistics > Materials Management > Inventory Management > Goods Movement > Goods Receipt > MIGO – Goods Movement (MIGO)

2. Double-click the **MIGO – Goods Movement (MIGO)** activity (Figure 7.1). The **Goods Receipt Purchase Order – User Test** screen appears (Figure 7.17)

3. Enter the purchase order as 4500017048 (Figure 7.17).
4. Enter the document date in the **Document Date** text box. In our case, we have entered 19.11.2006 (Figure 7.17).
5. Enter the posting date in the in the **Posting Date** text box. In our case, we have entered 19.11.2006 (Figure 7.17).
6. Enter the plant in the **Plant** text box. In our case, we have entered 1000 (Figure 7.17).
7. Enter the goods receipt type in the **GR goods receipt** text box. In our case, we have entered 101, which refers to the goods receipt for purchase order (Figure 7.17).
8. Click the **Enter** (☑) icon, as shown in Figure 7.17:

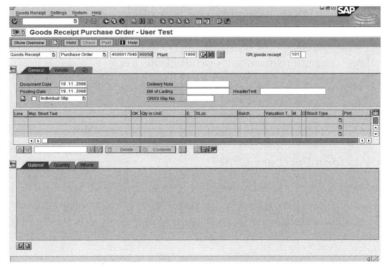

FIGURE 7.17 Displaying the Goods Receipt Purchase Order – User Test screen

The **Goods Receipt Purchase Order 4500017048 – User Test** screen appears (Figure 7.18). This screen displays the information from purchase order 4500017048 for goods receipt movement type 101.

9. Check the **Item OK** check box (Figure 7.18).
10. Click the **Check** button, as shown in Figure 7.18:

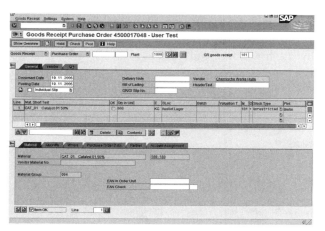

FIGURE 7.18   **Displaying the Goods Receipt Purchase Order 4500017048 – User Test screen**

The **Goods Receipt Purchase Order 4500017048 – User Test** screen appears (Figure 7.19). The green signal displayed in the **Stat** column shows that the status of purchase order is OK (Figure 7.19). The status bar also displays the message that the document is OK (Figure 7.19).

11. Click the **Post** button to post the goods receipt with the purchase order, as shown in Figure 7.19:

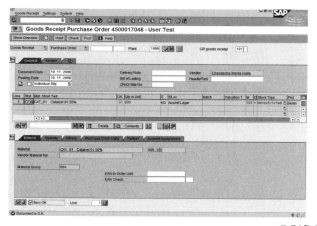

FIGURE 7.19   **Displaying the Goods Receipt Purchase Order 4500017048 – User Test screen**

The status bar of the **Goods Receipt Purchase Order – User Test** screen displays the message that goods receipt of the purchase order was posted successfully, as shown in Figure 7.20:

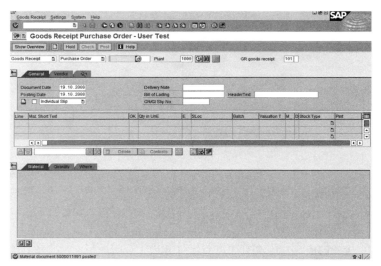

FIGURE 7.20   Displaying Goods Receipt Purchase Order – User Test screen

Let's now learn how to receive goods receipt without a purchase order.

Receiving Goods without a Purchase Order

Goods are received without a purchase order when the vendor does not provide the purchase order or the purchase documents are wrongly posted in the mySAP ERP system. Moreover, if there is a delay in entering the purchase order in the documents, goods may be received without a purchase order. Some organizations do not receive material without a purchase order at all to avoid undesirable circumstances, such as fraud and unauthorized deliveries.

Some organizations accept the goods receipt without a purchase order and place them in the blocked stock until all the items are verified. Only after proper verification and the posting of the goods receipt in the mySAP ERP system are the goods finally received in the stock. Goods received without the purchase order are posted in the mySAP ERP system as a goods receipt with the 501 movement type.

Perform the following steps to implement the goods receipt process without a purchase order:

1. Navigate the following menu path (Figure 7.1):

Menu Path

SAP menu > Logistics > Materials Management > Inventory Management > Goods Movement > MIGO – Goods Movement (MIGO)

2. Double-click the **MIGO – Goods Movement (MIGO)** activity (Figure 7.1). The **Goods Receipt Purchase Order – User Test** screen appears (Figure 7.21)
3. Enter the purchase order as 4500015525 (Figure 7.21).
4. Enter the document date in the **Document Date** text box. In our case, we have entered 19.11.2006.
5. Enter the posting date in the **Posting Date** text box. In our case, we have entered 19.12.2006 (Figure 7.21)
6. Enter the plant in the **Plant** text box. In our case, we have entered 1000 (Figure 7.21).
7. Enter the goods receipt type in the **GI receipt w/o PO** text box as 501 (Figure 7.21).
8. Click the **Enter** (⊘) icon, as shown in Figure 7.21:

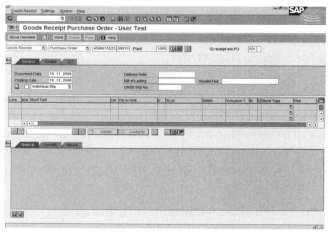

FIGURE 7.21   Posting the goods receipt without a purchase order

The **Goods Receipt Purchase Order – User Test** screen appears with the default dates, as shown in Figure 7.22:

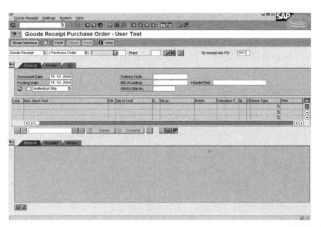

FIGURE 7.22   **Displaying the Goods Receipt Purchase Order – User Test screen**

Figure 7.22 displays the goods receipt transaction for receiving goods without the purchase order.

Now, let's discuss the goods received for a production order.

Receiving Goods for a Production Order

In cases where the goods are issued for internal production against a production order, the purchase unit receives the goods from the inventory and processes them as a goods receipt. The MIGO_GO transaction code is used to post the goods issued against a production order. However, the production order number must be entered in the mySAP ERP system to complete the posting process.

Perform the following steps to post the goods receipt for a production order:

1. Navigate the following menu path (Figure 7.23):

Menu Path

SAP menu > Logistics > Materials Management > Inventory Management > Goods Movement > Goods Receipt > MIGO_GO – GR for Order (MIGO)

2. Double-click the **MIGO_GO – GR for Order (MIGO)** activity, as shown in Figure 7.23:

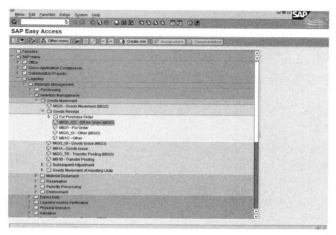

FIGURE 7.23   **Displaying the menu path to post the goods receipt for a production order**

The **Goods Receipt Order – User Test** screen appears (Figure 7.24).

3. Enter the relevant values in the text boxes of the **Goods Receipt Order – User Test** screen and click the **Enter** (☑) icon to post the goods receipt for a production order, as shown in Figure 7.24:

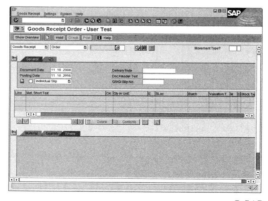

FIGURE 7.24   **Posting a goods receipt for a production order**

Now, let's discuss goods received without a production order.

Receiving Goods without a Production Order

If an organization does not maintain the production planning process, then the goods may be received without a production order. In this case, the goods receipt is treated as a miscellaneous goods receipt.

Perform the following steps to post the goods without a production order:

1. Navigate the following menu path (Figure 7.25):

Menu Path

SAP menu > Logistics > Materials Management > Inventory Management > Goods Movement > Goods Receipt > MB1C – Other

2. Double-click the **MB1C – Other** activity, as shown in Figure 7.25:

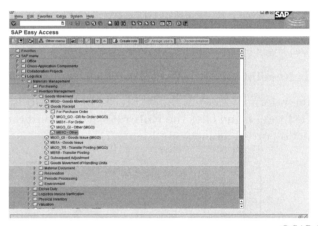

FIGURE 7.25   Displaying the menu path to post a goods receipt without a production order

The **Enter Other Goods Receipts: Initial Screen** appears (Figure 7.26).

3. Enter the document date in the **Document Date** text box. In our case, we have entered 19.12.2006 (Figure 7.26).
4. Enter the posting date in the **Posting Date** text box. In our case, we have entered 19.12.2006 (Figure 7.26).

5. Enter the movement type in the **Movement Type** text box. In our case, we have entered 521 (Figure 7.26).

6. Enter the plant in the **Plant** text box. In our case, we have entered 1000 (Figure 7.26). The 521 movement type is used to post a goods receipt without a production order into the unrestricted stock. Moreover, the goods receipt without a production order in the quality-inspection stock is posted by using the 523 movement type and in blocked stock by using the 525 movement type.

7. Click the **Enter** (✓) icon, as shown in Figure 7.26:

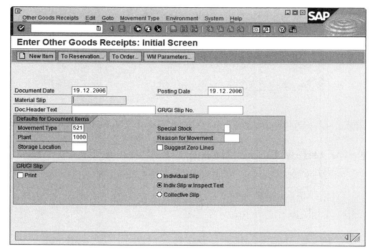

FIGURE 7.26   Displaying the Enter Other Goods Receipts: Initial Screen

The **Enter Other Goods Receipt: New Items** screen appears (Figure 7.27).

8. Enter the name of the material in the **Material** text box. In our case, we have entered GTS - 14009 (Figure 7.27).

9. Enter the quantity in the **Quantity** text box. In our case, we have entered 2 as the quantity of the material (Figure 7.27).

10. Enter the unit of measurement for the goods in the **UnE** text box. In our case, we have entered PC (Figure 7.27).

11. Enter the storage location in the **SLoc** text box. In our case, we have entered `0001` (Figure 7.27).

12. Click the **Enter** (◉) icon, as shown in Figure 7.27:

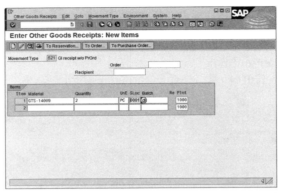

FIGURE 7.27   Displaying the Enter Other Goods Receipts: New Items screen

The **Enter Other Goods Receipt: Collective Processing** screen appears (Figure 7.28).

13. Click the **Save** (🖫) icon to post the goods receipt without a production order, as shown in Figure 7.28:

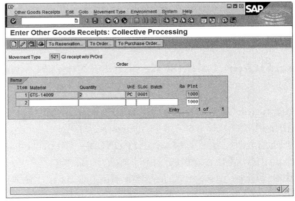

FIGURE 7.28   Displaying the Enter Other Goods Receipt: Collective Processing screen

The status bar shows that the goods receipt is posted without a production order, as shown in Figure 7.29:

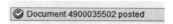

FIGURE 7.29 **Posting of a goods receipt without a production order**

Now, let's discuss the goods receipt for by-products.

Receiving Goods for By-Products

By-products are secondary products that are manufactured along with the scheduled products. For example, in the petroleum industry, diesel, kerosene oil, and bitumen are the by-products that are produced in the process of refining the crude oil. The by-products are directly consumed or used as a raw material for other products. The receipt of by-products from the production unit is posted in the mySAP ERP system by using the 531 movement type and the MB1C transaction code.

Perform the following steps to post the goods receipt for by-products:

1. Navigate the following menu path (Figure 7.25):

Menu Path

SAP menu > Logistics > Materials Management > Inventory Management > Goods Movement > Goods Receipt > MB1C – Other

2. Double-click the **MB1C – Other** activity (Figure 7.25). The **Enter Other Goods Reeipts: Initial Screen** appears (Figure 7.30).
3. Enter the document date as 20.11.2006 (Figure 7.30).
4. Enter the posting date as 20.12.2006 (Figure 7.30).
5. Enter the movement type and plant as 531 and 1000, respectively (Figure 7.30).

6. Click the **Enter** (☑) icon, as shown in Figure 7.30:

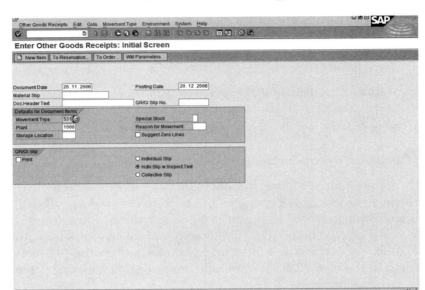

FIGURE 7.30   Displaying the Enter Other Goods Receipts: Initial screen

The **Enter Other Goods Receipt: New Items** screen appears (Figure 7.31).

7. Enter the name of the material in the **Material** text box. In our case, we have entered AS - 101 (Figure 7.31).
8. Enter the quantity in the **Quantity** text box. In our case, we have entered 20 (Figure 7.31).
9. Enter the unit of measure for the goods in the **UnE** text box. In our case, we have entered PC (Figure 7.31).
10. Enter the storage location in the **SLoc** text box. In our case, we have entered 0001 (Figure 7.31).
11. Click the **Enter** (☑) icon, as shown in Figure 7.31:

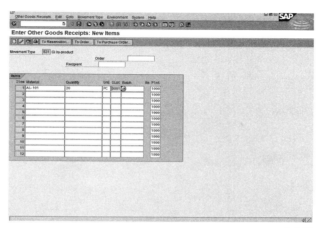

FIGURE 7.31   Displaying the Enter Other Goods Receipts: New Items screen

The **Enter Other Goods Receipts: Collective Processing** screen appears (Figure 7.32).

12. Click the **Save** (🖫) icon to post the transaction for goods receipt for by-products, as shown in Figure 7.32:

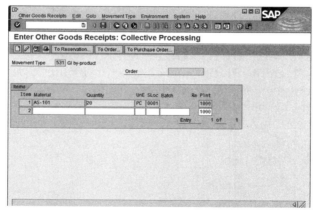

FIGURE 7.32   Displaying the Enter Other Goods Receipts: New Items screen

The status bar displays the message that the goods receipt for by-products was posted successfully, as shown in Figure 7.33:

FIGURE 7.33   **Posting of a goods receipt for by-products**

Now, after discussing the goods receipt for by-products, let's discuss receiving free goods.

Receiving Free Goods

An organization may receive goods from time to time without making any payment. For example, sample products are received free from vendors as a means to advertise their products. In the mySAP ERP system, the receipt of free goods is posted in a similar manner to other items by using the MB1C transaction code and the 511 movement type.

Perform the following steps to post a free goods receipt:

1. Navigate the following menu path (Figure 7.25):

Menu Path

SAP menu > Logistics > Materials Management > Inventory Management > Goods Movement > Goods Receipt > MB1C – Other

2. Double-click the **MB1C – Other** activity (Figure 7.25). The **Enter Other Goods Receipts: Initial Screen** appears (Figure 7.34).
3. Enter the document date as 19.11.2006 (Figure 7.34).
4. Enter the posting date as 19.12.2006 (Figure 7.34).
5. Enter the movement type and plant as 511 and 1000, respectively (Figure 7.34).
6. Click the **Enter** (✓) icon, as shown in Figure 7.34:

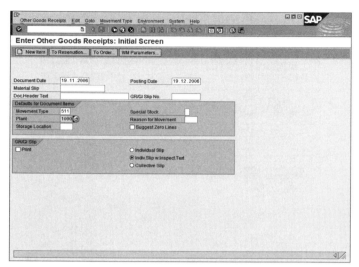

FIGURE 7.34   Displaying the Enter Other Goods Receipts: Initial Screen

The **Enter Other Goods Receipts: New Items** screen appears (Figure 7.35).

7. Enter the vendor in the **Vendor** text box. In our case, we have entered `4020` (Figure 7.35).

8. Enter the material name in the **Material** text box. In our case, we have entered `100-200` (Figure 7.35).

9. Enter the quantity in the **Quantity** text box. In our case, we have entered `2` (Figure 7.35).

10. Enter the unit of measurement for the goods in the **UnE** text box. In our case, we have entered `PC` (Figure 7.35).

11. Enter the storage location in the **SLoc** text box. In our case, we have entered `0001` (Figure 7. 35).

12. Click the **Enter** (✓) icon, as shown in Figure 7.35:

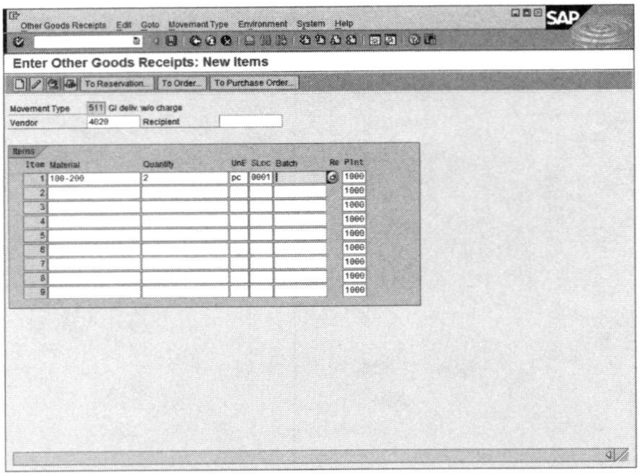

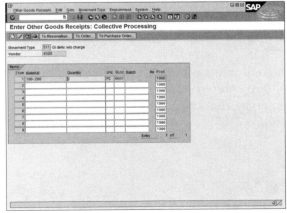

FIGURE 7.35   Displaying the Enter Other Goods Receipts: New Item screen

The **Enter Other Goods Receipts: Collective Processing** screen appears (Figure 7.36).

13. Click the **Save** (💾) icon to post the goods receipt for free products, as shown in Figure 7.36:

FIGURE 7.36   Displaying the Enter Other Goods Receipts: Collective Processing screen

The status bar displays the message that the goods receipt for free products was posted successfully, as shown in Figure 7.37:

FIGURE 7.37 **Posting of a free goods receipt**

Let's now discuss the process of returning goods to vendors.

RETURNING GOODS

An organization may return materials to the vendor for a variety of reasons, such as defective material, over delivery of the material, and returnable packaging materials. The goods are returned to vendors from the unrestricted stock, the quality-inspection stock, the blocked stock, or the goods receipt blocked stock. Vendors may reuse the packaging material or recycle the returned material at their end. The commitment to replace damaged material or return reusable material is mentioned in the purchase agreement created between the vendors and the organization. In addition, the purchase agreement contains information regarding the quantity, date of returning, and method of recycling the material (if recycling is done at the customer's end).

You need to perform the following activities to implement the goods return process in the mySAP ERP system:

- Creating a goods return document
- Configuring the reasons for goods return
- Creating a material document

Let's now discuss each of these activities in detail.

Creating a Goods Return Document

In the mySAP ERP system, the goods return document is created to specify the details of the goods that need to be returned to the vendor. Perform the following steps to create the goods return document in the mySAP ERP system:

1. Navigate the following menu path (Figure 7.38):

Menu Path

SAP menu > Logistics > Materials Management > Inventory Management > Goods Movement > Goods Receipt > For Purchase Order > MIGO_GR – GR for Purchase Order (MIGO)

2. Double-click the **MIGO_GR – GR for Purchase Order (MIGO)** activity, as shown in Figure 7.38:

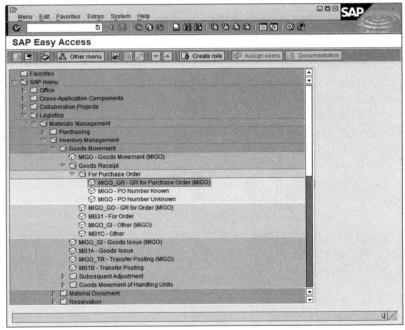

FIGURE 7.38 Displaying the menu path to create a goods return document

The **Return Delivery Material Document – User Test** screen appears (Figure 7.39).

3. Enter the material document type as `5000011985` (Figure 7.39).
4. Click the **Execute** (⊕) icon, as shown in Figure 7.39:

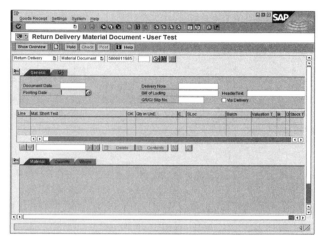

FIGURE 7.39   **Displaying the Return Delivery Material Document – User Test screen**

The **Return Delivery Material Document 5000011985 – User Test** screen appears (Figure 7.40). The screen displays the delivery details of the `5000011985` material document (Figure 7.40).

5. Select the **Where** tab, as shown in Figure 7.40:

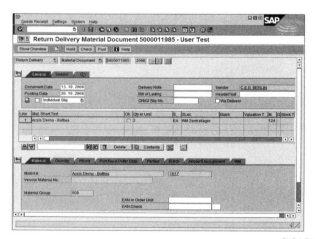

FIGURE 7.40   **Displaying the Return Delivery Material Document 5000011985 – User Test screen**

Figure 7.41 displays the details of the return delivery, such as movement type, stock name, plant, and storage location:

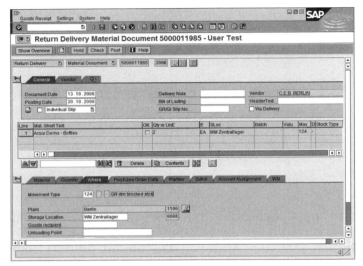

FIGURE 7.41   Displaying the Return Delivery Material Document 5000011985 – User Test screen

Note: You can use the `MIGO_GR` transaction code to access the **Return Delivery Material Document – User Test** screen.

Let's now learn to configure the reasons of goods return.

Configuring the Reasons for Goods Return

Returned goods, also known as return deliveries, refer to the goods or items that are returned to a customer or vendor. The returned deliveries comprise defective materials, surplus items, and packaging materials that are returned to the vendor after the delivery of products. In the mySAP ERP system, you can configure the reasons for creating a return delivery by using the `OMBS` transaction code.

Perform the following steps to configure the reasons for a delivery return:

1. Navigate the following menu path (Figure 7.42):

Menu Path

SAP Customizing Implementation Guide > Materials Management > Inventory Management and Physical Inventory > Movement Types > Record Reason for Goods Movements

2. Click the **IMG Activity** (⊕) icon, as shown in Figure 7.42:

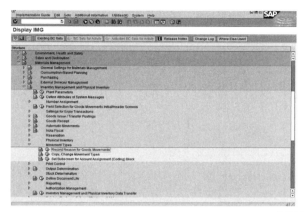

FIGURE 7.42   **Displaying the menu path to create reasons for a return delivery**

The **Reason for Movement** screen appears (Figure 7.43).

3. Click the **Reason for Movement** button, as shown in Figure 7.43:

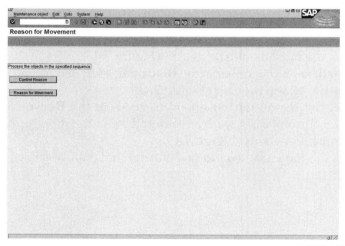

FIGURE 7.43   **Displaying the Reason for Movement screen**

The **Change View "Reason for Movement": Overview** screen appears (Figure 7.44).

4. Click the **New Entries** button, as shown in Figure 7.44:

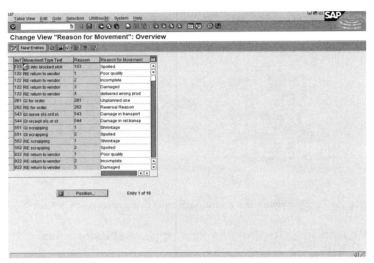

FIGURE 7.44 Displaying the Change View "Reason for Movement": Overview screen

The **New Entries: Overview of Added Entries** screen appears (Figure 7.45).

5. Enter the movement type as 122 (Figure 7.45).
6. Enter the reason number in the **Reason** header. In our case, we have entered 45 as the reason number (Figure 7.45).
7. Enter the reason for movement of goods in the **Reason for Movement** header. In our case, we have entered Spoiled Goods as the reason for movement of goods (Figure 7.45).
8. Click the **Save** (▣) icon to save the entered data, as shown in Figure 7.45:

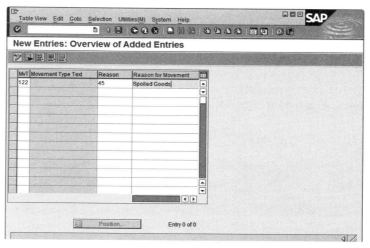

FIGURE 7.45   Displaying the New Entries: Overview of Added Entries screen

The status bar displays the message that the configuration details were saved successfully, as shown in Figure 7.46:

FIGURE 7.46   Displaying message after configuring the reason for goods return

Now, after configuring the reasons for goods return, let's create the material document.

Creating the Material Document

The material document contains the details of the goods returned, such as the posting date, delivery note, material, quantity, plant location, and movement type. The material document is prepared after the reasons for goods movement are configured. The 122 movement type and the MB03 transaction code are used to create the material document for returnable goods.

Perform the following steps to create a material document:

1. Navigate the following menu path (Figure 7.47):

Menu Path

SAP menu > Logistics > Materials Management > Inventory Management > Material Document > MB03 – Display

2. Double-click the **MB03 – Display** activity, as shown in Figure 7.47:

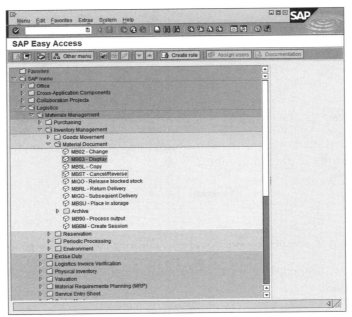

FIGURE 7.47   Displaying the menu path to create a material document

The **Display Material Document: Initial Screen** appears (Figure 7.48).

3. Enter the material document number as 4900033031 (Figure 7.48).
4. Click the **Enter** (☑) icon, as shown in Figure 7.48:

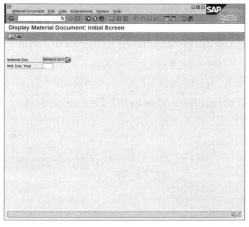

FIGURE 7.48 **Representing the Display Material Document: Initial Screen**

The **Display Material Document 4900033031: Overview** screen appears (Figure 7.49). The details of items, such as item number, quantity, unit of measurement, material description, plant, storage location, and movement type, contained in material document 49000033031 are shown in Figure 7.49:

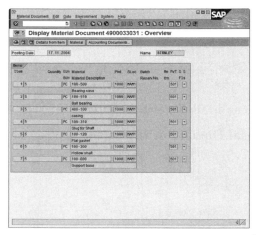

FIGURE 7.49 Displaying the Display Material Document 4900033031: Overview screen

Apart from creating the material document, you can also generate the list of material documents of the items that need to be returned. Perform the following steps to generate the list of material documents of the items that need to be returned to the vendor:

1. Select item 1 from the list of items (Figure 7.49).
2. Select **Environment > Material Document for Material**, as shown in Figure 7.50:

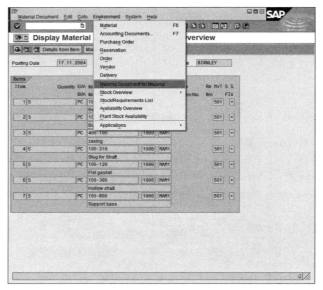

FIGURE 7.50   Showing the Display Material Document 4900033031: Overview Screen

The **Material Document List** screen appears, as shown in Figure 7.51:

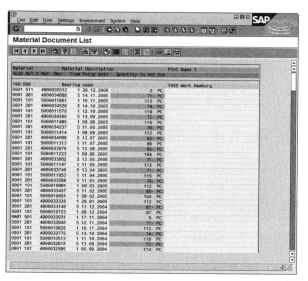

FIGURE 7.51 **Displaying the Material Document List screen**

Figure 7.51 displays the movement type, storage location, material document number, posting date, and quantity for a material document. For example, material document number 4900035512 contains the data for item 1 that was posted on 20.12.2006.

After discussing the material documents, let's discuss the reservation of stock.

RESERVING STOCK

The stock materials are reserved for various reasons, such as scheduled production, urgent delivery, and goods sampling. The reservation of the stock in the mySAP ERP system can be done either automatically or manually. The automatic reservation of stock is done on the basis of current stock level and the process cycle of material. In case of the shortage of materials in the stock, the mySAP ERP system automatically reserves the required amount of materials. You can view the quantity of automatically reserved material by using the MMBE transaction code. You can set the reservation of stocks at the plant level by configuring the following default values in the mySAP ERP system:

- **Setting goods movement for reservations**—Implies that you need to set the goods movement type associated with a reservation
- **Deleting reservations**—Implies that you need to set the default values for deleting wrong and incorrect reservations
- **Creating automatic reservations for storage locations**—Implies that you need to configure the automatic reservation of items under a plant
- **Posting goods movements reference to a reservation**—Implies that you need to set goods movement if a reservation is referenced
- **Setting indicators for creating a reservation**—Implies that you need to set an indicator for a reservation

Note: The reservation of material does not affect the quantity of material in the stock.

Apart from automatic reservation of stock, you can also reserve the stock manually in the mySAP ERP system by creating a manual reservation. In this section, you learn to create a manual reservation and use the reservation management system.

Let's first learn to create a manual reservation in the mySAP ERP system.

Creating a Manual Reservation

A manual reservation is a planned activity in comparison to automatic reservation. In contrast to an automatic reservation that is created based on the internal conditions of the inventory items, a manual reservation is created on the basis of the following external factors:

- **Movement type**—Represents the goods movement types associated with a manual reservation. The stock is reserved for internal consumption, transfer of goods to another stock, or futuristic evaluation. In each of these activities, proper movement types are used.
- **Requirement date**—Represents the date on which the forthcoming reservation is planned.
- **Quantity**—Represents the exact quantity of the reserved materials.
- **Movement indicator**—Represents the system tool to monitor the goods movement associated with reservation. Generally, this indicator is activated by default. If the goods movements are deferred in future, this option may be skipped.
- **FI indicator**—Represents the financial conditions and posting associated with a particular reservation. Similar to the movement indicator, it is enabled by default.
- **Deletion indicator**—Represents the deletion of a reservation in the mySAP ERP system. The storekeeper may delete a reservation if it is wrong or no longer needed.
- **Debit/Credit indicator**—Represents the accounting status of the reservation. If the reservation is allocated for the outbound process, it would be debited. However, if a stock is reserved for internal transfer, then it would be credited.

Perform the following steps to create a manual reservation of stock materials:

1. Navigate the following menu path (Figure 7.52):

Menu Path

SAP menu > Logistics > Materials Management > Inventory Management > Reservation > MB21 – Create

2. Double-click the **MB21 – Create** activity, as shown in Figure 7.52:

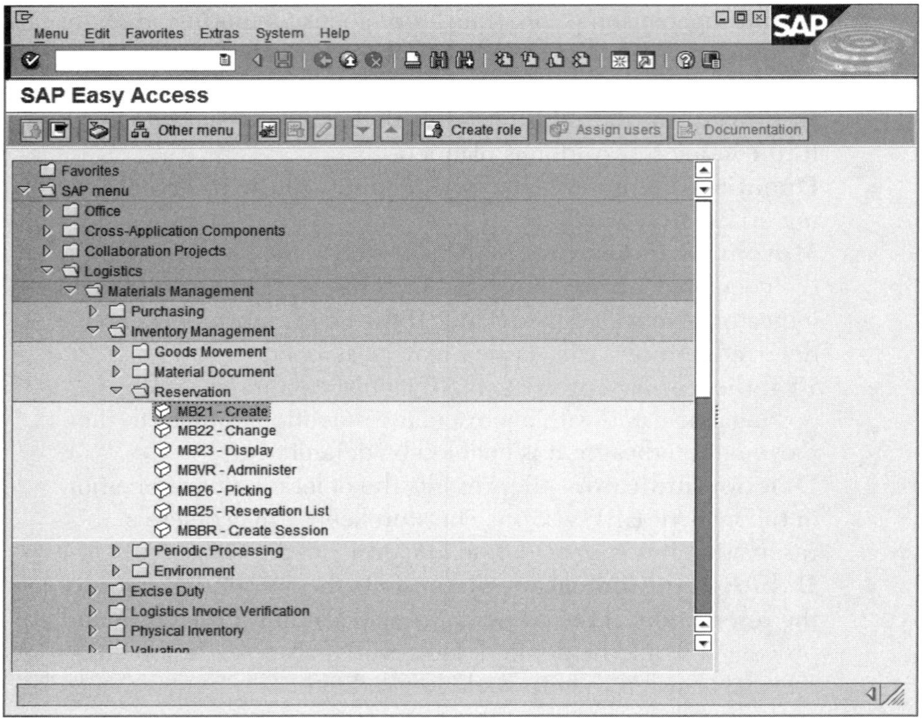

FIGURE 7.52   Displaying the menu path to create a manual reservation

The **Create Reservation: Initial Screen** appears (Figure 7.53).

3. Enter the base date in the **Base date** text box. In our case, we have entered `21.12.2009` (Figure 7.53).

4. Enter the movement type in the **Movement Type** text box. In our case, we have entered `501` (Figure 7.53).

5. Enter the plant in the **Plant** text box. In our case, we have entered `1000` (Figure 7.53).

6. Click the **Enter** (🗹) icon, as shown in Figure 7.53:

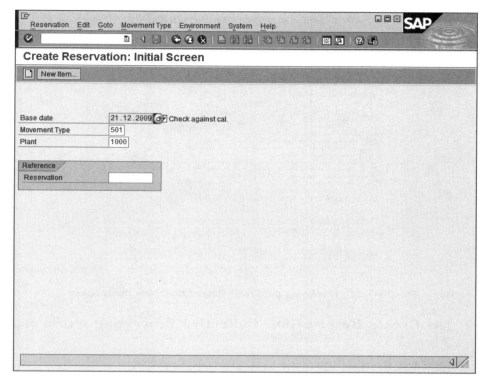

FIGURE 7.53   Displaying the Create Reservation: Initial Screen

The **Create Reservation: New Items** screen appears (Figure 7.54).

7. Enter the name of the material in the **Material** text box. In our case, we have entered `100-500` (Figure 7.54).
8. Enter the quantity in the **Quantity** text box. In our case, we have entered 2 (Figure 7.54).
9. Enter the unit of measurement in the **UnE** text box. In our case, we have entered `PC` (Figure 7.54).
10. Enter the plant in the **Plant** text box. In our case, we have entered `1000` (Figure 7.54).

11. Click the **Enter** (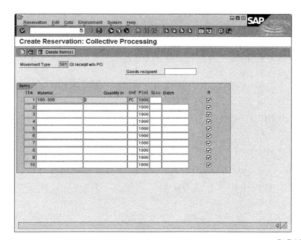) icon, as shown in Figure 7.54:

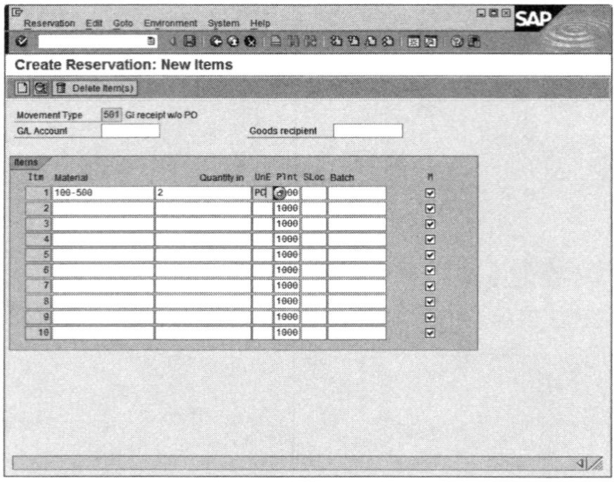

FIGURE 7.54   **Displaying the Create Reservation: New Items screen**

The **Create Reservation: Collective Processing** screen appears (Figure 7.55).

12. Click the **Save** (🖫) icon, as shown in Figure 7.55:

FIGURE 7.55   **Displaying the Create Reservation: Collective Processing screen**

The status bar displays the message that the manual reservation process completed successfully, as shown in Figure 7.56:

FIGURE 7.56   **Displaying the manual creation of a reservation**

Let's now discuss the use of the reservation management system.

Using the Reservation Management System

The reservation management system is used to manage stock reservation in the mySAP ERP system. The management of stock reservation is required for inventory management, production, and MRP processes. The stock material for periodic consumption should be planned and arranged before starting the production process. The primary function of maintaining the stock material before reservation is to ensure uninterrupted production flow. Therefore, before creating a reservation, the availability of sufficient materials in the stock should be ensured.

In the mySAP ERP system, the goods movement and allocated reserved quantity are examined on the basis of indicators. For example, the movement indicator checks the goods movement associated with a particular reservation.

Perform the following steps to control reservations in the mySAP ERP system:

1. Navigate the following menu path (Figure 7.57):

Menu Path

SAP menu > Logistics > Materials Management > Inventory Management > Reservation > MBVR – Administer

352

2. Click the **MBVR – Administer** activity as shown in Figure 7.57:

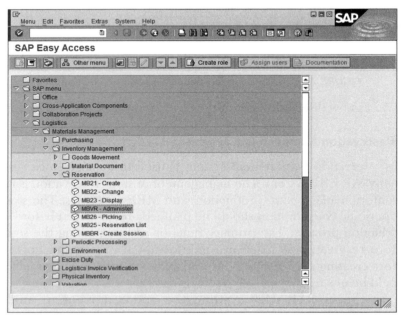

FIGURE 7.57   **Displaying the menu path to manage reservations**

The **Manage Reservations** screen appears (Figure 7.58).

3. Enter the reservation number in the **Reservation** text box. In our case, we have entered 4060 (Figure 7.58).
4. Click the **IMG Activity** (⊕) icon, as shown in Figure 7.58:

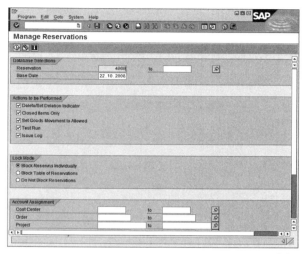

FIGURE 7.58   Displaying the Manage Reservations screen

The **Manage Reservations – Choose Reservations to be Deleted** screen appears (Figure 7.59).

5. Check the check box displaying the reservation number (Figure 7.59).
6. Click the **Save** (🖫) icon to save the changes, as shown in Figure 7.59:

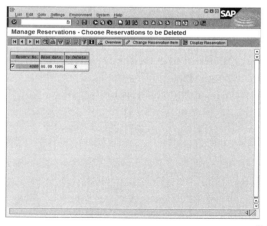

FIGURE 7.59   Displaying the Manage Reservations – Choose Reservations to be Deleted screen

The **Manage Reservations** screen appears again with a message displayed on the status bar confirming that the changes were saved (Figure 7.60).

7. Click the **Activity** (⊕) icon, as shown in Figure 7.60:

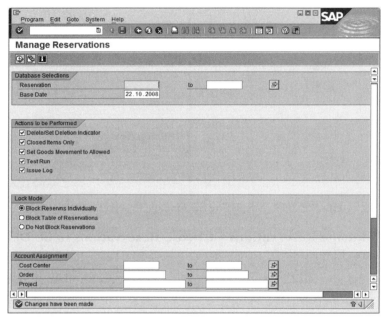

FIGURE 7.60 Displaying a message after deleting a reservation

The **Displaying Manage Reservations – Choose Reservations to be Deleted** screen appears again (Figure 7.61).

You should note that the reservation number, 4060, is not included in the list of reservation numbers, as shown in Figure 7.61:

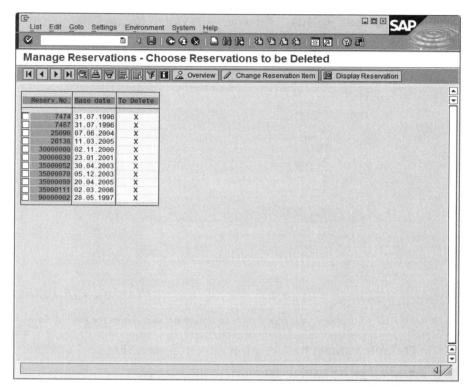

FIGURE 7.61   Displaying the reservation list after deletion

Apart from generating the reservation list, you can also change the retention date of a reservation.

Perform the following steps to change the retention date of a reservation:

1. Navigate the following menu path (Figure 7.62):

Menu Path

SAP Customizing Implementation Guide > Materials Management > Inventory Management and Physical Inventory > Reservation > Define Default Values

2. Click the **IMG Activity** (⊕) icon, as shown in Figure 7.62:

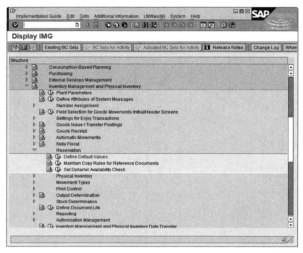

FIGURE 7.62   Displaying the menu path to define default values for reservations

The **Default Values: Reservation** screen appears (Figure 7.63).

3. Click the **Plant** button, as shown in Figure 7.63:

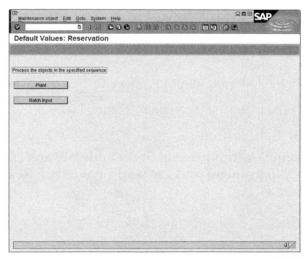

FIGURE 7.63   Displaying Default Values: Reservation screen

The **Change View "Setting: Reservation": Overview** screen appears (Figure 7.64).

4. Change the retention period of a plant, say the Hamburg plant denoted by plant code 0005, to 19 (Figure 7.64).
5. Click the **Save** (🖫) icon, as shown in Figure 7.64:

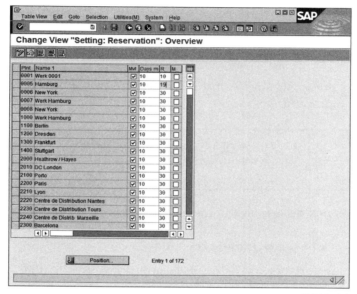

FIGURE 7.64   Displaying the Change View "Setting: Reservation": Overview screen

The status bar displays the message that the default values were changed successfully, as shown in Figure 7.65:

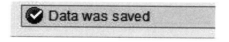

FIGURE 7.65   Displaying the successful changing of default retention time

Let's now discuss stock transfer in the next section.

TRANSFERRING STOCK

In an organization, stock is transferred from one storage location to another under a plant and from one plant to another under a particular company code. Stock can also be transferred from one company code to another.

In this section, you learn to:

- Transfer stock between storage locations
- Transfer stock between plants
- Transfer stock between company codes

The preceding stock transfers can be performed by using the one-step or two-step procedure.

> **Note:** The one-step and two-step stock transfer procedures are discussed in detail in Appendix A, Exploring the Procurement Processes under Various Business Scenarios.

Let's first discuss how to transfer stock between storage locations.

Transferring Stock between Storage Locations

Stock transfers between storage locations are usually done within a plant. The transferring of stock between one storage location to another helps an organization maintain a healthy stock reserve and reduces inventory carrying costs. In addition, proper stock transfer between a storage location and the production department helps provide an uninterrupted supply of materials. This also ensures that optimum stock levels are maintained at all times.

> **Note:** In the case of stock transfers between storage locations, the valuation of stock levels does not change.

As mentioned earlier, stock is transferred between storage locations by either the one-step or the two-step procedure. Let's now discuss and use both these procedures.

Transferring Stock Using the One-Step Procedure

As the name suggests, in the one-step procedure, material is transferred from one storage location to another in one step. The stock levels of the source and destination storage locations change in the one-step stock transfer. The MB1B transaction code is used to perform one-step stock transfer.

Perform the following steps to transfer stock by using the one-step transfer process:

1. Navigate the following menu path (Figure 7.66):

Menu Path

SAP menu > Logistics > Materials Management > Inventory Management > Goods Movement > MB1B – Transfer Posting

2. Double-click the **MB1B – Transfer Posting** activity, as shown in Figure 7.66:

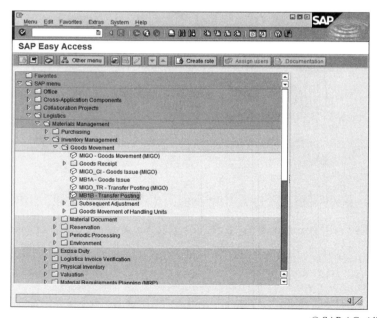

FIGURE 7.66   **Displaying the menu path to transfer stock**

The **Enter Transfer Posting: Initial Screen** appears (Figure 7.67).

3. Enter the document date in the **Document Date** text box. In our case, we have entered 22.11.2006 (Figure 7.67).
4. Enter the posting date in the **Posting Date** text box. In our case, we have entered 22.12.2006 (Figure 7.67).
5. Enter the movement type in the **Movement Type** text box. In our case, we have entered 311 (Figure 7.67).
6. Enter the plant in the **Plant** text box. In our case, we have entered 1000 (Figure 7.67).
7. Enter the storage location in the **Storage Location** text box. In our case, we have entered 0001 (Figure 7.67).
8. Click the **Enter** (✓) icon, as shown in Figure 7.67:

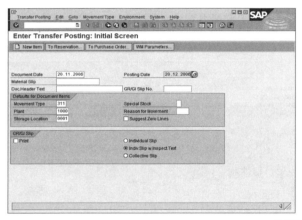

FIGURE 7.67   Displaying the Enter Transfer Posting: Initial Screen

The **Enter Transfer Posting: New Items** screen appears (Figure 7.68).

9. Enter the storage location to receive the stock in the **Rcvg SLoc** text box. In our case, we have entered the storage location code as 0002 (Figure 7.68).
10. Enter the name of the material in the **Material** text box. In our case, we have entered AS - 101 (Figure 7.68).
11. Enter the quantity in the **Quantity** text box. In our case, we have entered 20 (Figure 7.68).

12. Click the **Enter** (☑) icon, as shown in Figure 7.68:

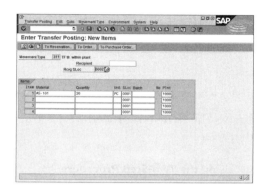

FIGURE 7.68   **Displaying the Enter Transfer Posting: New Items screen**

The **Enter Transfer Posting: Collective Processing** screen appears (Figure 7.69).

13. Click the **Save** (🖫) icon. The stock transfer is posted from storage location 0001 to 0002, as shown in Figure 7.69:

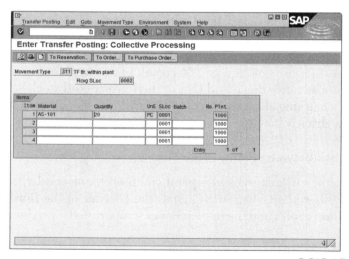

FIGURE 7.69   **Displaying the Enter Transfer Posting: Collective Processing screen**

The status bar displays the following message after the successful posting of the stock transfer, shown in Figure 7.70:

FIGURE 7.70   **Displaying a message after the successful posting of the stock transfer**

Let's now discuss the two-step procedure for transferring stock from one location to another location.

Transferring Stock Using the Two-Step Procedure

The two-step stock transfer procedure is used to transfer stock in two stages. The first stage consists of removing material from the source stock and placing it in the transit stock, which is then transported to the purchasing organization. In the second stage, the organization removes the material from the transit stock and places it in the destination stock. The two-step procedure is generally used to transfer stock from distant vendors. In addition, two-step stock transfers are made from the unrestricted stock.

In the mySAP ERP system, in the first step, the material is removed from a storage location by using the 313 movement type and placed in the transit stock. As a result, the stock level of the unrestricted stock in the source storage location comes down and the transit stock level goes up. The next step is to transfer the material from the transit stock to the receiving storage location by using the 315 movement type. As a result of this transfer, the stock level of the transit stock comes down and that of the unrestricted stock goes up.

After learning about the process of transferring stock from storage locations, let's now discuss how stock is transferred between plants.

Transferring Stock between Plants

The shortage of materials in a plant can be replenished by transferring stock from another plant. Activities such as the transfer of the finished stock to the distribution center and the movement of scrap from the production house to the recycling plant are covered under the transfer of stocks between plants. Similar to the transfer of stock between storage locations, stock transfer between plants is also implemented by using the one-step and two-step procedures.

Let's discuss stock transfer between plants using the one-step procedure.

Transferring Stock Using the One-Step Procedure

The one-step transfer procedure to transfer stock between two plants is similar to the one-step procedure to transfer stock between storage locations discussed earlier. The 301 movement type and the MB1B transaction code are used to transfer stock between plants in the one-step stock transfer procedure.

Perform the following steps to transfer stock between plants using the one-step transfer procedure:

1. Navigate the following menu path (Figure 7.66):

Menu Path

SAP menu > Logistics > Materials Management > Inventory Management > Goods Movement > MB1B – Transfer Posting

2. Double-click the **MB1B – Transfer Posting** activity (Figure 7.66). The **Enter Transfer Posting: Initial Screen** appears (Figure 7. 66).
3. Enter the document date in the **Document Date** text box. In our case, we have entered 11.11.2006 (Figure 7.71).
4. Enter the posting date in the **Posting Date** text box. In our case, we have entered 11.12.2006 (Figure 7.71).
5. Enter the movement type in the **Movement Type** text box. In our case, we have entered 301 (Figure 7.71).
6. Enter the code of the plant in the **Plant** text box. In our case, we have entered 3000 (Figure 7.71).
7. Enter the storage location in the **Storage Location** text box. In our case, we have entered 0001 (Figure 7.71).

8. Click the **Enter** (✓) icon, as shown in Figure 7.71:

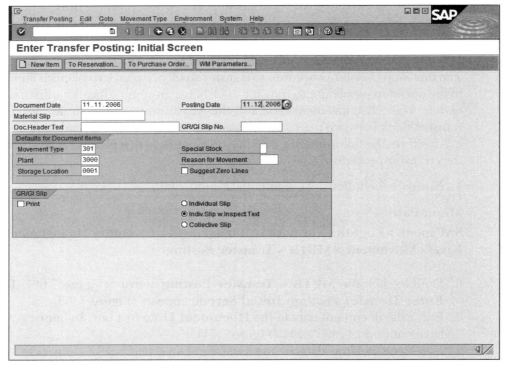

FIGURE 7.71   Displaying the Enter Transfer Posting: Initial Screen

The **Enter Transfer Posting: New Items** screen appears (Figure 7.72).

9. Enter the name of the material in the **Material** text box. In our case, we have entered EKH - 009 (Figure 7.72).
10. Enter the quantity in the **Quantity** text box. In our case, we have entered 1 (Figure 7.72).
11. Enter the unit of measurement in the **UnE** text box. In our case, we have entered EA (Figure 7.72).
12. Enter the batch number in the **Batch** text box. In our case, we have entered 0000000250 (Figure 7.72).
13. Click the **Enter** (✓) icon, as shown in Figure 7.72:

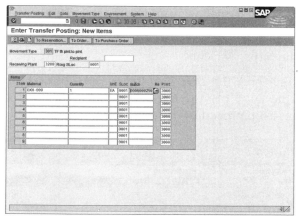

FIGURE 7.72 Displaying the Enter Transfer Posting: New Items screen

Note: In some cases, when you execute the data after entering the details in the **Enter Transfer Posting: Initial Screen** (Figure 7.71), the batch is automatically assigned, as shown in Figure 7.73:

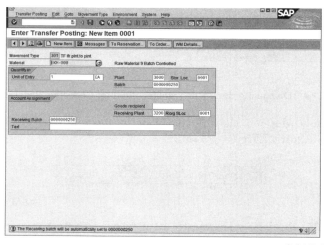

FIGURE 7.73 Displaying the Enter Transfer Posting: New Item 0001 screen

The **Enter Transfer Posting: Collective Processing** screen appears (Figure 7.74).

14. Click the **Save** (⊟) icon.

The stock transfer of the EKH - 009 material is posted from the 0001 storage location of the 3000 plant to the 0001 storage location of the 3200 plant by using the one-step procedure, as shown in Figure 7.74:

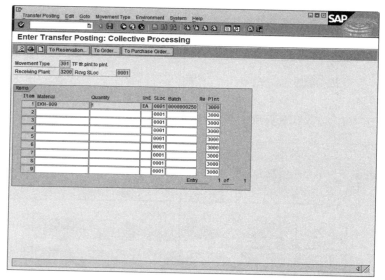

FIGURE 7.74   **Displaying the Enter Transfer Posting: Collective Processing screen**

The following message appears after the successful posting of the transaction, shown in Figure 7.75:

FIGURE 7.75   **Posting a stock transfer using the one-step stock transfer procedure**

Let's now discuss the two-step procedure.

Transferring Stock by Using the Two-Step Procedure

As the name suggests, the two-step stock procedure to transfer stock between plants consists of two stages. In the first stage, the material to be transferred is removed from the supplying plant by using the 303 movement type. As a result, the stock level of the supplying plant comes down. The next step is to move the material from the supplying plant to the receiving plant by using the 305 movement type. As a result, the stock level of the receiving plant goes up.

Next, let's discuss how to transfer stock between company codes.

Transferring Stock between Company Codes

Company code transfer refers to the transfer of stock between two company codes. Stock transfer between company codes is done either by using the one-step or two-step transfer procedure.

After discussing the various ways to transfer stock in an organization, let's move on to a new topic in which we discuss the traditional methods of inventory management.

USING TRADITIONAL METHODS OF INVENTORY MANAGEMENT

The physical inventory is the actual number of materials that can be counted in the inventory. The counting and management of the physical inventory items is done manually and is therefore termed as the traditional method of inventory management. The number of items in the physical inventory may be different from that calculated by the mySAP ERP system. The reasons for this are many, such as the posting of wrong or duplicate entries that the mySAP ERP system takes into account in the counting process.

The physical inventory management process produces quick and accurate results. This process allows you to bypass certain system-specific constraints in the mySAP ERP system.

After the physical inventory management process is completed, the result is compared with that produced by the mySAP ERP system. Any difference in the comparison is analyzed and an inventory variance document is produced. Thereafter, the necessary adjustments are made to match the results, which include rechecking the data and re-executing the counting process in the mySAP ERP system. The management of physical inventory involves counting of the unrestricted, quality-inspection, or blocked stock. In addition, returnable stock and consignments are also covered under physical inventory management. The physical inventory management process is performed periodically, say on a yearly basis. However, depending upon the specific requirements of an organization, it can also be implemented on a frequent basis.

In this section, you learn the following aspects of inventory management:

- Creating the physical inventory
- Creating the physical inventory document
- Entering the physical inventory count
- Preparing the difference list
- Resolving the missing items
- Recounting material
- Posting the physical inventory

Let's begin by discussing how to create the physical inventory.

Creating the Physical Inventory

A physical inventory is created when the items in the inventory are physically counted. Before creating the physical inventory, you need to configure the count procedure. For example, different counting methods are used for finished products and raw materials. In addition, you can set the priority for the way the items are to be counted. The configuration of the count procedure is important to ensure the transparency of the process and correctness of the results.

Variance may arise when the results of the manual process of counting and the one displayed by the mySAP ERP system are different. If the variance is slight, the business process is not affected. However, if the variance is large, then it may severely affect the production process. For example, variances in the count of finished goods may affect the delivery processes. Therefore, the process of counting the physical inventory must be conducted carefully. The following procedures are used to count the physical inventory:

- **Running the stock on hand report**—Refers to the process of estimating the number of goods in the unrestricted, quality inspection, and blocked stocks. This activity is performed to get an overview of the levels of stock before beginning the actual counting process. The MB52 transaction code is used to create the stock on hand report.

Perform the following steps to create a stock on hand report:

1. Enter the MB52 transaction code in the **SAP Easy Access** screen (Figure 7.76).
2. Press the **Enter** icon, as shown in Figure 7.76:

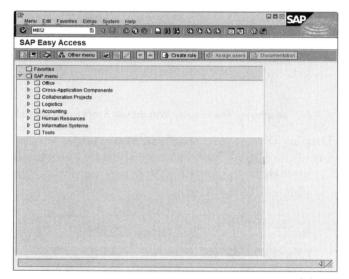

FIGURE 7.76   **Creating the physical inventory**

The **Display Warehouse Stocks of Material** screen appears (Figure 7.77).

3. Enter the name of the material in the **Material** text box. In our case, we have entered 100 - 300 (Figure 7.77).
4. Enter the plant in the **Plant** text box. In our case, we have entered 1000 (Figure 7.77).
5. Enter the storage location in the **Storage Location** text box. In our case, we have entered 0001 (Figure 7.77).

6. Click the **IMG Activity** (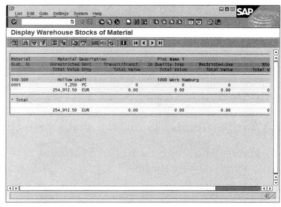) icon, as shown in Figure 7.77:

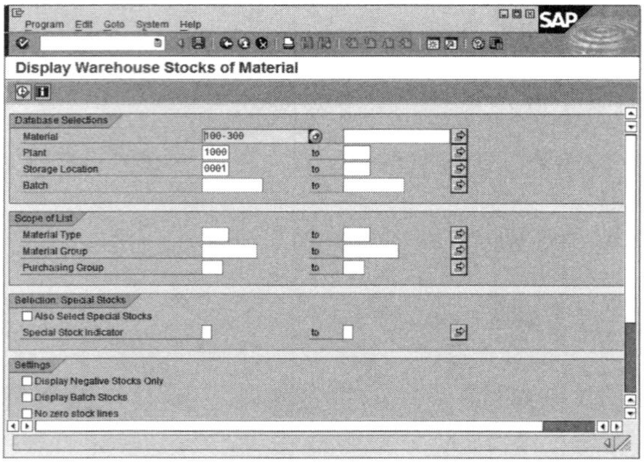

FIGURE 7.77   **Displaying the Display Warehouse Stocks of Material screen**

The **Display Warehouse Stocks of Material** screen displays the stock on hand report of the 100 - 300 material, which includes the description of the material (Hollow shaft), quantity (1,250 pieces), and value (254, 912.50 EUR), as shown in Figure 7.78:

FIGURE 7.78   **Displaying the stock on hand report**

- **Processing and posting items affecting count**—Refers to the factors that affect the physical count, such as the inward or outward movement of goods, goods receipts, stock transfers, inventory adjustments, and sales orders. You need to consider the factors affecting the physical count before posting the data in the relevant books. This helps in providing an updated result of the physical inventory count.
- **Separating the sold items**—Refers to isolating those items from the counting process for which the sales processes have been finalized. This is done to avoid data redundancy and confusion in the counting process.
- **Putting away the counted items**—Refers to the process of separating the counted items from the uncounted items.
- **Halting the goods movements**—Refers to halting the inward or outward goods movements during the physical inventory count process.

In the mySAP ERP system, the physical inventory count document is prepared after the completion of the physical inventory process.

Let's now learn to create the physical inventory document.

Creating the Physical Inventory Document

Physical inventory documents are used to keep a record of each physical inventory count in the mySAP ERP system. The MI01 transaction code is used to create the physical inventory document.

Perform the following steps to create the physical inventory document:

1. Navigate the following menu path (Figure 7.79):

Menu Path

SAP menu > Logistics > Materials Management > Physical Inventory > Physical Inventory Document > MI01 – Create

2. Click the **MI01 – Create** activity, as shown in Figure 7.79:

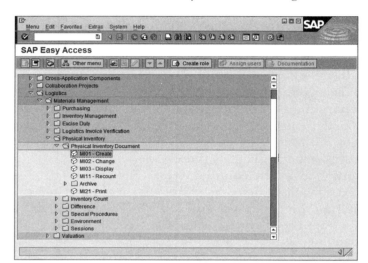

FIGURE 7.79 Displaying the menu path to create the physical inventory document

The **Create Physical Inventory Document: Initial Screen** appears (Figure 7.80).

3. Enter the document date in the **Document Date** text box. In our case, we have entered 19.11.2006 (Figure 7.80).
4. Enter the posting date in the **Posting Date** text box. In our case, we have entered 19.12.2006 (Figure 7.80).
5. Enter the plant in the **Plant** text box. In our case, we have entered 1000 (Figure 7.80).
6. Enter the storage location in the **Storage Location** text box. In our case, we have entered 0002 (Figure 7.80).
7. Click the **Enter** (🗹) icon to create the physical inventory document, as shown in Figure 7.80:

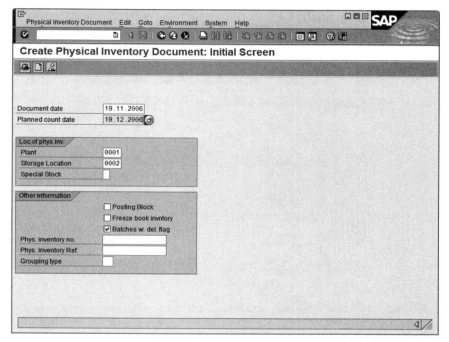

FIGURE 7.80   **Creating the physical inventory document**

Figure 7.80 displays the following check boxes that you can select to create the physical inventory document:

- **Posting Block**—Specifies that the goods are counted but not yet posted in the books. You can select the **Posting Block** check box when the planned date for the physical inventory count is different from the date on which the results of the counting are actually posted in the books, as shown in Figure 7.81:

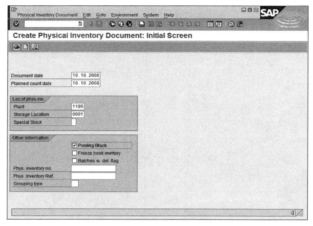

FIGURE 7.81   Specifying the posting block for the physical inventory document

- **Freezing book inventory**—Refers to the freezing of the book inventory balance if the physical inventory count process is not completed. In this situation, the **Freeze book inventory** check box is selected, as shown in Figure 7.82:

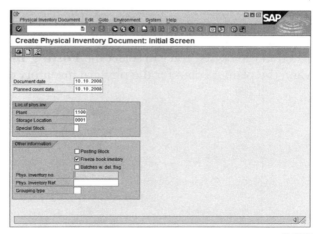

FIGURE 7.82   Freezing the book inventory for the physical inventory document

- **Batches w. del. flag**—Refers to counting the items that have been earlier flagged for deletion. The **Batches w. del. flag** check box is selected to include the deleted batch items when creating the physical inventory document, as shown in Figure 7.83:

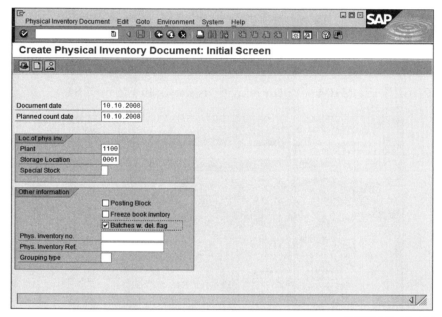

FIGURE 7.83   Including deleted items in the physical inventory document

After discussing the physical inventory document, let's learn to enter the physical inventory count in the mySAP ERP system.

Entering the Physical Inventory Count

After performing the prerequisite steps for the physical inventory count, such as preparing the stock on hand report and physical inventory document, you can begin with the process of counting the physical inventory. The results of the counting are entered in a sheet known as the physical inventory count sheet.

The actual counting process is done by the employees of the organization and the discrepancies in the counting are eliminated. After the counting process is completed, the result is entered in the mySAP ERP system by using the MI04 transaction code.

Perform the following steps to enter counting results in the count sheet to the physical inventory document:

1. Navigate the following menu path (Figure 7.84):

Menu Path

SAP menu > Logistics > Materials Management > Physical Inventory > Inventory Count > MI04 – Enter

2. Click the **MI04 – Enter** activity, as shown in Figure 7.84:

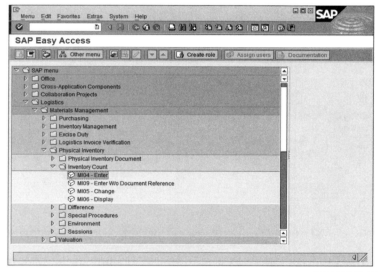

FIGURE 7.84   Displaying the menu path to enter the physical inventory count

The **Enter Inventory Count: Initial Screen** appears (Figure 7.85).

3. Enter the counting date and physical inventory count document number from the physical inventory count sheet, as shown in Figure 7.85:

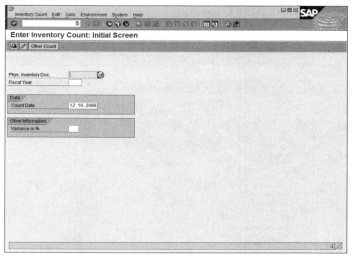

FIGURE 7.85 **Displaying Enter Inventory Count: Initial Screen**

If there is any error in counting the physical inventory items, you can restart the process by using the transaction code `MI05`.

Now, let's proceed to discuss the difference list.

Preparing the Difference List

The difference list is prepared after the counting process of the physical inventory is completed and the results have been matched with the inventory details of the mySAP ERP system. In case a difference arises in the results of the manual counting and the counting shown by the mySAP ERP system, a report is prepared to analyze the reasons for the difference, based on which the appropriate remedial actions can be taken.

Perform the following steps to prepare a difference list:

1. Navigate the following menu path (Figure 7.86):

Menu Path

SAP menu > Logistics > Materials Management > Physical Inventory > Difference > MI20 – Difference List

2. Click the **MI20 – Difference List** activity, as shown in Figure 7.86:

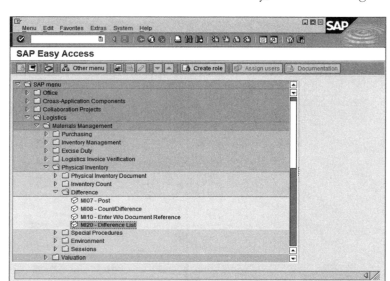

FIGURE 7.86 Displaying the menu path to create a difference list

The **List of Inventory Differences** screen appears (Figure 7.87).

3. Enter the name of the material in the **Material** text box. In our case, we have entered CPF10104 (Figure 7.87).
4. Enter the plant in the **Plant** text box. In our case, we have entered the plant as 0001 (Figure 7.87).
5. Enter the storage location in the **Storage Location** text box. In our case, we have entered 0002 (Figure 7.87).
6. Click the **Execute** (⊕) icon, as shown in Figure 7.87:

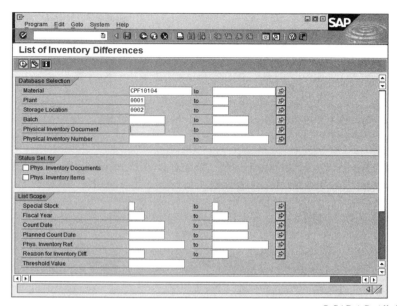

FIGURE 7.87   Displaying the List of Inventory Differences screen

The difference list is generated.

Let's now discuss the various ways used to resolve the issue of missing items after the physical inventory count.

Resolving the Missing Items Issue

While comparing the results of the counting of the physical inventory with the data in the mySAP ERP system, some of the items may be found to be missing. In other words, the items that were earlier shown to exist in the mySAP ERP system are not found while counting the physical inventory. Different organizations use different processes to deal with missing items. Sometimes, an auditor may be called to resolve the difference in the item count. If the items are found, then an adjustment is made to offset the difference. However, most of the time, a variance document is prepared to deal with the missing items. If the number of missing items is large, the physical inventory is recounted.

Recounting the Material

The decision to recount the physical inventory is taken if there is a large difference between the inventory count shown in the mySAP ERP system and the physical count. Perform the following steps to learn how to recount the physical inventory:

1. Navigate the following menu path (Figure 7.88):

Menu Path

SAP menu > Logistics > Materials Management > Physical Inventory > Physical Inventory Document > MI11 – Recount

2. Click the **MI11 – Recount** activity, as shown in Figure 7.88:

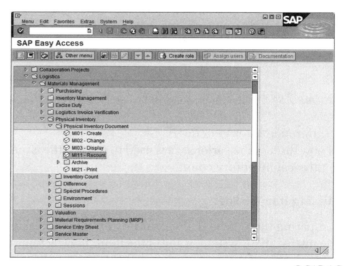

FIGURE 7.88   Displaying the menu path to recount the physical inventory

The **Enter Recount: Initial Screen** appears (Figure 7.89).

3. Enter the physical inventory document number in the **Phys. Inventory Doc**. text box (Figure 7.89).
4. Click the **Enter** (☑) icon, as shown in Figure 7.89:

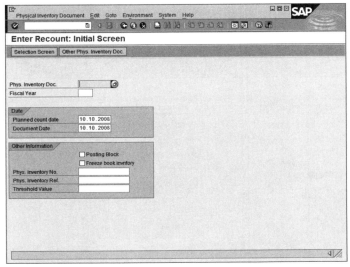

FIGURE 7.89   **Displaying the Enter Recount: Initial Screen**

The details of the recount are displayed on the screen.

Let's now learn to post the physical inventory in the mySAP ERP system.

Posting the Physical Inventory

After counting the physical inventory, the details of the count are entered in the mySAP ERP system. The results of the physical inventory count are posted on the basis of the physical inventory document. In this case, the physical inventory document number is entered in the mySAP ERP system along with the posting date. The `MI07` transaction code is used to post the details of the physical inventory count.

Perform the following steps to post the physical inventory by using the physical inventory document:

1. Navigate the following menu path (Figure 7.90):

Menu Path

SAP menu > Logistics > Materials Management > Physical Inventory > Difference > MI07 – Post

2. Click the **MI07 – Post activity**, as shown in Figure 7.90:

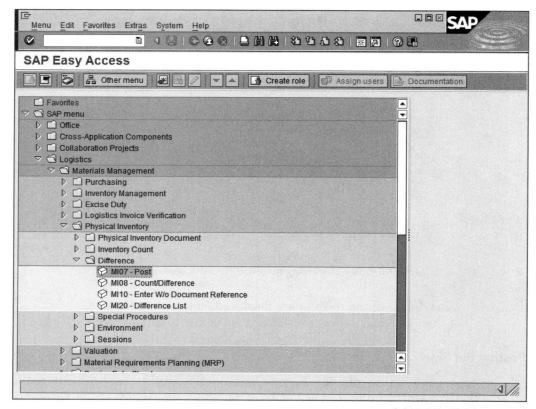

FIGURE 7.90   Posting the physical inventory with the physical inventory document

The **Post Inventory Difference: Initial Screen** appears (Figure 7.91).

3. Enter the physical inventory document number in the **Phys. Inventory Doc**. text box and the posting date in the **Posting Date** text box (Figure 7.91).

4. Click the **Enter** (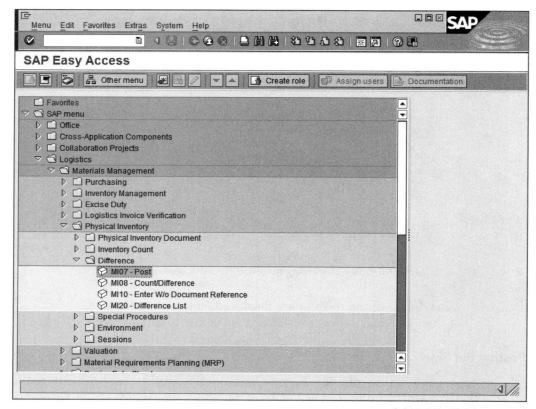) icon to post the physical inventory, as shown in Figure 7.91:

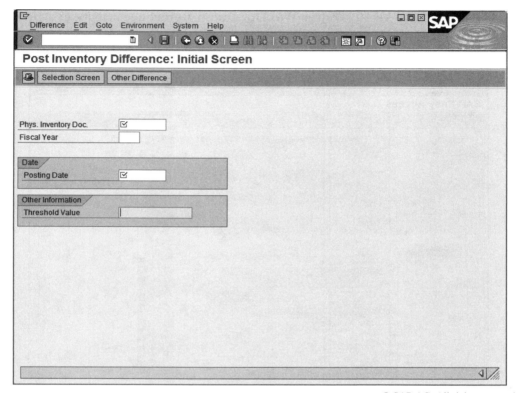

FIGURE 7.91   **Displaying the Post Inventory Difference: Initial Screen**

You can also post the physical inventory without the physical inventory document number by using the `MI10` transaction code.

Perform the following steps to post the physical inventory without using a physical inventory document number:

1. Navigate the following menu path (Figure 7.92):

Menu Path

SAP menu > Logistics > Materials Management > Physical Inventory > Difference > MI10 – Enter W/o Document Reference

2. Click the **MI10 – Enter W/o Document Reference** activity, as shown in Figure 7.92:

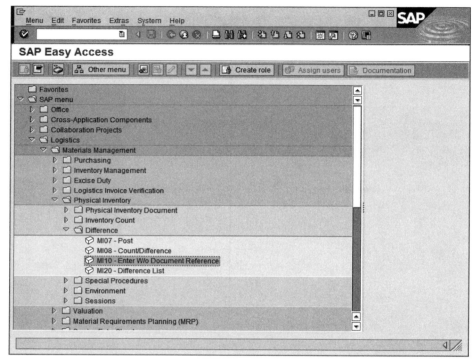

FIGURE 7.92   Displaying the menu path to post the physical inventory without the physical inventory document

The **Post Document, Count, and Difference: Initial Screen** appears (Figure 7.93).

3. Enter the count date in the **Count date** text box. In our case, we have entered 19.11.2006 (Figure 7.93).

4. Enter document date in the **Document date** text box. In our case, we have entered 11.12.2006 (Figure 7.93).
5. Enter the plant in the **Plant** text box. In our case, we have entered 1000 (Figure 7.93).
6. Enter the storage location in the **Storage Location** text box. In our case, we have entered 0001 (Figure 7.93).
7. Click the **Enter** (☑) icon, as shown in Figure 7.93:

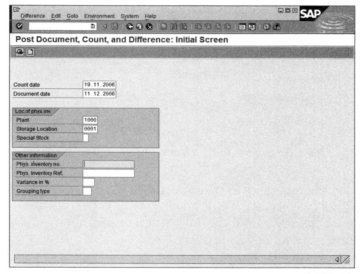

FIGURE 7.93 Displaying the Post Document, Count, and Difference: Initial Screen

The **Post Document, Count, and Difference: New Items** screen appears (Figure 7.94).
8. Enter the name of the material in the **Material Description** text box. In our case, we have entered AS - 100 (Figure 7.94).
9. Enter the quantity in the **Quantity** text box. In our case, we have entered 20 (Figure 7.94).

10. Click the **Save** (⊟) icon to post the data, as shown in Figure 7.94:

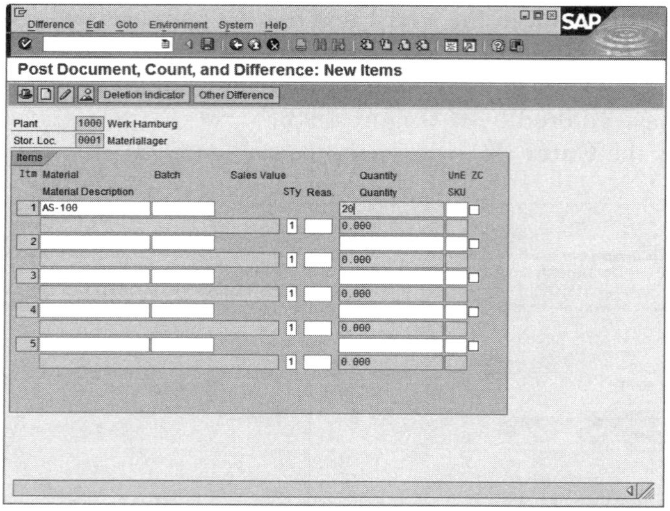

FIGURE 7.94 **Displaying the Post Document, Count, and Difference: New Items screen**

The status bar shows the following message after posting the physical inventory, as shown in Figure 7.95:

FIGURE 7.95 **Posting the physical inventory**

Let's now review the main topics discussed in the chapter.

SUMMARY

In this chapter, you learned about the implementation of the inventory management process in the mySAP ERP system. The different types of stock maintained in an organization, such as unrestricted, quality inspection, and blocked stock have been explained in detail. You also learned about the movement of goods in organizations, such as stock transfer from one plant, storage location, or company code to another. Toward the end, the chapter discussed the traditional method of inventory management.

In the next chapter, you will learn about how to implement the invoice verification process.

Chapter **8**

IMPLEMENTING THE INVOICE VERIFICATION PROCESS

Invoice verification refers to the process of checking the incoming invoices with respect to the price, content, and quantity of the material. This process ensures error-free transactions on both the vendor as well as customer's side. Invoice verification forms an important part not only of the Material Management (MM) module but also of the Financial Accounting (FI) module of the SAP® system. In the MM module, invoice verification is accomplished in three steps—verifying the purchase order sent to the vendor, verifying the goods received by the customer, and finally verifying the invoice sent by the vendor to the customer. If there is no problem in any of these three steps, the invoice is posted in the mySAP™ ERP system and the payment is sent to the vendor. In other words, invoice verification helps complete the material procurement process, which starts with a purchase requisition being sent from the customer to the vendor and ends with the goods or payment received from the vendor or the customer, respectively.

In this chapter, you will learn to work with the standard method of invoice verification, and the Evaluated Receipt Settlement (ERS) process. You also will learn how to park an invoice using the **Park Incoming Invoice** screen. The chapter further explores different types of variances, such as quantity variance and price variance. Next, various methods to block an invoice are discussed in detail. Finally, you will learn how to release a blocked invoice.

WORKING WITH THE STANDARD METHOD OF INVOICE VERIFICATION

The standard method of invoice verification ensures that the vendors are paid the correct amount at the right time. The steps included in the standard method of invoice verification are:

1. Recording the vendor invoice details
2. Matching of the details with the original invoices
3. Correcting the mismatches, if any
4. Releasing payment for the invoices that are recorded correctly
5. Recording the details for audit purposes

You can complete the process of invoice verification by just entering the invoice details and posting the invoice in the mySAP ERP system. However, it is recommended to follow all the steps to minimize/avoid the chances of any error in the invoice verification process.

In this section of the chapter, you will learn to enter the invoice details and post an invoice.

Entering the Invoice Details

An invoice consists of various types of information, such as the name of the organization that has issued the invoice, the transaction to which the invoice refers to, and the amount of tax the purchasing organization has to pay. When an invoice is received at the accounts payable department, the first step that is performed is the invoice verification process. To verify an invoice, you need to enter the invoice details in the system.

Let's perform the following steps to enter the invoice details in the system:

1. Navigate the following menu path (Figure 8.1):

Menu Path

SAP menu > Logistics > Materials Management > Logistics Invoice Verification > Document Entry > MIRO – Enter Invoice

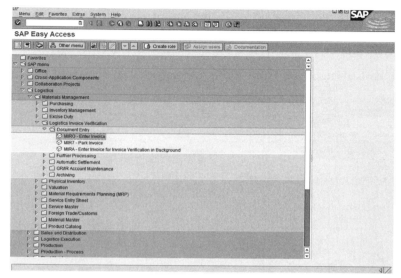

FIGURE 8.1   **Displaying the menu path to enter invoice details**

The **Enter Company Code** dialog box opens, as shown in Figure 8.2:

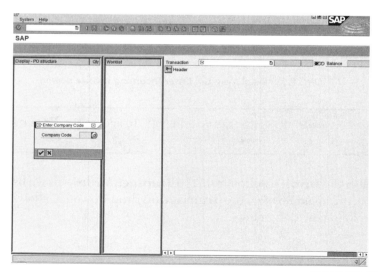

FIGURE 8.2   **Entering the company code**

2. Enter the company code of the organization for which you are creating the invoice in the **Company Code** text box (Figure 8.2) and press the ENTER key.

The **Enter Incoming Invoice** screen appears, as shown in Figure 8.3:

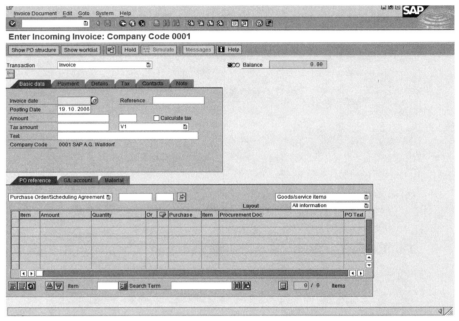

FIGURE 8.3   Displaying the Enter Incoming Invoice screen

Note: You can also use the MIRO transaction code to access the **Enter Incoming Invoice** screen directly.

3. Select the **Invoice** option from the **Transaction** drop-down list (Figure 8.3). Apart from an invoice, the **Transaction** drop-down list allows you to create the following documents:

        □ Credit memo
        □ Subsequent debit
        □ Subsequent credit

4. Enter the invoice date in the **Invoice date** text box (Figure 8.3) of the **Basic** data tab. You should note that a future date must not be entered as the invoice date.
5. Enter the amount of invoice in the **Amount** text box (Figure 8.3) of the **Basic data** tab. The amount of the invoice should be the same as shown in the invoice of the vendor.
6. Select the **Calculate tax** check box (Figure 8.3) of the **Basic data** tab. This check box helps in calculating the tax automatically when the invoice is posted.
7. Click the **Enter** (✅) icon to enter the invoice details.

After entering the invoice details in the system, you need to post the invoice. However, before actually posting the invoice, you can make a trial posting of the invoice. You can simulate the invoice posting by clicking **Invoice Document > Simulate Document** in the header menu. This process does not post the invoice, but only ascertains if the invoice posting is being performed successfully or not. If the simulation process is unable to post the invoice, error messages are posted to the message log indicating the reasons why the invoice cannot be posted.

Posting an Invoice

Posting an invoice helps in passing the invoice information to the FI module for updating the general ledger accounts. In other words, when you post an invoice, different modules of the SAP system are updated in the following ways:

- Invoice documents are generated in the MM and FI modules.
- The general ledger (G/L) accounts are debited and credited.
- The invoice posting is recorded in the production order (PO), and simultaneously the PO history is updated.
- The vendor is informed about the payment.

While posting an invoice, you should take care when executing the payment process. The payment process is defined in the FI module and can be executed by navigating through the following menu path:

Menu Path

SAP menu > Accounting > Financial Accounting > Accounts Payable > Periodic Processing > Payments. You can also use the F110 transaction code for defining the payment process while posting an invoice.

In this section of the chapter, you learned about the standard method of invoice verification. Let's now learn about the ERS process in SAP MM.

WORKING WITH THE EVALUATED RECEIPT SETTLEMENT PROCESS

The ERS process is used to settle purchase orders and goods receipts automatically. It is an alternative to the manual invoice entry process in the SAP MM module. In this process, the organization settles the vendor's liabilities and prepares the payment statement without the vendor submitting the invoice for payment. In other words, ERS can be defined as a two-way process, in which the goods receipts and purchase orders are matched and posted without an invoice. Since no invoice is involved in ERS, this process is mainly based on cooperation and trust between the customer and vendor; and therefore, is not a standard process for most companies. The ERS process is best suited in organizations where the sale and purchase of materials is between different departments of the same organization.

The various advantages of using the ERS process are:

- Checking for any variations in actual price and quantity with those mentioned in the invoices
- Making the purchasing process fast
- Paying the vendor on the receipt of goods

You can configure the ERS process by selecting the ERS indicator in the vendor master record. Let's perform the following steps to configure ERS in the vendor master record:

1. Navigate the following menu path (Figure 8.4):

Menu Path

SAP menu > Logistics > Materials Management > Purchasing > Master Data > Vendor > Central > XK02 – Change

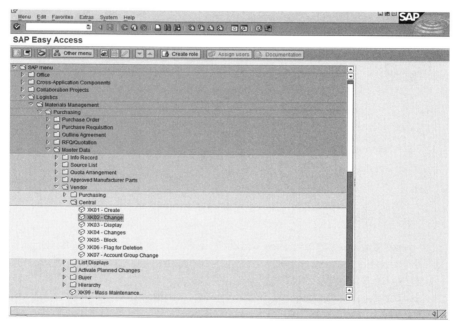

FIGURE 8.4   Displaying the menu path to change the vendor master record

After navigating the menu path, the **Change Vendor: Initial Screen** appears, as shown in Figure 8.5:

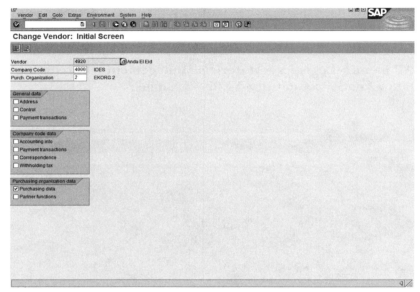

FIGURE 8.5   **Changing the vendor master record**

2. Enter the vendor number in the **Vendor** text box (Figure 8.5).
3. Enter the company code of the vendor in the **Company Code** text box (Figure 8.5).
4. Enter the purchasing organization of the vendor in the **Purch. Organization** text box (Figure 8.5).
5. Select the **Purchasing data** check box in the **Purchasing organization** data group (Figure 8.5) and press the ENTER key.

The **Change Vendor: Purchasing data** screen opens, as shown in Figure 8.6:

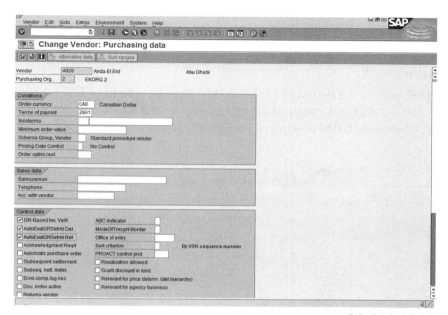

FIGURE 8.6   Displaying the Change vendor: purchasing data screen

6. Select the **GR-Based Inv. Verif., AutoEvalGRSetmt Del.,** and **AutoEvalGRSetmt Ret** check boxes in the **Control data** group of the **Change Vendor: Purchasing data** screen, as shown in Figure 8.6.
7. Click the **Save** (🖫) icon to save the changes.

A system message indicating that the changes have been made appears in the message log of the **Change Vendor: Initial Screen**.

Note: If you want to implement the default invoice verification process, clear the **GR-Based Inv. Verif., AutoEvalGRSetmt Del.,** and **AutoEvalGRSetmt Ret** check boxes in the **Change Vendor: Purchasing data** screen.

You can also implement the ERS process for a specific plant or vendor by navigating through the following menu path:

Menu Path

SAP menu > Logistics > Materials Management > Logistics Invoice Verification > Automatic Settlement > MRRL – Evaluated Receipt Settlement (ERS). Figure 8.7 shows the preceding menu path:

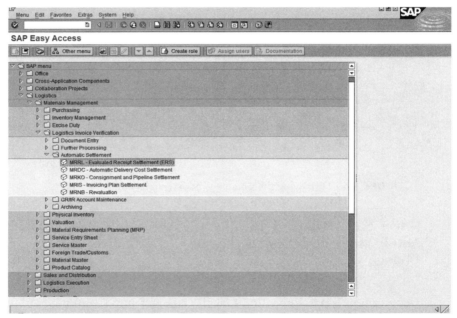

FIGURE 8.7   Displaying the menu path to configure ERS

The **Evaluated Receipt Settlement (ERS) with Logistics Invoice Verification** screen appears, as shown in Figure 8.8:

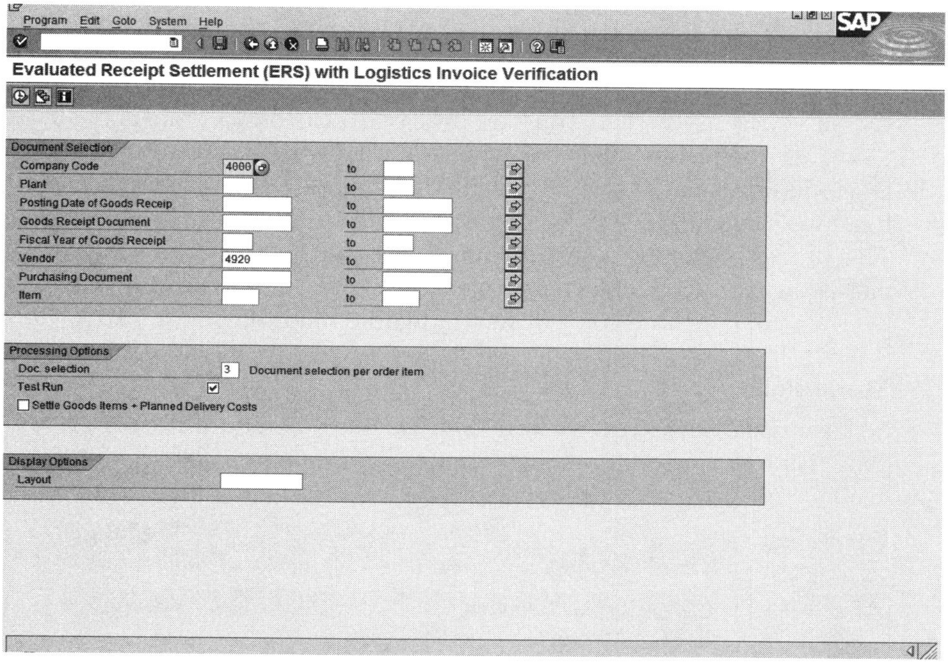

FIGURE 8.8   Configuring ERS with logistics invoice verification

Note: You can also use the MRRL transaction code to access the **Evaluated Receipt Settlement (ERS) with Logistics Invoice Verification** screen.

You can restrict the implementation of the ERS process to a certain plant or vendor by specifying the company code and vendor information in the **Company Code** and **Vendor** text boxes, respectively, in the **Evaluated Receipt Settlement (ERS) with Logistics Invoice Verification** screen.

After learning about the ERS process, let's now learn how to park an invoice.

PARKING AN INVOICE

Parking an invoice means to create an invoice with full detail, but not posting it. Consider a scenario where you have prepared an invoice and are about to post it. However, you just recollect that some other information, which is not available at the moment, also needs to be filled in before posting. Therefore, you put that invoice on hold, i.e., it is not posted until you get the required information. This process of putting an invoice on hold is known as parking an invoice. The parked invoice is editable, i.e., you can implement any type of changes in it.

You can park an invoice by navigating the following menu path:

Menu Path

SAP menu > Logistics Invoice Verification > Document Entry > MIR7 – Park Invoice. Figure 8.9 shows the preceding menu path:

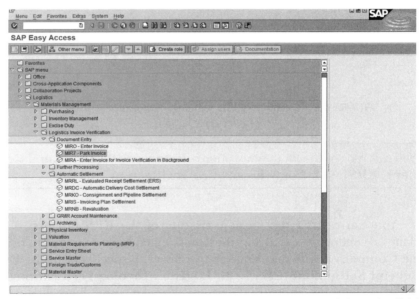

FIGURE 8.9   Displaying the menu path to park an invoice

The **Park Incoming Invoice** screen opens, as shown in Figure 8.10:

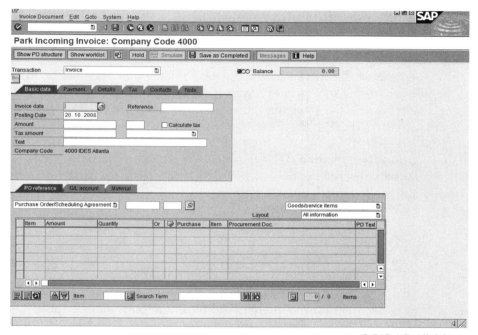

FIGURE 8.10   Parking an invoice

Note: You can also use the `MIR7` transaction code to access the **Park Incoming Invoice** screen.

In the **Park Incoming Invoice** screen, you need to provide the details of the invoice that you want to park. These details can be modified as and when required. In cases where you need to modify the details of an invoice at a later point of time, select **Edit > Switch to Document Parking** from the menu bar of the **Enter Incoming Invoice** screen to park the invoice. If you think that the information is complete and should be posted, select **Invoice Document > Save as Completed** from the menu bar.

In this section, you learned how to park an invoice. Let's now explore invoice variances.

EXPLORING INVOICE VARIANCES

When there are different values in the invoice and other documents, an invoice is said to have variance. For example, if the total amount in the vendor invoice is different from the total amount suggested by the system, the invoice has a variance. In SAP MM, there are four types of invoice variances:

- **Quantity variance (Q)**—Refers to the situation when the actual delivered quantity of products is different from that already recorded in the invoice.
- **Price variance (P)**—Refers to the situation when different prices are recorded for the same product in the purchase order and invoice.
- **Quantity and price variance**—Refers to the situation when there are differences in both price and quantity.
- **Order price quantity variance**—Refers to the situation when the price per ordered quantity is different in both the purchase order and invoice. For example, the price of a material was quoted as Rs. 9 per unit in the purchase order; however, in the invoice, the total amount has been calculated with price as Rs. 9.50 per unit.

There is a tolerance limit for every invoice variance. The tolerance limit is the limit up to which the variances or differences in an invoice can be tolerated. When there is a variance in the invoice, the system checks if the variance is within the tolerance limit. If the variance is within the tolerance limit, which can be either an absolute limit or a percentage limit, you can post the invoice in the system. On the other hand, if the variance is outside the limit, the invoice is posted, but with a warning message. In cases where the upper limit of the tolerance limit is exceeded, the invoice is posted; however, the payment is blocked. Thereafter, you need to release the blocked invoice for payment in a separate step.

The tolerance limits not only define the limit for invoice variances but also determine the amount above which an invoice item should be blocked.

Let's learn about blocking invoices in the next section of the chapter.

BLOCKING INVOICES

After invoice verification, the invoices are posted in the system. This is when the finance department of an organization comes into the picture. The finance department is responsible for making payments to the vendor. However, sometimes the invoice amount is not paid to the vendor as the invoice has been blocked. For example, there is a situation when the organization has received an invoice citing a higher amount than expected. In such a situation, the organization blocks the invoice until the difference in the amount is resolved. The following are the four ways in which an invoice can be blocked:

- Manual block
- Stochastic/Random block
- Block due to amount of an invoice item
- Block due to variance of an invoice item

Let's learn about each of them.

> **Note:** This chapter discusses the overview of the four ways in which an invoice can be blocked. The practical implementations of all these ways are covered in Appendix B: Exploring the Invoice Verification Process under Various Business Scenarios.

Blocking Invoices Manually

When an invoice is blocked while entering its details in the **Enter Incoming Invoice** screen, it is said to have been blocked manually. The entire invoice is blocked in such a case, which implies that this type of blocking is not set at the item level but at the invoice level. You can block an invoice manually in the **Payment** tab of the **Enter Incoming Invoice** screen, as shown in Figure 8.11:

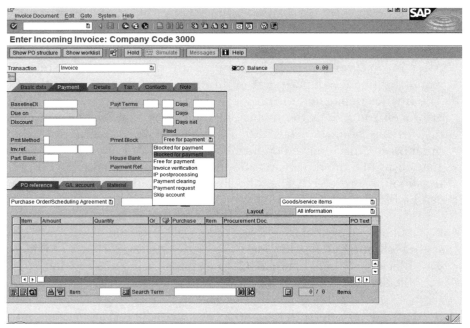

FIGURE 8.11   **Blocking an invoice manually**

In the **Payment** tab, select the **Blocked for payment** option from the **Pmnt Block** drop-down list, as shown in Figure 8.11, to block an invoice manually.

Blocking Invoices Randomly

You can also configure the mySAP ERP system to check invoices randomly and block those that do not satisfy specific requirements. This type of blocking is not set at the item level but at the invoice level, and is known as random or stochastic blocking. When random blocking occurs, the whole invoice is blocked for payment. There are two basic steps to blocking invoices randomly, which are as follows:

■ Activating random blocking at the plant level
■ Setting a threshold for each plant on the basis of which the invoice is checked for blocking

You can use the following menu path to configure random blocking:

Menu Path

SAP IMG > Materials Management > Logistics Invoice Verification > Invoice Block > Stochastic Block > Activate Stochastic Block. Figure 8.12 shows the preceding menu path:

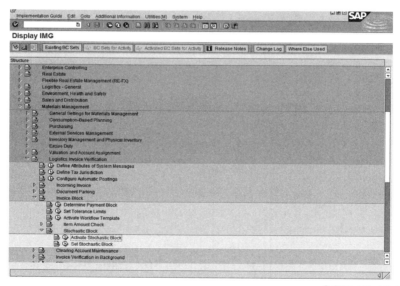

FIGURE 8.12   Displaying the menu path to block an invoice randomly

The **Change View "Stochastic Block: Activation": Overview** screen appears, as shown in Figure 8.13:

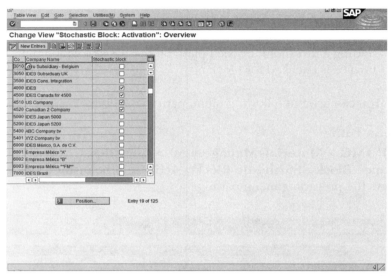

FIGURE 8.13   Displaying the Overview screen

In the **Change View "Stochastic Block: Activation": Overview** screen, select the check box of the company code for which you want to activate random blocking.

After activating random blocking, navigate the following menu path:

Menu Path

SAP IMG > Materials Management > Logistics Invoice Verification > Invoice Block > Stochastic Block > Set Stochastic Block. Figure 8.14 shows the preceding menu path:

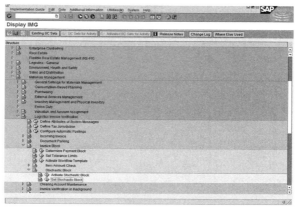

FIGURE 8.14   Displaying the menu path for setting random blocking

The **Change View "Stochastic Block: Values": Overview** screen opens, as shown in Figure 8.15:

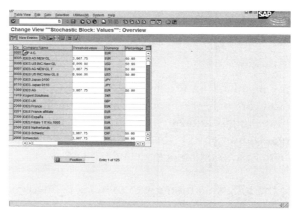

FIGURE 8.15   Setting random blocking

In the **Change View "Stochastic Block: Values": Overview** screen, you need to specify the degree of probability of an invoice getting blocked randomly. For example, if you configure a threshold value of Rs. 500 and the percentage of blocking as 50%, then every invoice above Rs. 500 will have a 50% chance of getting blocked. Similarly, an invoice of Rs. 250 has a 25% chance of getting blocked. If you require the same degree of probability for all the invoices, you should set the threshold value to 0.

> **Note:** If you set the threshold value to 0 and the percentage of blocking as 99.9%, then all the invoices are blocked.

In the **Change View "Stochastic Block: Values": Overview** screen, enter the threshold value and the percentage for the company code in the **Threshold value** and **Percentage** columns, respectively. The percentage value determines the degree of probability of blocking an invoice. If an invoice exceeds the amount specified in the **Threshold value** column, the invoice is blocked with the degree of probability specified in the **Percentage** column.

Blocking Based on Amount

If there is any mismatch in the amount of the invoice entered in the system and the amount shown in the vendor's invoice, the invoice should be blocked. This type of blocking is known as blocking an invoice based on amount. This helps the organization ensure that the vendors are not paid a higher amount incorrectly. The first step in blocking an invoice based on amount is to activate blocking.

Navigate the following menu path to block an invoice based on amount:

Menu Path

SAP IMG > Materials Management > Logistics Invoice Verification > Invoice Block > Item Amount Check > Activate Item Amount Check. Figure 8.16 shows the preceding menu path:

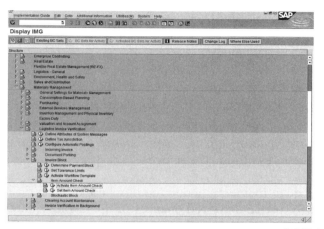

FIGURE 8.16   Displaying the menu path to block an invoice based on amount

The **Change View "Activate Block Due to Item Amount": Overview** screen opens, as shown in Figure 8.17:

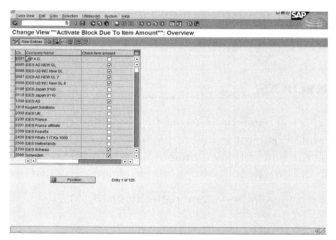

FIGURE 8.17   Displaying the Change View "activate block due to item amount": Overview screen

In the **Change View "Activate Block Due to Item Amount": Overview** screen, select the check box of the company code for which you want to block the invoice based on amount.

Blocking Based on Variance

As learned earlier, variances refer to the differences in the received and posted invoices. When invoice variances occur, they should be blocked. This is known as blocking an invoice based on variance. An invoice can be blocked due to the following reasons:

- If the quantity mentioned in the purchase order is different from the actual delivered quantity or the invoice quantity
- If the price specified in the purchase order does not match with the price mentioned in the invoice
- If the goods are delivered before or after the scheduled date
- If the quality of the received goods is not satisfactory

In any of the preceding situations, the invoice is blocked to stop the payment.

After learning to block an invoice, let's now learn how to release a blocked invoice.

RELEASING INVOICES

A blocked invoice can be released by cancelling the blocking indicator that was set while posting the invoice. When you release an invoice, the system deletes all the blocks that you might have set while posting the invoice.

Let's perform the following steps to release a blocked invoice:

1. Navigate the following menu path (Figure 8.18):

Menu Path

SAP menu > Logistics > Materials Management > Logistics Invoice Verification > Further Processing > MRBR – Release Blocked Invoices

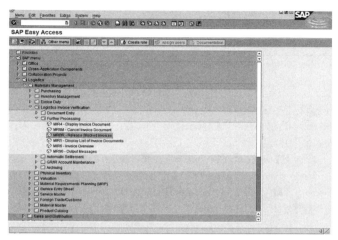

FIGURE 8.18 Displaying the menu path to release blocked invoices

The **Release Blocked Invoices** screen appears, as shown in Figure 8.19:

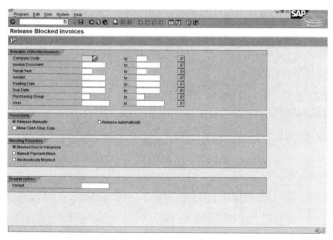

FIGURE 8.19 Releasing blocked invoices

Note: You can use the `MRBR` transaction code to access the **Release Blocked Invoices** screen.

2. Specify the company code related to the invoice in the **Company Code** text box (Figure 8.19).
3. Select the **Release Manually** radio button in the **Processing** group (Figure 8.19).
4. Select the **Blocked Due to Variances** radio button in the **Blocking Procedure** group (Figure 8.19).
5. Press the F8 key. The **Release Blocked Invoices** screen appears, as shown in Figure 8.20:

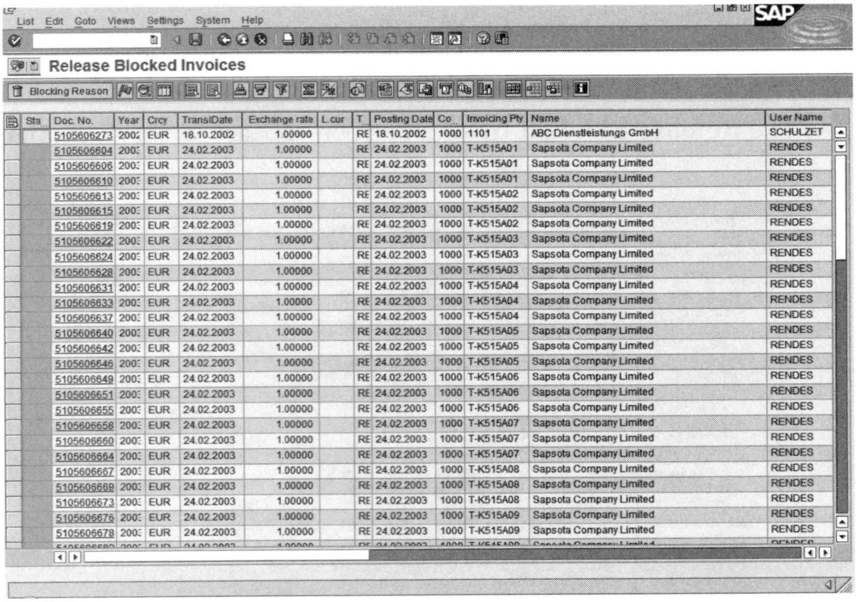

FIGURE 8.20   Displaying the Release Blocked Invoices screen

In the **Release Blocked Invoices** screen, select the invoice that you want to release from the **Doc. No**. column and press the F9 key.

SUMMARY

In this chapter, you learned to implement the standard method of invoice verification, in which the system ensures that the vendors receive the correct amount on time. You also learned about ERS, which is an automatic method to set the purchase orders and goods receipts. Next, you learned to park an invoice, that is, enter the invoice details in the system and post it on a later date. The chapter also explored different types of invoice variances that might arise due to various reasons, such as differences in the quantity delivered and the invoice quantity, price differences between the purchase order and invoice, differences in both price and quantity, and differences in price per ordered quantity. You also learned various ways to block an invoice, such as manual, random, blocking based on amount, and blocking based on variance. Finally, you learned to release a blocked invoice when the issues for which the invoice was blocked are resolved.

In the next chapter, you learn how to implement the inventory valuation process in the SAP MM module of the mySAP ERP system.

IMPLEMENTING THE INVENTORY VALUATION PROCESS IN THE MM MODULE

9

Inventory, in a general sense, is the total amount of goods or materials that are stored in an organization at a given point of time. However, in accounts, inventory is also considered as an asset of an organization that can either be sold directly or used as a raw material to produce goods. Since inventory is considered as an asset of an organization, it is valuated like any other asset, and a proper record of the incoming and outgoing stock value is maintained. This process of recording any changes in the stock is called inventory valuation. The inventory valuation process allows an organization to monitor inventory in the balance sheet, which can help identify an excess of stock or avoid any out-of-stock situation. This process also helps in planning the movement of goods within and outside the organization, which helps in stock maintenance.

In this chapter, you will learn to implement the inventory valuation process in SAP MM. The chapter discusses different valuation areas, valuation methods, and the split valuation process in detail. You will also learn to valuate inventory in the balance sheet of the organization.

Let's first explore the different valuation areas in the SAP® MM module.

EXPLORING VALUATION AREAS

The valuation area is the organizational level at which you can valuate materials. There are two types of valuation areas—plant level and company code level. The material valuated at the plant level can have different prices in different plants; whereas, the price of the material valuated at the company code level has to be same in all the plants. The valuation area can be defined in the **Valuation Level** screen, which can be accessed by navigating the following menu path:

Menu Path

SAP IMG > Enterprise Structure > Definition > Logistics – General > Define valuation level. Figure 9.1 shows the preceding menu path:

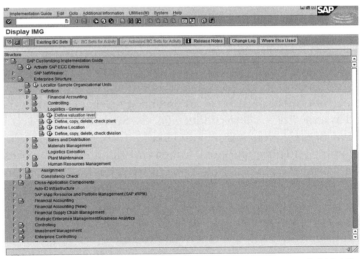

FIGURE 9.1   **Displaying the menu path to define the valuation level**

The **Valuation Level** screen appears, as shown in Figure 9.2:

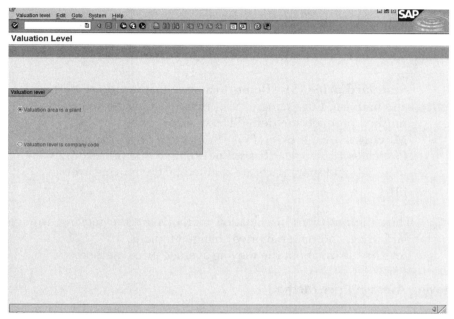

FIGURE 9.2   **Displaying the Valuation Level screen**

You can see in Figure 9.2 that the valuation level is not editable. This implies that the valuation level has already been defined. After learning about the levels at which an item is valuated, let's discuss the various methods employed to valuate them.

WORKING WITH VALUATION METHODS

The inventory valuation process in an organization is implemented using different valuation methods, such as the moving average price and the standard price method. The valuation methods are important not only for accounting purposes but also for knowing the actual value of the assets of the organization. The valuation methods also help the organization in determining the price at which the assets should be sold. The type of valuation method implemented in the SAP system depends upon the price control set in it. You can set the following two types of price control in the SAP system:

- **Standard price (S)**—Refers to a price that is pre-established and uniform. For example, the prices of semi-finished goods and finished products are defined as standard price.
- **Moving average price (V)**—Refers to a price that has fluctuates on a regular basis. For example, the prices of raw materials and spare parts are defined by the moving average price.

The different types of valuation methods are the moving average price, standard price, and material price change methods.

Let's first learn about the moving average price method.

The Moving Average Price Method

The moving average price method is used to calculate the weighted average price of a material. In this method, the system calculates the price of received goods at the purchase order (PO) price and the price of goods issued at the current market price of the material. Any sort of movement of material, such as the issue or receipt of material, affects its moving average price. The moving average price method is mainly used to valuate the inventory for raw materials.

The moving average price of a material can be calculated by using the following formula:

Moving average price = Total stock value/Total stock quantity

Consider the following example to calculate the moving average price of a material:

You have an initial stock of 100 pieces of Product1 at $10 per unit. Recently, you have ordered an additional 100 pieces of Product1 at $12 per unit. After receiving 100 pieces from the vendor, you make an entry of the goods receipt in your records. When you make an entry, the stock account is debited with $1200 (100 × 12) and the goods receipt (GR) account is credited with $1200.

The total stock of Product1 is 200 units (100 + 100) and the total value of the stock is $2200 ([100 × 10] + [100 × 12]). The moving average price of the stock is $11 (2200 / 200). The material master record of Product1 is updated with the current moving average price, which is $11 in this case.

The main advantage of using the moving average price method is that in this method, a new material price is calculated after every goods receipt; and therefore, it causes an update in the price and stock value of the material. The new material price represents the current delivered price of the material, which is calculated from the total inventory value and quantity of the material in stock.

The disadvantage of using the moving average price method is that the price, which is used to valuate the consumption of material, is dependent on the time the goods issue is posted in the system. This implies that the material is not valuated at its actual procurement cost. For example, a vendor receives an invoice for 10 pieces of a material on 15th of a month, but does not record the invoice receipt in the system. The vendor sends the material to the purchaser on the 16th of the next month and records the invoice receipt and goods issue on the same day in the system. In this case, the invoice receipt is posted in the system after the goods receipt was entered. Therefore, the material is valuated not at the procurement cost but at the cost prevailing in the market. The moving average price method may also lead to incorrect material valuation as the goods posted in the previous period are valuated with the current moving average price.

Note: The material master record of a material is always updated with the current moving average price, which can be checked using transaction code MM03.

The Standard Price Method

The standard price of a material refers to the price that is recorded in its material master record. This method of pricing is used for products that do not have a tendency toward frequent price fluctuation, such as finished or semi-finished products. The standard price method is used to valuate the materials whose price remains constant for at least one period. The standard price is based on the planned values and not the actual values of a material.

The advantage of using the standard price method is that it ensures consistency in the price of the material, as the materials are valued at the same price for at least one period.

Consider the following example to calculate the standard price of a material:

You have an initial stock of 100 pieces of Product1 at $10 per unit. Recently, you have raised a PO for Product1 at $12 per unit. After receiving the material, you enter the goods receipt for the PO. The accounts department debits the stock account by $1000 (100 × 10), in spite of the PO listing the price as $12 per unit. However, the GR account will be credited by $1200 as the GR account is based on the price in the PO and not the standard price. The price difference account is debited by $200, because of the difference in the cost credited in the GR account and the stock account.

This implies that in the standard price method, the standard price is always fixed and any difference between the standard price and the PO price is recorded in the price difference account.

The Material Price Change Method

Any change in the market affects the price of a material and this change should be reflected in the account of the respective material. In the SAP system, you can implement the price changes and simultaneously revaluate the stock of the material at the current market price. For example, an organization has 100 pieces of stock of a material at $10 per piece. The current market price of the material is $6 per piece. In such a situation, the organization should update the stock valuation of the material as per the current market price. This revaluation of stock according to the current market price is called the material price change method in the SAP system. There can be three instances of change in the material price:

The price of the material changes in the current year.

The price of the material had changed in the previous year and the change is effective only for the current year.

The price of the material had changed in the previous year and the change is effective in the current year.

Let's discuss each of these three instances with examples.

In the first case, the price of the material changes in the current year. Consider a scenario where an organization has 100 pieces of a material at

$100 per piece. The total value of the stock is $10,000. The market price of the material has increased to $150 per piece. You now need to revaluate the stock according to the current market price and also post the same in the price change document and the accounting document. In the accounting document, the stock general ledger (G/L) account is debited by $5000 ($10,000 – 15,000) and the expense/revenue from revaluation G/L account is credited by $5000. This completes the process of material price change and the new price of the material in the accounts is $150 per piece.

In the second case, the price of the material had changed in the previous year and the change is effective only in that year. This implies that if there is a change in the material price in the previous year, the current price of the material remains the same. In such a situation, two accounting documents are created, one for the previous year and another for the current year. For example, when the price of the material changed from $100 to $150 in the previous period, the stock G/L account, which is the accounting document, should be debited by $5000 and the expense/revenue from revaluation G/L account should be credited by $5000. In the current year, the stock account is credited and the expense from revaluation account is debited by $5000. This helps in keeping the same price; i.e., $100 per piece in the current year.

In the third case, the price of the material had changed in the previous year and the change is effective in the current year. This implies that the price, which was changed in the previous year, is carried forward to the current year. In such a situation, two accounting documents are created, with the first posted for the previous year and the second posted for the current year. Consider a situation in which the total stock of material was 100 pieces at $10 per piece in the previous year and had increased to $12 per piece in that year. The current stock of material is 120 pieces at $15 per piece. In the first accounting document, which represents the previous year, $200 ([$12 – 10] × 100) is debited to the stock G/L account and the same amount is credited to revenue from revaluation G/L account. In the current year, posting will be done in the second accounting document. Firstly, there will be a reversal of the amount ($200) posted in the accounting document of the previous year, which is credited to the stock G/L account, and then debited to the expense from revaluation G/L account. Secondly, the new price, which is $3 per piece, needs to be carried over in the current year. Therefore, the stock G/L account is debited with $360 ($3 × 120) and the same amount is credited to the revenue from revaluation G/L account. The net effect of the two postings would be that the stock G/L account is credited with $160 ($360 – 200) and the same amount is debited in the expense from revaluation G/L account. Therefore, $160 will be debited in the stock G/L account and credited in the expense from revaluation G/L account in the accounting document of the current year to implement the material price change method.

You can change the material price by navigating the following menu path:

Menu Path

SAP menu > Logistics > Materials Management > Valuation > MR21 – Change in Material Prices. Figure 9.3 shows the preceding menu path:

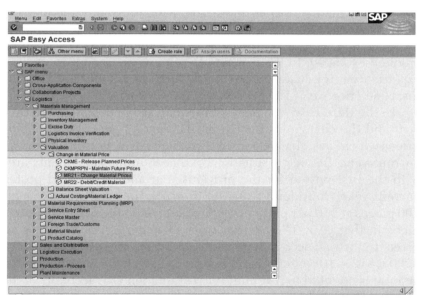

FIGURE 9.3   Displaying the menu path to change the material price

The **Price Change – Overview Screen** appears, as shown in Figure 9.4:

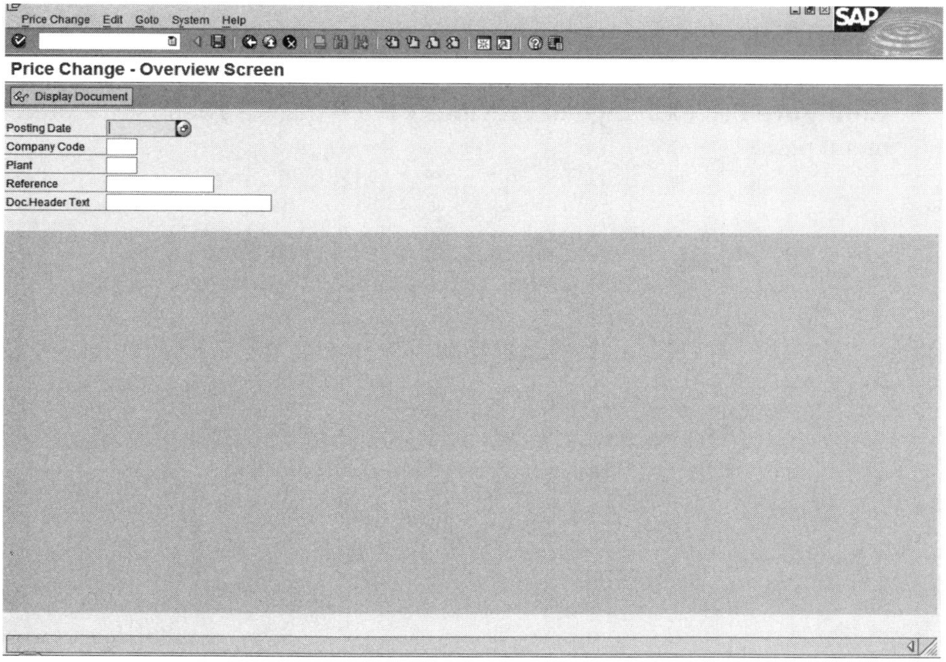

FIGURE 9.4   **Displaying the Price Change – Overview Screen**

Note: You can also use the MR21 transaction code to access the **Price Change – Overview Screen**.

You can also configure the price change in the previous year to be applied to the current year by navigating the following menu path:

Menu Path

SAP IMG > Materials Management > Valuation and Account Assignment > Configure Price Change in Previous Period. Figure 9.5 shows the preceding menu path:

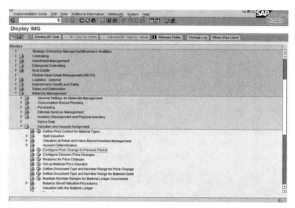

FIGURE 9.5   Displaying the menu path to configure a price change

The **Change View "Price Change in Previous Period, not in Current Period":** screen appears, as shown in Figure 9.6:

FIGURE 9.6   Displaying the Change View screen for configuring a price change

In the **Change View "Price Change in Previous Period, not in Current Period":** screen, you can select the **Price carry over** check box of the material whose price you want to carry over to the current year.

CONFIGURING THE VALUATION PROCESS

The moving average price (V) and the standard price (S) are the predefined price control methods in the mySAP™ ERP system. At the time of creating the material master record, you need to assign the price control method manually to configure the valuation process of the material. However, you can also configure the mySAP ERP system to assign the price control method to a material automatically. You can do so by assigning the price control method to the material type.

Navigate the following menu path to assign a price control method to a material type:

Menu Path

SAP IMG > Logistics – General > Material Master > Basic Settings > Material Types > Define Attributes of Material Types. Figure 9.7 shows the preceding menu path:

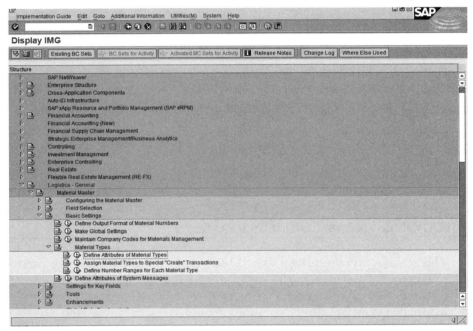

FIGURE 9.7   Displaying the menu path to configure the valuation process

The **Change View "Material types": Overview** screen appears, as shown in Figure 9.8:

FIGURE 9.8   Displaying the Change View "Material types": Overview screen

In the **Change View "Material types": Overview** screen, click any material to configure its settings. The **Change View "Material types": Details** screen of the respective material appears, as shown in Figure 9.9:

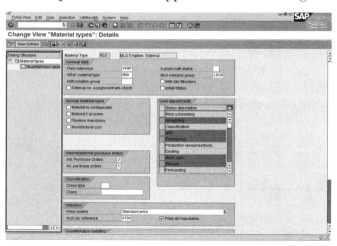

FIGURE 9.9   Displaying the Details screen

In the **Valuation** group of the **Change View "Material types": Details** screen, you can configure the valuation method, which is used by the system as the default valuation method for this material type. You can select the **Price ctrl mandatory** check box in the **Valuation** group to make the selected valuation method mandatory, which means that a user cannot change the default valuation method while creating the material master record.

In this section, you have learned about the valuation methods used while creating the material master record. Let's now learn to configure the split valuation process in SAP MM.

CONFIGURING THE SPLIT VALUATION PROCESS

The spilt valuation process allows you to divide material stock in small parts, so that each part can be valuated in different ways. This method is employed when you need to sort the materials according to various parameters, such as:

- **Country of origin**—Valuates materials according to the country from where the material is purchased. For example, the same material can be purchased from different countries.
- **Procurement type**—Valuates materials according to the way materials are procured, such as internal or external. Internal procurement implies procuring materials or services from internal resources, such as from some other plant of the same organization. External procurement implies procuring materials or services from an external supplier.
- **Quality of material**—Valuates materials according to their quality, such as good, damaged, or poor quality.

> **Note:** The materials that are valuated using the split valuation process can only be valuated through the moving average price method.

Consider a scenario where a watch manufacturing company has ordered watch straps from two companies: Company1 and Company2. Company1 is a domestic company and Company2 is a foreign company. The price charged by Company2 is greater than the price charged by Company1. Therefore, the company has decided to valuate the stocks separately. The company is procuring 60 pieces of the material at $10 per unit from the domestic company and 40 pieces at $15 per unit from the foreign company. The stock value of the material procured from Company1 and Company2 is $600.

Figure 9.10 shows how the materials are split according to their country of origin:

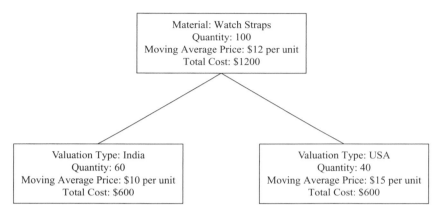

FIGURE 9.10   Displaying the split valuation process

Let's perform the following steps to configure spilt valuation in the mySAP ERP system:

1. Navigate the following menu path to assign a price control method to a material type:

Menu Path

SAP IMG > Materials Management > Valuation and Account Assignment > Split Valuation > Configure Split Valuation. Figure 9.11 shows the preceding menu path:

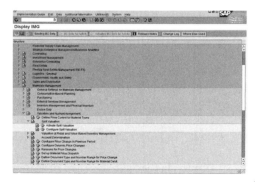

FIGURE 9.11   Displaying the menu path to configure split valuation

The **QSL1 Valuation Area** dialog box appears, as shown in Figure 9.12:

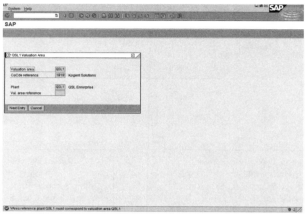

FIGURE 9.12   Displaying the QSL1 Valuation Area dialog box

2. Click the **Cancel** button. The **QSL1 Valuation Area** dialog box closes and the **Split Valuation of Materials** screen appears, as shown in Figure 9.13:

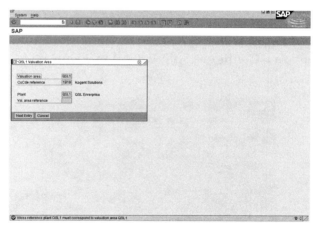

FIGURE 9.13   Displaying the Split Valuation of Materials screen

3. Click the **Global Types** button on the **Split Valuation of Materials** screen. The **Global Valuation Types** screen appears, as shown in Figure 9.14:

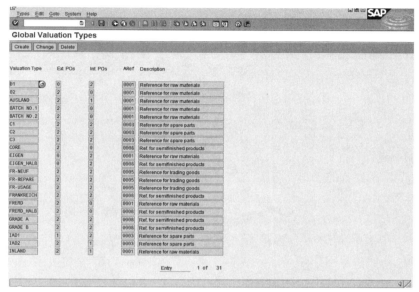

FIGURE 9.14   **Displaying the Global Valuation Types screen**

The **Global Valuation Types** screen allows you to define the following attributes:

- □ **External PO**—Specifies whether external POs are allowed or not
- □ **Internal PO**—Specifies whether internal POs are allowed or not
- □ **Account Category Reference**—Groups the valuation classes and specifies the account category reference for the valuation type

Note: You can also create the valuation types in the **Global Valuation Types** screen by clicking the **Create** button.

4. Press the F3 key to return to the **Global Valuation Types** screen and click the **Global Categories** button. The **Global Valuation Categories** screen appears, as shown in Figure 9.15:

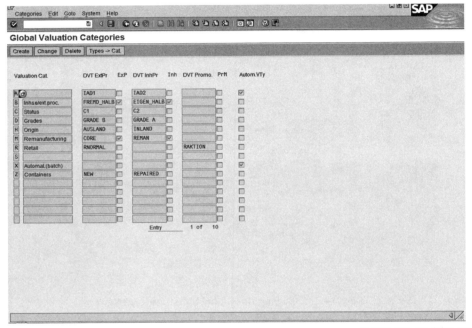

FIGURE 9.15 Displaying the Global Valuation Categories screen

The **Global Valuation Categories** screen allows you to define the following attributes:

- **Default External Procurement**—Specifies the valuation type proposed at the time of PO creation
- **External Procurement Mandatory**—Specifies that the default valuation type is mandatory and cannot be changed in the PO
- **Default In-house**—Specifies the valuation type that is proposed at the time of PO creation
- **In-house Mandatory**—Specifies that the default valuation type is mandatory and cannot be changed in the PO
- **Valuation Type Automatic**—Determines the valuation type at the time of goods receipt

5. Click the **Types > Cat.** button in the **Global Valuation Categories** screen. The **Valuation Category A: Allocate Valuation Types** screen appears, as shown in Figure 9.16:

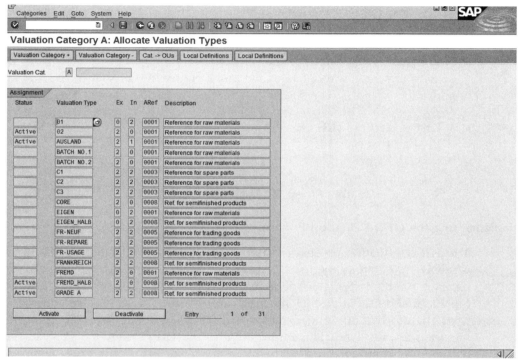

FIGURE 9.16   **Displaying the Valuation Category screen**

6. Select the valuation type you want to activate from the **Valuation Type** column and click the **Activate** button.
7. Click the **Save** (🖫) button to save the changes.

After learning how to configure split valuation in the mySAP ERP system, let's learn about valuing inventory in a balance sheet.

VALUING INVENTORY IN A BALANCE SHEET

A balance sheet is the financial statement of an organization that specifies the financial position of the organization at a given point of time. A balance sheet is used to provide information about the sources of funds of the organization and also helps to decide how these funds are used or invested. Inventories are generally valuated in the balance sheet of an organization because they are treated as assets that can be sold or utilized in the future.

There are three ways of valuating an inventory in the balance sheet of an organization:

- Last in, first out (LIFO)
- First in, first out (FIFO)
- Lowest value

Let's first learn about the LIFO valuation process.

Implementing the LIFO Valuation Process

The LIFO valuation process is based on the principle that the material that is received last should be used first. For example, 100 units of a material are received on the first day and 50 units are received on the second day. In when the material is used, the stock received on the second day would be consumed first. Therefore, there is no change in the value of old materials when the new materials are received. This implies that in the LIFO valuation process, the old material is not affected by the higher or lower price of the new material; and therefore, the old material is not valuated at the new material price. Let's consider a scenario to understand the LIFO valuation process better.

The opening balance of a material in an organization, as on January 1st of a specific year, is 800 units at $6 per unit. On January 5th, 200 units at $7 per unit are purchased. On January 10th, an additional purchase of 200 units at $8 per unit is made. The total stock of material on January 10th is $7800 ([800 × 6] + [200 × 7] + [200 × 8]). On January 11th, 800 units are issued, the total price of which was $5400 (1600 + 1400 + 2400). The valuation of the price of 800 units is as follows:

> 200 units (received on January 10th) at $8 per unit = $1600
> 200 units (received on January 5th) at $7 per unit = $1400
> 400 units (balance of materials on January 1st) at $6 per unit = $2400

After issuing 800 units, a total of 400 units are left in stock at $6 per unit. On January 15th, an additional stock of 400 units at $8 per unit is received. On January 17th, 500 units worth $3800 (3200 + 600) are issued. The valuation of the price of 500 units is as follows:

400 units (received on January 15th) at $8 per unit = $3200
100 units (balance of materials on January 1st) at $6 per unit = $600

Therefore, the final balance of materials left with the organization is 300 units at $6 per unit.

To use the LIFO valuation process for valuating the inventory, you need to first activate it in the mySAP ERP system. Navigate the following menu path to activate the LIFO valuation process:

Menu Path

SAP IMG > Materials Management > Valuation and Account Assignment > Balance Sheet Valuation Procedures > Configure LIFO/FIFO Methods > General Information > Activate/Deactivate LIFO/FIFO Valuation. Figure 9.17 shows the preceding menu path:

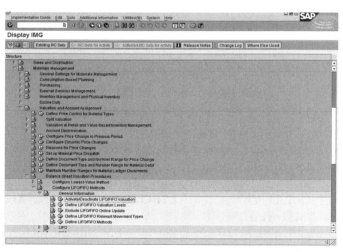

FIGURE 9.17   Displaying the menu path to activate LIFO

The **Activate Balance Sheet Valuation** screen appears, as shown in Figure 9.18:

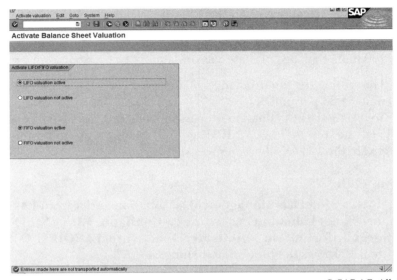

FIGURE 9.18   Activating LIFO

Note: You can use the transaction code OMWE to open the **Activate Balance Sheet Valuation** screen. You should remember that the entries in OMWE are not transported automatically for further use.

In the **Activate Balance Sheet Valuation** screen, select the **LIFO valuation active** radio button to activate the LIFO valuation process. Next, prepare the material master record for LIFO valuation by selecting the **LIFO/FIFO-relevant** check box in the **LIFO data** group in the **Accounting** tab of the **Create Material** screen.

You can also update the LIFO flag after creating the material master record by navigating the following menu path:

Menu Path

SAP menu > Logistics > Materials Management > Valuation > Balance Sheet Valuation > LIFO Valuation > Prepare > MRL6 – Select materials. Figure 9.19 shows the preceding menu path:

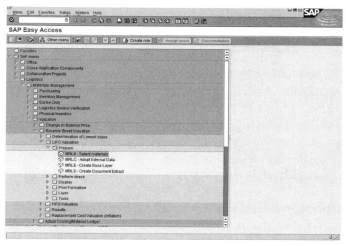

FIGURE 9.19 **Displaying the menu path to prepare the material record for LIFO valuation**

When you select the preceding menu path, the **Select LIFO-Relevant Materials** screen appears, as shown in Figure 9.20:

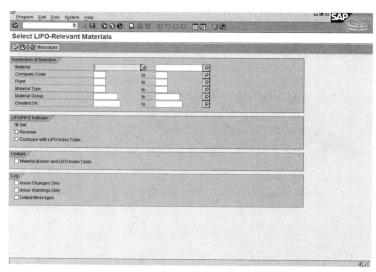

FIGURE 9.20 **Preparing materials for LIFO valuation**

Note: You can also use the `MRL6` transaction code to open the **Select LIFO-Relevant Materials** screen.

In the **Select LIFO-Relevant Materials** screen, specify the number of the material that needs to be valuated in the **Material** text box and select the **Set** radio button in the **LIFO/FIFO indicator** group. Press the F8 key to finally prepare the material for LIFO valuation.

After configuring and preparing the material, you can execute the LIFO valuation in the following three ways:

On individual level (MRL1)—Specifies that the material is valuated individually

On pool level (MRL2)—Specifies that the material is grouped and is valuated with the group

Comparison of Lowest Values (MRL3)—Compares the lowest values

Navigate the following menu path to execute the LIFO valuation in any of the preceding three ways:

Menu Path

SAP menu > Logistics > Materials Management > Valuation > Balance Sheet Valuation > LIFO Valuation > Perform check. Figure 9.21 shows the preceding menu path:

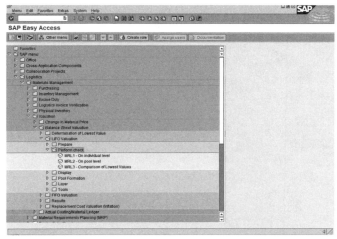

FIGURE 9.21 Displaying the menu path to perform check for LIFO valuation

In this case, we have selected the **On individual level** option, so that the material is valuated individually. The **LIFO Valuation for Individual Materials** screen opens, as shown in Figure 9.22:

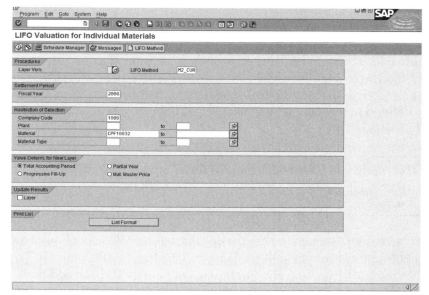

FIGURE 9.22   Valuating individual materials

In the **LIFO Valuation for Individual Materials** screen, perform the following steps to prepare the material for LIFO valuation:

1. Specify the period for which you want to valuate the stock in the **LIFO Method** text box.
2. Specify the fiscal year for which you want to valuate the stock in the **Fiscal Year** text box.
3. Specify the company code of the material in the **Company Code** text box.
4. Specify the material code in the **Material** text box.
5. Select the **Total Accounting Period** radio button in the **Value Determined for New Layer** group.
6. Press the F8 key to execute the LIFO valuation.

The transaction is executed and the result is displayed in the **LIFO Valuation for Individual Materials** screen.

Implementing the FIFO Valuation Process

In the FIFO valuation process, the material that is purchased or received first is sold or issued first. This method of valuation is best suited for materials that either have an expiry date or degrade with time. This is the most common method, as it helps the organization to dispose of older materials and display the new materials as assets in the balance sheet. In the SAP system, FIFO valuation is defined in the valuation area level and hence receipt data will be updated at the valuation area level.

> **Note:** This method is not advantageous if the company is planning to reduce the amount of tax being paid to the government. The LIFO method is a more popular method for saving on taxes.

Consider a scenario where the opening balance of materials in an organization is 800 units at $6 per unit on January 1st of a specific year. On January 5th, 200 units at $7 per unit are purchased. On January 10th, an additional purchase of 200 units at $8 per unit is made. Therefore, the total stock of material on January 10th is $7800 ([800 × 6] + [200 × 7] + [200 × 8]). On January 11th, 1000 units worth $6200 (4800 + 1400) are issued. The valuation of the price of 800 units is as follows:

800 units (balance of materials on January 1st) at $6 per unit = $4800
200 units (received on January 5th) at $7 per unit = $1400

After issuing 1000 units, 200 units were left in stock at $8 per unit. On January 15th, 400 more units were received at $8 per unit. On January 17th, 500 units were issued, the total price of which was $4000 (1600 + 2400). The valuation of 500 units is as follows:

200 units (received on January 10th) at $8 per unit = $1600
300 units (received on January 15th) at $8 per unit = $2400

After all the preceding transactions, the final balance of materials left with the organization is 100 units at $8 per unit.

To use the FIFO valuation process for valuating the inventory, you need to first check that FIFO is active. Navigate the following menu path to activate the FIFO valuation process (Figure 9.17):

Menu Path

SAP IMG > Materials Management > Valuation and Account Assignment > Balance Sheet Valuation Procedures > Configure LIFO/FIFO Methods > General Information > Activate/Deactivate LIFO/FIFO Valuation

After navigating the menu path, the **Activate Balance Sheet Valuation** screen (Figure 9.18) appears. Select the **FIFO valuation active** radio button to activate the FIFO valuation process.

After configuring the FIFO valuation process, you can prepare the material master record for FIFO valuation by selecting the **LIFO/FIFO-relevant** check box in the **LIFO data** group in the **Accounting** tab of the **Create Material** screen.

You can also update the FIFO flag after creating the material master record by navigating the following menu path:

Menu Path

SAP menu > Logistics > Materials Management > Valuation > Balance Sheet Valuation > FIFO Valuation > Prepare > MRF4 – Select Materials. Figure 9.23 shows the preceding menu path:

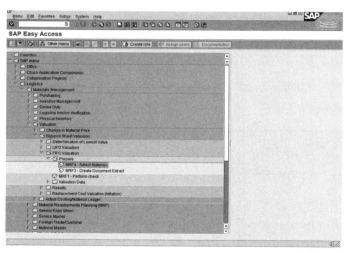

FIGURE 9.23 Displaying the menu path to prepare the material record for FIFO valuation

When you select the menu path, the **FIFO Valuation: Flag Materials** screen appears, as shown in Figure 9.24:

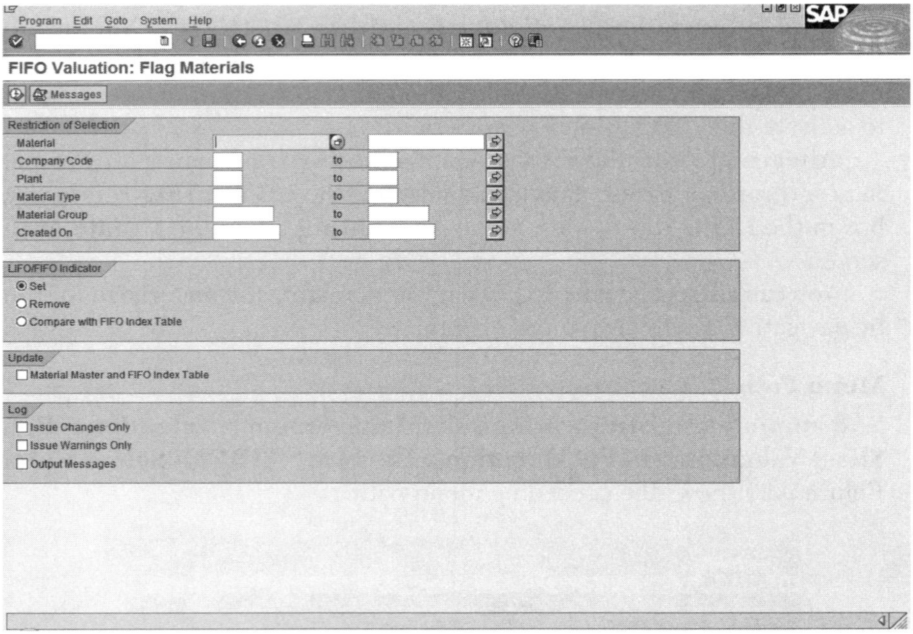

FIGURE 9.24 **Displaying the FIFO Valuation screen**

Note: You can use the MRF4 transaction code to open the **FIFO Valuation: Flag Materials** screen.

In the **FIFO Valuation: Flag Materials** screen, specify the material number in the **Material** text box and select the **Set** radio button in the **LIFO/FIFO Indicator** group. Press the F8 key to finally prepare the material for FIFO valuation.

After configuring and preparing the material for FIFO valuation, you can execute the FIFO valuation by navigating the following menu path:

Menu Path

SAP menu > Logistics > Materials Management > Valuation > Balance Sheet Valuation > FIFO Valuation > MRF1 – Perform check. Figure 9.25 shows the preceding menu path:

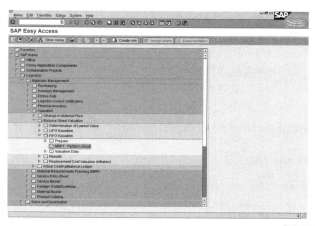

FIGURE 9.25   Displaying the menu path to perform check for FIFO valuation

The **Execute FIFO Valuation** screen appears, as shown in Figure 9.26:

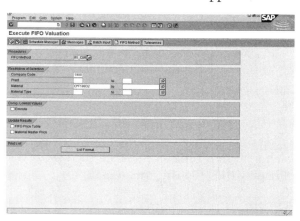

FIGURE 9.26   Displaying the Execute FIFO Valuation screen

> **Note:** You can also use the MRF1 transaction code to open the **Execute FIFO Valuation** screen.

In the **Execute FIFO Valuation** screen, perform the following steps to prepare the material for FIFO valuation:

1. Specify the FIFO method in the **FIFO Method** text box.
2. Specify the company code of the material in the **Company Code** text box.
3. Specify the material number in the **Material** text box.
4. Press the F8 key to execute the FIFO valuation.

The transaction is executed and the result is displayed in the **Execute FIFO Valuation** screen.

Determining the Lowest Value

The lowest value of an inventory is calculated by using the lowest value principle (LVP) method. It is a method of valuating stocks for balance sheet purposes. This method is used to valuate the material stock as accurately as possible so that there is minimum loss of material. The lowest value of an inventory can be calculated using the following three types of value determination:

- Market prices
- Range of coverage
- Movement rate

Let's now discuss each of these determinations in detail.

Market Prices

The market price value determination calculates the lowest value of an inventory based on market prices. It calculates the lowest price from the different prices stored for each material. You can calculate the lowest value based on market prices by navigating the following menu path:

Menu Path

SAP menu > Logistics > Materials Management > Valuation > Balance Sheet Valuation > Determination of Lowest Value > MRN0 – Market Price. Figure 9.27 shows the preceding menu path:

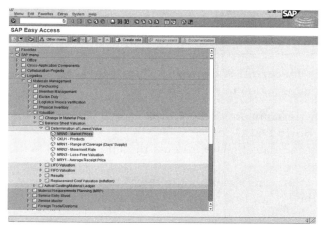

FIGURE 9.27   **Displaying the menu path to calculate the lowest value based on market prices**

The **Determine Lowest Value: Market Prices** screen appears, as shown in Figure 9.28:

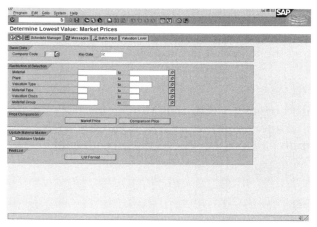

FIGURE 9.28   **Determining the lowest value based on market prices**

> **Note:** You can use the MRN0 transaction code to open the **Determine Lowest Value: Market Prices** screen.

In the **Determine Lowest Value: Market Prices** screen, enter the following information to calculate the lowest value based on market prices:

1. Specify the company code of the material in the **Company Code** text box in the **Basic Data** group.
2. Specify the date that represents the end of fiscal year in the **Key Date** text box.
3. Specify the material number in the **Material** text box.
4. Press the F8 key to execute the transaction.

The lowest value of the material, according to the market price, is displayed in the **Determine Lowest Value: Range of Coverage** screen.

Range of Coverage

The range of coverage value determination checks if the price of the material should be devaluated. In this method, the SAP system defines the range of coverage of the material, which is calculated by dividing average stock by average consumption. You can calculate the lowest value based on the range of coverage by navigating the following menu path:

Menu Path

SAP menu > Logistics > Materials Management > Valuation > Balance Sheet Valuation > Determination of Lowest Value > MRN1 – Range of Coverage (Days' Supply). Figure 9.29 shows the preceding menu path:

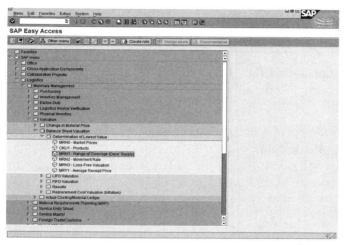

FIGURE 9.29   Displaying the menu path to calculate lowest value based on range of coverage

The **Determine Lowest Value: Range of Coverage** screen appears, as shown in Figure 9.30:

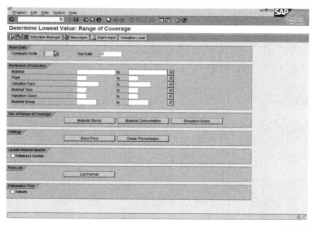

FIGURE 9.30   Determining the lowest value based on range of coverage

> **Note:** You can use the MRN1 transaction code to open the **Determine Lowest Value: Range of Coverage** screen.

In the **Determine Lowest Value: Range of Coverage** screen, enter the following information to calculate the lowest value based on the range of coverage:

1. Specify the company code of the material in the **Company Code** text box in the **Basic Data** group.
2. Specify the date that represents the end of fiscal year in the **Key Date** text box.
3. Specify the material number in the **Material** text box.
4. Press the F8 key to execute the transaction.

The lowest value of the material according to the range of coverage is displayed in the **Determine Lowest Value: Range of Coverage** screen.

Movement Rate

The lowest value determination based on movement rate allows you to determine the value of the material based on the rate of movement of the material. The movement rate is calculated as a percentage value, which is calculated by dividing the total quantity of material receipt by material in stock and then multiplying the figure by 100. You can calculate the lowest value based on movement rate by navigating the following menu path:

Menu Path

SAP menu > Logistics > Materials Management > Valuation > Balance Sheet Valuation > Determination of Lowest Value > MRN2 – Movement Rate. Figure 9.31 shows the preceding menu path:

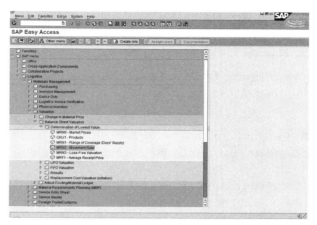

FIGURE 9.31   Displaying the menu path to calculate the lowest value based on movement rate

The **Determine Lowest Value: Movement Rate** screen appears, as shown in Figure 9.32:

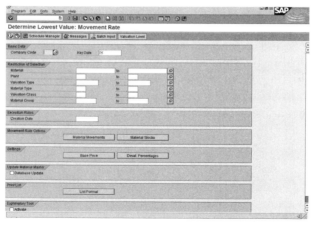

FIGURE 9.32   Determining the lowest value based on movement rate

> **Note:** You can use the MRN2 transaction code to open the **Determine Lowest Value: Movement Rate** screen.

In the **Determine Lowest Value: Movement Rate** screen, enter the following information to calculate the lowest value based on movement rate:

1. Specify the company code of the material in the **Company Code** text box in the **Basic Data** group.
2. Specify the date that represents the end of fiscal year in the **Key Date** text box.
3. Specify the material number in the **Material** text box.
4. Press the F8 key to execute the transaction.

The lowest value of the material according to the movement type is displayed in the **Determine Lowest Value: Movement Type** screen.

SUMMARY

In this chapter, you learned to implement the inventory valuation process in SAP MM. The chapter discussed different valuation areas and valuation methods implemented in SAP to valuate materials. You also learned to configure the valuation process. Next, you learned about the split valuation process, which helps in valuating the stock of a material in small parts. You also learned different ways of valuating the inventory in the balance sheet of an organization.

Appendix A explores different procurement processes under various business scenarios within the SAP MM Module.

Exploring the Procurement Process under Various Business Scenarios

Appendix A

Procurement refers to the acquisition of goods or services from a company, institution, or person at the lowest possible cost. The procurement process begins from the requirement of a material or service and ends when the payment is made to the supplier. In industrial terms, this procurement process is known as the procure to pay (P2P) cycle. The mySAP™ ERP system provides certain standard procurement processes that can be customized according to customer requirements. Depending upon what is procured and how it is being procured, you can select any of the following procurement processes:

- Direct material procurement
- Indirect material procurement

- Consumable material procurement
- Services procurement
- Consignment procurement
- Subcontracting procurement
- Third-party procurement
- Procurement process for stock transfers

Consider a scenario where a car manufacturing organization, ABC, procures some car parts from other manufacturers to assemble a car, such as engines, suspensions, brakes, and wheels. In addition to the car parts, the organization procures stationery from suppliers for its employees to perform paperwork. In this scenario, the procurement of car parts and stationery comes under two types of procurement processes—direct procurement and indirect procurement. As the procured car parts are directly consumed by the manufacturing process, they are said to be procured by the direct procurement process; whereas, the process employed to procure stationary is known as the indirect procurement process. In both these procurement processes, the organization first needs to determine the requirements and then plan for the procurement of materials.

In the mySAP ERP system, the item category specified in the procurement documents is used to determine the type and the procedure to procure the items. The mySAP ERP system provides the standard item categories from 0 to 9, each having an external representation and description. For example, in the mySAP ERP system, the 1 item category is externally represented as B and its description is Limit. You need to select the appropriate item category in a purchasing document depending upon the procedure used to procure items.

This appendix explores the P2P cycle and discusses the role of various P2P documents, such as purchase requisition and purchase order, in procuring the materials. In addition, various types of procurement processes are described in detail, with the help of specific business scenarios, along with their configuration in the mySAP ERP system.

EXPLORING THE P2P CYCLE

The P2P cycle is a process to obtain and manage the raw materials required to manufacture final goods. Let's consider the scenario of an organization that manufactures bikes. The organization requires many components, such as shifters, stems, and wheel sets to manufacture a bike. The planning department analyzes the sales forecasts and generates purchase requisitions specifying the material requirements. After that, the organization procures these components externally from a third-party vendor. After deciding on the type of material, quantity of material, and delivery date, the purchase requisition is passed to the purchasing department, which generates the purchase order. The supplier then sends the material to the organization on the basis of these details.

The Inventory Management module helps to verify that the material is received in the correct quantity and at the right time, and issues a goods receipt, which is sent to the finance department. Finally, the finance department generates the invoice and ensures that the payment is sent to the supplier. Figure A.1 shows the P2P cycle:

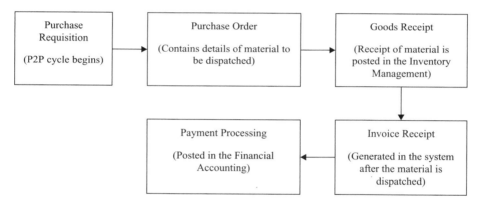

FIGURE A.1   **Displaying the P2P cycle**

Figure A.1 shows that the P2P cycle begins with the generation of a purchase requisition in which the requirements of various departments are specified. Based on the purchase requisition, a request is made to the purchasing department to procure the required materials and services. Further, the purchase requisition is converted into a purchase order and sent to the supplier to procure materials. Then, on the basis of the delivery date and quantity of materials to be supplied specified in the purchase order, the supplier dispatches the materials. After receiving the materials, the goods receipt is posted in the mySAP ERP system and an invoice is generated. Toward the end, the invoice posting payment is processed.

After discussing the P2P cycle in detail, let's discuss the documents that are processed in the P2P cycle.

In the P2P cycle, various documents, such as purchase requisitions, purchase orders, request for quotations (RFQs), goods receipts, and invoice receipts are used for the internal and external transactions of an organization. The documents used for maintaining the internal transactions of an organization are called internal documents. For example, a purchase requisition is used by various departments of an organization to request that the purchasing department procure materials or services. External documents, on the other hand, are used to send information to external business dealers, such as vendors. For example, a purchase order is used to send information to vendors outside the organization. The list of P2P documents are as follows:

- **Purchase requisition**—Represents the request of various departments for the procurement of materials or services. You can create a purchase requisition either manually with the help of the ME51N transaction code or automatically in the material requirements planning (MRP) process by selecting the auto purchase requisitions option. While creating a purchase requisition, you need to provide details in various fields, such as material or service, quantity, source of supply, and delivery date. You should note that these fields vary depending on the type of procurement. In the mySAP ERP system, the document types are predefined for various procurement types. For example, the NB document type is used for the standard procurement type and the UB document type is used for the stock transfer procurement type. The purchase requisition document is used to create RFQs, purchase orders, or outline agreements.
- **RFQ**—Serves as an external document that is used by the purchasing department to locate a vendor. In the mySAP ERP system, an RFQ can be created either automatically, with reference to a purchase requisition, or manually. In addition, the mySAP ERP system predefines AN as the RFQ document type. While creating an RFQ, you need to provide details in various fields, such as material or service description, quantity, and required-by date. The vendor's responses on RFQs are received and updated in the mySAP ERP system. Further, the purchasing department can send a purchase order to a selected vendor. However, if the price or conditions quoted by a vendor are not

acceptable by the purchasing department, a rejection letter can be sent to the vendor.

▪ **Purchase order**—Represents the request made to the vendor to supply materials or services under the defined conditions that specify the required quantity and delivery date. In the mySAP ERP system, a purchase order can be created with or without a reference to a purchase requisition, RFQ, or contracts. You can define a purchase order by either using the ME59 transaction code or automatically converting a purchase requisition into a purchase order. While creating a purchase order as much information as possible, such as terms of payment and ordering address, is retrieved from the master records. The standard SAP document type for purchase order is FO.

▪ **Goods receipt**—Serves as an acknowledgement indicating that the goods have been received at the right time and in the correct quantity. The goods receipt helps in updating the inventory status, verifying under-delivery or over-delivery of materials, and generating the following documents:

   ▫ **Material document**—Updates the stock in the Inventory Management (IM) module
   ▫ **Accounting document**—Updates the books of accounts in the Financial Accounting (FI) module

In the mySAP ERP system, the goods receipt is generated on the basis of the purchase order.

▪ **Invoice verification**—Helps to process payments to suppliers and post an invoice in the mySAP ERP system. You can post an invoice with or without reference to a purchase order. When generating an invoice with reference to a purchase order, the mySAP ERP system automatically uses the information, such as material, quantity, terms of payment, and amount, provided in the purchase order. After posting the invoice, the payment is processed by the finance department.

After discussing P2P documents, let's explore the various types of procurement processes.

EXPLORING THE DIRECT MATERIAL PROCUREMENT PROCESS

The process of procuring materials that are directly used for production purposes is known as the direct material procurement process. Consider the scenario of an enterprise that produces washing machines. The parts or components of a washing machine, such as electromechanical buzzers, suppressors, and electronic timers, are procured from external sources. As these parts are directly used in the manufacturing of washing machines, they are purchased, stored in the inventory, and issued to the production department, depending upon the department's need.

Figure A.2 shows the direct material procurement process:

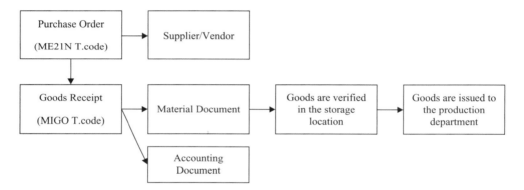

FIGURE A.2   Displaying the direct procurement process

Figure A.2 shows that in the direct procurement process, the purchase order is first created through the ME21N transaction code. Then, the purchase order is transferred to the supplier or vendor and used to create the goods receipt document through the MIGO transaction code. The goods receipt document is used as a material document to verify the goods received at the storage location. The goods receipt document is also used as an accounting document and posted in the FI module. Finally, the goods stored in the storage location are issued to the production department for production purposes.

You need to perform the following steps to implement direct material procurement in the mySAP ERP system:

1. Create a purchase requisition
2. Create a purchase order

3. Post a goods receipt
4. Post an invoice

Let's perform each of these steps in the given sequence.

Creating a Purchase Requisition

In the mySAP ERP system, you can create a purchase requisition by using the ME51N transaction code. While creating a purchase requisition, you should select NB as the document type. Perform the following steps to create a purchase requisition:

1. Enter the ME51N transaction code in the transaction code text box and press the ENTER key, as shown in Figure A.3:

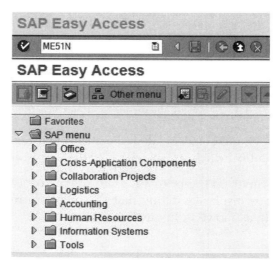

FIGURE A.3   Displaying the ME51N transaction code

The **Create Purchase Requisition** screen appears (Figure A.4).

2. Enter the required details in the **Create Purchase Requisition** screen, as shown in Figure A.4:

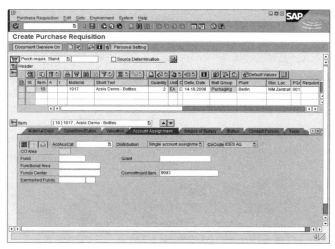

FIGURE A.4   Specifying the details for a purchase requisition

Figure A.4 shows the details related to material, delivery date, material group, plant, and quantity, which are specified for the new purchase requisition.

3. Click the **Save** (⊟) icon to save the details of a purchase requisition. A message is displayed stating that the purchase requisition was created successfully, as shown in Figure A.5:

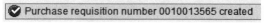

FIGURE A.5   Displaying the message indicating the successful creation of a purchase requisition

Now, let's learn to create a purchase order based on this purchase requisition.

Creating a Purchase Order

A purchase order contains the details of the material requirements specified in the purchase requisition. In the mySAP ERP system, you can create a purchase order with the help of the `ME21N` transaction code.

Perform the following steps to create a purchase order:

1. Enter the `ME21N` transaction code in the transaction code field of the **SAP Easy Access** screen and press the ENTER key, as shown in Figure A.6:

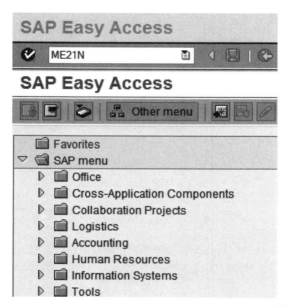

FIGURE A.6   Displaying the transaction code to create a purchase order

The **Create Purchase Order** screen appears (Figure A.7).

2. Enter the details, such as the purchasing organization, purchasing group, company code, vendor, material, delivery date, net price, and currency, as shown in Figure A.7:

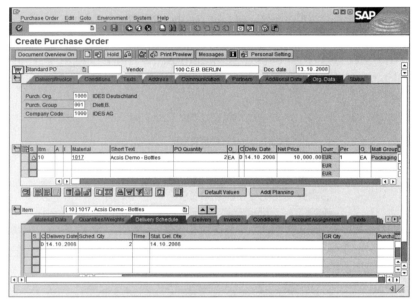

FIGURE A.7 **Displaying the Create Purchase Order screen**

3. Click the **Save** (🖫) icon to create the purchase order. The message confirming the successful creation of a purchase order is displayed, as shown in Figure A.8:

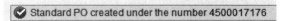

Standard PO created under the number 4500017176

FIGURE A.8 **Displaying the message confirming the successful creation of a purchase order**

Based on the standard purchase order, you can now post the goods receipt, as discussed in the following subsection.

Posting the Goods Receipt

After receiving the goods, their details are posted in the mySAP ERP system with reference to the purchase order. You can use the `MIGO` transaction code to post the goods receipt.

Perform the following steps to post the goods receipt in the mySAP ERP system:

1. Enter the `MIGO` transaction code in the transaction code text box and press the ENTER key, as shown in Figure A.9:

FIGURE A.9   **Displaying the transaction code to post a goods receipt**

The **Goods Receipt Purchase Order – User Test** screen appears (Figure A.10).

2. Enter `4500017176` as the purchase order in the **Goods Receipt Purchase Order – User Test** screen (Figure A.10).

3. Click the **Execute** (⊕) icon, as shown in Figure A.10:

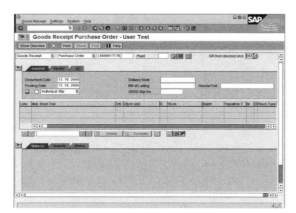

FIGURE A.10   Displaying the Goods Receipt Purchase Order – User Test screen

The details of the material are displayed in the **Header Data** and **Detail Data**
sections (Figure A.11).

4. Check the **Item OK** check box (Figure A.11).
5. Click the **Check** button, as shown in Figure A.11:

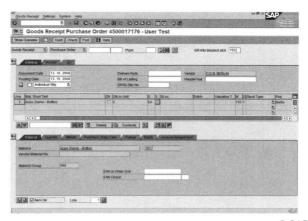

FIGURE A.11   Displaying the Goods Receipt Purchase Order 4500017178 – User Test screen

A traffic light appears displaying whether or not the details of the material entered in the **Header Data** and **Detail Data** sections are correct. The following are the colors of the traffic light:

- **Red**—Indicates that an error has occurred
- **Yellow**—Indicates a warning message
- **Green**—Indicates that the details entered in the purchase order document are correct

In our case, the green light appears and the **Document is O.K.** message is displayed, as shown in Figure A.12:

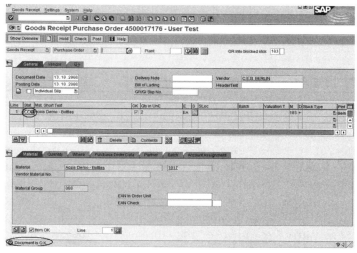

FIGURE A.12   **Displaying the successful verification of the goods receipt**

After checking the details of the goods receipt, you need to post the goods receipt for further payment processing in the FI module.

6. Click the **Post** button to post the goods receipt (Figure A.12). A message appears, indicating the successful posting of the goods receipt, as shown in Figure A.13:

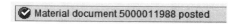

FIGURE A.13   **Displaying the message indicating the successful posting of the goods receipt**

After posting the goods receipt, the invoice is posted with reference to the purchase order.

Posting the Invoice

When the invoice is received from a vendor, it is posted in the mySAP ERP system by using the `MIRO` transaction code. You need to provide details, such as the document date, posting date, and purchase order number, to post an invoice. The details of the specified purchase order are retrieved by the mySAP ERP system. You can check whether or not the transaction is posted in the correct account by clicking the **Simulate** button.

After understanding the direct material procurement process, let's now explore the indirect material procurement process and learn how to implement it in the mySAP ERP system.

EXPLORING THE INDIRECT MATERIAL PROCUREMENT PROCESS

The process of procuring materials that are used indirectly in the production of finished goods is known as the indirect material procurement process. The stationery used by the employees of an organization or the spare parts of a machine that are required to fix a damaged machine are some examples of indirectly used materials. Let's consider a scenario to understand the indirect material procurement process. An organization, which manufactures washing machines, procures components of machines from external sources for direct production purposes. However, the employees of the organization also require stationery, printers, and computers to perform day-to-day activities. Out of these materials, stationery is stored in the storage locations; however, computers as well as printers are procured depending upon the requirements. As the costs of these materials are directly posted in the consumption accounts, they are not managed on the value basis in the IM module.

You should note that indirect materials are procured for direct consumption but for indirect manufacturing purposes. Due to their direct consumption, the indirect materials should be assigned a consumption category in the purchase order. In the mySAP ERP system, the consumption category is assigned on the basis of the account assignment category. The account assignment category is used to determine the cost elements for a specific category. In other words, this category specifies whether or not accounting of an item would be affected through an auxiliary account, such as project, cost center, and sales order.

You can implement the indirect material procurement process in the mySAP ERP system by performing the following steps:

1. Create a purchase requisition by specifying the account assignment category
2. Create a purchase order on the basis of the specified account assignment category
3. Post the goods receipt
4. Post the invoice

The preceding steps are similar to the ones discussed in the *Exploring the Direct Material Procurement Process* section.

Sometimes, the customer requirements are not met by the account assignment categories that are defined in the mySAP ERP system. In such situations, you need to create an account assignment category and a material master record in the mySAP ERP system, which we learn next.

Creating an Account Assignment Category

In the mySAP ERP system, there are a few predefined account assignment categories, such as A representing assets, C representing sales order, and K representing cost center. In addition to these predefined categories, you can define a new account assignment category by performing the following steps:

1. Navigate the following menu path to create an account assignment category:

Menu Path

SAP Customizing Implementation Guide > Materials Management > Purchasing > Account Assignment > Maintain Account Assignment Categories

2. Click the **IMG Activity** (⊕) icon beside the **Maintain Account Assignment Categories** activity, as shown in Figure A.14:

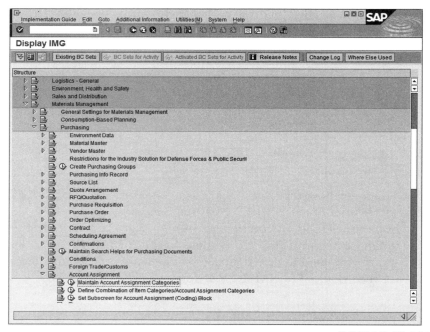

FIGURE A.14   Displaying the menu path to create an account assignment category

The **Change View "Account Assignment Categories": Overview** screen appears (Figure A.15).

3. Click the **New Entries** button, as shown in Figure A.15:

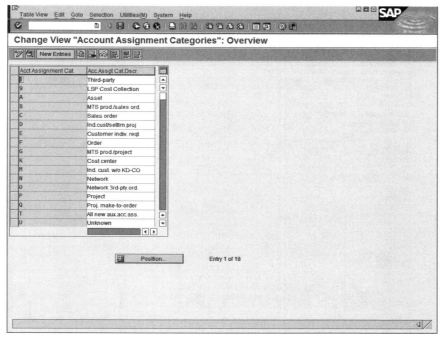

FIGURE A.15   **Displaying the Change View "Account Assignment Categories": Overview screen**

The **New Entries: Details of Added Entries** screen appears (Figure A.16).

4. Enter the account assignment category in the **Acct. Assignment Cat.** field. In our case, we have entered S in the **Acct. Assignment Cat.** field and Nw. Accnt. Assignment as the description (Figure A.16).

5. Enter the consumption indicator in the **Consumption posting** field. In our case, we have entered P as the consumption indicator (Figure A.16).

6. Click the **Save** (🖫) icon to save the entered details, as shown in Figure A.16:

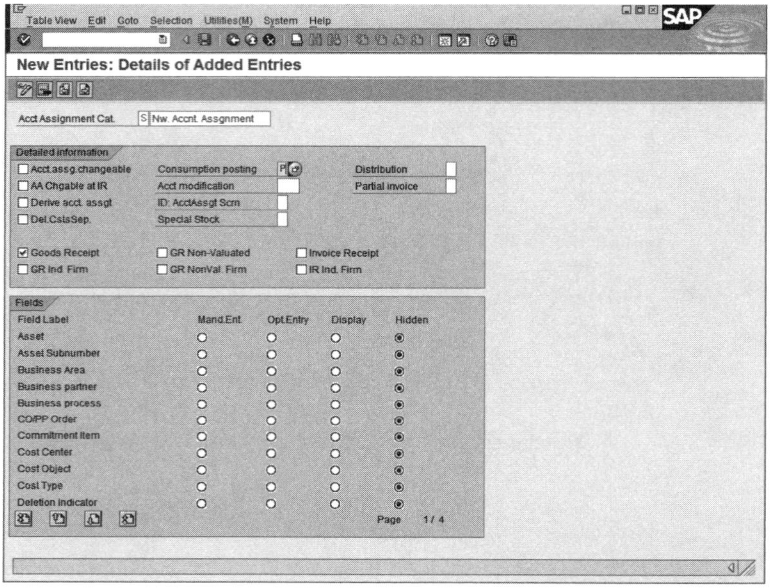

FIGURE A.16   Displaying the New Entries: Details of Added Entries screen

Figure A.16 shows the controlling options for the new account assignment category.

After clicking the **Save** (🖫) icon, a message appears on the status bar of the **New Entries: Details of Added Entries** screen confirming that the data is saved.

> **Note:** You can also check the check boxes, such as **Goods Receipt, GR Non-Valuated**, and **Invoice Receipt**, shown in Figure A.16, depending upon the requirements. For example, if you want the mySAP ERP system to verify whether a goods receipt is required or not, you should select the **Goods Receipt** indicator. Similarly, the **GR Non-Valuated** check box specifies whether the goods receipt should be valuated or not. In our case, we have checked the **Goods Receipt** check box.

Let's now learn how to create material master records for indirect materials.

Creating the Material Master Record for an Indirect Material

While creating material master records, you need to specify the material type as it helps to decide whether a material should be maintained on the basis of quantity, value, or both. The UNBW or NLAG material type is used to indicate that the indirect materials are not valuated. Perform the following steps to create the material master record for an indirect material:

1. Navigate the following menu path to create the material master record:

Menu Path

SAP Customizing Implementation Guide > Logistics-General > Material Master > Basic Settings > Material Types > Define Attributes of Material Types. The **Display IMG** screen appears (Figure A.17).

2. Click the **IMG Activity** (🌐) icon beside the **Define Attributes of Material Types** activity, as shown in Figure A.17:

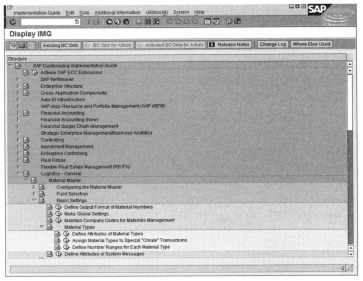

FIGURE A.17   **Displaying the menu path to define the material master record for an indirect material**

The **Change View "Material types": Overview** screen appears (Figure A.18).

3. Select the NLAG material type and double-click the **Quantity/value updating** folder, as shown in Figure A.18:

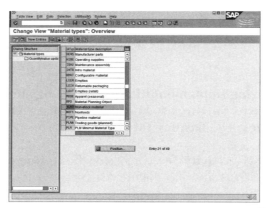

FIGURE A.18   Displaying the Change View "Material Types": Overview screen

The **Quantity/value updating** details of the materials under the NLAG material type are displayed, as shown in Figure A.19:

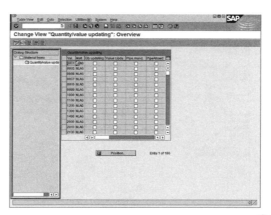

FIGURE A.19   Displaying the Change View "Quantity/value updating": Overview screen

Figure A.19 shows the **Qty updating**, **Value updating**, **Pipe mandatory**, and **PipeAllowd** check boxes, which can be used to configure the material types.

After understanding the implementation of the indirect material procurement process, let's explore the concept of a blanket purchase order.

EXPLORING A BLANKET PURCHASE ORDER

A blanket purchase order facilitates avoiding repetitive data entry and the creation of multiple purchase orders for a supplier from whom materials are regularly purchased at a fixed price. It is a long-term agreement valid for a specified period of time between a company and its supplier. This type of purchase order uses a single purchase order number for multiple purchases and allows you to limit the type of goods or services and the order value.

In the mySAP ERP system, the B item category and the FO document type is used for a blanket purchase order. While creating a blanket purchase order, you should specify its description and validity period. Let's consider a scenario to understand the concept of a blanket purchase order in detail. Imagine an organization wants to create an annual agreement with the landscaping service providers to clean the lawn on a monthly basis. The company cannot directly pay for the entire year; instead, a blanket purchase order is created so that the monthly amount is paid for lawn servicing. In the mySAP ERP system, the organization creates the blanket purchase order for 12 months by using a single purchase order number. The monthly amount to be paid is also included in the blanket purchase order. In addition, the organization creates the blanket order rules to set the expiration date, that is, 12 months from the current date. Each month, the landscaping service provider cleans the lawn and receives invoices for it. In other words, the organization generates a release order for each month to pay the invoice. When the 12 releases are made against the blanket purchase order, the purchase order finally gets completed. The organization needs to perform the following steps to complete the processing of the blanket purchase order:

1. Create a purchase requisition by selecting the FO document type and enter B as the item category.
2. Create a purchase order with reference to the purchase requisition.
3. Post an invoice by retrieving the details from the purchase order.

In the mySAP ERP system, the FO document type allows you to enter the validity period at the header level of the purchase order and select the B (Limit) item category.

After understanding the blanket purchase order, let's explore the service procurement process.

EXPLORING THE SERVICE PROCUREMENT PROCESS

The process of procuring external services, such as painting, repairing electric fitting, and plumbing, from a supplier is known as the service procurement process. Consider a scenario where a company hires an external vendor to repair electric fittings. The procurement of external services is similar to the procurement of consumable materials, as these services are also procured for consumption.

To procure these services, you need to create and send a service purchase order to the vendor. As compared to material procurement, no goods receipt is posted in the case of service procurement. Instead of a goods receipt, a service entry sheet is maintained to record the details of the services provided by the vendor. Figure A.20 shows the implementation of the service procurement process in the mySAP ERP system:

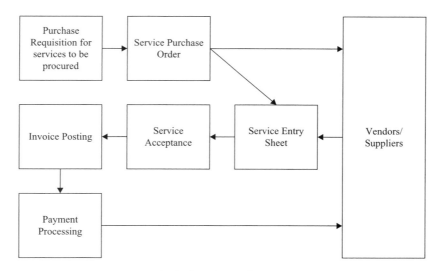

FIGURE A.20 **Displaying the service procurement process**

Figure A.20 shows that a purchase requisition is created to define the services that need to be procured. Next, a service purchase order is created with reference to the purchase requisition, which is then sent to a vendor or supplier. In addition, the service entry sheet is maintained to keep records of the services provided by the vendor or supplier. Further, an invoice is posted in the mySAP ERP system and the payment is processed.

You need to create the following documents for the service procurement process:

- **Service entry sheet**—Maintains the records of the services availed by an organization from an external vendor. When the services are availed completely, the service entry sheet is signed off and the invoice postings are made.
- **Invoice verification document**—Maintains the invoice details after the service entry sheet is signed off. You should note that invoice verification is performed with reference to purchase orders.

Let's now learn how to create the service master record required to implement the service procurement process.

Creating the Service Master Record

In the mySAP ERP system, the service master record is used to maintain the records of the external services procured from vendors. You can create a service master record by using the AC03 transaction code and then entering important details, such as a description of the services as well as the unit of measure. You need to enter the AC03 transaction code in the transaction code field, as shown in Figure A.21:

FIGURE A.21 **Displaying the transaction code to create a service master record**

The **Display Service SVCS – 002** screen appears, as shown in Figure A.22:

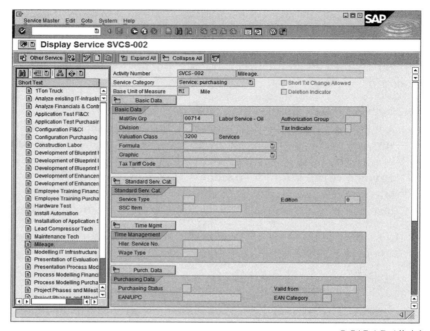

FIGURE A.22 Showing the Display Service SVCS – 002 screen

Figure A.22 shows the service description and unit of measure.

You can also assign a price to a service master record in which the service conditions are defined in the following ways:

- **Defining or maintaining service conditions at the service level**—Use the ML45 transaction code to add or define service conditions. You can change the service conditions with the help of the ML46 transaction code. Moreover, the ML47 transaction code is used to display the service conditions, as shown in Figure A.23:

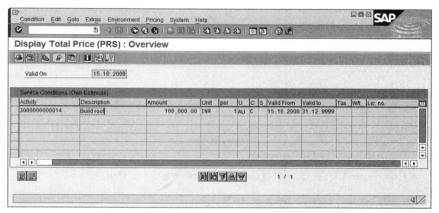

FIGURE A.23   **Displaying the service condition**

- **Defining or maintaining service conditions at the service and vendor level**—Use the ML39 transaction code to add the service condition at the service as well as vendor level. After entering the ML39 transaction code, you need to select the vendor and enter prices on the basis of services provided by the vendor. In addition, you can use the ML40 or ML41 transaction code to change or display the service conditions, respectively.
- **Defining or maintaining service conditions at the service, vendor, and plant level**—Use the ML33 transaction code to add the service conditions at the service, vendor, and plant levels. After entering the ML33 transaction code, you need to select the vendor, plant combinations, and prices for the services. In addition, you can use the ML34 or ML35 transaction

code to change or display the service conditions at the service, vendor, and plant level.

After discussing how to create the service master record and define service conditions, let's learn how to implement the service procurement process in the mySAP ERP system. You need to perform the following steps to implement the service procurement process:

1. Create a purchase order
2. Create, maintain, and accept the service entry sheet
3. Verify the invoice

Let's now discuss each of the preceding steps in detail.

Creating a Purchase Order for the Service Procurement Process

While creating the purchase order for the service procurement process, the item category D (services) and account assignment category K (cost center) or U (unknown) should be selected. The service master number and quantity should be entered in the item details, while prices are automatically retrieved from the condition records.

Perform the following steps to create a purchase order for services:

1. Enter the ME21N transaction code in the transaction code field and press the ENTER key (Figure A.6). The **Create Purchase Order** screen appears (Figure A.24).
2. Select K or U as the account assignment category and D as the item category (Figure A.24).
3. Enter the details for the items in the **Item Details** section, as shown in Figure A.24:

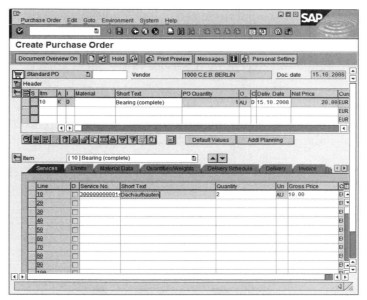

FIGURE A.24   **Displaying purchase order details for services**

Figure A.24 shows the details retrieved from the condition records.

4. Click the **Save** (🖫) icon to save the purchase order. The **Standard PO created under the number 4500017177** message appears, as shown in Figure A.25:

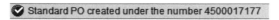

FIGURE A.25   **Displaying the message indicating the successful creation of a purchase order**

After creating the purchase order, let's learn how to create, maintain, and accept a service entry sheet in the mySAP ERP system.

Creating, Maintaining, and Accepting a Service Entry Sheet

To keep record of the services provided by the vendor, you need to maintain a service entry sheet. After availing the services, the service entry sheet is signed off. In the mySAP ERP system, perform the following steps to create, maintain, and accept the service entry sheet:

1. Enter the ML81N transaction code in the transaction code field and press the ENTER key, as shown in Figure A.26:

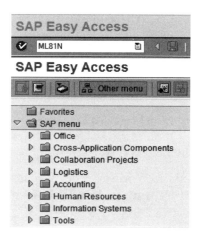

FIGURE A.26   **Displaying the transaction code to maintain a service entry sheet**

The **Service Entry Sheet** screen appears (Figure A.27).

2. Click the **Other Purchase Order** push button, as shown in Figure A.27:

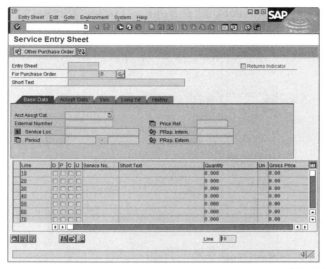

FIGURE A.27   Displaying the Service Entry Sheet screen

The **Select Purchase Order/Entry Sheet** dialog box appears (Figure A.28).

3. Enter the 4500017177 purchase order number in the **Purchase Order** field (Figure A.28).
4. Click the **Continue** (☑) icon, as shown in Figure A.28:

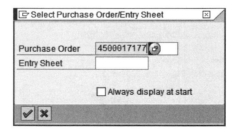

FIGURE A.28   Displaying the Select Purchase Order/Entry Sheet dialog box

The **Service Entry Against Purchase Order 4500017177** screen appears (Figure A.29).

5. Click the **Create** (⬜) icon, as shown in Figure A.29:

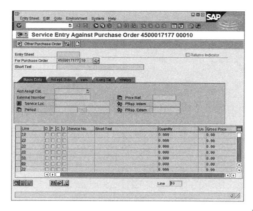

FIGURE A.29   Displaying the Service Entry Against Purchase Order 4500017177 screen

The **100000263 Create Entry Sheet** screen appears (Figure A.30).

6. Select **Cost center** as the account assignment category and enter Service Procurement Process in the **Short Text** box, as shown in Figure A.30:

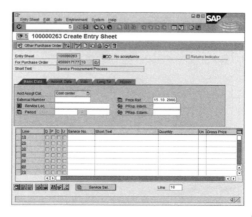

FIGURE A.30   Displaying the 100000263 Create Entry Sheet screen

Figure A.30 shows various tabs, such as **Basic Data, Accept Data, Vals, Long Txt**, and **History**, which can be selected depending upon the type of data to be provided. When all the services are recorded in the service entry sheet, you need to accept the sheet. The traffic light on the **100000263 Create Entry Sheet** screen indicates the status of the service entry sheet. The following are the colors of the traffic light:

- **Red**—Indicates that the service entry sheet is not accepted
- **Yellow**—Indicates that the service entry sheet is accepted but is not saved
- **Green**—Indicates that the service entry sheet is accepted and saved

7. Click the **Save** (▣) icon to save the entered details (Figure A.30).

After maintaining and accepting the service entry sheet, post the invoice for the direct procurement process.

Let's now explore the consignment procurement process.

EXPLORING THE CONSIGNMENT PROCUREMENT PROCESS

The process, in which a vendor keeps the material with a company, while the ownership is retained by the vendor until the material is sold or used, is known as the consignment process. In the consignment procurement process, a consignment agreement should be created between a company and a vendor. In such a situation, the company should pay the vendor before issuing material to the production department.

Let's consider a scenario where a washing machine manufacturing company procures suppressors from a vendor and keeps the stock of suppressors in its warehouse. Even if the stock is stored in the company's warehouse, the vendor remains the owner of the stock. The company would pay the vendor for the suppressors stock only if the suppressors are issued to the production department. In such a case, the vendor would be regularly informed about the issue of suppressors to the production department and invoices would be generated accordingly.

The prices and conditions of the consignment procurement process are specified in the consignment info records, instead of the consignment purchase order. In other words, the consignment info records are created to maintain the prices and conditions of a consignment. As the invoices are settled on a periodic basis, the prices and conditions are retrieved by the mySAP ERP system from the consignment info records.

You need to perform the following steps to implement the consignment procurement process in the mySAP ERP system:

1. Create a consignment info record
2. Create a consignment purchase order
3. Post the goods receipt
4. Post the goods issue
5. Settle the consignment liabilities

Let's now perform each of these tasks.

Creating a Consignment Info Record

In the case of consignment procurement, you need to create consignment info records that are different from the info records maintained for stock material procurement. In the mySAP ERP system, you need to select the **Consignment** category to create a consignment info record (Figure A.32). The consignment price and conditions are specified in the consignment info record (Figure A.33).

Perform the following steps to create a consignment info record:

1. Enter the ME11 transaction code in the transaction code field and press the ENTER key, as shown in Figure A.31:

FIGURE A.31 Displaying the transaction code to create an info record

The **Create Info Record: Initial Screen** appears (Figure A.32).

2. Enter the vendor details in the **Vendor** field. In our case, we have entered 1000 as the vendor (Figure A.32).
3. Enter the material number in the **Material** field. In our case, we have entered I-22600 as the material number (Figure A.32).
4. Enter the code for purchasing organization in the **Purchasing Org.** field. In our case, we have entered 1000 as the purchasing organization code (Figure A.32).
5. Enter the plant code in the **Plant** field. In our case, we have entered 1300 as plant code (Figure A.32).
6. Click the **Enter** (✓) icon, as shown in Figure A.32:

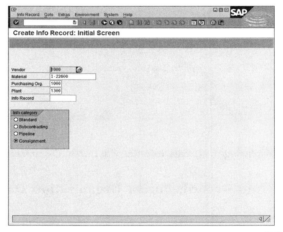

FIGURE A.32   Displaying the Create Info Record: Initial Screen

The **Create Info Record: Purch. Organization Data 1** screen appears (Figure A.33).

7. Enter the quantity in the **Standard Qty** field. In our case, we have entered 2 (Figure A.33).

8. Enter the net price in the **Net Price** field. In our case, we have entered 100 (Figure A.33).

9. Click the **Enter** (☑) icon, as shown in Figure A.33:

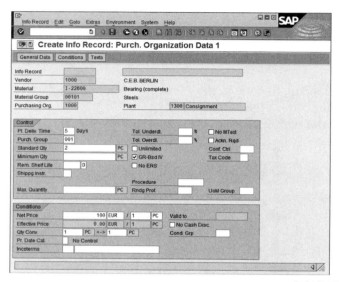

FIGURE A.33   Displaying the Create Info Record: Purch. Organization Data 1 screen

The **Create Info Record: Purch. Organization Data 2** screen appears (Figure A.34).

10. Enter the quotation in the **Quotation** field. In our case, we have entered 10 as the quotation (Figure A.34).

11. Click the **Enter** (☑) icon, as shown in Figure A.34:

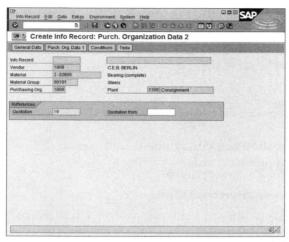

FIGURE A.34   **Displaying the Create Info Record: Purch. Organization Data 2 screen**

The **Create Info Record: Text Overview** screen appears (Figure A.35).

12. Enter the text in the **Info record note** field (Figure A.35).
13. Click the **Save** (🖫) icon, as shown in Figure A.35:

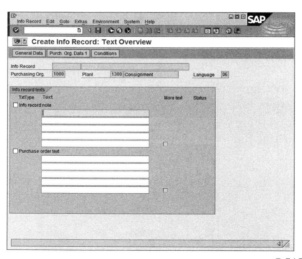

FIGURE A.35   **Displaying the Create Info Record: Text Overview screen**

The message indicating the successful creation of the purchasing info record is displayed, as shown in Figure A.36:

FIGURE A.36   **Displaying the message indicating the successful creation of an info record**

After creating the consignment info record, let's learn how to create a consignment purchase order.

Creating a Consignment Purchase Order

A consignment purchase order is similar to a standard purchase order. Therefore, the steps to create a consignment purchase order are similar to those of creating a purchase order, as discussed in the *Creating a Purchase Order* subsection of the *Exploring the Direct Material Procurement Process* section.

The ME21N transaction code is used to create a consignment purchase order. However, while creating a consignment purchase order, you do not need to specify the price and conditions. In addition, you need to select the K item category, which represents the consignment scenario, to create a consignment purchase order.

Let's now learn how to post the goods receipt in the consignment procurement process.

Posting the Goods Receipt

To post the goods receipt in the consignment procurement process, select 201 K as the movement type. In the 201K movement type, K serves as a special stock indicator for consignment material.

Perform the following steps to post the goods receipt for consignment procurement:

1. Enter MIGO as the transaction code to post the goods receipt (Figure A.9).

The **Goods Receipt Purchase Order – User Test** screen appears (Figure A.37).

2. Enter `4500017047` as the vendor code and `1100` as the plant code (Figure A.37).
3. Select `201 K` to represent consignment of material (Figure A.37).
4. Click the **IMG Activity** (⚙) icon, as shown in Figure A.37:

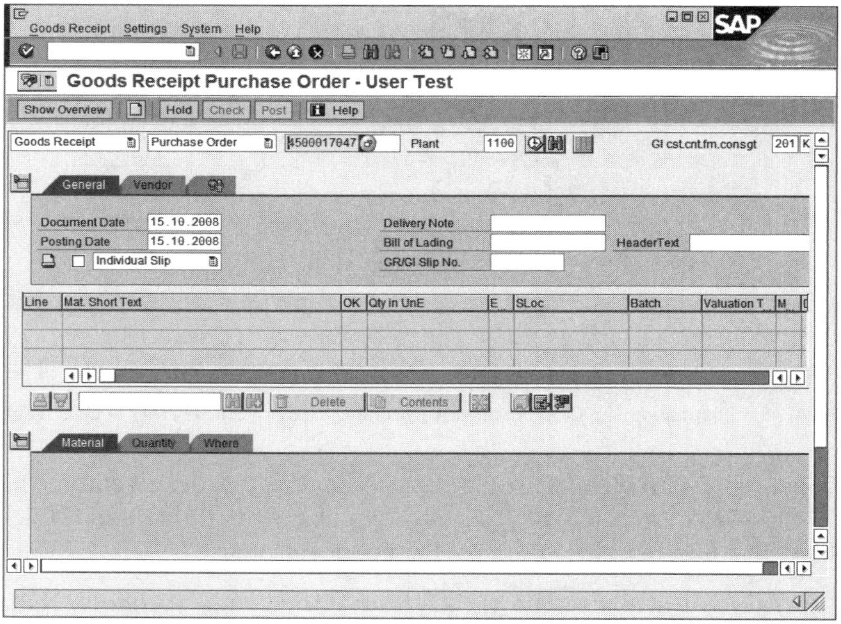

FIGURE A.37 **Displaying the Goods Receipt Purchase Order – User Test screen**

The details of the material appear in the **Item Details** header, as shown in Figure A.38:

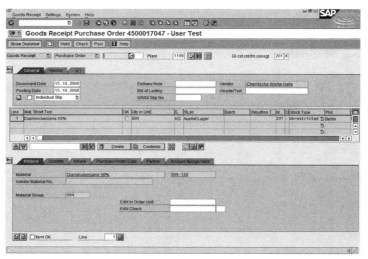

FIGURE A.38   Displaying the Goods Receipt Purchase Order 4500017047 – User Test screen

5. Click the **Check** button to check whether the item details entered are correct or not. The green light is displayed indicating that the item is OK.
6. Click the **Post** button to post the goods receipt.

You can also use the MMBE transaction code to check the vendor's consignment stock.

Let's now learn how to post goods that are issued from consignment stock.

Posting the Goods Issue for Consignment Stock

With the consignment procurement process, an organization can either issue the goods to the production department or transfer the goods from consignment stock to the organization's stock. When issuing goods to the production department, you need to access the `MIGO_GI` transaction code, select `201 K` as the movement type, and enter the following details in the mySAP ERP system:

- Vendor code
- Quantity
- Storage location
- Cost center

After entering the preceding details, the material and accounting documents are created and the consignment liability is generated. In other words, the account payable is credited and the consumption account is debited.

However, when transferring the goods to the organization's stock, the `MIGO_TR` transaction code is used and the `411 K` movement type is selected. You also need to provide the following details in the mySAP ERP system:

- Vendor code
- Quantity
- Storage location

In this case, the consignment liability is generated by crediting the account payable and debiting the stock account.

Let's now discuss how to settle consignment liabilities.

Settling the Consignment Liabilities

When the consignment goods are used by an organization, the organization is liable to pay the vendor. The organization periodically settles the consignment liabilities against a vendor. In the mySAP ERP system, the `MRKO` transaction code is used to settle the consignment liabilities through either an online or on the batch basis. You need to enter the company code, plant, and vendor details in the **Consignment and Pipeline Settlement** screen. Next, you should select the **Settle** option and click the **Execute** icon in the mySAP ERP system. The list of materials and invoice documents that are pending for settlement is displayed.

Let's now learn the subcontracting procurement process.

EXPLORING THE SUBCONTRACTING PROCUREMENT PROCESS

Subcontracting is an outsourcing process in which an enterprise hands over raw materials to a subcontractor to produce and return the final or semi-finished products. In other words, the raw components are sent to a subcontractor for manufacturing purposes and the finished or semi-finished materials are returned into the inventory of the enterprise. Consider a scenario where a washing machine manufacturing company issues the raw materials to a subcontractor to produce the suppressors of the machine. The subcontractor utilizes the raw material to produce the suppressors according to the design and quality standards specified by the manufacturing company, and is paid for the labor by the manufacturing company in turn.

Figure A.39 shows the implementation process flow of the subcontract procurement process in the mySAP ERP system:

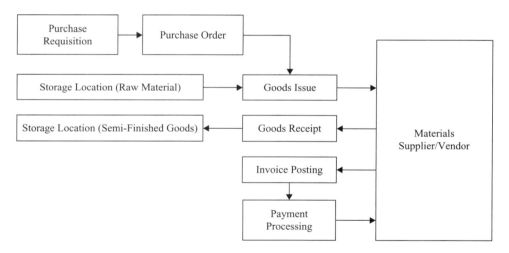

FIGURE A.39   Displaying the process flow of the subcontracting procurement process

Figure A.39 shows the process flow of the subcontract procurement process, illustrating that the raw materials are issued to the subcontractor and the semi-finished goods are received in return. When the goods are received, the goods receipt is posted in the mySAP ERP system. You can see that no records are maintained in the books of accounts when the raw material is issued to the subcontractor; however, the raw material issued is valuated during the stock valuation process and displayed in the stock overview reports. The material and accounting documents are maintained when the goods receipt is posted; whereas, the bill of material (BOM) and subcontract info records are maintained during the subcontract procurement process. The BOM contains a list of materials required to manufacture a component.

You need to perform the following steps to implement the subcontract procurement process in the mySAP ERP system:

1. Create subcontract info records
2. Create a BOM
3. Create a subcontract purchase order
4. Post the goods issue
5. Post the goods receipt
6. Post the invoice
7. Post the settlement

Let's now learn to perform each of these steps.

Creating Subcontract Info Records

The info records maintained for the subcontract procurement process are different from the info records maintained for the material procurement process. While creating subcontract info records, ensure that the **Subcontracting** option is selected in the **Create Info Record: Initial Screen**. In the mySAP ERP system, the conditions defined in the info records are copied into the subcontract purchase order.

Perform the following steps to create subcontract info records:

1. Enter the ME11 transaction code in the transaction code field (Figure A.31). The **Create Info Record: Initial Screen** appears (Figure A.40).
2. Enter vendor details in the **Vendor** field. In our case, we have entered 1007 as the vendor code (Figure A.40).
3. Enter the material code in the **Material** field. In our case, we have entered 100-200 as the material code (Figure A.40).

4. Enter the purchasing organization code in the **Purchasing Org.** field. In our case, we have entered `1000` as the purchasing organization code (Figure A.40).
5. Enter the plant code in the **Plant** field. In our case, we have entered `1000` as the plant code (Figure A.40).
6. Select the **Subcontracting** radio button (Figure A.40).
7. Click the **Enter** (✓) icon, as shown in Figure A.40:

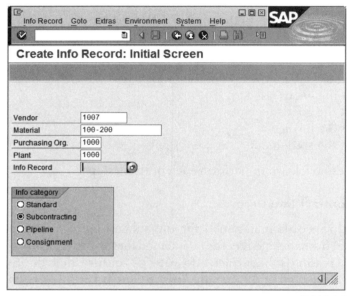

FIGURE A.40   Displaying the Create Info Record: Initial Screen

The **Create Info Record: General Data** screen appears (Figure A.41).

8. Enter the relevant details in the **Create Info Record: General Data** screen and click the **Enter** (✅) icon, as shown in Figure A.41:

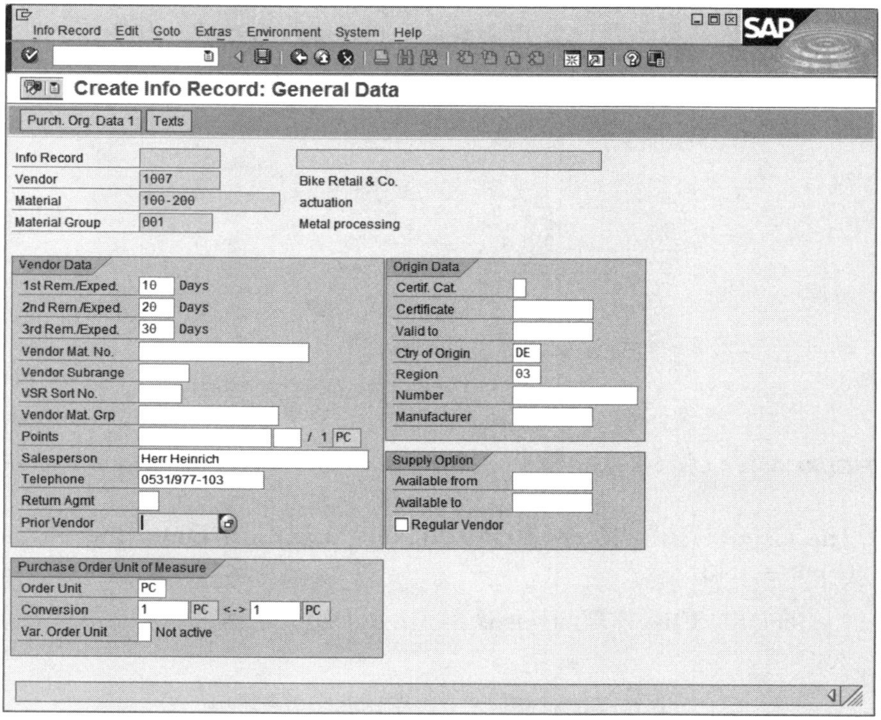

FIGURE A.41   **Displaying the Create Info Record: General Data screen**

The **Create Info Record: Purch. Organization Data 1** screen appears (Figure A.42).

9. Enter 2 as the standard quantity in the **Standard Qty** field (Figure A.42).

10. Enter 100 in the **Net Price** field and click the **Enter** () icon, as shown in Figure A.42:

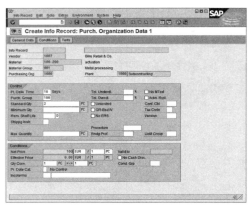

FIGURE A.42   Displaying the Create Info Record: Purch. Organization Data 1 screen

The **Create Info Record: Purch. Organization Data 2** screen appears (Figure A.43).

11. Click the **Enter** () icon, as shown in Figure A.43:

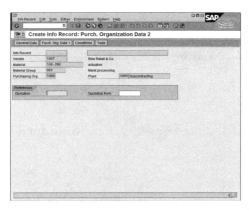

FIGURE A.43   Displaying the Create Info Record: Purch. Organization Data 2 screen

The **Create Info Record: Text Overview** screen appears (Figure A.44).

12. Enter `New Info Record for Subcontracting` in the text box under the **Info record note** check box and click the **Save** (🖫) icon, as shown in Figure A.44:

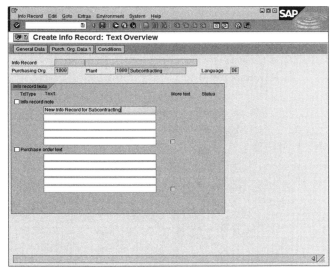

FIGURE A.44   Displaying the Create Info Record: Text Overview screen

The **Purchasing info record 5300005726 1000L 1000 created** message appears, as shown in Figure A.45:

FIGURE A.45   Displaying the message indicating the successful creation of an info record

After creating the subcontract info record, let's discuss how to create a BOM.

Creating a BOM

While creating a purchase requisition, purchase order, or scheduling agreement, you need to specify one or more sub-items with each subcontract item, and the prior requirement for this is the availability of the bill of material structure and the proper hierarchy setup. These sub-items can also be created manually while creating purchasing documents or copied from an existing BOM.

Perform the following steps to create a BOM:

1. Enter CS01 as the transaction code in the transaction code field and press the ENTER key, as shown in Figure A.46:

FIGURE A.46   **Displaying the transaction code to create a BOM**

The **Create material BOM: Initial Screen** appears (Figure A.47).

2. Enter the material number in the **Material** field. In our case, we have entered RX_5000 in the **Material** field (Figure A.47).
3. Enter the plant code in the **Plant** field. In our case, we have entered 0001 as the plant code (Figure A.47).
4. Enter the BOM code in the **BOM Usage** field. In our case, we have entered 4 as the BOM code (Figure A.47).
5. Click the **Enter** (🗸) icon, as shown in Figure A.47:

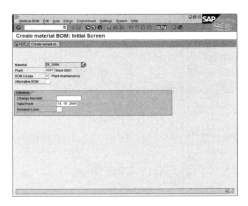

FIGURE A.47   Displaying the Create material BOM: Initial Screen

The **Create material BOM: General Item Overview** screen appears (Figure A.48).

6. Enter the item details in the **Material** tab, as shown in Figure A.48:

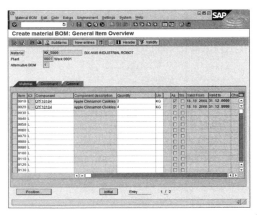

FIGURE A.48   Displaying the Create material BOM: General Item Overview screen

The **Creating BOM for material RX_5000** message appears, as shown in Figure A.49:

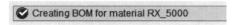

FIGURE A.49   Displaying the message indicating the successful creation of a BOM

After creating a BOM, let's learn how to create a subcontract purchase order.

Creating a Subcontract Purchase Order

You can create a subcontract purchase order in the same way you created a standard purchase order. You should note that while creating a subcontract purchase order, the L item category is selected. In addition, you can enter the item details in the mySAP ERP system either manually or by using a BOM explosion. Item details, such as delivery date, vendor code, quantity, and account assignment category, are entered to create a subcontract purchase order. You can create a subcontract purchase order by using the ME21N transaction code.

Let's now learn how to post the goods issue.

Posting the Goods Issue

After issuing the purchase order, the materials need to be issued to a subcontractor. You can monitor the goods issue to a subcontractor by using the ME20 transaction code. When you enter the ME20 transaction code, the **SC Stock Monitoring for Vendor** screen appears, as shown in Figure A.50:

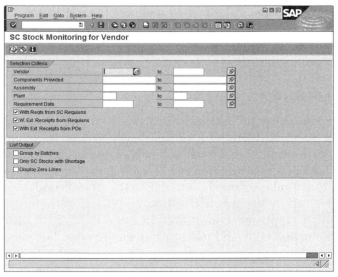

FIGURE A.50   Displaying the SC Stock Monitoring for Vendor screen

Figure A.50 shows various details related to the vendor code, plant code, and components that are used to select the appropriate criterion to display the report of the goods issued. After entering the details, click the **Execute** icon to generate a report displaying the items on the basis of the selected criteria. You can select an item from the report and click the **Post Goods Issue** button to post the goods issue.

Alternatively, you can post the goods issue by using the MIGO_TR transaction code and selecting the 541 movement type. When the MIGO_TR transaction code is used, you need to enter the purchase order number to determine the material and quantity that need to be issued to the subcontractor.

After the goods are issued to a subcontractor, the mySAP ERP system creates the material document. As the goods are still owned by the company, the accounting document is not created.

Let's now discuss how to post the goods receipt.

Posting the Goods Receipt

The subcontractor produces the materials on the basis of the subcontract purchase order and supplies the finished goods to the company. When the company receives the goods, the details of the transaction are posted in the mySAP ERP system with reference to a purchase order. After posting the goods receipt, the number of goods available in the stock is updated. In addition, the materials used by the subcontractor are updated in the mySAP ERP system. The goods receipts are then posted in the mySAP ERP system by using the `MIGO` transaction code and the `101` movement type. You should note that the materials required to produce final goods are posted with the `543` movement type and the co-products are posted with the `545` movement type.

After posting the goods receipt, let's learn to post the invoice for payment processing.

Posting the Invoice

In the mySAP ERP system, the `MIRO` transaction code is used to post an invoice. You need to provide the document date, purchase order number, and posting date to post an invoice. The details, such as quantity, amount, price, and item, are retrieved from the purchase order. Before saving the invoice, you must verify the account posting to avoid the posting of any wrong entry by clicking the **Simulate** button.

Let's now learn how to post the settlement of payment.

Posting the Settlement

When the goods receipt is posted in the mySAP ERP system, the subcontractor informs the organization about over- and under-consumption so that the organization can make further provisions accordingly. In other words, the adjustments for over- and under-consumption are made with reference to a purchase order by using the `MIGO_GS` transaction code. If under-consumption is posted, the stock to be received from the subcontractor is listed in the mySAP ERP system. The `544` movement type represents under-consumption and `543` represents over-consumption. The under-consumption movement type shows that a specified quantity of stock needs to be returned by the subcontractor. However, with the over-consumption movement type, a specified quantity of stock should be provided to the subcontractor.

Let's now discuss the third-party procurement process.

EXPLORING THE THIRD-PARTY PROCUREMENT PROCESS

In the third-party procurement process, a company instructs a supplier to supply the required goods to a third party. Consider a scenario where an enterprise sells and distributes wood to a furniture manufacturing firm. The enterprise procures wood from a wood manufacturing company and asks this company to supply wood to the firm engaged in manufacturing furniture. Such a scenario demonstrates the third-party procurement process where the enterprise provides the address of the third party to whom wood needs to be delivered. In this scenario, the wood manufacturing company is the delivering party and the furniture manufacturing firm is the third party. Figure A.51 illustrates this scenario to help you clearly understand the third-party procurement process:

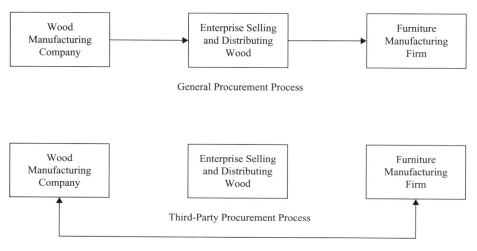

FIGURE A.51   Displaying the third-party procurement scenario

Figure A.51 shows the general procurement process in which the enterprise that is selling and distributing wood procures wood from the wood manufacturing company. Further, the enterprise sells wood to a furniture manufacturing firm. In such a scenario, the general procurement process consumes a lot of time; thereby, the third-party procurement process can be implemented. In the third-party procurement process, the enterprise that distributes wood asks the wood manufacturing company to directly supply wood to the furniture manufacturing firm. So, with the third-party procurement process, while placing an order to a supplier, the address of the third party where the goods need to be finally shipped should be provided. The intermediate party, i.e., the enterprise engaged in selling and distributing wood, posts a statistical goods receipt in the mySAP ERP system to confirm that the goods are shipped to the third party. The process steps for invoice verification for the third-party procurement process are similar to those of other procurement processes.

You can perform the following steps to implement the third-party procurement process in the mySAP ERP system:

1. Create the purchase order by using the `ME21N` transaction code and specify the subcontracting vendor code in the **Delivery Address** tab displayed in the **Item Details** header. After providing the subcontract vendor details, the mySAP ERP system retrieves the delivery address from the vendor master record.

2. Post the goods receipt by using the purchase order. In addition, the material and accounting documents are created while posting the goods receipt. For the third-party procurement process, the `MIGO` transaction code and the `101 O` movement type are used.

3. Post the invoice by using the `MIRO` transaction code in the mySAP ERP system.

After understanding the third-party procurement process, let's learn about the procurement process for a stock transfer.

EXPLORING THE PROCUREMENT PROCESS FOR A STOCK TRANSFER

The movement of stock from one storage location, plant, or company to another is known as stock transfer. Consider a scenario where a washing machine manufacturing company has two plants. Depending on the quantity of components required to produce washing machines, it is possible that during the production process, the company needs to transfer some of the components from one plant to another. You can transfer stock from one plant to another by using stock transport orders, which specify the delivery costs of the stock. Mostly for companies where the warehouses or production units are distributed across different geographical locations, the stock transport order is used to assign the units or subunits (with storage capacity) as plants and then implement the stock transfer process.

Perform the following steps to transfer goods through stock transport orders:

1. Create the stock transport order by using the `ME21N` transaction code and selecting the `UB` document type. In addition, you should enter `U` as the item category for stock transport orders.
2. Post the goods issue from the issuing plant by using the `MIGO_GI` transaction code. Further, select the `351` movement type and enter a stock transport order number.
3. Post the goods receipt for the receiving plant by using the `MIGO_GR` transaction code. You also need to specify the stock transport order number and select the `101` movement type.

Apart from transferring stock through stock transport orders, a company can transfer stock in two different ways—one-step stock transfer and two-step stock transfer.

Let's explore each of these in detail.

The One-Step Stock Transfer Process

The process of transferring stock from one location to another in one step is known as the one-step stock transfer process. You can implement this process in the mySAP ERP system at two levels—storage location and plant. You can implement the one-step stock transfer process at the storage location level by using the `MIGO_TR` transaction code and selecting the `311` movement type. You also need to specify the locations between which the stock is being transferred. After entering the details, the transaction is posted and the stock is transferred from one storage location to another in the mySAP ERP system.

When transferring stock from one plant to another in the mySAP ERP system, the `MIGO_TR` transaction code is used. You need to enter the details such as material plant and storage location and select the `301` movement type.

After specifying the details, save the transaction to transfer the specified quantity from the source plant to the destination plant in the mySAP ERP system. You can verify the successful transfer of stock by using the `MMBE` transaction code.

The Two-Step Stock Transfer Process

In the two-step stock transfer process, the goods are issued from an issuing point and received at a receiving point in two steps. In the mySAP ERP system, the `MIGO_TR` transaction code is used to transfer stock on the basis of the two-step stock transfer process. You also need to enter the details such as material, quantity, from plant, and to plant and select the `303` movement type. After posting these details in the mySAP ERP system, the status of stock is displayed as stock in transit since it has been dispatched from the issuing plant. In addition, the accounting document is created if the stock valuation is performed at the plant level.

In this appendix, you learned to implement the procurement process under various business scenarios, such as subcontracting, third-party transactions, and stock transfers.

EXPLORING THE INVOICE VERIFICATION PROCESS UNDER VARIOUS BUSINESS SCENARIOS

Invoice verification is an important part of the MM module of the mySAP™ ERP system. The procurement process, as you already learned in *Appendix A: Exploring the Procurement Process under Various Business Scenarios*, ends with the invoice verification process in the MM module. The invoice verification process mainly deals with the payments made to vendors by an organization for the purchase of material, and is generally handled by the finance and accounting department.

An invoice is sent by the vendor to the buyer of items, which, in our case, is an organization. It is a legal document and contains basic information about the items, such as the name of the item(s), the cost per unit, the discount offered, the taxes levied, and the terms of payment. After receiving the invoice, the purchasing department of the organization checks it for any discrepancies and then posts it in the mySAP ERP system. The finance and accounting department processes the full and final payment to the vendor after going through the checking.

There are two types of invoice verification implemented in the SAP® system: purchase order (PO)-based and goods receipt (GR)-based invoices. The PO is a commercial document that contains information about the goods or services the seller provides to the buyer, such as the type of goods/ service, its quantity, and the price agreed upon. The PO helps to protect the interests of the seller in case the buyer refuses to pay for the goods or services purchased by him. With PO-based invoice verification, you can post an invoice in the SAP system, even if the goods have not been delivered. In this type of invoice verification, all the items of the PO can be settled together, irrespective of the fact that the items have not been received. In addition to this, if the items are not received in a single delivery, then the total of the multiple deliveries is posted in the system as a single item. After the invoice is posted in the system, the PO number is automatically generated by the system. With GR-based invoice verification, you are allowed to post the invoice only after the goods receipt has been posted in the system and the quantity mentioned in the invoice is matched with the quantity received. After the goods are received and the invoice is posted, the PO number is automatically generated by the system.

In this appendix, the invoice verification process is discussed by using various business scenarios. The appendix first explores the content of an invoice in the mySAP ERP system as well as the invoices for account-assigned POs. Next, you learn to configure the tolerance limit for a blanket purchase order, and to configure Evaluated Receipt Settlement (ERS) and invoicing plans. You also learn about subsequent debit/credit, credit memos and reversals, and invoice verification in background processing. In addition, you learn to implement invoice reduction. The concept of invoices with variances, taxes in invoice verification, and discounts in invoices are also discussed in this appendix. Toward the end, you learn about blocking an invoice, maintaining a goods receipt/invoice receipt (GR/IR) account, and checking duplicate invoice entries.

Let's begin by exploring the content of an invoice.

EXPLORING THE CONTENT OF AN INVOICE

An invoice is a document that contains information about the payment that is to be made by a buyer (the organization in our case) to a seller or vendor for material or services purchased. The invoice includes details regarding the person or organization issuing the invoice, the reference of the transaction for which the invoice is made, and the amount that the buyer of the material has to pay. You can enter the details of an invoice for the invoice verification process in the **Incoming Invoice: Company Code 1000** screen, as shown in Figure B.1:

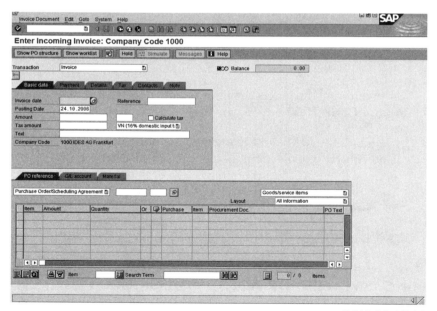

FIGURE B.1   Displaying the Enter Incoming Invoice: Company Code 1000 screen

As you can see in Figure B.1, the **Incoming Invoice: Company Code 1000** screen contains the following user interface (UI) elements:

- **Transaction**—Allows you to select various types of transactions: Invoice, Credit Memo, Subsequent Debit, and Subsequent Credit. The screen layout changes according to the option you select.
- **Basic data** tab—Consists of various fields, such as:
  - **Invoice date**—Refers to the date printed on the invoice
  - **Posting Date**—Refers to the date on which the invoice is posted in the mySAP ERP system
  - **Amount**—Refers to the price of the material, which is entered in the invoice

- **PO reference** tab—Contains the PO reference number, which is used to post the invoice.
- **Layout**—Allows you to determine which columns should be displayed in the item list for the invoice.
- **Hold**—Contains an invoice that has insufficient information. You can save such an invoice and post it at a later date when the missing information is available.
- **Balance**—Displays the balance between gross invoice amount, the tax amounts, the unplanned delivery costs, and the net total.

After entering the preceding information in the **Enter Incoming Invoice: Company Code 1000** screen, you can post the invoice to:

- Generate the MM and Financial Accounting invoice documents
- Enter the respective debit and credit entries in the various general ledger (G/L) accounts
- Update the PO history to reflect the invoice posting
- Process the payment to the vendor

Let's now explore the invoices for account-assigned POs.

EXPLORING INVOICES FOR ACCOUNT-ASSIGNED POs

An account-assigned PO is issued for materials that are procured for internal consumption within the organization. This implies that such materials are neither sold outside the organization nor subject to inventory management. In an account-assigned PO, you need to enter an account assignment category for each item. Therefore, the account assignment category is an important field as it helps in determining the materials procured for direct usage or consumption.

When you post an invoice for an account-assigned PO, two kinds of situations may occur:

- **Valuated goods receipt is defined for the PO item**—Refers to the situation in which a posting a made in the cost account of a PO and an offsetting entry is made to the goods receipt/invoice receipt (GR/IR) clearing account when the goods are received.
- **Non-valuated goods receipt is defined for the PO item**—Refers to the situation in which no posting is made when the goods are received. This implies that at the time of goods receipt, posting is made directly to the account specified in the PO.

In this section of the appendix, you learn to define the account assignment category and check the invoice for an account-assigned PO.

Defining an Account Assignment Category

The account assignment category defines an account assignment for the material. While implementing invoice verification, you cannot change the amount and quantity of the items mentioned in the invoice. However, you can change both the quantity as well as the amount of the item after invoice verification in the account assignment screen. For example, consider a situation when an organization has purchased five computers to sell them to a client. All the computers are part of the inventory. However, the organization decides to use one computer internally. In this case, the organization needs to make an entry to remove one computer from the inventory. The organization, therefore, needs to define an account assignment category for the computer, which is no longer subject to inventory management.

Let's perform the following steps to define an account assignment category:

1. Navigate the following menu path to define an account assignment category:

Menu Path

SAP IMG > Materials Management > Purchasing > Account Assignment > Maintain Account Assignment Categories. Figure B.2 shows the preceding menu path:

FIGURE B.2   **Maintaining account assignment categories**

The **Change View "Account Assignment Categories": Overview** screen appears, as shown in Figure B.3:

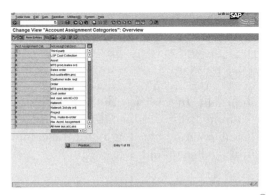

FIGURE B.3   **Displaying the Change View "Account Assignment Categories": Overview screen**

2. Select an account assignment category and click the **Details** (▣) icon.

The **Change View "Account Assignment Categories": Details** screen appears, as shown in Figure B.4:

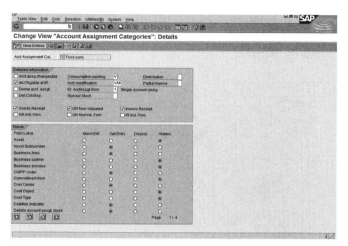

FIGURE B.4   **Displaying the Change View "Account Assignment Categories": Details screen**

3. Select the **AA Chgable at IR** and **GR Non-Valuated** check boxes in the **Change View "Account Assignment Categories": Details** screen.

By doing this, you can change the account assignment category defined in the PO when the invoice is posted.

Checking an Invoice for an Account-Assigned PO

After posting an invoice by using the `MIRO` transaction code, you can check whether or not an account-assigned PO is enabled for that invoice.

Perform the following steps to check an invoice for an account-assigned PO:

1. Navigate the following menu path:

Menu Path

SAP menu > Logistics > Materials Management > Logistics Invoice Verification > Document Entry > Enter Invoice. Figure B.5 shows the preceding menu path:

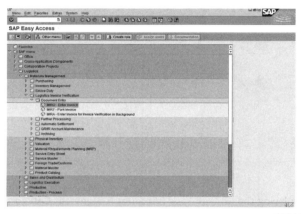

FIGURE B.5   Displaying the menu path to enter an invoice

The **Enter Company Code** dialog box appears, as shown in Figure B.6:

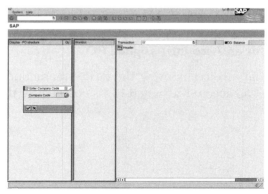

FIGURE B.6   Displaying the Enter Company Code dialog box

2. Enter the company code of the organization for which you are entering the invoice in the **Company Code** text box, and press the ENTER key. In our case, we have entered 1000 as the company code.

The **Enter Incoming Invoice: Company Code 1000** screen appears, as shown in Figure B.7:

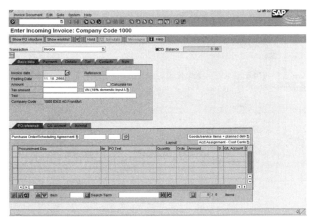

FIGURE B.7   **Displaying the Enter Incoming Invoice: Company Code 1000 screen**

Note: You can also use the MIRO transaction code to open the **Enter Incoming Invoice** screen.

3. Enter the invoice date in the **Invoice date** text box (Figure B.8) of the **Basic data** tab. In our case, we have entered 09.10.2008.
4. Select the **Purchase Order/Scheduling Agreement** option from the **Reference Document Category** drop-down list in the **PO reference** tab (Figure B.8).
5. Enter the purchasing document number in the **Purchasing Document Number** text box of the **PO reference** tab (Figure B.8). In our case, we have entered 4500015695.
6. Select the **Goods/services items + planned delivery** option from the **Goods Items/Delivery Costs/Both** drop-down list of the **PO reference** tab (Figure B.8).
7. Select the **Acct Assignment – Cost Center** option from the **Invoice Items Layout** drop-down list of the **PO reference** tab (Figure B.8).

The options selected in the **Enter Incoming Invoice: Company Code 1000** screen are shown in Figure B.8:

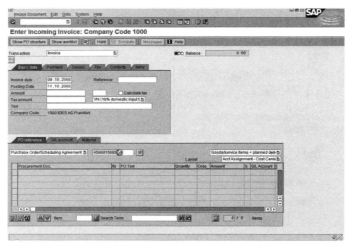

FIGURE B.8   Displaying the details entered in the screen

8. Press the ENTER key. The **Enter Incoming Invoice: Company Code 1000** dialog box appears, as shown in Figure B.9:

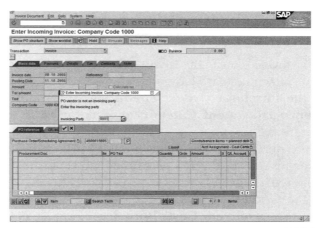

FIGURE B.9   Displaying the Enter Incoming Invoice: Company Code 1000 dialog box

9. Enter the invoice party number in the **Invoicing Party** text box of the **Enter Incoming Invoice** dialog box (Figure B.9). In our case, we have entered 9001.

10. Press the ENTER key. The final details of the invoice are displayed in the **Enter Incoming Invoice: Company Code 1000** screen, as shown in Figure B.10:

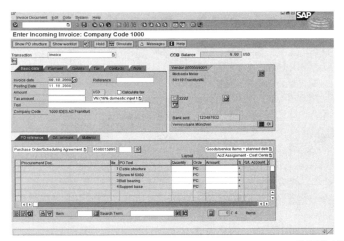

FIGURE B.10   **Displaying the final invoice details**

As shown in Figure B.10, four items from the PO (whose number is 4500015695 in our case) are displayed in the item list. In this case, all four items are defined as a valuated goods receipt in the PO. This is because the account assignment, which is specified in the **Acct. Assgt**. column of the **PO reference** tab is in the display mode and cannot be changed (Figure B.11):

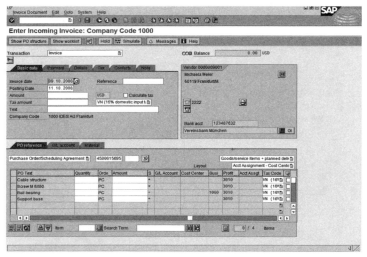

FIGURE B.11   Checking the account assignment category

Note: If any of the items has been assigned the category K in the Acct. Assgt. column of the PO reference tab, this implies that the line item is defined as a non-valuated goods receipt in the PO.

In this section of the appendix, you explored invoices for an account-assigned PO. Let's now learn to configure a tolerance limit for a blanket purchase order.

CONFIGURING A TOLERANCE LIMIT FOR A BLANKET PURCHASE ORDER

An organization may regularly purchase material from a supplier at a fixed price. For each purchase, a new PO has to be created in the system. This repetitive entry of data and the creation of multiple POs can be avoided by creating a blanket purchase order. A blanket purchase order uses a single PO number for multiple purchases from the single vendor and is valid for a specified period of time. The advantage of using a blanket purchase order is that its validity is longer than that of a normal PO.

> **Note:** You have already learned about creating a blanket purchase order in *Appendix A: Exploring the Procurement Process under Various Business Scenarios*.

When you post an invoice for a blanket purchase order, the system checks the invoice for two criteria: validity date and tolerance limits, which are defined in the PO. Tolerance limit is the limit up to which the variances or differences in an invoice can be tolerated. You can also configure tolerance limits for a blanket purchase order, which means that if an invoice exceeds the tolerance limit, the invoice will be blocked.

Navigate the following menu path to configure the tolerance limit for a blanket purchase order:

Menu Path

SAP IMG > Materials Management > Logistics Invoice Verification > Invoice Block > Set Tolerance Limits. Figure B.12 shows the preceding menu path:

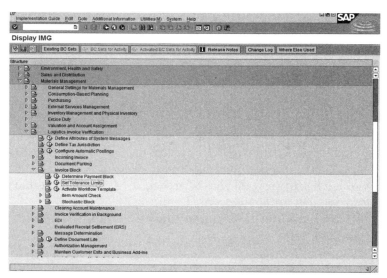

FIGURE B.12   Setting the tolerance limit

The **Change View "Tolerance Limits": Overview** screen appears, as shown in Figure B.13:

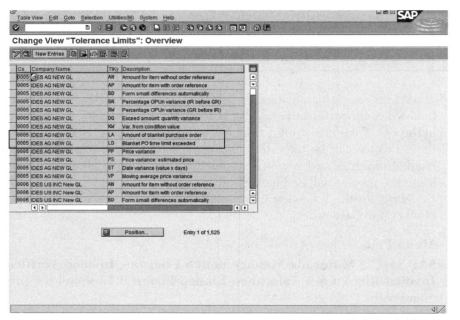

FIGURE B.13 Displaying the Change View "Tolerance Limits": Overview screen

The **TlKy** column in Figure B.13 helps determine the tolerance limits that you want to check. For example, the key LA defines the tolerance limit for the amount of the blanket purchase order and the key LD defines the time limit for the blanket purchase order. In other words, the tolerance key LA specifies that the amount of material in the blanket purchase order has exceeded the tolerance limit and the tolerance key LD specifies that the time for delivery of the material has exceeded the time limit.

Double-click the row that has tolerance key value LA to define the tolerance limit for a blanket purchase order (Figure B.13).

The **Change View "Tolerance Limits": Details** screen opens, as shown in Figure B.14:

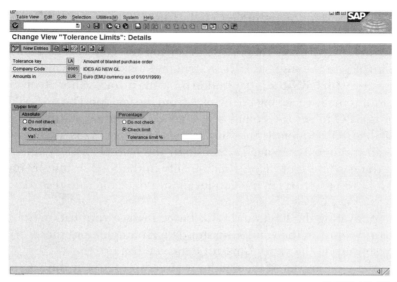

FIGURE B.14   Changing the tolerance limit

In the **Change View "Tolerance Limits": Details** screen, you can specify the maximum allowed variance in the **Val.** text box of the **Absolute** group. This implies that an invoice value can be lower than the value calculated from the PO and the goods receipt. However, it cannot be larger than the value specified in the **Val.** text box.

After learning to configure a tolerance limit for a blanket purchase order, let's now learn to configure Evaluated Receipt Settlement (ERS).

CONFIGURING ERS

ERS is an alternate method of processing the invoices sent by vendors. In this method, the organization settles the vendor liabilities and generates the payment statement. The mySAP ERP system automatically posts the invoices after the goods receipt is entered in the system. The ERS method not only helps reduce paperwork but also minimizes data entry errors. You should implement ERS if you regularly update the POs in the system.

Let's consider an example to understand ERS in a better way. Suppose an organization receives a specific quantity of goods mentioned in the PO at the specified delivery schedule. After receiving the goods, the organization posts the invoice in the mySAP ERP system and makes the payment to the vendor. However, with ERS, the organization posts the invoices after receiving the goods, without actually receiving the invoice from the vendor. The mySAP ERP system uses the PO to get the details of the goods, including price and the discounts available. Subsequently, the information that the PO is settled is sent to the vendor through a message generated by the mySAP ERP system.

You can configure ERS functionality in the SAP system by implementing the following settings in the vendor master data and info record:

- Activating the ERS- and GRS-based invoice verification indicators in the vendor master data. To implement these settings in the vendor master data, you can use the XK02 transaction code if the vendor is already defined or the XK01 transaction code if you are creating a new vendor.
- Activating the ERS indicator for the goods and defining the tax code in the info record. You can use the ME11 transaction code to implement this setting in the info record.

The following are the broad-level steps to configure ERS:

1. Create a PO
2. Post the GR in the SAP system
3. Execute the settlement program for ERS

Let's first learn to create a PO.

Creating a PO

The first step in configuring ERS is to create a PO. A PO contains the details of the material specified in the purchase requisition.

Let's perform the following steps to create a PO:

1. Navigate the following menu path:

Menu Path

SAP menu > Logistics > Materials Management > Purchasing > Purchase Order > Create > Vendor/Supplying Plant Known. Figure B.15 shows the preceding menu path:

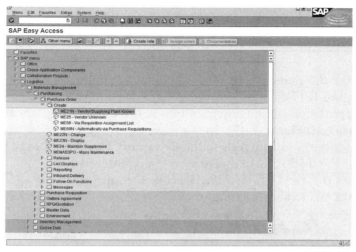

FIGURE B.15 Displaying the menu path to create a PO

The **Create Purchase Order** screen opens, as shown in Figure B.16:

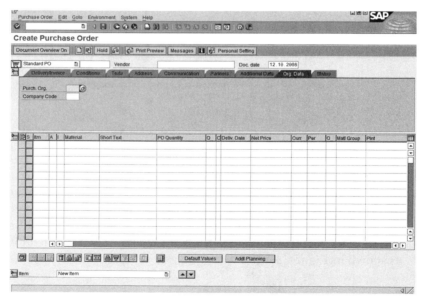

FIGURE B.16 Displaying the Create Purchase Order screen

Note: You can also use the `ME21N` transaction code to access the **Create Purchase Order** screen.

2. Enter the name of the supplying plant (vendor) in the **Vendor** text box (Figure B.17).
3. Enter the purchasing organization in the **Purch.Org.** text box of the **Org. Data** tab (Figure B.17). In our case, we have entered 1000.
4. Enter the company code in the **Company Code** text box of the **Org. Data** tab (Figure B.17). In this case, we have entered 1000.
5. Press the ENTER key. The **Purch. Group** text box is added in the **Org. Data** tab, as shown in Figure B.17:

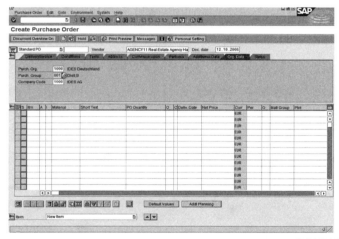

FIGURE B.17   **Entering the purchasing details**

6. Enter the purchasing group number of the PO in the **Purch. Group** text box of the **Org. Data** tab (Figure B.17). In our case, we have entered 001.
7. Enter the material number and plant number in the **Material** and **Plant** columns, respectively, and press the ENTER key. The **Item** section expands, as shown in Figure B.18:

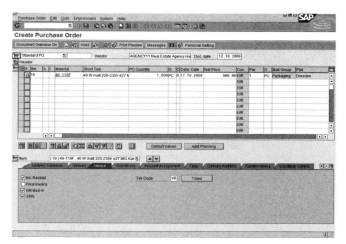

FIGURE B.18   Creating a PO

8. Select the **Inv. Receipt**, **GR-Bsd IV**, and **ERS** check boxes in the **Invoice** tab of the **Item** group (Figure B.18).

9. Click the **Save** (💾) icon to create the PO.

A system message specifying that a standard PO, which in our case is `4500017180`, has been created appears in the **Create Purchase Order** screen.

Posting a GR

The second step in configuring ERS is to post a GR. The GR is posted after the goods are received and the PO is created. In our example, the details of the received goods are posted in the SAP system with reference to the PO that was created in the first step, discussed in the previous section.

Perform the following steps to post the GR in the SAP system.

1. Enter the `MIGO` transaction code in the transaction code text box and press the ENTER key, as shown in Figure B.19:

FIGURE B.19   **Displaying the transaction code to post a GR**

The **Goods Receipt Purchase Order – User Test** screen appears (Figure B.20).

2. Select the **Purchase Order** option from the **Reference Document for MIGO Transaction** drop-down list (Figure B.20).
3. Enter 4500017180 as the PO in the **Goods Receipt Purchase Order – User Test** screen (Figure B.20).
4. Click the **Execute** (🌐) icon, as shown in Figure B.20:

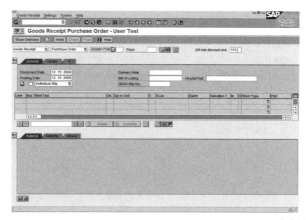

FIGURE B.20   **Displaying the Goods Receipt Purchase Order – User Test screen**

The details of the PO of the material are displayed in the **Header Data** and **Detail Data** sections, as shown in Figure B.21:

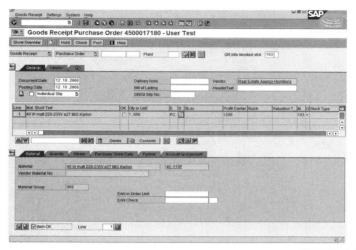

FIGURE B.21   **Displaying the Goods Receipt Purchase Order 4500017180 – User Test screen**

5. Select the **Item OK** check box in the **Detail Data** section (Figure B.21).
6. Click the **Check** button (Figure B.21).

A green light appears in the **Header Data** section, indicating that the details of the goods receipt have been checked and no error has been found in them. In addition, the **Document is OK** message appears in the System Message Line of the screen.

7. Click the **Post** button to post the goods receipt. A message appears in System Message Line of the screen, informing you that the goods receipt has been successfully posted in the system.

After posting the goods receipt, the invoice is posted with reference to the PO.

Executing the Settlement for ERS

After successfully creating the PO and posting the GR in the SAP system, the next step for configuring ERS is to execute the settlement for ERS to create an invoice document.

Perform the following steps to execute the settlement for ERS:

1. Enter the MRRL transaction code in the transaction code text box and press the ENTER key, as shown in Figure B.22:

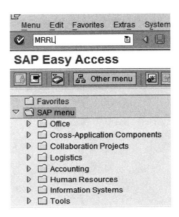

FIGURE B.22   Entering the MRRL transaction code

The **Evaluated Receipt Settlement (ERS) with Logistics Invoice Verification** screen opens, as shown in Figure B.23:

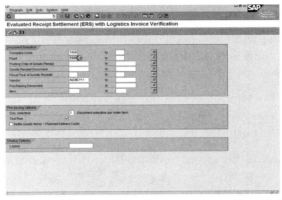

FIGURE B.23   Displaying the Evaluated Receipt Settlement (ERS) with Logistics Invoice Verification screen

2. Enter the company code of the PO in the **Company Code** text box of the **Document Selection** group (Figure B.23). In our case, we have entered 1000.
3. Enter the plant code of the PO in the **Plant** text box of the **Document Selection** group (Figure B.23). In our case, we have entered 1000.
4. Enter the vendor code of the PO in the **Vendor** text box of the **Document Selection** group (Figure B.23). In our case, we have entered AGENCY11.
5. Click the **Execute** (⊕) icon.

The system creates the invoice document and configures ERS.

In this section of the appendix, you learned to configure ERS. Let's now learn to configure invoicing plans.

CONFIGURING INVOICING PLANS

In a PO, an invoicing plan is defined for repetitive transactions, such as rental and leasing payments. For example, an organization can use an invoicing plan to automatically generate invoices for monthly office rent, which is a repetitive transaction. An invoicing plan helps in reducing the time taken to enter data in the accounts of the purchasing and invoice verification departments. It also helps in scheduling the dates for creating invoices independent of the actual receipt of goods.

In short, you can define an invoicing plan as a utility that allows you to specify when you want to create an invoice, and for what amount. The creation of an invoice in the invoicing plan is independent of the receipt of the goods or services. Two types of invoicing plans are available in the SAP MM module:

- **Periodic invoicing plan**—Refers to the invoicing plan used for recurring transactions, such as payment of rent or lease.
- **Partial invoicing plan**—Refers to the invoicing plan used for transactions that are paid in phases. For example, the payment of a construction project is made in installments rather than making a single payment of the full amount. Note that the payment in a partial invoicing plan is not made at regular intervals, but depends on the phases of completion of a project.

In this section, you learn to customize and create invoicing plans.

Customizing Invoicing Plans

Before creating an invoicing plan, it has to be customized to control the procedure to create the invoicing schedule. You can customize an invoicing plan after considering various parameters, such as the invoicing plan type, date categories, and date proposal.

In this section, you learn to maintain a periodic invoicing plan, a partial invoicing plan, the date ID, the date category, and the date proposal.

Maintaining a Periodic Invoicing Plan

As already explained, a periodic invoicing plan refers to a plan that is used for transactions that are recurring in nature, such as rental or leasing payments. In this type of invoicing plan, the total amount of the PO is paid on each due date. For example, a monthly rent of Rs. 5000 is charged for a rented office, which is represented by a single item in the PO. This rent is paid on the first day of each month.

You can maintain a periodic invoicing plan by navigating the following menu path:

Menu Path

SAP IMG > Materials Management > Purchasing > Purchase Order > Invoicing Plan > Invoicing Plan Types > Maintain Periodic Invoicing Plan Types. Figure B.24 shows the preceding menu path:

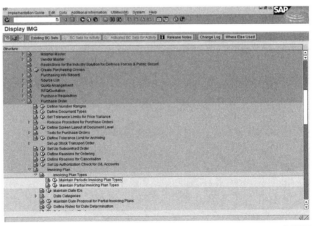

FIGURE B.24   Displaying the menu path to maintain a periodic invoicing plan

The **Change View "Maintain Invoicing Plan Types: Periodic Invoices":
Overview** screen opens, as shown in Figure B.25:

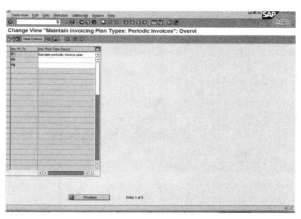

FIGURE B.25 Displaying the Change View "Maintain Invoicing Plan Types: Periodic Invoices": Overview screen

Double-click any row in the **Inv. Pl Ty.** column (Figure B.25).

The **Change View "Maintain Invoicing Plan Types: Periodic Invoices":
Detail** screen appears, as shown in Figure B.26:

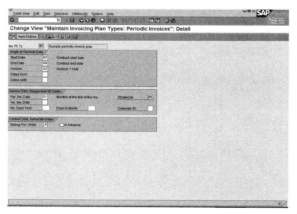

FIGURE B.26 Displaying the Change View "Maintain Invoicing Plan Types: Periodic Invoices": Detail screen

In Figure B.26, you can define the periodic invoicing plan type by entering the relevant details in the **Start Date, End Date**, and **Horizon** text boxes in the **Origin of General Data** section. Note that the horizon date is the last planned billing date of the invoice. In addition, you can specify the periodic invoice date to determine the next billing in the **Per. Inv. Date** text box in the **Invoice Data: Suggestion for Dates** section.

Maintaining a Partial Invoicing Plan

As you know, a partial invoicing plan refers to a plan that is paid in installments. In this type of invoicing plan, each installment is shown separately in the invoice. For example, a PO is created for a building project, which has a total value of Rs. 900,000. The organization pays 33.3% of the total value of the project on the completion of the first phase of construction. Another 33.3% is paid on the completion of the second phase, and the final 33.3% is paid on the completion and acceptance of the final phase of the building.

You can maintain a partial invoicing plan by navigating the following menu path:

Menu Path

SAP IMG > Materials Management > Purchasing > Purchase Order > Invoicing Plan > Invoicing Plan Types > Maintain Partial Invoicing Plan Types. Figure B.27 shows the preceding menu path:

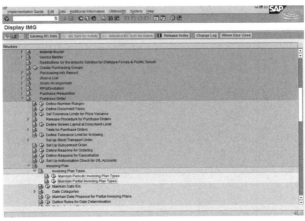

FIGURE B.27   Displaying the menu path to maintain a partial invoicing plan

The **Change View "Maintain Invoicing Plan Types: Partial Invoice": Overview** screen opens, as shown in Figure B.28:

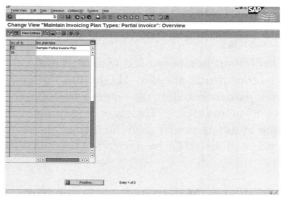

FIGURE B.28   Displaying the Change View "Maintain Invoicing Plan Types: Partial Invoice": Overview screen

Double-click any row in the **Inv. Pl. ty.** column (Figure B.28).

The **Change View "Maintain Invoicing Plan Types: Partial Invoice": Details** screen appears, as shown in Figure B.29:

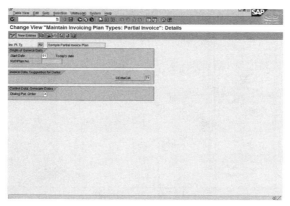

FIGURE B.29   Displaying the Change View "Maintain Invoicing Plan Types: Partial Invoice": Details screen

You can specify the relevant control date and define the partial invoicing plan types in the **Change View "Maintain Invoicing Plan Types: Partial Invoice": Details** screen. In addition, you can specify the start date of the invoice in the **Start Date** text box.

Maintaining Date IDs

The date ID refers to numbers used to describe the different dates used in an invoice. In other words, the date ID defines the function that needs to be performed on a particular billing plan date. For example, suppose the date ID of a date is 0008 in an invoice. The date description associated with the date ID implies that at the particular date the invoice needs to be closed.

You can maintain date IDs by navigating the following menu path:

Menu Path

SAP IMG > Materials Management > Purchasing > Purchase Order > Invoicing Plan > Maintain Date IDs. Figure B.30 shows the preceding menu path:

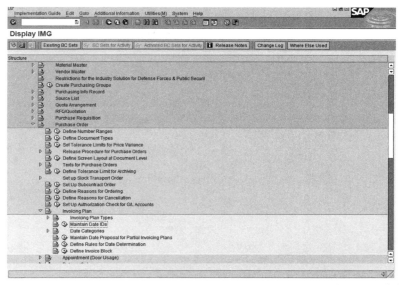

FIGURE B.30   Displaying the menu path to maintain date IDs

The **Change View "Maintain Date Descriptions for Invoicing Plan": Overview** screen opens, as shown in Figure B.31:

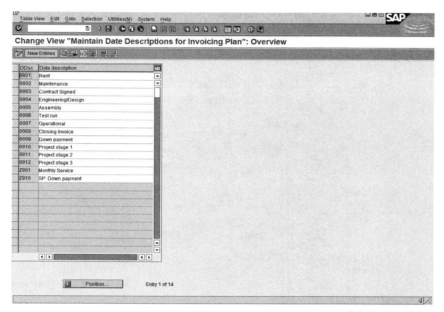

FIGURE B.31   Displaying the Change View "Maintain Date Descriptions for Invoicing Plan": Overview screen

You can define the date description by clicking the **New Entries** button in the **Change View "Maintain Date Descriptions for Invoicing Plan": Overview** screen (Figure B.31).

Maintaining a Date Category

A date category refers to a code, which is an alphanumeric combination. You can define a date category with reference to partial and periodic invoice plan types. For example, the date category T3 is defined with reference to partial invoice plans. You can either define a new date category or implement changes in the existing date category to maintain the date category.

Navigate the following menu path to maintain a date category:

Menu Path

SAP IMG > Materials Management > Purchasing > Purchase Order > Invoicing Plan > Date Categories > Maintain Date Category for Invoicing Plan Type. Figure B.32 shows the preceding menu path:

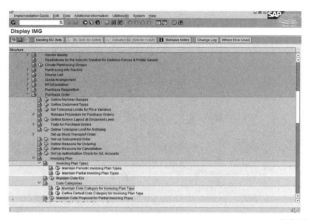

FIGURE B.32 Displaying the menu path to maintain a date category

The **Change View "Maintain Date Category for Invoicing Plan Type": Overview** screen opens, as shown in Figure B.33:

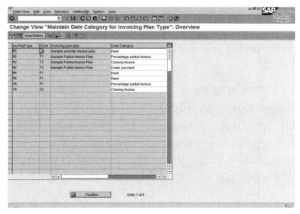

FIGURE B.33 Displaying the Change View "Maintain Date Category for Invoicing Plan Type": Overview screen

Double-click any row in the **Inv. Plan Type** column (Figure B.33).

The **Change View "Maintain Date Category for Invoicing Plan Type": Details** screen appears, as shown in Figure B.34:

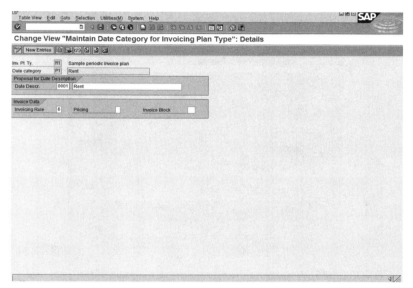

FIGURE B.34   Displaying the Change View "Maintain Date Category for Invoicing Plan Type": Details screen

You can specify one or more date categories for each invoicing plan type in Figure B.34. You can specify the date category in the **Date Category** text box and enter the description for the date in the **Date Descr**. text box.

Maintaining a Date Proposal

A date proposal refers to a proposed date mentioned in the invoice to perform a specific operation. You can maintain a date proposal only for partial invoicing plan types. Date proposals can help by enabling the creation of a standard billing plan for the PO.

Navigate the following menu path to maintain a date proposal:

Menu Path

SAP IMG > Materials Management > Purchasing > Purchase Order > Invoicing Plan > Maintain Date Proposal for Partial Invoicing Plans. Figure B.35 shows the preceding menu path:

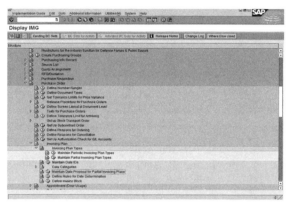

FIGURE B.35   Displaying the menu path to maintain a date proposal

The **Change View "Maintain Date Proposal for Invoicing Plan Type": Overview** screen opens, as shown in Figure B.36:

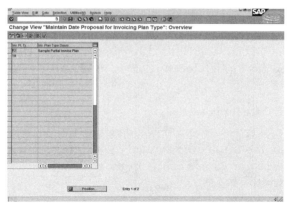

FIGURE B.36   Displaying the Change View "Maintain Date Proposal for Invoicing Plan Type": Overview screen

Double-click any row in the **Inv. Pl. Ty.** column (Figure B.36).
The **Change View "Maintain Date Proposal for Invoicing Plan Type":**
Details screen appears, as shown in Figure B.37:

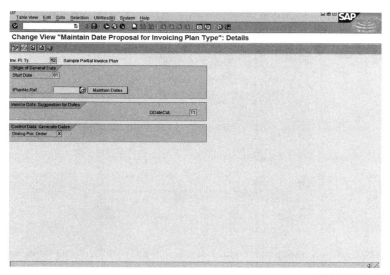

FIGURE B.37   Displaying the Change View "Maintain Date Proposal for Invoicing
Plan Type": Details screen

You can maintain the date proposal for partial invoicing plans in Figure B.37.
Let's now learn to create an invoicing plan.

Creating an Invoicing Plan

Creating an invoicing plan involves the steps of creating a PO and executing
the invoicing plan.

Perform the following steps to create a PO and then execute the invoicing plan:

1. Enter the ME21N transaction code in the transaction code text box and press the ENTER key. The **Create Purchase Order** screen opens, as shown in Figure B.38:

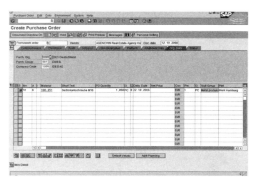

FIGURE B.38   Entering the relevant details in the Create Purchase Order screen

2. Select the **Framework order** option from the **Order Type** drop-down list (Figure B.38).
3. Enter the vendor number and name in the **Vendor** text box (Figure B.38).
4. Enter the relevant details in the **Purch. Org.**, **Purch. Group**, and **Company Code** text boxes in the **Org. Data** tab (Figure B.38).
5. Enter the start date of the PO in the **Validity Start** text box in the **Additional Data** tab, as shown in Figure B.39:

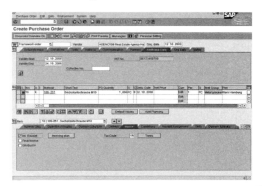

FIGURE B.39   Entering additional data in the Create Purchase Order screen

6. Enter the material and plant number in the **Material** and **Plant** columns (Figure B.39).
7. Enter K as the account assignment category in the **Account Assignment Category** column (Figure B.39) and press the ENTER key. The **Item** group expands.
8. Click the **Invoicing plan** button in the **Invoice** tab of the **Item** group. A dialog box appears, displaying the various invoicing plan types.
9. Select the required type of invoicing plan from the dialog box and click the **Continue** (✓) icon to close the dialog box.
10. Click the **Save** (🖫) icon to create the PO (Figure B.39).

A system message indicating that the standard PO has been created appears in the System Message Line of the screen.

After creating the PO, you can use the MRIS transaction code to execute the invoicing plan settlement. The **Invoicing Plan Settlement with Logistics Invoice Verification** screen opens, as shown in Figure B.40:

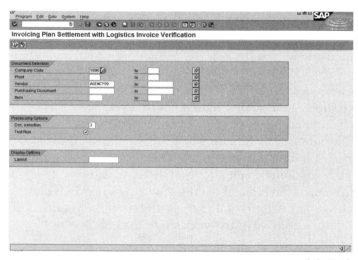

FIGURE B.40   **Displaying the Invoicing Plan Settlement with Logistics Invoice Verification screen**

In the **Invoicing Plan Settlement with Logistics Invoice Verification** screen, enter the relevant details in the **Company Code, Plant**, and **Vendor** text boxes in the **Document Selection** group, and click the **Execute** (⊕) icon.

Let's now explore subsequent debit/credit.

EXPLORING SUBSEQUENT DEBIT/CREDIT

Subsequent debit/credit refers to the process in which an invoice or a credit memo for items is received from a vendor after posting the invoice or credit memo in the system. In addition, it is applicable only in cases where the quantity of material in the original invoice posted in the system and the invoice received from the vendor does not change.

When you post subsequent debit/credit in the system, the relevant transaction is updated only on the basis of price and not on the basis of quantity. For example, if the invoice originally sent by the vendor contained prices that were too low or too high, the vendor can send the invoice again. The maximum quantity that you can post in a subsequent debit/credit entry is the quantity specified in the original invoice.

In this section, you learn to post the subsequent debit/credit entries in the accounts as well as post the transaction in the SAP system.

Posting in Accounts

When a subsequent debit/credit entry is posted in the accounts, the G/L account is updated on the basis of different situations, which are as follows:

- If the stock material is valuated with a standard price (S), then the subsequent debit/credit amount is posted in the vendor account and the price difference account.
- If the stock of material is valuated with a moving average price (V), then the subsequent debit/credit amount is posted in the vendor account and the GR/IR account.
- If the material is listed in an account-assigned PO, then the subsequent debit/credit entry is posted in the vendor account and the offsetting entry is posted to the cost account.
- If there is a subsequent debit/credit transaction before receiving the goods receipt, then the entries are posted in the vendor and GR/IR accounts. When the goods are received, the entries are posted in the respective accounts depending on the type of price control method (S or V) used in the organization.

Posting a Transaction

You can post a transaction related to subsequent debit/credit by using the `MIRO` transaction code. The **Enter Incoming Invoice: Company Code** screen opens, as shown in Figure B.41:

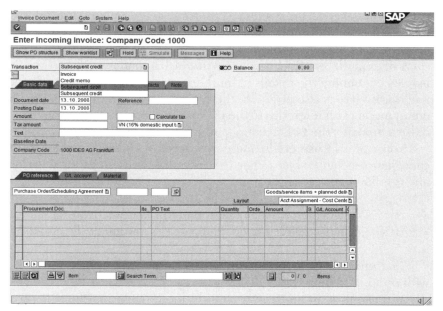

FIGURE B.41   **Selecting the subsequent debit option**

In comparison to a normal invoice, when you post a subsequent debit/credit entry, you have to select the **Subsequent debit** or the **Subsequent credit** option in the **Transaction** drop-down list (Figure B.41).

After selecting the required option, enter the PO number in the **Purchasing Document Number** text box in the **PO reference** tab and press ENTER to display the information about the material and its quantity. Next, enter the amount of the invoice and save the transaction to update the PO history in the system.

After learning about subsequent debit/credit, let's now explore credit memos and reversals.

EXPLORING CREDIT MEMOS AND REVERSALS

With a subsequent debit/credit, you can only make changes in the price of the material. However, there may be situations when excess quantity is invoiced by the vendor. In such a situation, the organization issues a credit memo to adjust the amount owed to the vendor. Therefore, a credit memo is used for invoices that are posted with more than the received quantity that need to be updated in the mySAP ERP system.

For example, consider a situation in which a vendor sends an organization an invoice containing the details of more material than what is actually delivered, and this invoice is also posted in the system. In such a situation, you can post a credit memo with reference to the PO for the excess quantity. The credit memo, in turn, updates the G/L account and PO history in the system.

You can also use credit memos in case of reversals, which refer to the cancellation of an invoice. There are two different effects of reversals, which are as follows:

- If you cancel an invoice, a credit memo is automatically created.
- If you cancel a credit memo, an invoice is automatically created.

Therefore, with reversals, the credit memo will update the G/L account with opposite debit/credit entries.

You can post an invoice for a credit memo by using the `MIRO` transaction code, which opens the **Enter Incoming Invoice: Company Code 1000** screen, as shown in Figure B.42:

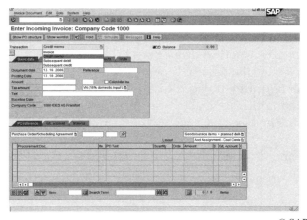

FIGURE B.42 Entering the details related to a credit memo

The procedure to post a credit memo is similar to posting a normal invoice, except that you have to select the **Credit memo** option from the **Transaction** drop-down list while posting the credit memo (Figure B.42).

After selecting the desired option, enter the posting date in the **Basic data** tab and the PO number in the **PO reference** tab to generate the required information about the material. After the system provides the information about the total invoiced quantity and amount, implement the necessary changes and save the transaction to update the PO history in the system.

Let's now explore invoice verification in background processing.

EXPLORING INVOICE VERIFICATION IN THE BACKGROUND

Normally the invoices you receive are posted in the SAP system by using the `MIRO` transaction code. However, when the invoices are large and have multiple line items, posting can take a lot of time. However, you can save time by processing such invoices in the background. This procedure is known as invoice verification in the background.

In this process, you need to enter and save general invoice data, such as the amount of the invoice, the tax levied, and the date on which the invoice was created, in the invoice document. The different items are not entered manually, but are created by using the settlement program. The mySAP ERP system checks the total quantity and the amount invoiced from the PO and performs various actions in the following situations:

- If the total amount is within the tolerance limit, the system implements invoice verification in the background.
- If the total amount exceeds the tolerance limit, the invoice document is created and the line items are entered in it. This invoice document is processed later. In such a situation, the `RMBABG00` settlement program is used for background processing.

The implementation of invoice verification in the background is a two-step process: enter the details of the invoice in the system and execute the settlement program to post the invoice.

Let's learn to perform both these steps in the following sections.

Entering an Invoice

The first step in implementing invoice verification in the background is to enter the details of the invoice in the SAP system.

Perform the following steps to enter the invoice details:

1. Enter the MIRA transaction code in the transaction code text box and press the ENTER key, as shown in Figure B.43:

FIGURE B.43   Entering the MIRA transaction code

The **Enter Incoming Invoice: Company Code 1000** screen opens, as shown in Figure B.44:

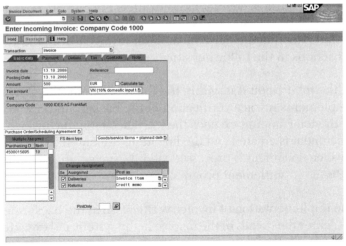

FIGURE B.44   Entering the invoice information

2. Select the **Invoice** option from the **Transaction** drop-down list (Figure B.44).
3. Enter the date of the invoice in the **Invoice date** text box in the **Basic data** tab (Figure B.44).
4. Enter the amount of the invoice in the **Amount** text box in the **Basic data** tab (Figure B.44).
5. Enter the currency in the **Currency Key** text box in the **Basic data** tab (Figure B.44).
6. Select the **Purchase Order/Scheduling Agreement** option from the **Reference Document Category** drop-down list (Figure B.44).
7. Enter the purchasing document number in the **Purchasing Doc.** column (Figure B.44).
8. Enter the quantity of material in the **Item** column (Figure B.44) and press the ENTER key. The **Enter Incoming Invoice: Company Code 1000** dialog box opens, as shown in Figure B.45:

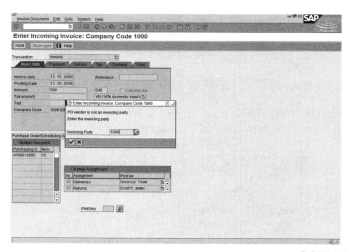

FIGURE B.45   Entering the vendor number

9. Enter the invoicing party number in the **Invoicing Party** text box of the **Enter Incoming Invoice** dialog box and click the **Continue** (☑) icon (Figure B.45).

The details of the invoice are displayed on the **Enter Incoming Invoice: Company Code 1000** screen, as shown in Figure B.46:

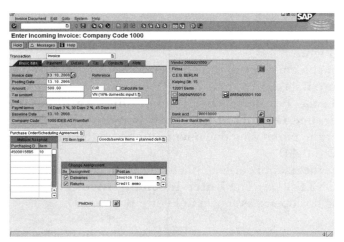

FIGURE B.46   Displaying the invoice information

10. Click the **Save** (⊟) icon (Figure B.46).

The system saves the invoice and generates an invoice document number in the System Message Line of the screen, as shown in Figure B.47:

FIGURE B.47   Displaying the invoice document number

The system message indicates that you have successfully entered the invoice details in the system.

Executing the Settlement Program

After entering the invoice details in the system and generating the invoice document number, the final step in implementing invoice verification in the background is to execute the settlement program. This step also posts the invoice in the system.

Perform the following steps to execute the settlement program:

1. Enter the SA38 transaction code in the transaction code text box and press the ENTER key, as shown in Figure B.48:

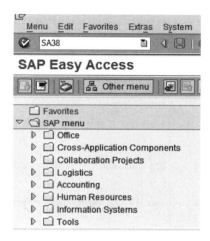

FIGURE B.48   Entering the SA38 transaction code

The **ABAP: Program Execution** screen opens, as shown in Figure B.49:

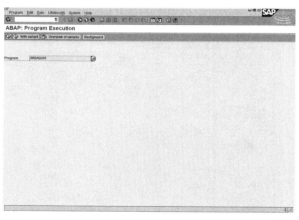

FIGURE B.49   Entering the program number

2. Enter RMBABG00 in the **Program** text box (Figure B.49) and click the **Execute** (⊕) icon. The **Logistics Invoice Verification – Verification in Background** screen opens, as shown in Figure B.50:

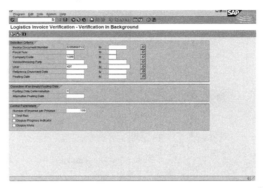

FIGURE B.50 Displaying the Logistics Invoice Verification – Verification in Background screen

3. Enter the invoice document number (which you have already created) in the **Invoice Document Number** text box of the **Selection Criteria** group (Figure B.50).
4. Enter the company code in the **Company Code** text box of the **Selection Criteria** group (Figure B.50).
5. Click the **Execute** (⊕) icon. The **Logistics Invoice Verification – Verification in Background** screen opens, as shown in Figure B.51:

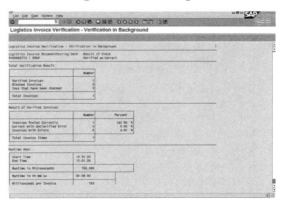

FIGURE B.51 Displaying the result

Figure B.51 displays a report containing the result of the background processing of the invoice. This screen displays error logs for the invoice documents that contain errors. These invoices need to be changed and posted again manually.

Let's now learn to implement invoice reduction.

IMPLEMENTING INVOICE REDUCTION

Invoice reduction refers to the process when the original amount of an invoice is reduced and the invoice is posted again with the reduced amount. This is done when the vendor has entered an incorrect quantity or price in the invoice by mistake. For example, suppose a PO is issued to a vendor for 100 pieces of an item costing Rs. 10 per piece. However, the vendor delivers only 60 pieces of the material and the goods receipt of 60 pieces is posted in the system. Later, the vendor sends an invoice for 100 pieces of the item instead of 60 pieces. In such a situation, you can post the invoice by implementing the reduction feature to avoid paying for the undelivered quantity.

With invoice reduction, two accounting documents are created. The first document contains the actual quantity and amount and the second document contains the credit memo for the difference between the amount mentioned in the original invoice and actual invoice. Therefore, in the invoice reduction feature, you do not reduce the amount in the original invoice. You first post the invoice with the actual quantity and amount specified by the vendor, and then the system posts a credit memo for amount that needs to be reduced from the original invoice.

Invoice reduction is a three-step process, which includes creating a PO, posting a GR, and posting an invoice with the reduction.

The first step for implementing invoice reduction is to create a PO. In our case, we are creating a PO for two pieces of an item at Rs. 1000 per item. You can create a PO by entering the ME21N transaction code in the transaction code text box and pressing the ENTER key, as shown in Figure B.52:

FIGURE B.52   **Displaying the ME21N transaction code**

The **Create Purchase Order** screen opens, as shown in Figure B.53:

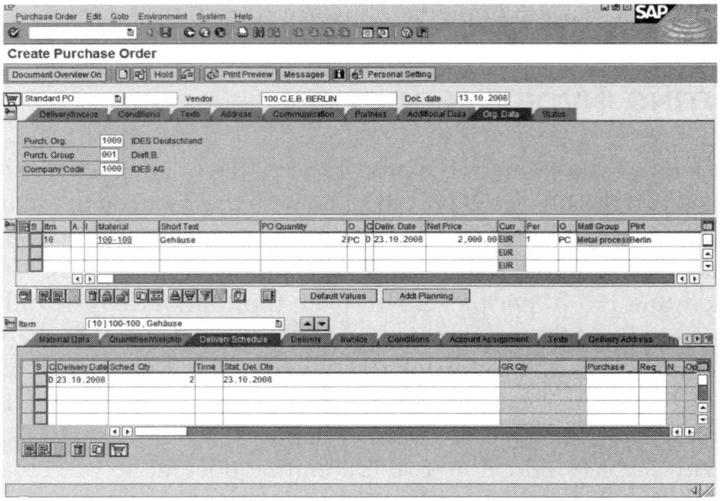

FIGURE B.53   **Displaying the Create Purchase Order screen**

In the **Create Purchase Order** screen, enter the required information to create the PO for the items. Next, click the **Save** (🖫) icon. A system message specifying that a standard PO under the entered number is created is displayed in the System Message Line of the screen, as shown in Figure B.54:

Standard PO created under the number 4500017184

FIGURE B.54   **Displaying the PO number**

After creating the PO, the next step for implementing invoice reduction is to post a GR. In our case, we are posting a goods receipt of 1 piece at Rs. 1000. Enter the `MIGO` transaction code in the transaction code text box and press the ENTER key to post the GR, as shown in Figure B.55:

FIGURE B.55   Displaying the MIGO transaction code

The **Goods Receipt Purchase Order – User Test** screen opens, as shown in Figure B.56:

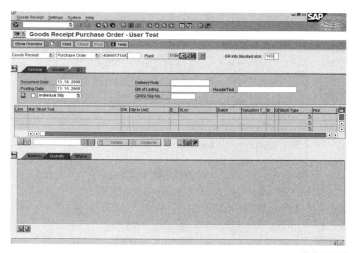

FIGURE B.56   Entering values in the general tab

In Figure B.56, enter the purchasing document number of the PO (created in the previous step) and the plant number in the **Purchasing Document Number** and **Plant** text boxes, respectively (Figure B.56). After entering the required information, press the ENTER key. The information related to the PO is displayed, as shown in Figure B.57:

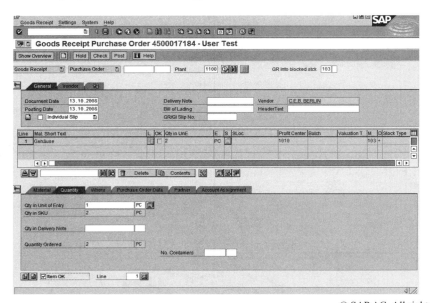

FIGURE B.57   **Displaying the relevant information in the quantity tab**

In the **Quantity** tab of the **Detail Data** section, change the quantity from 2 to 1 in the **Qty in Unit of Entry** text box, as shown in Figure B.57. In addition, select the **Item OK** check box.

After changing the quantity and selecting the check box, click the **Post** button. The goods receipt is posted in the system and a system message specifying the material document number is displayed in the System Message Line of the screen, as shown in Figure B.58:

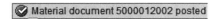

FIGURE B.58   **Displaying the material document number**

The last step in implementing invoice reduction is to post the invoice with the reduction. In this case, we have created a PO of 2 items but posted only 1 item, at Rs. 1000.

Perform the following steps to post the invoice with the reduction:

1. Enter the MIRO transaction code in the transaction code text box and press the ENTER key, as shown in Figure B.59:

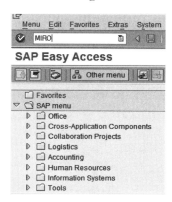

FIGURE B.59   Displaying the MIRO transaction code

The **Enter Incoming Invoice: Company Code 1000** screen opens, as shown in Figure B.60:

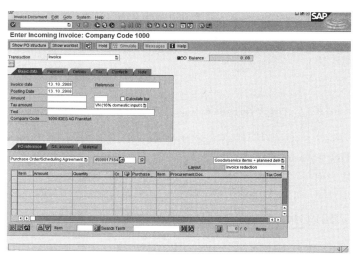

FIGURE B.60   Entering relevant information in the Enter Incoming Invoice: Company Code 1000 screen

2. Enter the date of the invoice in the **Invoice date** text box of the **Basic data** tab (Figure B.60).

3. Enter the number of the PO in the **Purchasing Document Number** text box of the **PO reference** tab (Figure B.60).

4. Select the **Invoice reduction** option in the **Layout** drop-down list (Figure B.60) and press the ENTER key. The system displays the information about the PO in the **PO reference** tab, as shown in Figure B.61:

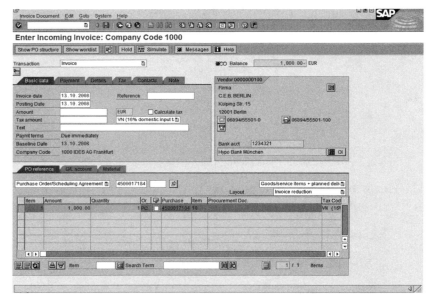

FIGURE B.61 Displaying the entered information in the PO reference tab

In Figure B.61, you can see that the invoice is posted with 1 piece in the **Quantity** column.

Let's now explore invoices with variances.

EXPLORING INVOICES WITH VARIANCES

We learned earlier that if an invoice contains variances, which means a difference between the quantity or amount invoiced in a PO in comparison to a value that the mySAP ERP system proposes, it is called an invoice with variance. This implies that the total amount or price in the vendor invoice and the total amount or price of the original invoice posted in the mySAP ERP system is different. Four different types of variances can occur, which are as follows:

- **Quantity variance**—Refers to a difference between the quantity delivered and the quantity invoiced.
- **Price variance**—Refers to a difference between the price in the invoice and the price in the PO.
- **Quantity and price variance**—Refers to a combination of quantity and price variance.
- **Order price quantity variance**—Refers to a difference between the ratio in the invoice and the ratio in the goods receipt.

In invoices with several items, it is difficult to find the item causing the variance. For example, suppose a vendor supplies several components of a material, which consists of more than 200 items. In this case, it is very difficult and time-consuming to identify the item responsible for the variance. Therefore, the organization decides to post an invoice reduction without any reference to a specific item.

You can correct the problem of variance in invoices by implementing the following two functions:

- **Total-based invoice reduction**—Creates two accounting documents. The first document contains the invoice posting and the second contains the credit memo for the difference amount. For example, while posting a vendor invoice of Rs. 100, the system displays the total amount as Rs. 90. In this case, the variance is of Rs. 10. Therefore, the invoice should be posted again using the total-based invoice reduction function.
- **Total-based invoice acceptance**—Posts the difference amount in a non-operating expense or revenue account. This implies that the system automatically generates a difference in the income and expense account.

While posting invoices with variances, the system decides whether to post the invoice by using total-based invoice reduction or total-based invoice acceptance. If the variance is within the tolerance limit, the invoice is posted by using total-based invoice acceptance. If the variance is not within the tolerance limit, the system checks for the difference limit for implementing total-based invoice reduction. If the difference is within the limit, the invoice is posted using total-based invoice reduction and if the difference exceeds the limit, the invoice cannot be posted.

In the following section, you learn how to define vendor-specific tolerance as well as how to assign a tolerance group in the vendor master record to post an invoice with variance.

Defining Vendor-Specific Tolerance

While posting an invoice, first the tolerance group for each company code is created and then the created tolerance group is assigned to the vendors in the vendors' master records. You can define a vendor-specific tolerance for both total-based invoice reduction and total-based invoice acceptance.

Perform the following steps to define a vendor-specific tolerance:

1. Navigate the following menu path:

Menu Path

SAP IMG > Materials Management > Logistics Invoice Verification > Incoming Invoice > Configure Vendor-Specific Tolerances. Figure B.62 shows the preceding menu path:

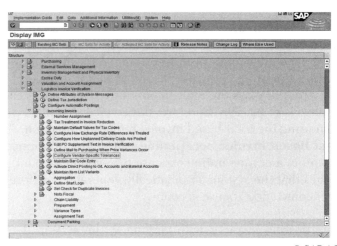

FIGURE B.62   Displaying the menu path to define vendor-specific tolerances

The **Change View "Vendor-Specific Tolerances": Overview** screen opens, as shown in Figure B.63:

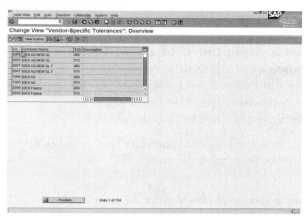

FIGURE B.63   **Displaying the Change View "Vendor-Specific Tolerances": Overview screen**

2. Click the **New Entries** button. The **New Entries: Details of Added Entries** screen opens, as shown in Figure B.64:

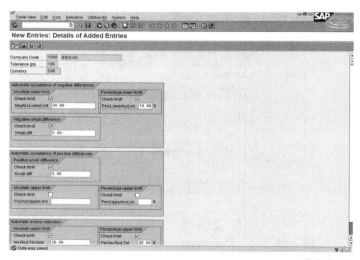

FIGURE B.64   **Displaying the New Entries: Details of Added Entries screen**

3. Enter the company code for which you want to define the tolerance limit in the **Company Code** text box (Figure B.64).
4. Enter the tolerance group for the vendor in the **Tolerance grp** text box (Figure B.64).
5. Enter the difference limits for negative and positive differences in the **Automatic acceptance of negative differences** and **Automatic acceptance of positive differences** groups, respectively (Figure B.64).
6. Enter the absolute and percentage value for the upper limit in the **Automatic invoice reduction** group (Figure B.64).
7. Click the **Save** (🖫) icon to save the changes.

A message specifying that the data was saved is displayed in the System Message Line of the screen (Figure B.64).

Assigning a Tolerance Group in the Vendor Master Record

After defining the tolerance limit for a vendor, you can assign the tolerance group in the vendor master record to post the invoice with variances.

Perform the following steps to assign a tolerance group in the vendor master record:

1. Enter the XK02 transaction code in the transaction code text box and press the ENTER key, as shown in Figure B.65:

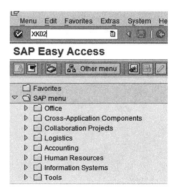

FIGURE B.65   Displaying the XK02 transaction code

The **Change Vendor: Initial Screen** opens, as shown in Figure B.66:

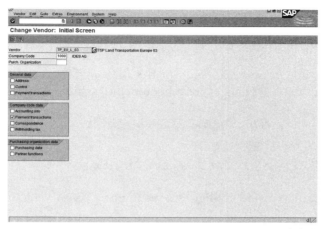

FIGURE B.66   Displaying the Change Vendor: Initial Screen

2. Enter the vendor number in the **Vendor** text box (Figure B.66).
3. Enter the company code number in the **Company Code** text box (Figure B.66).
4. Select the **Payment transactions** check box in the **Company code data** group (Figure B.66) and press the ENTER key. The **Change Vendor: Payment transactions Accounting** screen opens, as shown in Figure B.67:

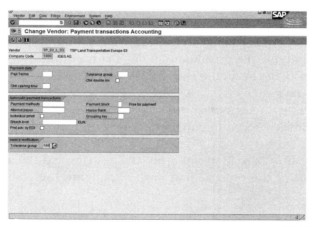

FIGURE B.67   Displaying the Change Vendor: Payment transactions Accounting screen

5. Enter the tolerance group number in the **Tolerance group** text box in the **Invoice verification** group (Figure B.67).
6. Click the **Save** (⊞) icon to save the data (Figure B.67).

A system message appears in the System Message Line of the screen specifying that the changes have been made, as shown in Figure B.68:

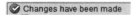

FIGURE B.68   **Saving the changes**

Let's now learn to configure taxes in invoice verification.

CONFIGURING TAXES IN INVOICE VERIFICATION

The material included in an invoice is taxable, which implies that you need to enter the tax amount while posting an invoice. Taxes are calculated during the purchase and sale of goods and are paid by the end customers. The tax collected from the customers is finally paid to the tax authorities. Therefore, handling taxes is an important part of invoice verification.

There are two options to configure taxes while posting an invoice, which are as follows:

- Selecting a tax code from the **Sales Tax Code** drop-down list and entering the tax amount in the **Tax amount** text box to calculate the tax in the **Basic data** tab of the **Enter Incoming Invoice** screen
- Selecting the **Calculate tax** check box in the **Basic data** tab of the **Enter Incoming Invoice** screen

Before an organization enters tax data in an invoice, the financial accounting department of the organization has to configure the codes and procedures related to taxes. For this, the SAP MM module provides various default tax code values.

Perform the following steps to define a default tax code for each company code:

1. Navigate the following menu path:

Menu Path

SAP IMG > Materials Management > Logistics Invoice Verification > Incoming Invoice > Maintain Default Values for Tax Codes. Figure B.69 shows the preceding menu path:

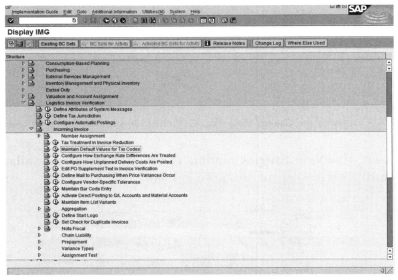

FIGURE B.69   Displaying the menu path to define the default tax code

The **Change View "Tax Defaults in Invoice Verification": Overview** screen opens, as shown in Figure B.70:

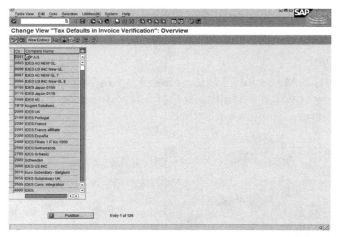

FIGURE B.70   Displaying the Change View "Tax Defaults in Invoice Verification": Overview screen

2. Click the **New Entries** button. The **New Entries: Details of Added Entries** screen opens, as shown in Figure B.71:

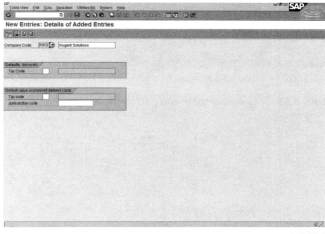

FIGURE B.71   Displaying the New Entries: Details of Added Entries screen

3. Enter the company code in the **Company Code** text box and press the ENTER key. The name of the company is displayed in the **Name of Company Code or Company** text box (Figure B.71).

4. Enter the code of the tax in the **Tax Code** text box in the **Defaults, domestic** group and press the ENTER key. The name of the tax is displayed in the **Name for value-added tax** text box, as shown in Figure B.72:

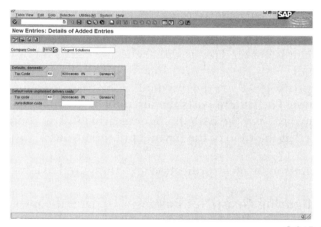

FIGURE B.72   **Displaying the new entries in the New Entries: Details of Added Entries screen**

5. Enter the code of the tax in **Tax code** text box in the **Defaults value unplanned delivery costs** group and press the ENTER key. The name of the tax is displayed in the **Name for value-added tax** text box (Figure B.72).

6. Click the **Save** (🖫) icon to save the information (Figure B.72).

A system message specifying that the data is saved is displayed in the System Message Line of the screen.

Let's now learn to configure discounts in invoice verification.

CONFIGURING DISCOUNTS IN INVOICE VERIFICATION

A vendor can offer discounts on the purchase price if you are ready to pay the amount within a specified period of time. For example, a vendor may give you a discount of 10% if the payment is made within 10 days of purchase, a discount of 5% if payment is made within 15 days of the purchase, and no discount if the payment is made 15 days after the purchase.

You can configure discounts while defining the terms of payment of an invoice. The discounts are posted in the system in the following ways:

- **Gross posting**—Posts the discount to the G/L account at the time of payment. This means that the system ignores the discount during the posting of the invoice. The amount of discount is not credited to either the stock account or the cost account.
- **Net posting**—Posts the discount to the cash discount clearing account. The system posts the discount at the time of posting the invoice, and the cash discount clearing G/L account is cleared at the time of the payment of the invoice.

Discounts in invoice verification are configured in a two-step process:

- **Configuring Gross/Net Posting**—Updates the invoice in the Financial Accounting module
- **Configuring Payment Terms**—Changes or updates the terms of payment mentioned in the invoice in the Financial Accounting module

Let's now learn to block invoices.

BLOCKING INVOICES

After verifying and posting the invoice in the system, the finance department of the organization makes the required payment to the vendors. However, sometimes an invoice is blocked and its payment is not made to the vendor. This may happen when, for example, the organization receives an invoice citing a higher amount than is expected. In such a situation, the organization blocks the invoice until the difference in the amount is resolved.

In the next section, we explore how to block invoices under the following topics:

- Blocking invoices based on quantity variance
- Blocking invoices based on price variance
- Blocking invoices randomly
- Blocking invoices manually

In addition to these, you can also define a tolerance limit in the mySAP ERP system for each variance type. When you post an invoice in the mySAP ERP system, it checks the invoice for variances. If the variance is more than the tolerance limit, the system blocks the invoice.

Blocking Invoices Based on Quantity Variance

Quantity variance refers to the situation in which the quantity of goods mentioned in an invoice is more than the quantity received. For example, an organization sends a PO for 100 items at Rs. 100 per item to the vendor, but the vendor delivers only 80 items. The invoice sent by the vendor is for 100 pieces, which means that the invoiced quantity is more than the received quantity. In such a situation, the invoice can be blocked due to quantity variance. The blocked invoice is released when the organization receives the balance quantity, which is 20 items, by posting another goods receipt.

Therefore, in the case of an invoice with quantity variance, three accounting documents are created: a goods receipt for 80 items, an invoice receipt for 100 items, and a goods receipt for 20 items.

Blocking Invoices Based on Price Variance

A price variance refers to a situation in which the price quoted in an invoice is different from that quoted in the PO. Such a situation results in a mismatch between the amount mentioned in the PO and the invoice of the vendor; therefore, the invoice is blocked. This is known as blocking an invoice based on price variance. This helps the organization in ensuring that the vendors are not paid a higher amount.

For example, suppose an organization sends a PO for 100 items at Rs. 100 per item. However, when the items are received, it is discovered that the invoice from the vendor had priced the items at Rs. 110 per piece. In such a situation, the invoice is blocked until the price variance is sorted out.

When blocking invoices based on price variance, accounting posting depends on the price control defined in the material master record. If the standard price valuation is followed for the material master record, the amount of difference in the prices, which is Rs. 10 per piece, is posted to the price difference G/L account. If the material master record is calculated by using the moving average price, the amount of difference in posted in the stock account.

Blocking Invoices Randomly

You can also configure the system to check invoices randomly and block those that do not satisfy specific requirements. This type of blocking is set at the invoice level and is known as random or stochastic blocking. With random blocking, the whole invoice is blocked for payment. There are two basic steps of blocking invoices randomly, which are as follows:

- Activate random blocking at the plant level
- Set a threshold for each plant, based on which the invoice is checked for blocking

Blocking Invoices Manually

When you block an invoice while entering its details in the **Enter Incoming Invoice** screen, the invoice is said to have been blocked manually. The entire invoice is blocked in this case. You can block an invoice manually by selecting the **Blocked for payment** option from the **Pmnt Block** drop-down list of the **Payment** tab in the **Enter Incoming Invoice: Company Code 3000** screen, as shown in Figure B.73:

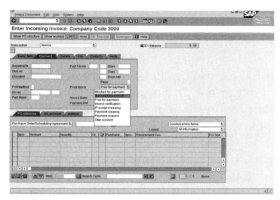

FIGURE B.73   Blocking an invoice manually

You can also block a particular item while posting multiple items in an invoice. In this case, the whole invoice is not blocked. To block a single item, select the **Manual Blocking Reason** check box of the item you want to block, as shown in Figure B.74:

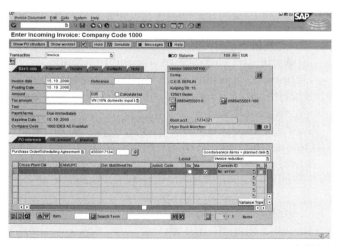

FIGURE B.74   Blocking a single item

In this way, you can block invoices manually.

Defining a Tolerance Limit

There is a tolerance limit for every variance of an invoice. A tolerance limit is the limit up to which the variances or differences in an invoice are tolerated. When there is variance in an invoice, the system checks whether the variance is within the tolerance limit or not. If the variance is within the tolerance limit, which can be either an absolute limit or a percentage limit, the invoice can be posted in the system. On the other hand, if the variance is outside the tolerance limit, the invoice is posted with a warning message; however, the payment is blocked. You need to release the blocked invoice for payment in a separate step.

Tolerance limits not only define the limit for variances of an invoice but also determine the maximum amount after which the invoice item is blocked. The tolerance keys defined in the mySAP ERP system are as follows:

- **AN**—Defines the amount for an item without the order reference
- **AP**—Defines the amount for an item with the order reference
- **BD**—Specifies that the differences are checked automatically
- **BR**—Defines the percentage order price quantity unit variance
- **BW**—Defines the percentage order quantity unit variance
- **DQ**—Specifies the quantity variance
- **DW**—Specifies that the goods receipt quantity is equal to zero
- **KW**—Specifies the variance from condition value
- **LA**—Defines the amount of a blanket purchase order
- **LD**—Specifies that the time limit of a blanket purchase order has been exceeded
- **PP**—Specifies the price variance
- **PS**—Defines the price variance of the estimated price
- **ST**—Specifies the date variance
- **VP**—Specifies the moving average price variance

You can configure the tolerance limit of the variance in an invoice by navigating the following menu path:

Menu Path

SAP IMG > Materials Management > Logistics Invoice Verification > Invoice Block > Set Tolerance Limit. Figure B.75 shows the preceding menu path:

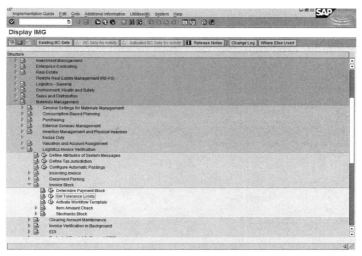

FIGURE B.75 Displaying the menu path to configure the tolerance limit

The **Change View "Tolerance Limits": Overview** screen opens, as shown in Figure B.76:

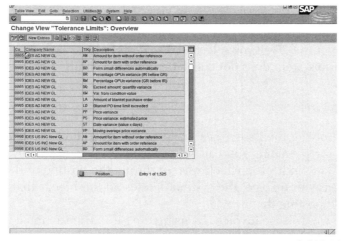

FIGURE B.76 Displaying tolerance keys

In Figure B.76, you can view a list of the tolerance keys for each company code. You can define the tolerance limit by selecting the company code and clicking the **Details** (⬚) icon. The **Change View "Tolerance Limits": Details** screen opens, as shown in Figure B.77:

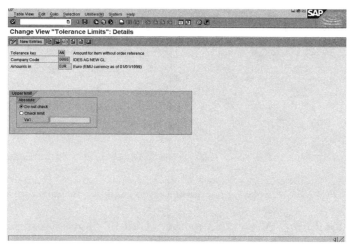

FIGURE B.77   Displaying the Change View "Tolerance Limits": Details screen

In Figure B.77, if you select the **Do not check** radio button in the **Absolute** group, the system does not check the tolerance limit.

Releasing Invoices

After resolving the issue of variance in a blocked invoice, you can release the invoice for payment. You can release a blocked invoice only after cancelling the blocking indicator, which was set during the posting of the invoice. When you release an invoice, the system deletes all the blocks that you might have set while posting the invoice.

You can release invoices by using the MRBR transaction code and entering the required information in the **Release Blocked Invoices** screen. You have two options in the **Release Blocked Invoices** screen for releasing invoices:

■ **Release Manually**—Displays blocked invoices in a list format that match the criteria entered in the **Selection of Blocked Invoices** group
■ **Release Automatically**—Automatically releases the invoices for which the blocking reasons have been deleted

Let's now learn to maintain the GR/IR account.

MAINTAINING THE GR/IR ACCOUNT

The GR/IR account is an intermediate account used to clear goods and invoice receipts. There are multiple instances when the GR/IR account is not cleared, such as:

■ The quantity mentioned in the invoice is greater than the received quantity. In such a situation, another goods receipt is required for the PO to clear the balance.
■ The received quantity is greater than the quantity mentioned in the invoice. In such a situation, another invoice is required for the PO to clear the balance.

Therefore, the GR/IR account is cleared when the quantity received from the vendor and the invoiced quantity are the same. Any difference results in a balance in the GR/IR account.

You can maintain the GR/IR account by using the MR11 transaction code in the transaction code text box, as shown in Figure B.78:

FIGURE B.78 **Displaying the MR11 transaction code**

The **Maintain GR/IR Clearing Account** screen opens, as shown in Figure B.79:

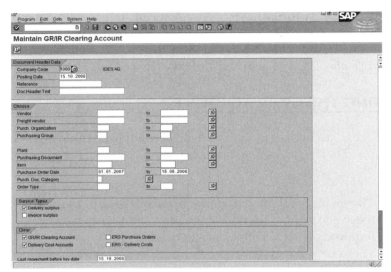

FIGURE B.79   Displaying the Maintain GR/IR Clearing Account screen

In Figure B.79, enter the relevant information and execute the transaction. The GR/IR clearing account is updated in the PO history.

Let's now learn to check duplicate invoices.

CHECKING DUPLICATE INVOICES

The mySAP ERP system provides you the functionality to check duplicate invoices. In some situations, a vendor may send you an invoice twice and you can post the same invoice twice in the system. The duplicate check functionality helps by preventing you from posting an invoice twice and thereby paying for the same transaction again.

You can check duplicate invoices by navigating the following menu path:

Menu Path

SAP IMG > Materials Management > Logistics Invoice Verification > Incoming Invoice > Set Check for Duplicate Invoices. Figure B.80 shows the preceding menu path:

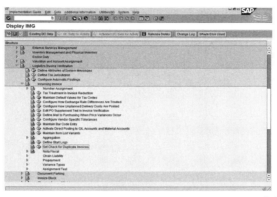

FIGURE B.80   Displaying the menu path to check duplicate invoices

The **Change View "Duplicate Invoice Check": Overview** screen opens, as shown in Figure B.81:

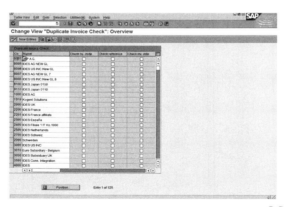

FIGURE B.81   Displaying the Change View "Duplicate Invoice Check": Overview screen

The **Change View "Duplicate Invoice Check": Overview** screen displays three columns that are used to check duplicate entries:

- **Check co. code**—Checks an invoice for duplicate company codes
- **Check references**—Checks an invoice for duplicate reference document numbers
- **Checks inv. date**—Checks an invoice for duplicate invoice dates

You can select any of the check boxes in the respective columns to check for duplicate invoices.

EXPLORING VARIOUS CONFIGURATIONS IN THE SAP MM MODULE

C

In the mySAP™ ERP system, various settings need to be configured to implement a release procedure, pricing procedure, and automatic account determination process. Consider the scenario of an organization in which external documents, such as contracts, purchase orders, and scheduling agreements, should be approved on the basis of the value limit of the material. In this scenario, the value limit set by the organization is as follows:

- For low value, that is, value below $30, no approval is required.
- For medium value, within the range of $30 to $100, the approval of the manager is required.
- For high value, that is, value above $100, the approval of both the manager as well as the vice president is required.

To implement this scenario, you need to configure various settings in the mySAP ERP system. This appendix helps you to explore the following topics to understand key configurations that may need to be implemented in the mySAP ERP system for various business scenarios:

- Release procedure
- Pricing procedure
- Automatic account determination process

The release procedure varies on the basis of the customer requirements; however, the pricing procedure as well as the automatic account determination process is implemented uniformly for all business processes. In general a maximum of 8 levels can be set in a release strategy.

CONFIGURING A RELEASE PROCEDURE

The process of approving various documents, such as purchase requisitions and purchase orders, is known as a release procedure; and the process of configuring a release procedure is known as a release strategy. For a release strategy, the document is first approved by an authorized person and then it is passed to the purchasing department. The approval procedure can be performed either manually or online. However, the process of approving the document online is more efficient and less time consuming as compared to the manual process. Consider the scenario of a manufacturing company in which the external documents need to be approved on the basis of the value limit. The documents of value $30 to $100 need to be approved by the manager; however, the documents valued more than $100 should be approved by both the manager and the vice president. You should define the range in such a way that there should not be any conflict. If a range is from $30 to $100, then the next range should be from $101 onwards. In such a case, there will not be any conflict when the value is exactly $100. Figure C.1 shows the release procedure for the purchase requisition and purchase order documents:

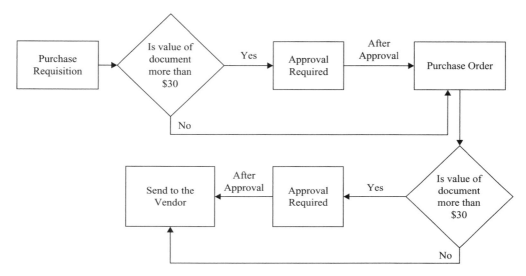

FIGURE C.1   Displaying the process flow of the release procedure

Figure C.1 shows that if the value of the documents is more than $30, approval is required and the release procedure should be implemented. However, if the document value is less than $30, no approval is required.

After learning the basics about the release procedure, you should learn how to implement a release procedure, without classification as well as with classification, in the mySAP ERP system. Let's learn each of these procedures in detail.

Configuring a Release Procedure without Classification

A release procedure without classification is configured for the purchase requisition documents and can be set on the basis of plant, value, material group, and account assignment category. You should note that a release procedure without classification is not used for the purchase order and request for quotation documents.

Before understanding the implementation process for a release procedure, you should know the key terms discussed in Table C.1:

Terms	Description
Release strategy	Provides a release procedure by defining the release conditions, release codes, and release prerequisites.
Release code	Represents a two character key of an individual or department. A release code is required to approve an external document.
Release conditions	Helps to identify the appropriate release strategy for a specific purchasing document. For example, the release strategy for a 3000 valued document valued at 3000 would vary from the strategy for a document valued at 10000 valued document.
Release prerequisite	Helps to set the order in which the document should be approved.
Release status	Depicts the current status of the document, whether the document is fully or partially approved.

TABLE C.1   Describing the key terms related to a release procedure

In the mySAP ERP system, you can set up a release procedure without classification by navigating the following menu path:

Menu Path

SAP Customizing Implementation Guide > Materials Management > Purchasing > Purchase Requisition > Release Procedure > Set Up Procedure Without Classification. Figure C.2 shows the preceding navigated menu path:

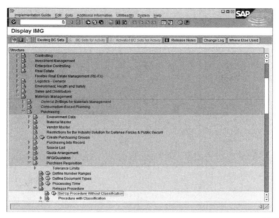

FIGURE C.2   **Displaying the menu path to set a release procedure without classification**

After navigating the preceding menu path, click the **IMG Activity** (⊕) icon. The **Choose Activity** dialog box appears, as shown in Figure C.3:

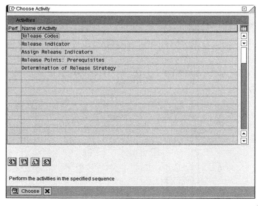

FIGURE C.3   **Displaying the Choose Activity dialog box**

Figure C.3 shows various activities that you need to perform while setting the release procedure without classification. Let's perform each of these activities.

Defining Release Codes

In the mySAP ERP system, each person responsible for approving documents is assigned a release code, which should be used during the approval process. Perform the following steps to define a release code:

1. Click the **IMG Activity** (⊕) icon after navigating the following menu path (Figure C.2):

Menu Path

SAP Customizing Implementation Guide > Materials Management > Purchasing > Purchase Requisition > Release Procedure > Set Up Procedure Without Classification. The **Choose Activity** dialog box appears (Figure C.3).

2. Select the **Release Codes** activity from the **Choose Activity** dialog box (Figure C.3).
3. Click the **Choose** push button (Figure C.3).

The **Change View "Release Codes": Overview** screen appears, displaying the release codes already defined in the mySAP ERP system (Figure C.4).

4. Click the **New Entries** button, as shown in Figure C.4:

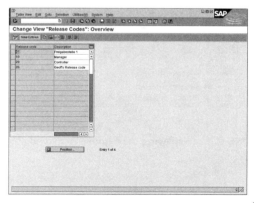

FIGURE C.4   **Displaying the release codes available in the mySAP ERP system**

The **New Entries: Overview of Added Entries** screen appears (Figure C.5).

5. Enter a release code and its description in the **Release code** and **Description** text boxes, respectively. In our case, we have entered `05` as the release code and `New Release Code` as its description (Figure C.5).

6. Click the **Save** (🖫) icon to save the new release code, as shown in Figure C.5:

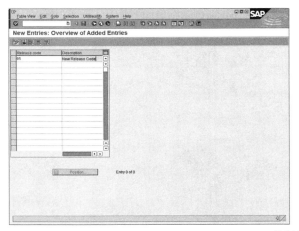

FIGURE C.5   Displaying the New Entries: Overview of Added Entries screen

The **Data was saved** message appears, as shown in Figure C.6:

FIGURE C.6   Displaying the message indicating the successful creation of a release code

After defining a new release code, let's learn how to create a release indicator.

Defining Release Indicators

In the mySAP ERP system, a release indicator depicts the current status of a purchase requisition document. You can define a release indicator by specifying a one-digit code and its description. In addition, you should also define the controlling indicators and field selection key for the new release indicator. Perform the following steps to define a release indicator:

1. Select the **Release indicator** activity from the **Choose Activity** dialog box (Figure C.3).
2. Click the **Choose** push button (Figure C.3). The **Change View "Release Indicator": Overview** screen appears, displaying the release indicators already defined in the mySAP ERP system (Figure C.7).
3. Click the **New Entries** button, as shown in Figure C.7:

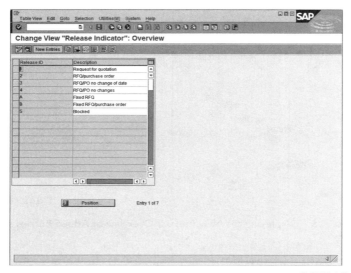

FIGURE C.7 **Displaying the release indicators defined in the mySAP ERP system**

The **New Entries: Details of Added Entries** screen appears (Figure C.8).

4. Enter a release ID and its description. In our case, we have entered 5 as the release ID and `New Release ID` as its description (Figure C.8). Figure C.8 shows the following fields that are used to define controlling indicators for the release indicator:

   ▫ **Firmed for Req. Planning**—Helps to define whether or not the purchase requisition should be changed on the basis of Material Requirements Planning (MRP). In other words, if you check the **Firmed for Req. Planning** check box, the purchase requisition document cannot be modified by the MRP process.

   ▫ **Released for Quotation**—Helps to specify whether or not the quotations and request for quotation (RFQ) should be processed with reference to the purchase requisition. In other words, if you check the **Released for Quotation** checkbox, the purchase requisition is used to process the quotations and RFQ.

   ▫ **Released for issue of PO**—Helps to specify whether or not a purchase order should be processed with reference to the purchase requisition. In other words, if you check the **Released for issue of PO** check box, the purchase requisition is used to generate the purchase order.

   ▫ **Field Selection Key**—Helps to define whether or not specific fields in the purchase requisition should be changed during approval of the purchase requisition document. For example, if you want the requested quantity in the purchase requisition document not to be changed after setting the release indicator, you should select the **Display Only** option in the **Field Selection Key** field.

   ▫ **Changeable**—Helps to define the procedure to be followed if the purchasing document is changed after starting a release procedure.

   ▫ **Value Change**—Helps to provide the percentage of the value of the material that can be changed after starting a release procedure.

5. Click the **Save** (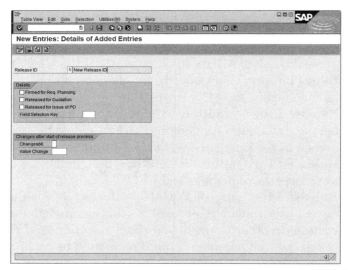) icon to save the details entered for a new release indicator, as shown in Figure C.8:

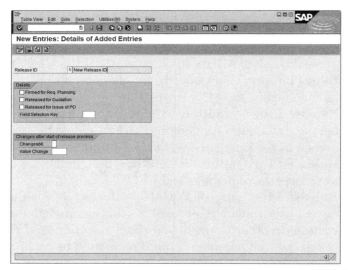

FIGURE C.8 Displaying the details of the new release indicator

The **Data was saved** message appears (Figure C.6).

After defining the release indicator, let's now assign the release indicator to the release code.

Assigning Release Indicators

We have defined the 5 release indicator and the 05 release code in the preceding sections; let's now assign the release indicator to the release code. Perform the following steps to assign release indicators:

1. Select the **Assign Release Indicators** activity and click the **Choose** push button in the **Choose Activity** dialog box (Figure C.3). The **Change View**

"Assign Release Indicators": Overview screen appears, as shown in Figure C.9:

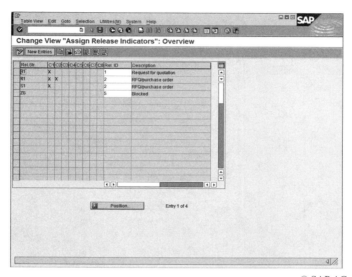

FIGURE C.9   Displaying the Change View "Assign Release Indicators": Overview screen

In Figure C.9, the 1 release indicator set for the R1 release strategy implies that the RFQ document can be created with the help of the purchase requisition document. In addition, the 2 release indicator is also set for the R1 release strategy, which implies that the RFQ and purchase order documents can be created. You should note that the 2 release indicator would be set for the R1 release strategy only after the 1 release indicator has been set.

2. Click the **New Entries** button on the **Change View "Assign Release Indicators": Overview** screen to assign a release indicator (say 5) to a release code (say 05). The **New Entries: Overview of Added Entries** screen appears (Figure C.10).

3. Enter the details, such as release strategy and release ID, as shown in Figure C.10:

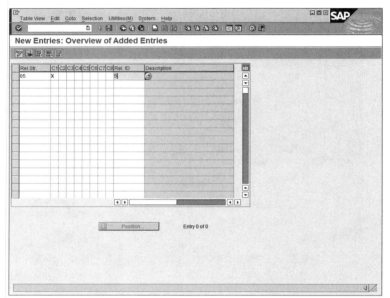

FIGURE C.10   Displaying the New Entries: Overview of Added Entries screen

4. Click the **Save** (🖫) icon to assign the release indicator.

Let's now learn how to define release points for the release procedure.

Defining Release Points: Prerequisites

Let's now define the release points and prerequisites for the release strategies. Perform the following steps to define prerequisites for a release strategy in the mySAP ERP system:

1. Select the **Release Points: Prerequisites** activity from the **Choose Activity** dialog box (Figure C.3).

2. Click the **Choose** push button (Figure C.3). The **Change View "Release Points: Prerequisites": Overview** screen appears, displaying the prerequisites already defined in the mySAP ERP system (Figure C.11).
3. Click the **New Entries** button, as shown in Figure C.11:

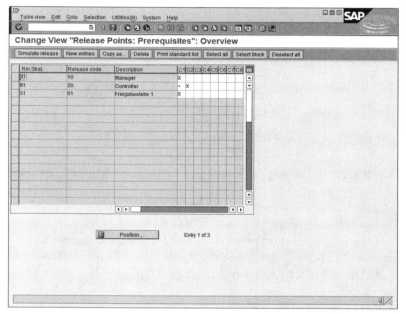

FIGURE C.11   **Displaying the Change View: "Release Points: Prerequisites": Overview screen**

The **New Entries: Overview of Added Entries** screen appears (Figure C.12).

4. Enter a code for the release strategy in the **Rel. Strat.** header. In our case, we have entered 05 as the release strategy (Figure C.12).
5. Enter a unique number for the release code in the **Release code** header. In our case, we have entered 05 as the release code (Figure C.12).
6. Enter a standard prerequisite in the **C1** header. In our case, we have entered X as the prerequisite (Figure C.12).

7. Click the **Save** (■) icon to save the entered details, as shown in Figure C.12:

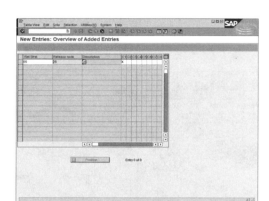

FIGURE C.12   **Displaying the New Entries: Overview of Added Entries screen**

Apart from defining prerequisites for a release strategy, you can also test the sequence and prerequisites of a release strategy. For example, if you want to test the sequence and prerequisites of the R1 release strategy, you should select the R1 strategy and click the **Simulate release** button (Figure C.11). The **Release Simulation for Strategy R1** dialog box appears, as shown in Figure C.13:

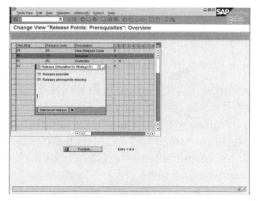

FIGURE C.13   **Displaying the release codes for the R1 release strategy**

Figure C.13 shows that the `R1` release strategy has release codes `10` and `20`, which allows you to create the RFQ document even though the purchasing document has not been released by release code `20`. In addition, when the purchase requisition document is released by release code `10`, release indicator `1` is set for the R1 release strategy.

After defining release codes as well as release strategies and assigning release codes and prerequisites, let's now discuss how to determine a release strategy for a purchase requisition document.

Determining a Release Strategy

When setting a release procedure without classification, you can configure a release strategy on the basis of account assignment, material group, plant, and value. Perform the following steps to determine a release strategy for a purchase requisition:

1. Select the **Determination of Release Strategy** activity from the **Choose Activity** dialog box (Figure C.3).
2. Click the **Choose** push button (Figure C.3). The **Change View "Determination of Release Strategy": Overview** screen appears, displaying the release strategies defined for the plant, value, material group, and account assignment categories (Figure C.14).
3. Click the **New Entries** button, as shown in Figure C.14:

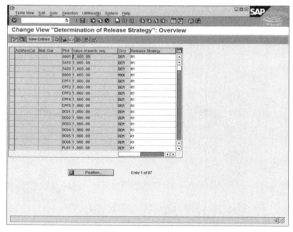

FIGURE C.14   **Displaying the Change View "Determination of Release Strategy": Overview screen**

The **New Entries: Details of Added Entries** screen appears (Figure C.15).

4. Enter an account assignment category in the **Acct. Assignment Cat.** text box. In our case, we have entered K as the account assignment category (Figure C.15).
5. Enter a material code group in the **Material** text box. In our case, we have entered 0001 as the material code (Figure C.15).
6. Enter a plant code in the **Plant** text box. In our case, we have entered 1100 as the plant code (Figure C.15).
7. Enter the currency type in the **Currency** text box. In our case, we have entered EUR as the currency (Figure C.15).
8. Enter a release procedure code in the **Release Strategy** field. In our case, we have entered 05 as the release procedure code (Figure C.15).
9. Click the **Enter** (✓) icon, as shown in Figure C.15:

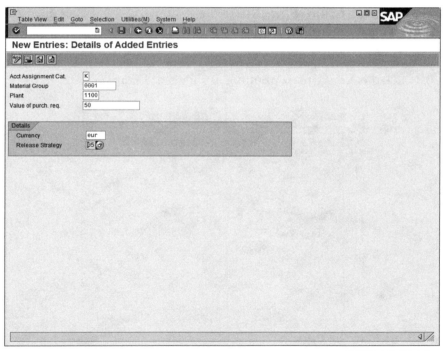

FIGURE C.15 Displaying the New Entries: Details of Added Entries screen

The **Data was saved message** appears, as shown in Figure C.16:

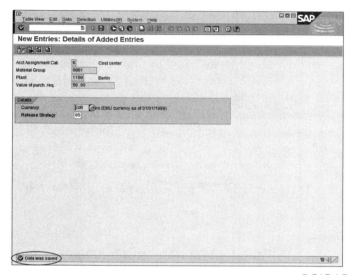

FIGURE C.16   **Displaying the message after successful assignment of a release strategy**

After configuring the release procedure without classification, let's now learn how to configure a release procedure with classification.

Configuring a Release Procedure with Classification

A release procedure with classification helps you to define release procedures for internal as well as external documents on the basis of the characteristics and class of a material. In the mySAP ERP system, a release procedure with classification is used for internal documents, such as purchase requisitions. Apart from internal documents, a release procedure with classification is also used for external documents, such as purchase orders, RFQs, contracts, and scheduling agreements. You should perform the following steps to configure a release procedure with classification in the mySAP ERP system:

1. Define characteristics
2. Define a class
3. Define a release strategy for a purchase order

Let's perform each of these steps in detail.

Defining Characteristics for a Release Procedure

In a release procedure, the characteristics serve as the conditions on the basis of which a release procedure is assigned to a purchasing document. For example, if the characteristic value for a release procedure is set to more than $100, or in other words, if the total value of a purchase order is more than $100, the release procedure would be assigned to the purchase order.

In the mySAP ERP system, the CEBAN table is defined for mapping the characteristics of the purchase requisition document and the CEKKO table is used to map the characteristics of the purchase order document. With respect to these tables, different characteristics are used for different fields. For example, the BSART characteristic is used for the order type field. Perform the following steps to define the characteristics for a release procedure:

1. Click the **IMG Activity** (⊕) icon after navigating the following menu path in the mySAP ERP system:

Menu Path

SAP Customizing Implementation Guide > Materials Management > Purchasing > Purchase Order > Release Procedure for Purchase Order > Edit Characteristics. Figure C.17 shows the preceding navigated menu path in the **Display IMG** screen:

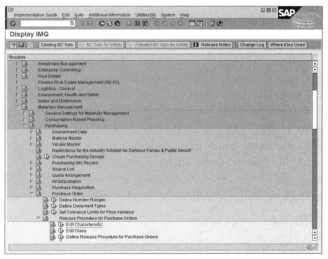

FIGURE C.17   Displaying the menu path to edit characteristics

The **Characteristics** screen appears (Figure C.18).

2. Enter the name or code of the new characteristic in the **Characteristic** text box. In our case, we have entered NEWCHAR as the name of the new characteristic (Figure C.18).

3. Click the **Create** (□) icon, as shown in Figure C.18:

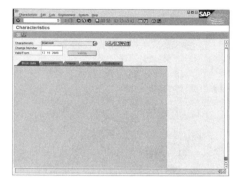

FIGURE C.18   **Displaying the Characteristics screen**

The **Create Characteristic** screen appears (Figure C.19).

4. Enter the details of the new characteristic in the fields displayed under the **Basic data** tab. In our case, we have entered New Characteristics as the description, Released as the status, and INR as the currency type, as shown in Figure C.19:

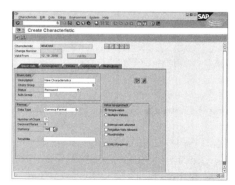

FIGURE C.19   **Displaying the basic data tab of the Create Characteristic screen**

5. Select the **Addnl data** tab and enter the table name and field name in the **Table Name** and **Field Name** text boxes, respectively. In our case, we have entered CEKKO as the table name and GNETW as the field name (Figure C.20).
6. Click the **Save** (■) icon to save the entered details, as shown in Figure C.20:

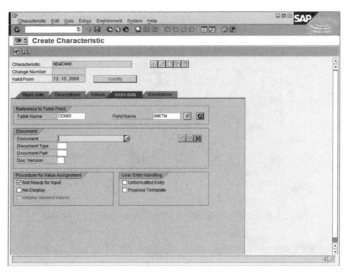

FIGURE C.20 Displaying the Addnl data tab of the Create Characteristic screen

The **Characteristic NEWCHAR saved** message appears, as shown in Figure C.21:

FIGURE C.21 Displaying the message indicating successful creation of a characteristic

Similarly, you can create other characteristics for a release procedure, after which you should group the characteristics in a class.

Let's discuss how to create a class for a release procedure.

Defining a Class for a Release Procedure

In the mySAP ERP system, you can define a class for a release procedure and group together various characteristics used for the release procedure. Perform the following steps to define a class for a release procedure:

1. Click the **IMG Activity** (⊕) icon after navigating the following menu path in the mySAP ERP system (Figure C.17):

Menu Path

SAP Customizing Implementation Guide > Materials Management > Purchasing > Purchase Order > Release Procedure for Purchase Order > Edit Classes. The **Class** screen appears (Figure C.22).

2. Enter the name of the class in the **Class** text box. In our case, we have entered NewClass as the name of the class (Figure C.22).
3. Enter the class type in the **Class type** text box. In our case, we enter 032 as the class type (Figure C.22).
4. Click the **Create** (🗋) icon, as shown in Figure C.22:

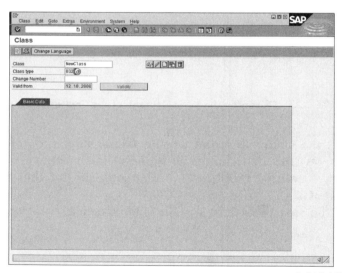

FIGURE C.22   **Displaying the Class screen**

The **Create Class:** screen appears (Figure C.23).

5. Enter the description, status, and class group of the new class in the **Basic Data** tab of the **Create Class:** screen, as shown in Figure C.23:

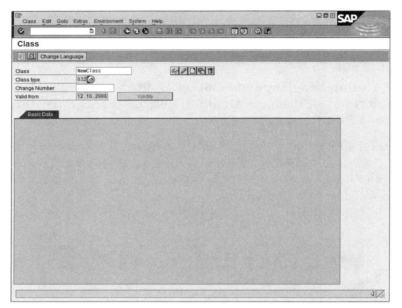

FIGURE C.23 **Displaying the Basic Data tab of the Create Class: screen**

6. Select the **Char** tab of the **Create Class:** screen to enter the different characteristics that should be grouped in the new class. In our case, we have entered the NEWCHAR characteristic for the NEWCLASS class (Figure C.24).

7. Click the **Save** (🖫) icon to save the entered details, as shown in Figure C.24:

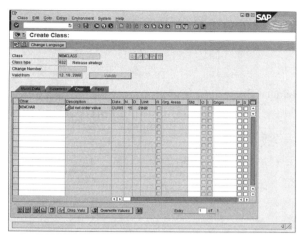

FIGURE C.24   Displaying the Char tab of the Create Class: screen

The **Class type 032: Class NEWCLASS** created message appears, as shown in Figure C.25:

FIGURE C.25   Displaying the message indicating successful creation of the NEWCLASS class

You should note that the characteristics and classes are known as master data in the mySAP ERP system, as they cannot be transported from a development server to quality and production clients through transport requests. Instead, you either need to manually create the characteristics as well as classes on each client, or automatically download them from the middleware tools provided by SAP, such as Application Link and Enabling (ALE). You can use the BD91, BD92, and BD93 transaction codes to transfer characteristics and classes through ALE.

After defining the characteristics and classes, the final step is to define a release procedure for a purchase order, which is discussed in the following subsection.

Defining a Release Procedure for a Purchase Order

While defining a release procedure for a purchase order, you need to perform various tasks, such as defining release groups, release codes, and release indicators, assigning the release groups to a release strategy, and defining the workflow. In the mySAP ERP system, navigate the following menu path to define a release procedure for a purchase order:

Menu Path

SAP Customizing Implementation Guide > Materials Management > Purchasing > Purchase Order > Release Procedure for Purchase Order > Define Release Procedure for Purchase Orders

After navigating the preceding menu path, click the **IMG Activity** (⊕) icon. The **Choose Activity** dialog box appears, displaying the list of activities to be performed to define a release procedure, as shown in Figure C.26:

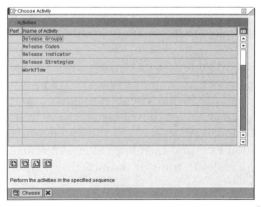

FIGURE C.26   Displaying the activities to be performed while defining a release procedure

Let's perform each of the listed activities to define a release procedure.

Defining Release Groups

In the mySAP ERP system, a release group is defined to group one or more strategies. You should remember that you can define a release strategy for various release groups. For example, the 01 release group is defined for the purchase requisition document and the 02 release group is defined for the purchase order document. In this example, you can define a release strategy for both the 01 and 02 release groups.

   Perform the following steps to define a release group:

1. Select the **Release Groups** activity from the **Choose Activity** dialog box (Figure C.26).
2. Click the **Choose** push button in the **Choose Activity** dialog box (Figure C.26).

The **Change View "Release Groups: External Purchasing Document": Overview** screen appears (Figure C.27).

3. Click the **New Entries** button, as shown in Figure C.27:

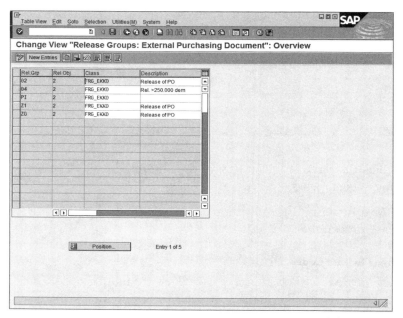

FIGURE C.27   **Displaying the details of existing release groups**

The **New Entries: Overview of Added Entries** screen appears (Figure C.28).

4. Enter the details for the new release group (Figure C.28).
5. Click the **Enter** (☑) icon, as shown in Figure C.28:

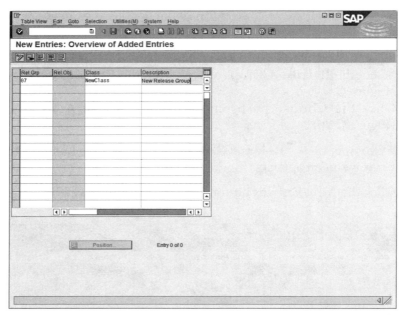

FIGURE C.28   Displaying the New Entries: Overview of Added Entries screen

6. Click the **Save** (🖫) icon to save the entered details. The **Data was saved** message appears.

After creating the release groups, you need to define release codes for release procedures.

Defining Release Codes

In the mySAP ERP system, release codes are unique codes that are assigned to release groups. We know that each person or department authorized for approving internal documents is assigned a release code. By using the release code, the authorized person can approve or reject the purchase requisition or purchase order documents. Perform the following steps to define a release code:

1. Select the **Release Codes** activity from the **Choose Activity** dialog box (Figure C.26).
2. Click the **Choose** push button in the **Choose Activity** dialog box (Figure C.26).

The **Change View "Release Codes: External Purchasing Documents": Overview** screen appears (Figure C.29).

3. Click the **New Entries** button, as shown in Figure C.29:

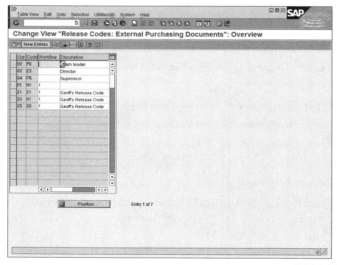

FIGURE C.29 **Displaying the details of existing release codes**

The **New Entries: Overview of Added Entries** screen appears (Figure C.30).

4. Enter the details of the new release code (Figure C.30).

5. Click the **Save** (🖫) icon to save the entered details, as shown in Figure C.30:

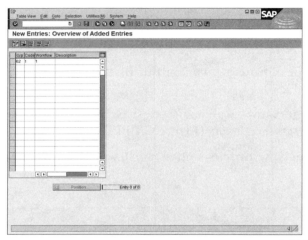

FIGURE C.30   **Displaying the New Entries: Overview of Added Entries screen**

The **Data was saved** message appears.

After defining the release codes, let's move ahead to define the release indicators.

Defining Release Indicators

In the mySAP ERP system, a release indicator depicts the status of a release strategy. In other words, if the approval process is complete, the release strategy can be released. However, if the approval process is in progress, then the release strategy is blocked. Perform the following steps to define a release indicator:

1. Select the **Release indicator** activity from the **Choose Activity** dialog box (Figure C.26).
2. Click the **Choose** push button in the **Choose Activity** dialog box (Figure C.26).

The **Change View "Release Indicator: Purchasing Document": Overview** screen appears (Figure C.31).

3. Click the **New Entries** button, as shown in Figure C.31:

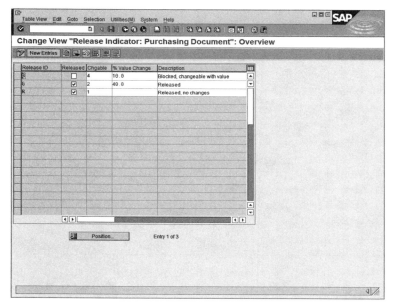

FIGURE C.31   Displaying the details of existing release indicators

The **New Entries: Overview of Added Entries** screen appears (Figure C.32).

4. Enter the details of a release indicator for purchasing documents (Figure C.32).

5. Click the **Save** (🖫) icon to save the details, as shown in Figure C.32:

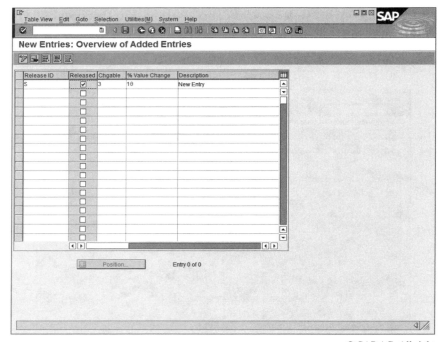

FIGURE C.32   Displaying the New Entries: Overview of Added Entries screen

The **Data was saved** message appears.

Let's now learn how to define release strategies.

Defining Release Strategies

In the mySAP ERP system, you can define a release strategy by assigning a release code and release group. Perform the following steps to define a release strategy:

1. Select the **Release Strategies** activity from the **Choose Activity** dialog box (Figure C.26).

2. Click the **Choose** push button in the **Choose Activity** dialog box (Figure C.26).

The **Change View "Release Strategies: External Purchasing Documents"**: **Overview** screen appears (Figure C.33).

3. Click the **New Entries** button, as shown in Figure C.33:

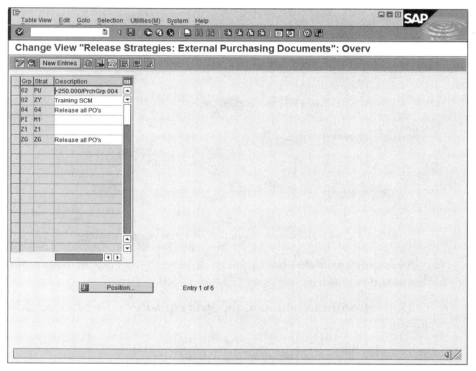

FIGURE C.33 Displaying the details of the existing release strategies

The **New Entries: Details of Added Entries** screen appears (Figure C.34).

4. Enter the release group code in the **Release Group** field. In our case, we have entered 01 as the release group code (Figure C.34).
5. Enter the release strategy code in the **Release Strategy** field. In our case, we have entered 05 as the release strategy code (Figure C.34).
6. Enter a release code in the **Release codes** field. In our case, we have entered EX as the release code (Figure C.34).

7. Click the **Release prerequisites** button, as shown in Figure C.34:

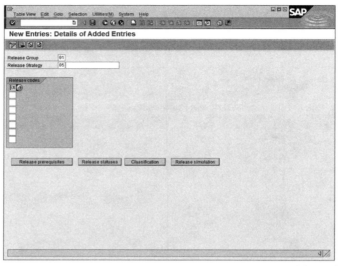

FIGURE C.34   **Displaying the details of a new release strategy**

The **Prerequisites** dialog box appears, displaying the code or release prerequisites of the new release strategy (Figure C.35).

8. Click the **Continue** button in the **Prerequisites** dialog box, as shown in Figure C.35:

FIGURE C.35   **Displaying the Prerequisites dialog box**

The **New Entries: Details of Added Entries** screen appears (Figure C.34).

9. Click the **Release statuses** button (Figure C.34). The **Release Statuses** dialog box appears (Figure C.36).
10. Click the **Continue** button, as shown in Figure C.36:

FIGURE C.36   **Displaying the Release Statuses dialog box**

The **New Entries: Details of Added Entries** screen appears (Figure C.34).

11. Click the **Classification** button in the **New Entries: Details of Added Entries** screen (Figure C.34). The **New Entries: Classification** screen appears (Figure C.37).
12. Enter the relevant details in the **New Entries: Classification** screen (Figure C.37).
13. Click the **Next Screen** (⊞) icon, as shown in Figure C.37:

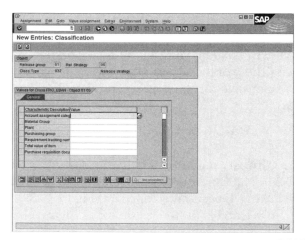

FIGURE C.37   **Displaying the New Entries: Classification screen**

The **New Entries: Details of Added Entries** screen appears (Figure C.34).

14. Click the **Release Simulation** button (Figure C.34). The **Release Strategy** dialog box appears (Figure C.38).
15. Click the **Continue** (☑) icon, as shown in Figure C.38:

FIGURE C.38   **Displaying the Release Strategy dialog box**

The **New Entries: Details of Added Entries** screen appears (Figure C.34).

16. Click the **Save** (🖫) icon to save the entered details (Figure C.34). The **Data was saved** message appears.

After defining a release strategy, let's learn how to define a workflow for a release strategy.

Defining a Workflow for a Release Strategy

In the mySAP ERP system, you can define a workflow for a release strategy. While defining the workflow, you need to configure an agent for a release code that is responsible for the approval process. Perform the following tasks to define a workflow:

1. Select the **Workflow** activity from the **Choose Activity** dialog box (Figure C.26).
2. Click the **Choose** push button in the **Choose Activity** dialog box (Figure C.26). The **Change View "Assignment of Role to Release Code: Ext. Purchasing Docs.** screen appears (Figure C.39).
3. Click the **New Entries** button, as shown in Figure C.39:

FIGURE C.39   Displaying the Change View "Assignment of Role to Release Code: Ext. Purchasing Docs. screen

The **New Entries: Overview of Added Entries** screen appears (Figure C.40).

4. Enter the relevant details in the **New Entries: Overview of Added Entries** screen (Figure C.40).

5. Click the **Save** (🖫) icon to save the entered details, as shown in Figure C.40:

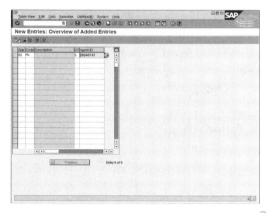

FIGURE C.40   Displaying the New Entries: Overview of Added Entries screen

The entered details are saved and you can now create a purchasing document for which the release strategy will be automatically assigned.

Let's now configure the pricing procedure, which is used to determine the price of a material in a purchase order.

CONFIGURING THE PRICING PROCEDURE

In an organization, the price of a material is based on the discounts, surcharges, taxes, and freight charges that are charged or allowed to a customer. Consider a scenario of a soap manufacturing enterprise that plans to purchase soap lather from a vendor. The vendor offers the soap lather at 10% discount and charges 12% VAT. Therefore, the price of soap lather is set on the basis of the discount and tax. In the SAP system, the pricing procedure is followed to calculate the price of a material to be provided in a purchase order.

While configuring the pricing procedure, you first need to define price, discount, surcharges, and freight charges in the form of condition types. Each condition type has various condition records that are defined in condition tables. Next, you need to define an access sequence, which holds the sequence of condition records. Further, the calculation schema is defined to group various condition types in a sequence. Finally, a schema group is defined to maintain the vendor details.

Therefore, the broad-level steps to configure the pricing procedure in the mySAP ERP system are as follows:

1. Define a condition type
2. Define an access sequence
3. Define a calculation schema
4. Define a schema group

Let's discuss all these in detail.

Defining a Condition Type

In the SAP system, a condition type depicts various elements that are used to determine prices, such as discounts, surcharges, taxes, or delivery costs.

For example, in the mySAP ERP system, the `0001` condition type is defined for gross price, which maintains the condition records until its validity period expires. Perform the following steps to define a condition type:

1. Click the **IMG Activity** (⊕) icon after navigating the following menu path:

Menu Path

SAP Customizing Implementation Guide > Materials Management > Purchasing > Conditions > Define Price Determination Process > Define Condition Types. Figure C.41 shows the preceding menu path in the **Display IMG** screen:

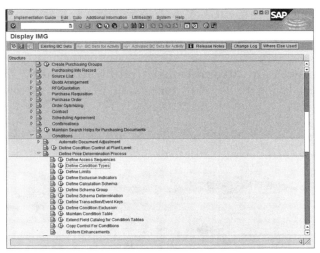

FIGURE C.41   **Displaying the menu path to define a condition type**

The **Choose Activity** dialog box appears (Figure C.42).

2. Select the **Define Condition Type** activity from the **Choose Activity** dialog box (Figure C.42).

3. Click the **Choose** push button, as shown in Figure C. 42:

FIGURE C.42   **Displaying the activities associated with condition types**

The **Change View "Conditions: Condition Types": Overview** screen appears, displaying the list of existing condition types in the mySAP ERP system (Figure C.43).

4. Click the **New Entries** button, as shown in Figure C.43:

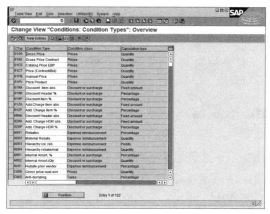

FIGURE C.43   **Displaying the list of existing condition types**

The **New Entries: Details of Added Entries** screen appears (Figure C.44).

5. Enter the following details in the **New Entries: Details of Added Entries** screen (Figure C.44):

    □ **Condition type**—Specifies a unique condition type in the **Condit. type** field. In our case, we have entered PB00 as the condition type and Gross Price as its description.

    □ **Access sequence**—Specifies the access sequence code in the **Access seq.** field. In our case, we have entered 0002 as the access sequence.

    □ **Condition class**—Specifies a condition class to group the identical condition types in the **Cond. class** field. In our case, we have entered B as the condition class, which represents the group of condition types for prices.

    □ **Calculation type**—Specifies a calculation type, which helps to determine how a condition value should be calculated. In other words, the specified calculation type can be used to determine whether the condition results lead to a positive or negative amount. You should note that the condition value can be calculated on the basis of quantity, weight, or volume of a material. In our case, we have entered C as the calculation type in the **Calculat. type** field.

    □ **Condition category**—Specifies the category in which the condition type lies. In our case, we have entered H as the condition category in the **Cond. category** field.

6. Check the relevant check boxes depending on the business scenario (Figure C.44).

7. Click the **Save** (🖫) icon to save the entered details, as shown in Figure C.44:

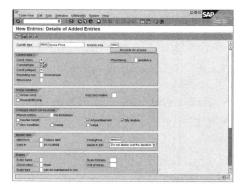

FIGURE C.44 **Displaying the details of a condition type**

The condition type has been created. Let's now learn how to define an access sequence.

Defining an Access Sequence

In the SAP system, an access sequence serves as a search strategy that is used to identify a valid condition record on the basis of a specific condition type. You should assign an access sequence for the condition types that need to be maintained. Perform the following steps to define an access sequence:

1. Click the **IMG Activity** (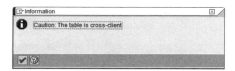) icon after navigating the following menu path (Figure C.41):

Menu Path

SAP Customizing Implementation Guide > Materials Management > Purchasing > Conditions > Define Price Determination Process > Define Access Sequence

The **Information** dialog box (Figure C.45) appears, displaying the message that the table used in the **Define Access Sequence** activity is cross-client; thereby, the changes made in an access sequence would be applicable for all clients.

2. Click the **Continue** (☑) icon, as shown in Figure C.45:

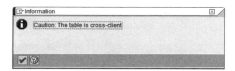

FIGURE C.45   Displaying the Information dialog box

The **Change View "Access Sequences": Overview** screen appears, displaying the list of access sequences already defined in the mySAP ERP system (Figure C.46).

3. Select an access sequence from the list of access sequences. In our case, we select 0002 as the access sequence (Figure C.46).

4. Double-click the **Accesses** folder displayed in the tree menu, as shown in Figure C.46:

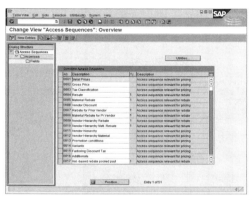

FIGURE C.46   Displaying the list of access sequences available in the mySAP ERP system

The **Change View "Accesses": Overview** screen appears, displaying the accesses provided for the 0002 access sequence (Figure C.47).

5. Click the **New Entries** button, as shown in Figure C.47:

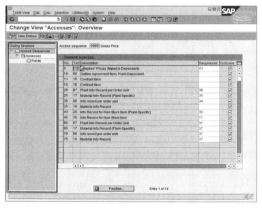

FIGURE C.47   Displaying the accesses of the 0002 access sequence

The **New Entries: Overview of Added Entries** screen appears (Figure C.48).

6. Enter the relevant details to create a new access for the 0002 access sequence (Figure C.48).

7. Click the **Save** (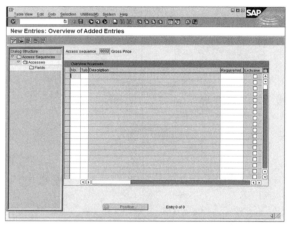) icon to save the entered details, as shown in Figure C.48:

FIGURE C.48   Displaying the New Entries: Overview of Added Entries screen

The new access for the 0002 access sequence is defined.
Let's now learn how to define a calculation schema.

Defining a Calculation Schema

A calculation schema defines a complete structure of various condition records, along with their sequence and control parameters. When you create a purchase order, the SAP system locates the calculation schema, which is used to identify the value of each condition defined within the schema. Perform the following steps to define a calculation schema:

1. Click the **IMG Activity** (⊕) icon after navigating the following menu path (Figure C.41):

Menu Path

SAP Customizing Implementation Guide > Materials Management > Purchasing > Conditions > Define Price Determination process > Define Calculation Schema. The **Change View "Schemas": Overview** screen appears (Figure C.49).

2. Select a schema from the list of schema procedure codes displayed in the **Change View "Schemas": Overview** screen. In our case, we select RM0000 as the schema, which represents the calculation schema for the purchasing document (Figure C.49).

3. Double-click the **Control data** folder displayed on the tree menu, as shown in Figure C.49:

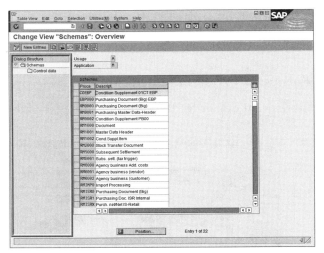

FIGURE C.49   **Displaying the list of existing schemas in the mySAP ERP system**

The **Change View "Control data": Overview** screen appears, displaying the control parameters of the RM0000 schema (Figure C.50).

4. Click the **New Entries** button to create a control parameter for the `RM0000` schema, as shown in Figure C.50:

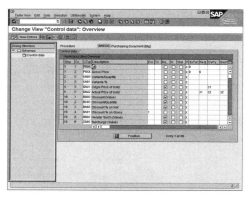

FIGURE C.50   Displaying the control data of the RM0000 schema

The **New Entries: Overview of Added Entries** screen appears (Figure C.51).

5. Enter the relevant details for the control parameter of the `RM0000` schema (Figure C.51).
6. Click the **Save** (⊟) icon to save the entered details, as shown in Figure C.51:

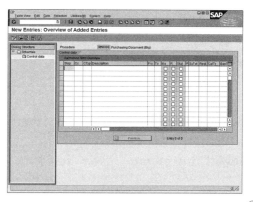

FIGURE C.51   Displaying the screen to enter the control data for the RM0000 schema

After defining the control data for the `RM0000` schema, let's discuss how to define a schema group.

Defining a Schema Group

In an organization, there are various calculation schemas for purchasing organizations or vendors. On the basis of similar calculation schemas, the purchasing organizations or vendors are grouped under a schema group. You can define a schema group by navigating the following menu path:

Menu Path

SAP Customizing Implementation Guide > Materials Management > Purchasing > Conditions > Define Schema Group

After navigating the preceding menu path, click the **IMG Activity** (🌐) icon. The **Choose Activity** dialog box appears, listing the activities to be performed while defining a schema group. Figure C.52 shows the **Choose Activity** dialog box:

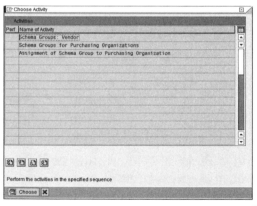

FIGURE C.52   **Displaying the activities to be performed to define a schema group**

Let's first define a schema group for vendors.

Defining Schema Groups for Vendors

Perform the following steps to define a schema group for vendors:

1. Select the **Schema Groups: Vendor** activity (Figure C.52).

2. Click the **Choose** push button (Figure C.52). The **Change View "Schema Groups for Vendors": Overview** screen appears, displaying the list of existing schema groups defined in the mySAP ERP system (Figure C.53).

3. Click the **New Entries** button, as shown in Figure C.53:

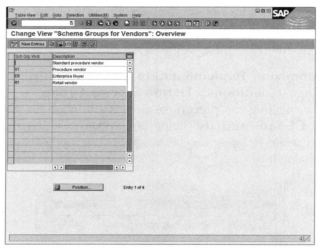

FIGURE C.53   **Displaying the list of existing schema groups for vendors**

The **New Entries: Overview of Added Entries** screen appears (Figure C.54).

4. Enter a unique code and description in the **Sch. Grp. Vndr.** And **Description** text boxes, respectively. In our case, we have entered Z1 and New Schema Group for Vendors (**Figure C.54**).

5. Click the **Save** (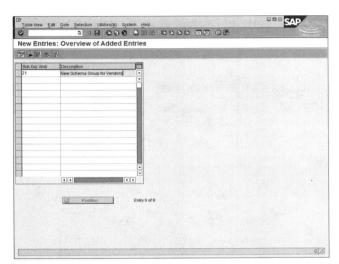) icon, as shown in Figure C.54:

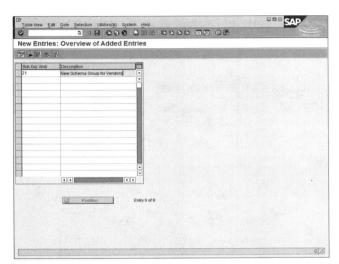

FIGURE C.54   Displaying the details of the new schema group for vendors

The new schema group for vendors, Z1, is created.
Let's now define a schema group for a purchasing organization.

Defining a Schema Group for a Purchasing Organization

Perform the following steps to define a schema group for a purchasing organization:

1. Select the **Schema Groups for Purchasing Organizations** activity from the **Choose Activity** dialog box (Figure C.52).

2. Click the **Choose** push button (Figure C.52). The **Change View "Schema Groups for Purchasing Organizations": Overview** screen appears (Figure C.55).

3. Click the **New Entries** button, as shown in Figure C.55:

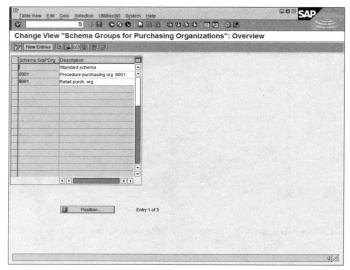

FIGURE C.55   **Displaying the list of existing schema groups for purchasing organizations**

The **New Entries: Overview of Added Entries** screen appears (Figure C.56).

4. Enter the unique code and description for the new schema group for purchasing organizations. In our case, we have entered Z01 and New Schema Group for Purch. Org. (Figure C.56).

5. Click the **Save** (🖫) icon, as shown in Figure C.56:

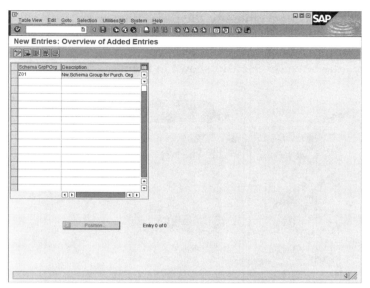

FIGURE C.56   Displaying the details of the new schema group for a purchasing organization

The new schema group for a purchasing organization, Z01, is created. Let's now assign a schema group to a purchasing organization.

Assigning a Schema Group to a Purchasing Organization

Perform the following steps to assign a schema group to a purchasing organization:

1. Select the **Assignment of Schema Group to Purchasing Organization** activity from the **Choose Activity** dialog box (Figure C.52).
2. Click the **Choose** push button (Figure C.52). The **Change View "Assignment of Schema Group to Purchasing Organization": O** screen appears (Figure C.57).

3. Enter the schema group for the purchasing organization in the **Sch. Grp. Pur. Org.** header. In our case, we have entered `0001` as the schema group for the purchasing organization (Figure C.57).
4. Click the **Save** (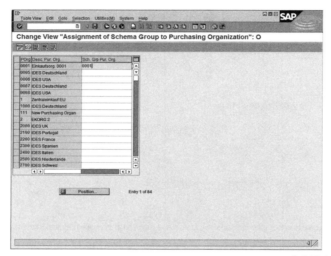) icon, as shown in Figure C.57:

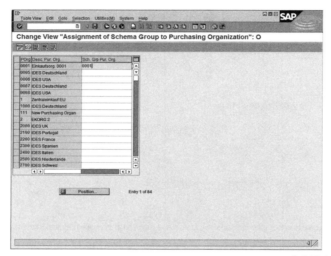

FIGURE C.57   **Displaying the list of purchasing organizations for schema groups**

The schema group is assigned to a purchasing organization. This ends the discussion on the pricing procedure; let's now configure the settings for automatic account determination.

CONFIGURING THE AUTOMATIC ACCOUNT DETERMINATION SETTINGS

While entering the details of various transactions, such as issuing of goods, receiving invoices, and receiving goods, the mySAP ERP system automatically determines the G/L accounts associated with the transactions and posts them. This automatic determination of G/L accounts is due to the automatic account determination settings configured in the mySAP ERP system. This section helps you to learn how to configure the automatic account determination settings in the mySAP ERP system.

You can configure automatic account determination settings in either of the following two ways:

- By using the automatic determination wizard
- By manually configuring the settings without using the wizard

Before exploring these two ways, you should be aware of few basic terms that are associated with the automatic account determination process. Table C.2 describes the key terms related to the automatic account determination process:

Terms	Description
Valuation area	Represents an organization unit that helps to divide and subdivide the organization to uniformly and completely value the material stocks. You can define a valuation area either at the company code or plant level.
Chart of accounts	Provides a framework to record the values and generate G/L accounts. Each G/L account has an account number, account name, and technical information.
Valuation class	Helps to determine a G/L account on the basis of the material type to which a valuation class is assigned.
Transaction key	Helps to determine accounts or post keys for line items that are defined in the mySAP ERP system and cannot be changed by any user.

TABLE C.2   **Key terms related to the automatic account determination process**

After a brief overview of the key terms, let's now explore the two ways to configure automatic account determination settings.

Using the Automatic Account Determination Wizard

The mySAP ERP system provides the automatic account determination wizard to configure the settings for automatic determination of G/L accounts. Perform the following steps to configure the settings with the help of the wizard:

1. Navigate the following menu path in the mySAP ERP system:

Menu Path

SAP Customizing Implementation Guide > Materials Management > Valuation and Account Assignment > Account Determination > Account Determination Wizard

2. Click the **IMG Activity** (⊕) icon beside the **Account Determination Wizard** activity, as shown in Figure C.58:

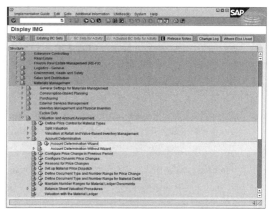

FIGURE C.58   Displaying the menu path for the Account Determination Wizard activity

The **Welcome** screen of the wizard (**MM Account Determination Wizard: Screen 1 of 15**) appears (Figure C.59).

3. Click the **Continue** push button to continue the configuration of the automatic account determination process, as shown in Figure C.59:

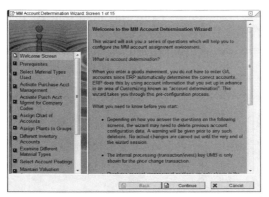

FIGURE C.59   Displaying the Welcome screen of the Wizard

The **Prerequisites** screen appears, displaying the settings that you have already set up before starting the automatic account determination process (Figure C.60).

4. Click the **Continue** push button, as shown in Figure C.60:

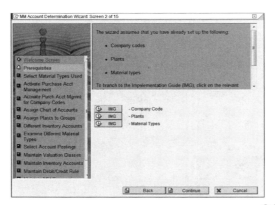

FIGURE C.60   Displaying the Prerequisites screen of the Wizard

The **Select Material Types Used** screen appears (Figure C.61).

5. Select the material types from the material list displayed on the **Select Material Types Used** screen (Figure C.61).
6. Click the **Continue** push button, as shown in Figure C.61:

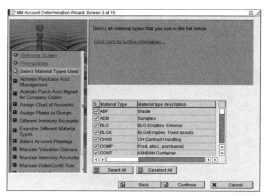

FIGURE C.61 Displaying the Select Material Types Used screen

The **Activate Purchase Acct Management** screen appears (Figure C.62).

7. Click the **Continue** push button, as shown in Figure C.62:

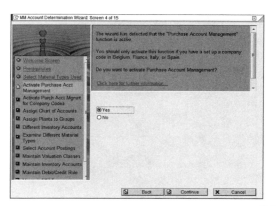

FIGURE C.62 Displaying the Activate Purchase Acct Management screen

The **Activate Purch Acct Mgmnt for Company Codes** screen appears (Figure C.63).

8. Select the company code from the list of company codes displayed on the **Activate Purch Acct Mgmnt for Company Codes** screen (Figure C.63).

9. Click the **Continue** push button, as shown in Figure C.63:

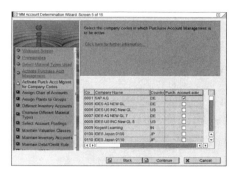

FIGURE C.63   Displaying the Activate Purch Acct Mgmnt for Company Codes screen

The **Assign Chart of Accounts** screen appears (Figure C.64).

10. Enter the code of the chart of accounts in the **Chart of Accounts** field (Figure C.64). In our case, we have entered ACIA as the code of the chart of accounts (Figure C.64).

11. Click the **Continue** push button, as shown in Figure C.64:

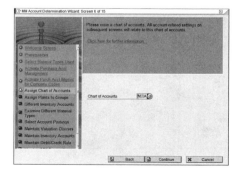

FIGURE C.64   Displaying the Assign Chart of Accounts screen

The **Assign Plants to Groups** screen appears (Figure C.65).

12. Enter a plant code and group in the **Plant** and **Group** text boxes, respectively (Figure C.65).

13. Click the **Continue** push button, as shown in Figure C.65:

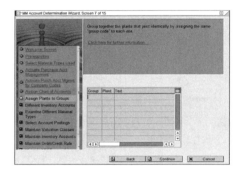

FIGURE C.65 Displaying the Assign Plants to Groups screen

The **Examine Different Material Types** screen appears (Figure C.66).

14. Select the **Yes** radio button if you want to examine other material types. Otherwise, select the **No** radio button. In our case, we select the **No** radio button (Figure C.66).

15. Click the **Continue** push button, as shown in Figure C.66:

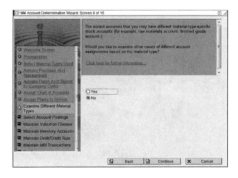

FIGURE C.66 Displaying the Examine Different Material Types screen

The **Maintain Valuation Classes** screen appears, displaying the list of valuation classes assigned to material types (Figure C.67).

16. Click the **Continue** push button, as shown in Figure C.67:

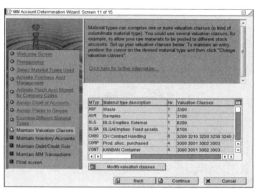

FIGURE C.67   Displaying the Maintain Valuation Classes screen

The **Maintain Inventory Accounts** screen appears (Figure C.68).

17. Enter the account numbers in the **Account** header for the various classes displayed on the **Maintain Inventory Accounts** screen (Figure C.68).
18. Click the **Continue** push button, as shown in Figure C.68:

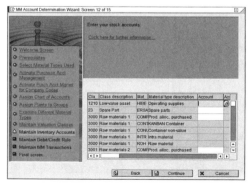

FIGURE C.68   Displaying the Maintain Inventory Accounts screen

The **Maintain Debit/Credit Rule** screen appears (Figure C.69).

19. Select the check boxes depending upon the debit or credit rule that you want to define (Figure C.69).
20. Click the **Continue** push button, as shown in Figure C.69:

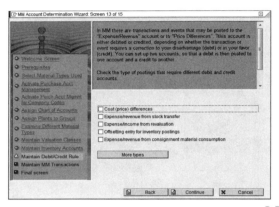

FIGURE C.69 Displaying the Maintain Debit/Credit Rule screen

The **Maintain MM Transactions** screen appears (Figure C.70).

21. Click the **Continue** push button, as shown in Figure C.70:

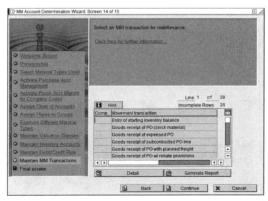

FIGURE C.70 Displaying the Maintain MM Transactions screen

The **Final** screen appears (Figure C.71).

22. Click the **Continue** push button, as shown in Figure C.71:

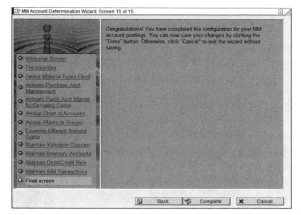

FIGURE C.71   Displaying the Final screen

The **MM Account Determination saved** message appears, as shown in Figure C.72:

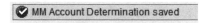

FIGURE C.72   Displaying the message indicating successful configuration of automatic account determination

After learning how to configure the automatic account determination settings with the help of the **Automatic Account Determination** wizard, let's now manually configure the settings.

Configuring the Automatic Account Determination Settings Manually

While configuring the settings for automatic determination of G/L accounts manually, you need to perform the following steps:

1. Define valuation control
2. Group valuation areas

3. Define valuation classes
4. Define an account group for movement types
5. Configure automatic postings

You can perform these steps by navigating the following menu path:

Menu Path

SAP Customizing Implementation Guide > Materials Management > Valuation and Account Assignment > Account Determination > Account Determination Without Wizard. Figure C.73 displays the preceding menu path in the **Display IMG** screen:

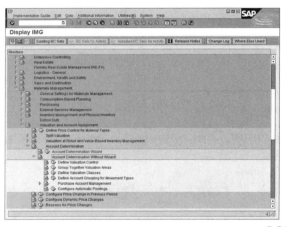

FIGURE C.73 Displaying the menu path for Account Determination Without Wizard

Let's perform each of the activities shown in Figure C.73.

Defining Valuation Control

The **Define Valuation Control** activity allows you to group the valuation areas by activating the valuation grouping code. The process of activating the valuation grouping code simplifies the task of configuration of automatic posting of transactions. You can define valuation control by clicking the **IMG Activity** (⊕)

icon beside the **Define Valuation Control** activity (Figure C.73). The **Valuation Control** screen appears, displaying the options of activating or deactivating the valuation posting. You should select the **Valuation grouping code active** radio button to implement the automatic account determination process, as shown in Figure C.74:

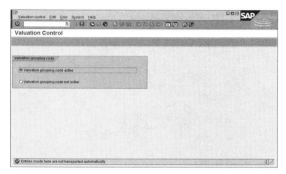

FIGURE C.74   Displaying the Valuation Control screen

Figure C.74 shows that you can activate or deactivate the valuation grouping code. You should note that by default, the **Valuation grouping code active** radio button is selected.

Let's now discuss how to group valuation areas.

Grouping Valuation Areas

You can group valuation areas by assigning a valuation grouping codes to valuation areas. A valuation grouping code helps you to easily configure the automatic account determination process. In other words, you can assign a single valuation grouping code to various valuation areas that need to be assigned to a similar G/L account. For example, the 0001 valuation grouping code is assigned to the 0001 valuation area and 0001 company code. You can click the **IMG Activity** icon (⊕) beside the **Group Together Valuation Areas** activity (Figure C.73) to group valuation areas. The **Change View "Acct Determination for Val. Areas": Overview** screen appears, as shown in Figure C.75:

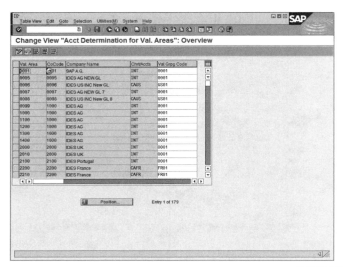

FIGURE C.75   **Displaying the valuation grouping codes assigned to valuation areas**

Figure C.75 shows that a single valuation grouping code is assigned to multiple valuation areas.

Let's now learn how to define valuation classes.

Defining Valuation Classes

To define valuation classes in the mySAP ERP system, you first need to define an account category reference. Next, you need to define a valuation class for each account category reference and finally assign the account category reference to the material type. Perform the following steps to define an account category reference and a valuation class:

1. Click the **IMG Activity** icon (⊕) beside the **Define Valuation Classes** activity (Figure C.73). The **Account Category Reference/Valuation Classes** screen appears (Figure C.76).
2. Click the **Account category reference** button, as shown in Figure C.76:

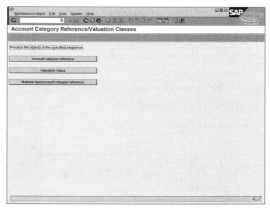

FIGURE C.76   **Displaying the Account Category Reference/Valuation Classes screen**

The **Change View "Account Category Reference": Overview** screen appears, displaying the account category references and their descriptions (Figure C.77).

3. Click the **New Entries** button, as shown in Figure C.77:

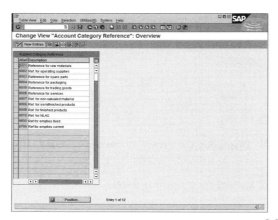

FIGURE C.77   **Displaying the list of account category references**

The **New Entries: Overview of Added Entries** screen appears (Figure C.78).

4. Enter the account category reference and its description. In our case, we have entered `001` as the account category reference and `New reference` as its description (Figure C.78).
5. Click the **Save** (⬛) icon to save the details of the new account category reference, as shown in Figure C.78:

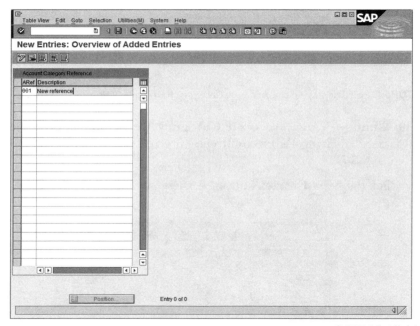

FIGURE C.78   Displaying the details of the new account category reference

The **Data was saved** message appears.

6. Click the **Back** (■) icon to navigate to the **Account Category Reference/ Valuation Classes** screen (Figure C.76).

7. Click the **Valuation Class** button on the **Account Category Reference/ Valuation Classes** screen (Figure C.76). The **Change View "Valuation Classes": Overview** screen appears displaying the details of the existing valuation classes (Figure C.79).

8. Click the **New Entries** button, as shown in Figure C.79:

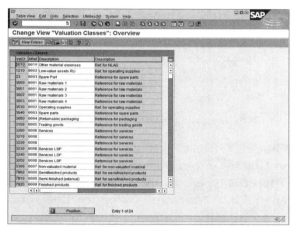

FIGURE C.79   **Displaying the details of existing valuation classes**

The **New Entries: Overview of Added Entries** screen appears (Figure C.80).

9. Enter the valuation class code, account category reference code, and description of the new valuation class. In our case, we have entered `0001` as the valuation class code as well as the account category reference code, and `New Valuation Class` as the description (Figure C.80).

10. Click the **Save** (⊞) icon to save the entered details, as shown in Figure C.80:

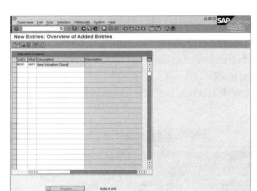

FIGURE C.80   **Displaying the details of the new valuation class**

11. Click the **Back** (◧) icon to navigate to the **Account Category Reference/ Valuation Classes** screen (Figure C.76).

12. Click the **Material type/account category reference** button (Figure C.76). The **Change View "Account Category Reference/Material Type": Overview** screen appears, displaying the account category reference assigned to material types, as shown in Figure C.81:

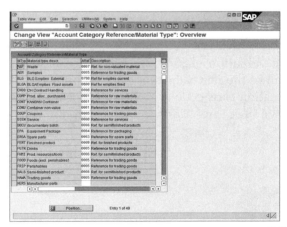

FIGURE C.81   **Displaying the account category reference assigned to material types**

You can edit the account category reference for a material type by entering a new account category code and clicking the **Save** (⊟) icon.

Let's now discuss how to define an account group for movement types.

Defining an Account Group for Movement Types

In this subsection, you learn how to define an account group for various movement types. Click the **IMG Activity** (⊕) icon beside the **Define Account Grouping for Movement Types** activity (Figure C.73). The **Change View "Account Grouping": Overview** screen appears, displaying the account group assigned to various movement types, as shown in Figure C.82:

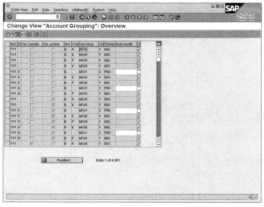

FIGURE C.82 Displaying the Change View "Account Grouping": Overview screen

Figure C.82 shows various account group details, such as account grouping code and movement type. You can edit the details of the account groups in the **Change View "Account Grouping": Overview** screen.

Let's now discuss how to configure automatic posting settings in the mySAP ERP system.

Configuring the Automatic Posting Settings

You need to configure various system settings, such as assigning a G/L account and simulating a transaction, in the mySAP ERP system for automatic posting of various transactions. You can configure these settings by clicking the **IMG Activity** (⊕) icon beside the **Configure Automatic Posting** activity (Figure C.73). The **Automatic Posting** screen appears, as shown in Figure C.83:

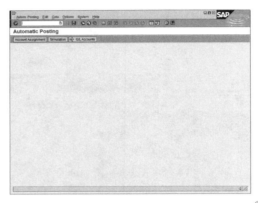

FIGURE C.83   **Displaying the Automatic Posting screen**

You can assign a G/L account to a transaction by clicking the **Account Assignment** button (Figure C.83). The **Maintain FI Configuration: Automatic Posting – Procedures** screen appears, displaying a list of transaction keys, as shown in Figure C.84:

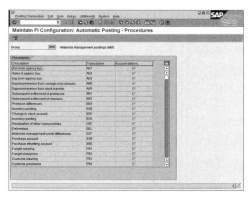

FIGURE C.84 **Displaying the list of transaction keys**

You can set the G/L accounts by double-clicking the transaction key. You also need to define the valuation grouping code, valuation class, and the G/L account to configure the automatic posting settings. Further, you can verify the settings by clicking the **Simulation** button (Figure C.83).

TRANSACTION CODES OF THE SAP MM MODULE

Appendix **D**

Transaction codes (T-codes) are shortcuts that allow you to directly access the relevant screens in the SAP® Graphical User Interface (GUI) instead of navigating through long menu paths. To perform a task in the mySAP™ ERP system, you need to enter its transaction code in the command field available on the **SAP Easy Access** screen and press the ENTER key. For example, to access the **Customizing: Execute Project** screen, enter the SPRO transaction code in the command field, as shown in Figure D.1:

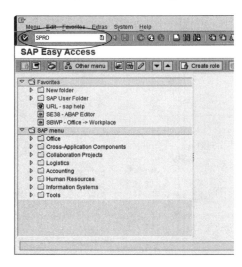

FIGURE D.1   Displaying the SAP Easy Access screen

After *entering* the transaction code and *pressing* the ENTER key, the **Customizing: Execute Project** screen appears, as shown in Figure D.2:

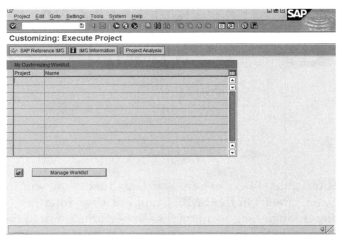

FIGURE D.2   Displaying the Customizing: Execute Project screen

In this way, you can perform various activities using the transaction codes in the mySAP ERP system. This appendix describes various transaction codes used in the SAP MM module.

Table D.1 lists the transaction codes used in the MM module of the mySAP ERP system:

Transaction Code	Description
MM01	Creates a material
MM02	Changes a material
MM03	Displays a material
MM04	Displays the changes made in a material
MM06	Flags (marks) a material for deletion
MK01	Creates the purchasing vendor

Continued

Transaction Code	Description
MK02	Changes the purchasing vendor
MK03	Displays the purchasing vendor
MK04	Changes the vendor account
MK05	Blocks/unblocks a vendor
MK06	Flags a vendor for deletion
AC03	Displays a service
AC05	Displays the list processing for a service master
AC06	Displays the list of services
MMNR	Defines the material master number range
XK01	Creates a vendor (centrally)
XK02	Changes a vendor
XK03	Displays a vendor
XK04	Makes changes in the vendor account
XK05	Blocks a vendor
XK06	Flags a vendor for deletion
XK07	Changes an account group
XKN1	Defines the number range of a vendor account
ME01	Maintains the source list
ME03	Displays the source list
ME04	Changes the source list
ME05	Generates the source list
ME06	Analyzes the source list
ME07	Deletes an info record
ME08	Sends the source list
ME11	Creates an info record

Continued

Transaction Code	Description
ME12	Changes an info record
ME13	Displays an info record
ME14	Changes the purchasing info record
ME15	Flags an info record for deletion
ME16	Deletes the proposal for info record
ME17	Archives administration
ME18	Sends the purchasing info record
MEMASSIN	Maintains mass (info record)
MEQ1	Maintains the quota arrangement
MEQ3	Displays the quota arrangement
MEQ4	Changes the quota arrangement
MEQ6	Analyzes the quota arrangement
MEQ7	Deletes the quota arrangement
MEQ8	Defines the quota arrangement for material
OMEO	Defines the number range for purchasing info records
MMBE	Defines the stock overview
MB51	Defines the material document list
MB52	Displays the warehouse stocks of material
MB53	Defines the availability of a plant
MB54	Displays the consignment stocks
MIGO	Defines goods movement (receipts/issues/transfers)
MIGO_GI	Displays the material document
MIGO_GR	Defines the goods receipt purchase order
MIGO_TR	Displays the material document for transfer posting

Continued

Transaction Code	Description
MIGO_GS	Displays the material document for subcontracting - subsequent adjustment
MBST	Cancels the material document
MBRL	Defines the return delivery
MB90	Displays the output from goods movement
MI01	Allows you to create the physical inventory document
MI02	Allows you to change the physical inventory document
MI03	Allows you to display the physical inventory document
MI04	Allows you to enter the inventory count
MI05	Allows you to change the inventory count
MI06	Allows you to display the inventory count
MI07	Allows you to define the post inventory difference
MI08	Allows you to define the post count and difference
MI09	Allows you to enter the inventory count without reference to the physical inventory document
MI10	Allows you to define the post document, count, and post inventory difference
MI11	Allows you to enter a recount
MI12	Allows you to change the physical inventory documents
ME51N	Allows you to create a purchase requisition
ME52N	Allows you to change a purchase requisition
ME53N	Allows you to display a purchase requisition
ME54N	Allows you to display the details of the purchase requisition
ME59N	Allows you to create the purchase orders from requisitions automatically
ME41	Allows you to create a request for quotation (RFQ) document

Continued

Transaction Code	Description
ME42	Allows you to change a RFQ
ME43	Allows you to display the details of a RFQ
ME44	Maintains the RFQ supplement
ME45	Releases the approved purchase documents
ME47	Maintains quotations
ME48	Displays quotations
ME49	Defines the price comparison list
ME51	Creates a purchase requisition
ME21N	Creates a purchase order
ME22N	Changes a purchase order
ME23N	Displays a purchase order
ME29N	Releases a purchase order
ME28	Releases a purchase document
ME31K	Creates a contract
ME32K	Changes a contract
ME33K	Displays a contract
ME34K	Maintains a contract
ME31L	Schedules an agreement
ME32L	Changes a scheduling agreement
ME33L	Displays a scheduling agreement
ME34L	Maintains a scheduling agreement
ME36	Displays an outline agreement schedule
ME37	Creates an outline agreement
ME38	Maintains the delivery schedule

Continued

Transaction Code	Description
ME39	Displays the scheduling agreement schedule
ME81N	Analyzes the purchase order values
MIRO	Enters an invoice
MIR7	Enters a parked invoice
MIRA	Enters the invoice verification in background processing
MIR4	Displays an invoice document
MIR5	Displays the list of invoice documents
MIR6	Displays the overview of an invoice
MRRL	Enters the evaluated receipt settlement (ERS) with logistics invoice verification
MRKO	Enters a consignment and pipeline settlement
MRIS	Enters an invoicing plan settlement
MR11	Maintains the GR/IR clearing account
MR21	Changes the material price
MR22	Enters the debited or credited material
OX08	Defines the purchase organization
OX09	Maintains the storage location
OX10	Defines a plant by copying, checking, and deleting the existing details of a plant
OX14	Defines the valuation level
OX15	Defines the internal trading partners
OX16	Assigns a company code to a company
OX17	Assigns a plant to a purchase organization
OX18	Assigns a plant to a company code
OX19	Defines the basic data for a material

Continued

Transaction Code	Description
OMS2	Defines the material types
IH09	Displays materials on the basis of material selection
MM50	Extends the material view(s)
MMI1	Creates the operating supplies
MMN1	Creates the non-stock material
MMS1	Creates a service
MMU1	Creates a non-valued material
ME5A	Displays the list of purchase requisitions
ME5J	Displays the list of purchase requisitions for a project
MELB	Defines the purchasing transactions per requirement tracking number
ME56	Assigns the source of supply to requisitions
ME57	Assigns and processes purchase requisitions
ME58	Orders the assigned purchase requisitions
ME59	Creates purchase orders from requisitions automatically
ME54	Releases a purchase requisition
ME55	Defines the collective release of purchase requisitions
ME5F	Defines the release (approval) reminder of purchase requisitions
MB21	Creates a reservation
MB22	Changes a reservation
MB23	Displays a reservation
MB24	Defines the reservation list inventory management by material
MB25	Defines the reservation list inventory management by account assignment
MB1C	Enters other goods receipts
MBRL	Enters the return delivery

Continued

Transaction Code	Description
MB90	Defines the output from goods movements
MB1B	Defines the transfer posting
MIBC	Defines the abc analysis for cycle counting (physical inventory)
MI31	Selects the data for physical inventory documents
MI32	Blocks the materials for physical inventory
MI33	Defines the batch input (freezes book investment balance for physical investment)
MICN	Defines the batch input (creates physical investment document for cycle counting)
MIK1	Selects data for physical inventory documents for a vendor consignment
MIQ1	Selects data for physical inventory documents for a project
MI21	Prints a physical inventory document
MI34	Defines the batch input (enters count with reference to a document)
MI35	Defines the batch input (posts zero count for uncounted materials)
MI37	Defines the batch input (posts differences)
MI38	Defines the batch input (enters count with reference to a document)
MI39	Defines the batch input (enters count without reference to a document)
MI40	Defines the batch input (enters count without reference to a document or post difference)
MI20	Displays the list of inventory differences
CT04	Defines a characteristic
CL01	Creates a class
CL02	Changes a class
CL03	Displays a class

Continued

Transaction Code	Description
CL04	Deletes a class
CL2B	Sets the class types
CL6C	Creates the class hierarchy
CT04	Defines characteristics
CL20N	Assigns an object to classes
CL24N	Assigns objects/classes to a class
CL22N	Assigns a class to superior classes
CL26	Defines the mass release for a class type/class
CLMM	Defines the mass change for assigned values
OMB3	Creates a storage location automatically
LS10	Defines the storage bins structure for automatic creation
V/76	Defines the materials product hierarchies
VE47	Defines foreign trade
VI69	Defines the stabilization and association process (EU) market product group
OB37	Assigns company code to the fiscal year variant
OWD1	Maintains the round profile
OV22	Displays the condition table
OP47	Defines the task list usage
CA10	Defines the standard text
VM01	Creates hazardous material
OMJ5	Defines the activate/deactivate expiration date check
OMLZ	Defines the storage section search
OMW6	Maintains the devaluation by slow/non-movement

Continued

Transaction Code	Description
OMW2	Configures the LIFO pools
OP88	Maintains the task list types
FS01	Edits the G/L account centrally
MSC1N	Creates a batch
MSC2N	Changes a batch
MM13	Activates the scheduled changes for the key data
MM71	Defines the archive administration: create archive files
MK12	Defines the plan vendor
ME21	Creates a purchase order
MKVZ	Displays the list of vendor's purchasing
ME61	Maintains the vendor evaluation
ME9F	Defines the message output
ME2A	Monitors the vendor confirmations
ML01	Creates the standard service catalog
ML45	Creates the total price condition (PRS)
MD05	Defines the MRP list
MD14	Converts the planned order to purchase requisition
MP80	Defines the forecast profile creation
OMJJ	Copies/changes the movement types
OMBS	Defines the reason for movement of goods
MBVR	Manages the reservation
MB1A	Enter the details of the goods issue
MIGO_GO	Defines the return delivery material document
MI20	Displays the list of inventory difference

Continued

Transaction Code	Description
F110	Defines the automatic payment transaction status
MRBR	Allows you to release the blocked invoices
OMWE	Activates the LIFO/FIFO valuation
MRL6	Defines the LIFO relevant materials
MRL1	Defines the LIFO valuation for individual materials
MRL2	Defines the LIFO valuation for pools
MRL3	Defines the LIFO valuation on lowest valuation comparison
OMW4	Changes the LIFO/FIFO movement types
MRF4	Defines the FIFO valuation for flagged materials
MRF1	Executes the FIFO valuation
MRF3	Creates document extract in FIFO valuation
MRN0	Determines the lowest value from market price
OMW5	Changes the lowest value devaluation by the range of coverage
MRN1	Determines the lowest value from the range of coverage
MRN2	Determines the lowest value from the movement rate
MRN3	Determines the lowest value for loss free valuation
OMX1	Changes the activation of material ledger
CKM3	Defines the material price analysis
CKMH	Defines the single level material price determination
CV01N	Creates a document

TABLE D.1   List of noteworthy transaction codes

The transaction codes, as listed in Table D.1, are used to perform various tasks in the MM module of the mySAP ERP system.

GLOSSARY

Access sequence

In the SAP system, an access sequence serves as a search strategy that is used to identify a valid condition record on the basis of a specific condition type. You should assign an access sequence for the condition types that need to be maintained.

Account-assigned PO

Issued for materials that are procured for consumption internally within the organization. This implies that such materials are neither sold outside the organization nor subject to inventory management.

Application layer

Executes the application logic in the SAP R/3 architecture. This layer consists of one or more Application servers and Message servers.

Backflushing

The process of automatic posting of a production order by the mySAP ERP system.

Balance sheet

The financial statement of an organization that specifies the financial position of the organization at a given point of time. A balance sheet is used to provide information about the sources of funds of the organization and also helps to decide how these funds are used or invested.

Batch management data

A batch refers to a collection of material grouped together for various reasons, such as the materials having the same characteristics or having been produced on the same day.

Blanket purchase order

Helps to avoid repetitive data entry and multiple purchase orders created for a supplier from whom the materials are regularly purchased at a fixed price.

Blocking invoices

After invoice verification, the invoices are posted in the system. This is when the finance department of an organization comes into the picture. The finance department is responsible for making payments to the vendor. However, sometimes the invoice amount is not paid to the vendor as the invoice has been blocked.

By-products
These products are secondary products that are manufactured along with the scheduled products.

Calculation schema
Defines a complete structure of various condition records, along with their sequence and control parameters.

Characteristic
In the SAP MM module, the characteristic component of a classification system specifies the properties of objects that are grouped together in a class. In other words, a characteristic represents a property, such as the length, color, or weight of an object.

Class
A prototype that defines the data and behavior common to the objects of a specific type. In a class, data is represented by class attributes and the behavior of an instance of the class is provided by class methods. In other words, we can say classes describe objects.

Class hierarchies
In the MM module, class hierarchies represent a list of superior and subordinate classes that are inherited or extended from a class.

Class type
Used to define objects associated with a class. It specifies whether objects should be classified under one class or different classes.

Classification system
Refers to a technique used to categorize various entities or materials in a structured format.

Company code
Refers to the organizational units under a client.

Condition type
In the SAP system, a condition type depicts various elements that are used to determine prices, such as discounts, surcharges, taxes, or delivery costs.

Consignment procurement process
The process, in which a vendor keeps the material with a company, while the ownership is retained by the vendor until the material is sold or used, is known as the consignment process.

Consumption-based planning
The process of determining the future material requirements based on the past consumption of a material is known as consumption-based planning.

Contract

An agreement made between a purchasing organization and a vendor to procure the specified quantity of a material over a period of time.

Customer service module

Provides support for customer services, such as monitoring service calls. In addition, this module helps a company to manage its service department, which improves customer service, reduces operating costs, and increases efficiency of the company.

Database layer

Comprises the central database system, which contains two components, DBMS and the database itself.

Date category

Refers to a code, which is an alphanumeric combination.

Date proposal

Refers to a proposed date mentioned in the invoice to perform a specific operation. You can maintain a date proposal only for the partial invoicing plan type, and date proposals can help in creating a standard billing plan for the PO.

Delivery documents

Refers to the creation of the delivery document after the products have been received by the customer. This document includes details, such as the purchase order date, the time of delivery, and the actual quantities delivered against the sales order.

Determining lowest value

The lowest value of the inventory is calculated by using the lowest value principle (LVP) method. It is a method of valuating stocks for balance sheet purposes.

Difference list

Prepared after the counting process of the physical inventory is completed and the results have been matched with the inventory details of the mySAP ERP system.

Direct material procurement process

The process of procuring materials that are directly used for production purposes is known as the direct material procurement process.

ERS

An alternate method of processing the invoices sent by vendors. In this method, the organization settles the vendor liabilities and generates the payment statement.

Evaluated receipt settlement

Used to settle the purchase orders and goods receipt automatically. It is an alternative to the manual invoice entry process in the SAP MM module.

External Service Management (ESM)

Refers to the process of managing the purchasing process of services in the MM module. In the MM module, the data for ESM is stored in the master records, which are located in the central database. These master records are used and processed by multiple applications.

Factory calendar

Refers to a calendar that contains information about the plant's activities, such as the planning, production, assembly, and delivery processes.

Field selections

A group of a material that helps you to identify whether or not entering a value in a particular field is mandatory or optional. You can define the field selection group in the **Change View "Field Groups": Overview** screen.

FIFO valuation process

In this valuation process, the material that is purchased or received first is sold or issued first. This method of valuation is best suited for materials that either have an expiry date or materials that degrade with time.

Forecast-based planning

Uses the past consumption values and the forecast values to plan for material procurement. During forecast-based planning, future requirements are determined on the basis of the forecasting program selected for a material.

Goods issuing

Refers to the process of transferring goods from stock for a variety of reasons, such as shipping goods to a customer, withdrawing goods for production, returning defective goods to vendors, and sending finished products to distributors.

Goods movement

The process of moving goods from one location to another. This movement of goods can be categorized as inbound or outbound. In the mySAP ERP system, each of these movements is assigned a unique movement type to prevent the unauthorized movement of goods.

Goods receipt blocked stock

When a stock of materials or goods is initially received from the vendor, it is kept in the goods receipt blocked stock to check whether or not the received materials are as per the order given by the organization.

Goods return document

In the mySAP ERP system, the goods return document is created to specify the details of the goods that need to be returned to the vendor.

GR/IR account

An intermediate account used to clear goods and invoice receipts.

Human Capital Management module

The HCM module is designed to plan and control activities related to human resources, and is also known as the Human Resources (HR) module. Employee relations and tasks related to resource planning are also managed by the HCM module.

Inbound movement process

The process of receiving goods from vendors, customers, or through purchase orders is known as the inbound movement process. In this process, the goods receipts are posted in the mySAP ERP system and a material document is created.

Indirect material procurement process

The process of procuring materials that are used indirectly in the production of finished goods is known as the indirect material procurement process.

Inventory management

Refers to the process of managing inventory items, such as raw materials, finished as well as semi-finished goods, and scrap or obsolete items of an organization.

Investment Management module

Designed to manage various investment securities, such as shares and bonds, to meet the investment goals for the benefit of the investors of a company. This module enables program management in SAP, which refers to the process of defining a hierarchy for multiple projects.

Invoice

Consists of various types of information, such as the name of the organization that has issued the invoice, the transaction to which the invoice refers to, and the amount of tax the purchasing organization has to pay.

Invoice reduction

Refers to the process when the original amount of an invoice is reduced and the invoice is posted again with the reduced amount. This is done when the vendor has entered incorrect quantity or price in the invoice by mistake.

Invoice verification

Refers to the process of checking the incoming invoices with respect to price, content, and quantity of the material. This process ensures error-free transactions on both the vendor as well as customer's side.

Invoices with variances

An invoice consists of variances, which implies a difference between the quantity or amount invoiced in a PO in comparison to a value that the mySAP ERP system proposes.

Invoicing plan

In a PO, an invoicing plan is defined for repetitive transactions, such as rental and leasing payments. For example, an organization can use an invoicing plan to automatically generate invoices for monthly office rent, which is a repetitive transaction.

LIFO valuation process
Based on the principle that the material that is received last should be used first.

Logistics Execution module
Designed to implement the shipping and delivery activities for the SD module. This module works closely with the MM and SD modules. In the LE module, the warehouse management process is implemented from the MM module, while the processes of delivery, shipping, and transportation are implemented from the SD module.

Material document
Contains the details of the goods returned, such as posting date, delivery note, material, quantity, plant location, and movement type.

Material master data
Refers to all the material master records that are stored in the system. In other words, material master data consists of the description of all the materials that an organization not only purchases but also produces and keeps in its stock.

Material master record
It comprises all the information that the company needs to manage a material. The data stored in the material master record is descriptive in nature, as it contains information, such as name, size, or dimension of the material.

Material price change method
Any change in the market affects the price of a material and this change should be reflected in the account of the respective material. In SAP, you can implement the price changes and simultaneously revaluate the stock of the material at the current market price.

Material requirements planning
A process to check the availability of materials in a storage location. The reports generated by this process help a company to decide whether the materials required for production are available in the organization or need to be procured from outside.

Materials Management module
Designed to procure and manage the material resources of a company. This module mainly deals with the material and vendor master data and handles inventory functions, such as purchasing, inventory management, and re-order processing.

Moving average price method
Used to calculate the weighted average price of a material. In this method, the system calculates the price of the received goods at the purchase order price and the price of goods issued at the current market price of the material.

MRP list

Serves as the initial working document for the MRP controller. The MRP list is a static list that reflects the changes of the planning results only when the next planning process is implemented. You can display the MRP list either of a single item or collectively of all items.

mySAP ERP Application

SAP introduced the mySAP ERP application as a follow-up product to the SAP R/3 software. With the passage of time, a need for a business suite that would run on a single database and offer a preconfigured system with various scenarios was felt.

Object

Defined as a pattern or instance of a class. For example, Maruti 800, Zen, and Tata Indica are objects and car is their class. An object can represent a real-world entity, such as a person, place, or a programming entity, such as constants, variables, and memory locations.

Organizational structure

A hierarchy that represents the units of an organization and the relationships among these units. The organizational structure provides a clear understanding of the organizational units and their functions.

Outbound movement process

The process in which goods are moved outside an organization, such as issuing goods to customers against a sales order, returning goods to vendors, sending finished products to suppliers and distributors for marketing, is known as the outbound movement process.

Outline purchase agreement

A long-term agreement made between a purchasing organization and a vendor.

P2P cycle

A process to obtain and manage the raw materials required to manufacture final goods.

Parking an invoice

It means to create an invoice with its full details, but not post it.

Physical inventory count document

Used to keep a record of each physical inventory count in the mySAP ERP system. The MI01 transaction code is used to create the physical inventory count document.

Planning process

The planning process in SAP ensures the availability of materials required for production purposes by an organization. To implement the planning process, you first need to calculate the material requirements at either the plant or the storage location level.

Plant

A centralized location in an organization where production, servicing, and maintenance facilities are performed.

Posting an invoice

Refers to passing the invoice information to the FI module for updating the general ledger accounts.

Presentation layer

Consists of one or more servers that act as an interface between the SAP R/3 system and its users, who interact with the system with the help of well-defined SAP GUI components. Using these components, users can enter a request to perform any task, for example, to display the contents of a database table.

Price variance

Refers to a situation in which the price quoted in an invoice is different from that quoted in the PO.

Pricing procedure

In an organization, the price of a material is based on the discounts, surcharges, taxes, and freight charges that are charged or allowed to a customer. In the SAP system, the pricing procedure is followed to calculate the price of a material to be provided in a purchase order.

Procurement process

It is the process of purchasing the required quantity of goods or materials by a company from another company at the optimum cost. The procurement process also monitors the activities related to quality inspection of the received material, invoice verification, and release of the invoice for payment.

Production Planning module

Designed to plan the production phase of a product, such as the type of the product and the quantity to be produced on the basis of demand. This module deals with the tasks related to the procurement, warehousing, and transportation of materials in a company. The company also plans for the transportation of intermediate products from one stage of production to another at the specified time.

Project System module

Helps the management to handle both small as well as large scale projects. For instance, it can handle large scale projects, such as building a factory, and small scale projects, such as organizing a schedule for recruitments.

Purchase order

A legal document that is issued by an organization to a vendor. It contains all the details of the required material or service, such as the description, quantity, delivery date, agreed prices, terms of delivery, and terms of payment.

Purchase order phase

In the purchase order phase, PO documents are issued by purchasing organizations to vendors for supplying the required materials or services at a specified delivery dates. A PO contains the details of the required materials or services, such as type, quantity, and price.

Purchase requisition

An internal document containing the details of the materials or services required by an organization. In the mySAP ERP system, a purchase requisition document can be created directly or indirectly. In the MM module, a purchase requisition document is created directly by executing the ME51N or ME54 transaction code in the Command field.

Purchasing group

Contains various persons or groups dealing with materials that are being purchased in the organization. To implement the activities of the purchasing organization, you can create purchasing groups in the mySAP ERP system.

Purchasing information records

The information related to the purchasing department of an organization is saved in the purchasing information record. In other words, the purchasing information record contains information about a specific material or service that is purchased from a specific vendor.

Purchasing organization

Used to perform all the purchase activities centrally in an organization. It helps to perform the tasks required to complete the purchase process, such as studying the requirements of the purchase, preparing the purchase requisition and request of quotation documents, analyzing the documents, and preparing purchase orders.

Purchasing process

Refers to the process of procuring materials or services required by an organization from an external source. Usually, an agreement, containing all the details of the transactions, such as the type of material, price, and delivery date, is drawn between the purchasing and the selling parties.

Quality Management module

Designed to check and enhance the quality of products developed by a company. In addition, it also monitors the performance of various processes, such as planning and execution. Quality management is incorporated in every step of the supply chain.

Quantity variance

Refers to the situation in which the quantity of goods mentioned in an invoice is more than the quantity received. For example, an organization sends a PO for 100 items at Rs. 100 per item to the vendor, but the vendor delivers only 80 items.

Quota arrangement

The method for determining the part of the material that can be procured from a specified source. For example, the switches of table lamps scheduled to be produced in a batch can be procured from a particular vendor.

Quotation phase

The phase in which an organization receives quotations from multiple vendors in response to the RFQ sent by it is known as the quotation phase.

Release codes

In the mySAP ERP system, release codes are unique codes that are assigned to release groups. We know that each person or department authorized for approving internal documents is assigned a release code.

Release indicator

In the mySAP ERP system, a release indicator depicts the status of a release strategy. In other words, if the approval process is complete, the release strategy can be released.

Release procedure with classification

Helps you to define release procedures for internal as well as external documents on the basis of the characteristics and classes of a material. In the mySAP ERP system, a release procedure with classification is used for internal documents, such as purchase requisitions.

Release procedure

The process of approving various documents, such as purchase requisitions and purchase orders, is known as the release procedure; and the process of configuring a release procedure is known as the release strategy.

Release strategy

In the mySAP ERP system, you can define a release strategy by assigning a release code and release group.

Releasing invoices

A blocked invoice can be released by cancelling the blocking indicator, which was set while posting the invoice. When you release an invoice, the system deletes all the blocks that you might have set while posting the invoice.

Reorder point

The stock level at which an organization should place new orders with the suppliers to bring the inventory level up. The average material requirements expected during the replenishment lead time and the safety stock should be included in the reorder point.

Request for quotation (RFQ)

An external document used by a purchasing organization to select a vendor or supplier to avail the material or service.

Reservation management system

Used to manage stock reservation in the mySAP ERP system. The management of stock reservation is required for inventory management, production, and MRP processes.

Reserving stock

The stock materials are reserved for various reasons, such as scheduled production, urgent delivery, and goods sampling. The reservation of the stock in the mySAP ERP system can be done either automatically or manually.

Returning goods

An organization may return materials to the vendor for a variety of reasons, such as defective material, over-delivery of the material, and returnable packaging materials. The goods are returned to the vendors from the unrestricted stock, the quality-inspection stock, the blocked stock, or the goods receipt blocked stock.

Sales and Distribution module

It is one of the logistics modules and helps to manage the sales and distribution activities in a company, such as checking for open sales orders and forecasting future material requirements. The SD module also helps in regulating all the activities, starting from receiving the order of a product till the product is delivered to the customer.

SAP

Developed by the SAP AG company, Germany, where SAP stands for Systeme, Anwendungen und Produkte in der Datenverarbeitung. The basic idea behind developing SAP was the need to introduce standard application software that helps in real-time business processing.

SAP Customizing Implementation Guide

It is the backbone of the mySAP ERP system and helps in determining how the system functions. It is a customizing screen introduced with the SAP R/3 system, which is used to perform various activities in the mySAP ERP system.

SAP GUI

A standard SAP user interface that displays menus to perform various business activities. The first initial screen of the SAP GUI is known as the **SAP Easy Access** screen.

SAP modules

The mySAP ERP application provides various SAP modules to handle the day-to-day business activities of a company, such as recording the payment of invoices, controlling financial accounts, and managing production resources.

SAP R/1

In SAP R/1 system, R stands for real-time data processing and 1 indicates the single-tier architecture, which means that the three networking layers, Presentation, Application, and Database, on which the architecture of SAP depends, are implemented on a single system.

SAP R/2

It was introduced in 1980, based on the two-tier architecture, and designed to work on mainframe databases, such as DB/2, IMS, and Adabas. The mainframe computer in SAP R/2 used the time-sharing feature to integrate the functions or business areas of an enterprise, such as accounting, manufacturing processes, supply chain logistics, and human resources. The two-tier client-server architecture of the SAP R/2 system enabled a SAP client to connect to a SAP server to access the data stored in the SAP database.

SAP R/3

It is based on the client-server model, and was officially launched on July 6, 1992. This version is compatible with multiple platforms and operating systems, such as UNIX and Windows.

Scheduling agreement

Created between a purchasing organization and vendor to procure materials on a predefined date specified in the agreement.

Schema group

In an organization, there are various calculation schemas for purchasing organizations or vendors. On the basis of similar calculation schemas, the purchasing organizations or vendors are grouped under a schema group.

Service entry sheet

Stores all the records of the transaction of services. This sheet is used to enter information about the partial or full completion of a service in the mySAP ERP system. You can enter data of a service in the service entry sheet by accessing the ML81N transaction code.

Service master record

Stores the master data of the purchasing process of services. You can create a service master record in the mySAP ERP system by using the AC03 transaction code.

Service procurement process

The process of procuring external services, such as painting, repairing electric fitting, and plumbing, from a supplier is known as the service procurement process.

Source list

A type of master data that specifies the sources of supply for a material. In other words, it lists the preferred sources from which the material can be procured.

Special stock

A type of stock that is stored outside the enterprise—at the customer's or vendor's premises—and contains items other than raw materials, such as subcontracts, consignments, and returnable packaging materials.

Spilt valuation process

Allows you to divide material stock in small parts, so that each part can be valuated in different ways. This method is employed when you need to sort the materials according to various parameters, such as country of origin, procurement type, and quality of material.

Standard price of a material

Refers to the price that is recorded in its material master record. This method of pricing is used for the products that do not have a tendency of frequent price fluctuation, such as finished or semi-finished products.

Standard Service Catalog (SSC)

A document used to store information of a service that does not have a service master record. Similar to master records, SSCs are stored centrally in the MM module.

Standard stock

Commonly used in an organization for the production or manufacturing process. It is stored in the common storage area having optimum temperature, light, and humidity conditions.

Stock/requirements list

Depicts the current requirements of material and available stock. As compared to the MRP list, the stock/requirements list is a dynamic list that is updated each time it is accessed.

Storage location

A physical place that is used to store a variety of items, such as raw materials, finished goods, and repair parts. In an organizational structure, a storage location is usually defined under a plant.

Subcontracting procurement process

An outsourcing process in which an enterprise hands over raw materials to a subcontractor to produce and return the final or semi-finished products.

Subsequent debit/credit

Refers to the process in which an invoice or a credit memo for items is received from a vendor after posting the invoice or credit memo in the system.

Third-party procurement process

In this type of procurement process, a company instructs a supplier to supply the required goods to a third party.

Time-phased planning

In cases where a vendor supplies the material on a specific date or day, time-phased planning is used to plan the material requirements. In such situations, you should ensure that the planning date set in the mySAP ERP system should be the date on which the vendor supplies the material.

Tolerance limit

Refers to the limit up to which the variances or differences in an invoice are tolerated. In the case of variance in an invoice, the system checks whether the variance is within the tolerance limit or not.

Traditional method of inventory management

The physical inventory is the actual number of materials that can be counted in the inventory. The counting and management of the physical inventory items is done manually and is therefore termed as the traditional method of inventory management.

Transaction codes (T-codes)

These are shortcuts that allow you to directly access the relevant screens in the SAP Graphical User Interface (GUI) instead of navigating through long menu paths.

Transferring stock

In an organization, stock is transferred from one storage location to another under a plant and from one plant to another under a particular company code. Stock can also be transferred from one company code to another.

Valuation area

The organizational level at which you can valuate the materials. There are two types of valuation areas—plant level and company code level.

Valuation classes

To define valuation classes in the mySAP ERP system, you first need to define an account category reference. Next, you need to define a valuation class for each account category reference and finally assign the account category reference to the material type.

Valuation methods

The inventory valuation process in an organization is implemented using different valuation methods, such as the moving average price and standard price method. The valuation methods are important not only for accounting purposes but also for knowing the actual value of the assets of the organization.

Valuation process

The moving average price (V) and the standard price (S) are the predefined price control methods in the mySAP ERP system. At the time of creating the material master record, you need to assign the price control method manually to configure the valuation process of the material.

Variances of invoices

When there are different values in the invoice and other documents, an invoice is said to have variance. For example, if the total amount in the vendor invoice is different from the total amount suggested by the system, it is called a variance of the invoice.

Vendor confirmation

It is defined in the mySAP ERP system either manually or automatically (in case the confirmation is sent from the vendor using EDI).

Vendor master record

A data file that contains the vendor-related information required by an organization for day-to-day business operations.

Warehouse Management module

Divides the storage location defined in the Inventory Management submodule into storage types and storage sections. The storage types are further divided into storage bins. This module maintains records of the movement of goods as well as current stock of the inventory.

Warehouse

An important part of an organization that is used to store finished products, semi-finished goods, scraps, and tools. It also contains separate storage types to store the particular type of material, such as bulk, liquid, chemicals, and metal ores.

Index

MBE Outlines

Subject-Matter Outlines for the Subjects Tested on the Multistate Bar Examination

AmeriBar
Phone (800) 529-2651 • Fax (800) 529-2652

MBE Outlines

Revised 2011
Copyright 2011 AmeriBar

ISBN 1-44049-256-5